The Vikings on Fil...

RAUBZUG DER WIKINGER

Richard Widmark · Sidney Poitier · Russ Tamblyn
Rosanna Schiaffino · Oscar Homolka
in **RAUBZUG DER WIKINGER**

mit Edward Judd · Lionel Jeffries · Beba Loncar · Drehbuch: Berkely Mather und Beverley Cross
Produktion: Irving Allen · Regie: Jack Cardiff · Ein Farbfilm der Warwick-Avala Produktion in Technicolor und Technirama

The Vikings on Film

*Essays on Depictions
of the Nordic Middle Ages*

Edited by
KEVIN J. HARTY

McFarland & Company, Inc., Publishers
Jefferson, North Carolina, and London

ALSO BY KEVIN J. HARTY
AND FROM MCFARLAND

The Reel Middle Ages: American, Western and Eastern European, Middle Eastern and Asian Films About Medieval Europe (1999; paperback 2006)

EDITED BY KEVIN J. HARTY

Cinema Arthuriana: Twenty Essays, rev. ed. (2002; paperback 2010)

King Arthur on Film: New Essays on Arthurian Cinema (1999)

FRONTISPIECE: **Reproduction of a German lobby card for *The Long Ships* (1964).**

LIBRARY OF CONGRESS CATALOGUING-IN-PUBLICATION DATA

The Vikings on film : essays on depictions of the
Nordic Middle Ages / edited by Kevin J. Harty.
p.   cm.
Includes filmography.
Includes bibliographical references and index.

ISBN 978-0-7864-6044-1
softcover : 50# alkaline paper ∞

1. Vikings in motion pictures.   2. Historical films —
History and criticism.   I. Harty, Kevin J.
PN1995.9.V465V55   2011   791.43'658 — dc22   2011006121

BRITISH LIBRARY CATALOGUING DATA ARE AVAILABLE

Front cover image: Kirk Douglas as Einar in
The Vikings, 1958 (editor's collection)

Manufactured in the United States of America

*McFarland & Company, Inc., Publishers
Box 611, Jefferson, North Carolina 28640
www.mcfarlandpub.com*

For Ginny Tobiassen,
friend, editor, and true mother of Thor!

Contents

Preface

In 1999, I coined the phrase *the "reel" Middle Ages* to define a cinematic genre that has, since Thomas Edison's 1895 *Execution of Joan of Arc*, reimagined the medieval for film audiences for more than a century. This present volume reflects a further refinement of the idea of the *reel* Middle Ages by discussing Viking films in a series of essays by diverse hands that demonstrate that such films are anything but monolithic in the way that they have chosen to depict our Scandinavian and Nordic forbearers.

The Vikings on Film is the first collection of essays to examine cinematic reimaginings of the Vikings and their exploits. Historically, the Viking Age did not last that long. Vikings make their entrance on to the historical stage in the late eighth century C.E. — famously, they sack the monastery at Lindisfarne in 793 — and all but disappear from the pages of Western European history in large part because of their assimilation into other cultures by the early twelfth century, though a distinctive Viking colony limped along in Greenland into the fifteenth century. In the intervening years, Vikings spread terror and trade, chaos and colonies from the steppes of present-day Russia to the Atlantic shores of North America. The Vikings, like so many other things medieval, were then "rediscovered" by the Victorians, and such nineteenth-century reimaginings of the Vikings in literature, art, and popular culture paved the way for the Viking film, the first of which, Lewin Fitzhamon's *The Viking's Bride*, was released in 1907. The most well-known Viking film remains Richard Fleischer's 1958 *The Vikings*, with its hauntingly familiar theme song and cast of well-known Hollywood stars that included Ernest Borgnine, Tony Curtis, Kirk Douglas, and Janet Leigh. The film spawned a short-lived television series, *Tales of the Vikings*, produced by Douglas, which aired for 39 thirty-minute episodes from September 1959 to June 1960, and inspired an Italian sword-and-sandal knock-off, Mario Bava's 1961 *Erik the Conqueror* (*Gli Invasori*).

The essays in this collection discuss Fleisher's *The Vikings* as well as other Hollywood and European Viking film epics, films (more or less) based on medieval sources as well as on comic strips, animated films, and cartoons. As a group, these films only contribute to the complicated legacy that the Vikings have left us. As Julian D. Richards notes in his *The Vikings: A Very Short Introduction* (Oxford: Oxford University Press, 2005), Vikings "have been alternately, noble savages, raiders, marauders and rapists, peaceful traders, entrepreneurs, explorers, early democrats, or IKEA sales personnel, according to what we want them to be" (132–133). As the essays that follow demonstrate, filmmakers and film audiences alike have, then, been in good company in reimagining the Vikings according to what *they* want them to be.

This collection of essays would never have been published without the kindness and generous help of many, many people. I owe debts of thanks to the contributors who, with imagined and real Viking songs in their hearts, agreed to write the essays that I commissioned them to write.

The true heroes of any research in the many areas of film studies are the staffs at film libraries and archives worldwide, and I want especially to thank specifically the following for their multiple — in many cases, continuing — kindnesses. (Blanche DuBois was only half correct; film researchers and scholars, I have found, always rely upon the kindness of friends and strangers!) I am as always indebted to the staff of the Library, Special Collections Division, Stills Archive, and Viewing Services at the British Film Institute in London, especially to David Sharp, Sean Delaney, Nathalie Morris, Kathleen Dickson, Emma Smart, Julian Granger, Nigel Arthur, and Dave McCall, whose devotion to preserving the history and scholarship of film for students of the genre like me is unflagging. I owe thanks as well to Rosemary Hanes at the Library of Congress in Washington, DC; to Nancy Goldman at the Pacific Film Archive in Berkeley; to Francis Poole and his staff in the Instructional Media Collection Department at the University of Delaware Library in Newark; and to Marc Dewey Bayer, Information Systems Librarian at the Butler Library at Buffalo State University.

At La Salle University, I am indebted to John Baky, Director of the Connelly Library, and to the members of his staff, especially Eithne Bearden, Chris Kibler, Samantha Smart, Georgina Murphy, Stephen Breedlove, and Nancy Tresnan; and to my colleagues in the Department of English who offered advice, suggestions, and encouragement: Eileen Barrett, John Beatty, Claire Busse, Jim Butler, Madeleine Dean, Br. Gabriel Fagan FSC, Craig Franson, Kevin Grauke, Ryan Hediger, Br. Emery Mollenhauer FSC, Judith Musser, Bryan Narendorf, and Steve Smith. My research into the general topic of Viking films was supported in part by a generous summer subvention from the Committee on Leaves and Grants and from the Office of the Provost at La Salle University. Elsewhere at La Salle, I am also indebted for assistance to Perry Golia, Anthony Machamer, and Matt Sullivan, and to the students enrolled in my honors seminar on the Vikings in literature, film, and popular culture.

I read an earlier version of my essay on films about the Vikings in North America at the Medieval Studies Conference held at Fordham University's Lincoln Center Campus in Manhattan in March 2010, and I am grateful to the many members of the audience, especially to Roberta Frank, who offered their suggestions and critiques of what I had to say.

Any number of friends offered their additional contributions to this volume, some of whom having put me up then had to put up with me as they sat through repeated screenings of multiple Viking films: Charlie Wilson and Matt McCabe, Richard Meiss and Peter Rudy, Kathleen Harty, Barbara Tepa Lupack, Olwen and Gordon Terris, Rick Fisher and Marcus Tozini, David Barrable and Simon Cunniffe, Sheena Napier, Judith Greenwood, Jeffrey Richards, Debra Mancoff, Rick Tempone, Donald Burns, Jeff Petraco, Linda Merians, Helena White, Russell Leib, Martha W. Driver, Michael Klossner, and Peter W. Travis. On all these kind folk, I invoke the blessings of Thor and Odin, and I wish them all long lives and eventual safe passage to Valhalla!

Kevin J. Harty • Spring 2011

Introduction:
"Save Us, O Lord, from the Fury of the Northmen"; or, "Do You Know What's in Your Wallet?"

KEVIN J. HARTY

The Anglo-Saxon Chronicle records the following terrifying entry for the year 793 C.E.: "In this year dire portents appeared over Northumbria and sorely frightened the people. They consisted of immense whirlwinds and flashes of lightning, and fiery dragons were seen flying in the air. A great famine immediately followed those signs, and a little after that in the same year, on 8 June, the ravages of heathen men miserably destroyed God's church at Lindisfarne with plunder and slaughter" (36). Subsequent raids at Lindisfarne and at other centers of monastic Christianity led the monks to add to their daily litanies the prayer: "Save us, O Lord, from the fury of the Northmen."

In 2000, as the pre–Christmas buying season was at its height, American television audiences were introduced to a commercial for the Capital One Card that featured a happily gift-ladened husband and wife suddenly set upon by marauding Vikings as a voice-over anticipating the shock of those post–Christmas credit card statements ominously asked, "Do you know what's in your wallet?" As the husband quickly displays his Capital One Card, the marauders sigh with frustration, but immediately set their sights on the neighbors' house in the hope that its occupants have been less financially savvy. The agency responsible for the television spot, D'Arcy World-wide in New York, first toyed with the idea of making the marauders Visigoths, but quickly changed them to bearded, horn-helmeted, skin-and-hide-wearing Vikings, and the commercials have continued to air though with an increasingly comic — if not slapstick — edge featuring bra-wearing Vikings on tropical beaches taking battering rams to sand castles and generally confused Vikings on the rim of the Grand Canyon assuming a sign saying "burro rides" means that they are to give rides to burros. This shift in advertising messages doubtless reflects the financial crisis at the end of the first decade of the twenty-first century in which Capital One and other banks lost the confidence and respect of their customers, and of the general public, thanks to their predatory lending practices. That crisis tarred all banks, and Capital One's television commercials have substituted humor for the now previously dubious claims of better customer service and care.[1]

How do we explain so drastic a shift in conceptions of the Vikings? For medieval Europe, the Vikings were the global terrorists of their day. Vikings began menacing the coast of Kent as early as 792. The 793 sack of the monastery of Lindisfarne was followed by raids on Skye,

3

Iona, and Raithlin in 795, and on the monastery of St-Philbert on Noirmoutier in 799 that
led Charlemagne in 800 to fortify the coast against their subsequent attacks north of the
estuary of the Seine. Vikings subsequently turned their attentions to Wessex. The monastery
at Iona was burned in 802, and another raid in 806 resulted in the killing of 68 members
of the monastic community there. Viking fleets attacked Frisia in 810, and began in that
same year to exact tribute from the inhabitants of the region. In 820, Viking attacks on
Flanders and on the Seine estuary were repelled, but an attack on the Aquitaine was more
successful for the Vikings, netting them extensive booty. In 835, the Isle of Sheppey in the
Thames estuary was the site of a Viking raid, and, in the following year, Viking raids
extended from the coast to deep into Ireland where they continued annually for decades.
The Vikings sacked Nantes in 840—and Toulouse, Galicia, and al-Andalus in 844. In 845,
Paris was held for ransom, and Hamburg was sacked. In 851, the inhabitants of Canterbury
and of London found themselves under attack by Vikings. In 859, Viking ships entered the
Mediterranean and laid siege to Nakur in the north of Africa. Subsequent Viking attacks
occurred in 859 in Winchester and present-day Russia, in 860 in Constantinople, in 865
in Poitiers, in 870 in Dumbarton, and elsewhere across Europe throughout the balance of
the ninth century.

   At the same time, Vikings began to establish settlements or assume control of territories
in Ireland, England, Scotland, Russia, the Faeroes, the Shetlands and the Orkneys, Iceland,
and eventually Greenland — the settlement at L'Anse aux meadows in Newfoundland generally thought to date from 999 and associated with the voyages of Leif Ericcson to Vinland
turns out to have been only a winter camp. These more permanent activities would eventually
lead to Viking assimilation with conquered peoples and the establishment of Viking kingdoms from the steppes of Russia to the Atlantic shores of North America. But just as suddenly
as they appeared, the Vikings disappeared. Shortly after the turn of the millennium, almost
all of Scandinavia was Christian — at least in name — and the defeat of Harald Hardrada
by William of Normandy sounded the initial death knell for the Viking Age as fully assimilated former Vikings, the Normans, conquered England. To the east, Viking culture adapted
to its Slavic counterpart. Viking settlements would continue, albeit haphazardly, in Greenland until the mid-fifteenth century, which also saw the beginning of the end for an independent Iceland. After that, the pages of history are silent about the Vikings.[2]

   Vikings were then absent from popular and high culture for almost four centuries until
the Victorian Age. We are indebted to the Victorians for "rediscovering," albeit on their
own terms, much that we today consider medieval. In the case of the Vikings, Wawn, whose
study of the Vikings and the Victorians remains the standard work on the subject, goes so
far as to assert that the Vikings were actually invented by the Victorians. Victorian England
increasingly looked back to its native Anglo-Saxon (and by extension Germanic) roots. In
doing so, they raised thorny questions about race, about state, about nationhood, about
heritages Anglo-Norman versus heritages Anglo-Saxon. The result was a more benign and
heroic view of the Vikings, which, like everything else in western culture they appropriated,
the Nazis would, following the lead of Wagner, subvert for their own purposes.[3] But the
Victorian Vikings would also soon find a home in film, in melodramas such as *The Viking
Bride* (1907), *The Viking's Daughter* (1908), *The Viking Queen* (1914), and *The Oath of a
Viking* (also 1914).[4] Such early film efforts were prefatory to the fuller tradition of Viking
films that the essays in this collection discuss. These films in turn further fueled popular
reimaginings of the Vikings in comic strips, in animated and print cartoons, and in *bandes
desinées* and graphic novels.[5]

Kathleen Coyne Kelly's essay on *The Vikings* (1958) begins this collection. Kelly uncovers what it is we actually do and don't see in the film, arguing that the director's touch is at times invisible and at other times all too visible in what is still the best-known Viking film. Donald L. Hoffman follows with an essay on yet another Hollywood Viking epic, *The Long Ships* (1964). The title of Hoffman's essay puns nicely on the title of one of co-star Sidney Poitier's more serious films. Specifically, Hoffman is interested in how desire plays a role in the film, and what its agendas are in terms of a judgment that all desire in the film is viewed at best as a form of deviance. Christopher A. Snyder follows with an analysis of the ways in which Clive Donner's 1969 biopic about King Alfred, the only English monarch to be called "the Great," fails to do justice to the complex life of the king and to the political realities of the times in which Alfred lived.

The longest running Viking comic strip is Hal Foster's *Prince Valiant*, whose run has outlived its creator who died in 1982, but who had already given up drawing the comic strip in 1971. Foster had previously drawn the *Tarzan* comic strip, and he began drawing *Valiant* in 1937 at the urging of William Randolph Hearst. The strip would inspire — and panels from it would be incorporated into — two films; see the study of Foster by Kane for more details. Alan Lupack sees the 1954 film directed by Henry Hathaway as reflective of contemporary politics at a time in American history when loyalty and betrayal were part of the national discussion and agenda. Joseph M. Sullivan follows with an analysis of the negative effect that poor financial decisions had on artistic outcomes in the 1997 European film based on the strip, *Prinz Eisenherz*. For Lupack, Foster's Vikings are valiant and villainous; for Sullivan, they are just silly, though without the panache, as Rostand's Cyrano would say, of that quintessential "silly place," the Python troupe's Camelot.

Susan Aronstein follows with a discussion of an anti–Viking Viking film, The Pythons' Terry Jones' *Erik the Viking* (1989), that is, in the final analysis, more affirmation than send-up. Fractured fairy tales remain, Aronstein effectively argues, fairy tales, but ones in which we can choose what we do and do not believe. In contrast, Joan Tasker Grimbert and Claudia Bornholdt discuss a film firmly grounded in the reality of the Icelandic sagas, Hrafn Gunnlaugsson's 1988 *Shadow of the Raven*. Their discussion takes two foci: Grimbert discusses the film's reworking of the complicated legend of Tristan and Iseult, and Bornholdt discusses the complex symbolism of the raven and veil in the film.

Roberta Davidson next offers a comparison of two films based on a medieval Sami folktale about the so-called Pathfinder, a Sami who is the sole survivor of a murderous raid on his or her village, who is used by the Sami's traditional enemies to lead them to other Sami villages on which to unleash their deadly fury. The second of those films sets the folktale on the shores of North America with less than successful results, and I follow Davidson's essay with a comparative analysis of a number of films that reimagine Viking incursions into North America at the beginning of the second millennium. Such films face a difficult decision as to whom they will demonize since traditionally Viking films have depicted Vikings as other to their fellow Europeans, while the film Western has depicted native Americans as other to white Americans and Europeans.

Part of the cultural legacy that the Anglo-Saxons brought with them to England included the background to and the sources of the epic poem *Beowulf*, which has had a checkered record when attempts have been made to bring it to the screen. Elizabeth S. Sklar analyzes a film once removed from Beowulf by way of its source, John McTiernan's 1999 film *The 13th Warrior*, based on Michael Crichton's 1976 fictional reworking of *Beowulf*, *The Eaters of the Dead*. Sklar argues that issues of genre impede the film's success, offering a laundry list of which generally accepted narrative and cinematic genres that the film does and does not easily fit into. David W. Marshall offers a reading of yet another film loosely-based on *Beowulf*, Howard McCann's 2008 film *Outlander*, which marries science fiction to the plot of the poem with the result that, in the end, it imagines the possibility of a kinder, gentler sort of Viking.

A different sort of Viking is definitely presented in the two films that Laurie A. Finke and Martin B. Shichtman discuss: Roger Corman's 1957 film *The Viking Women and the Sea Serpent* and Don Chaffey's 1967 film *The Viking Queen*—in both of which the Vikings find a home in the B-movie. Finke and Shichtman suggest ways in which these exploitation films subvert the examples of cinematic sexuality that they are supposed to present.

Earlier, David W. Marshall's essay on Howard McCann's *Outlander* argued that, in the final analysis, the film advocated for a kinder, gentler Viking. There are no kinder, gentler Vikings than Astérix and Obélix, the peripatetic duo from the long-running series of *bandes desinées*. In the 2005 animated film *Astérix and the Vikings*, the two take under their wing the nephew of their village chief, as Viking marauders threaten their village. In his essay on the film, Andrew B. R. Elliott wonders why a Gaul even fought the Normans in the film; his answer is rooted in a discussion of the film's comic and subversive perspectives on the story it tells. Animated Vikings are ubiquitous in cartoons as Michael N. Salda demonstrates in this collection's final essay. As he previously had done for the tradition of Arthurian animation (203–32), Salda catalogs how cartoon Vikings have taken a variety of forms since at least the late 1950s. This collection then concludes with my comprehensive filmography of full-length fiction films that treat the Vikings or their legacy as an essential part of their plots. The filmography provides basic information about the film's production, a brief plot summary, a selection of reviews, and, where appropriate, bibliographic data on significant longer discussions of a film.

Notes

1. The creative directors for the original commercial were Graham Woodall and Keith Goldberg, and the copywriter was Robert E. Lee. The original commercial can be viewed on YouTube at http://www.youtube.com/watch?v=drg08aySdFg.

2. The relative brevity of the Viking Age notwithstanding, the history of the Vikings is complicated and multi-faceted, and beyond the scope of this introductory essay. For more specifics, see the works by Arnold, Hall, Richards, Sawyer, and Seaver *passim*; the essays edited by Fitzhugh and Ward; and the reader edited by Somerville and McDonald. On the demise of Viking society, see also Diamond (178–276) and Wiesner (145–85). The ninth-century Viking raids on Paris are chronicled by Abbo of Saint-Germain-des Prés.

3. See, for instance, the Nazi poster reprinted by Hill (221).

4. For details about these early Viking films, see the filmography below, pp. 193–214.

5. While graphic novels have become a global phenomenon, *bandes desinées* remain unique to Belgian and French cultures. See the two studies by Miller and by Vessels. In the penultimate essay in this collection, Andrew B. R. Elliott discusses the animated *Astérix and the Vikings,* which is based on a *bande desinée.*

Works Cited

Abbo of Saint-Germain-des-Prés. *Bella parisiacae urbis.* Ed. Nirmal Dass. Dallas Medieval Texts and Translations 7. Paris: Peeters, 2007.

The Anglo-Saxon Chronicle. Rev. trans. and ed. Dorothy Whitelock et al. London: Eyre and Spottiswoode, 1961.

Arnold, Martin. *The Vikings, Wolves of War.* Lanham, MD: Rowman & Littlefield, 2007.

Diamond, Jared. *Collapse: How Societies Choose to Fail or Succeed.* New York: Viking, 2005.

Fitzhugh, William W., and Elisabeth I. Ward, eds. *Vikings: The North Atlantic Saga.* Washington, DC: Smithsonian Institution Press, 2000.

Hall, Richard. *The World of the* Vikings. New York: Thames & Hudson, 2007.

Kane, Brian H. *Hal Foster: Prince of Illustrators, Father of the Adventure Strip.* Lebanon, NJ: Vanguard Productions, 2001.

Miller, Ann. *Reading* bande desinée: *Critical Approaches to French-language Comic Strip.* Chicago: Intellect/University of Chicago Press, 2007.

Richards, Julian D. *The Vikings: A Very Short Introduction.* Oxford: Oxford University Press, 2005.

Salda, Michael N. "'What's Up, Duke?': A Brief History of Arthurian Animation." In Kevin J. Harty, ed. *King Arthur on Film: New Essays on Arthurian Cinema.* Jefferson, NC: McFarland, 1999.

Sawyer, Peter, ed. *The Oxford Illustrated History of the Vikings.* 1997; rpt. New York: Oxford University Press, 2001.

Seaver, Kristin A. *The Last Vikings.* London: Tauris, 2010.

Somerville, Angus A., and R. Andrew McDonald, eds. *The Viking Age, A Reader.* Toronto: University of Toronto Press, 2010.

Vessels, Joel E. *Drawing France, French Comics and the Republic.* Jackson: University Press of Mississippi, 2010.

Wawn, Andrew. *The Vikings and the Victorians, Inventing the Old North in 19th-Century Britain.* 2000; rpt. Woodbridge, Suffolk: Boydell & Brewer, 2002.

Wiesner, Merry E., et al. *Discovering the Global Past: A Look at the Evidence, Volume 1: To 1650.* 3d ed. Boston: Houghton Mifflin, 2007.

The Trope of the Scopic in *The Vikings* (1958)

KATHLEEN COYNE KELLY

"See for yourself."
— Lord Egbert to Einar

"It really was a Western set in the days of the Vikings."
— Kirk Douglas

As do the majority of film trailers, the trailer for *The Vikings* (Richard Fleischer, 1958)[1] offers a mixture of the diegetic; that is (in this case), excerpts from the narrative that constructs the world of '50s Hollywoodized Vikings, and the non- or extra-diegetic; that is, a voice-over and graphics promoting the film.[2] And, as is typical of earlier films (and true again with respect to the widespread use of CGI in contemporary Hollywood films), the trailer also advertises the technology used in the making of the story-world in such a way that technology itself is made a feature, even a star, of the film, as when (over a full-screen shot of a castle) we read:

IN HORIZON-SPANNING TECHNIRAMA AND MAGNIFICENT TECHNICOLOR.

In addition, the trailer also features Mario Nascimbene's magisterial score for the film, including the now-famous three-note fanfare intended to invoke the sound of a Viking horn: both sight and sound are offered as exercises in the authentic.[3]

The trailer begins with a low-angle shot of men shooting fiery arrows into the sky, against which is flashed:

ACROSS ALL THE CENTURIES!

followed by a cut to a long shot of a Viking ship in full sail, blazoned with the words: ACROSS ALL THE SEAS!, followed by a cut to a front-on shot of men rowing: ACROSS THE SCREEN COME ... *The Vikings.* The stirring voice-over declaims:

For the first time, the saga of the mighty Viking hordes who swept across the world, breaking every commandment of heaven and earth as they put an age to the torch.

Then, against scenes chosen to match the voice-over, we hear:

To a Viking there was no life except life in battle.
There was no death except death in battle.
There were no women except women taken in battle.

9

Against a montage we read:

NOTHING EVER MATCHED ITS VIOLENCE! ... ITS VENGEANCE! ... ITS VASTNESS!

Next, against a vista of sky, mountains, and fjords, we read:

Actually Filmed Amid the Ice-Capped Fjords of Norway!

Hyperbole, half-truths,[4] claims to historicity and authenticity — the assertion of film as a, or even *the*, medium for accurately registering the past — delineate the discursive field in which *The Vikings* participates. Those stark snowy fjords of Norway seem to rise out of history, promising us a connection to a visible and tangible past. If Jack Cardiff's stunning cinematography[5] allows us to "see" the age of the Vikings, then surely the camera also enables us to see into the hearts and minds and lives of the Vikings themselves. The trailer hopes to persuade that there is a there there, and, if reviews at the time of its premiere in theatres and after it was released on DVD in 2002 are any evidence, *The Vikings* succeeds in so persuading, diegetically because of its Technicolor scenery, and extra-diegetically because the publicity for the film asserts its authenticity so absolutely that no reviewer questions it, therefore becoming complicit in it.[6]

In his influential *The Imaginary Signifier*, Christian Metz argues against the "there" of cinema, saying that cinema dramatizes "the absence of the object seen ... the illusion ... of a state of desire which is not just imaginary" (61, 63). Cinema is not a transparent medium, but instead always and only signifies itself as a technology, shaping — better, naturalizing — the ways we see and the ways we are seen. *The Vikings* is a case study in how a Hollywood studio (here, United Artists and Kirk Douglas' company, Byrna Productions) banks on — literally — the processes by which everyone, from director to cinematographer to actors to audience, contributes to (reflexively or not) the pleasurable fiction that *The Vikings* is about medieval Norway and its inhabitants, and to the equally-pleasurable fiction that the cinema permits us to recover the past.

Still, we can identify fissures in these fictions in the ways that *The Vikings* and the apparatuses that first produced it and now maintain its place in the history of cinema constantly slide from *telos* to *techne*. In what follows, I hope to document this slippage by showing how *The Vikings* can be read/seen as a story about seeing and looking and the limits *of* and *on* seeing and looking. Such a story operates on both diegetic and extra-diegetic levels, as I have been suggesting. The hero of the film — or, better, antihero — Einar (Kirk Douglas) is blind in one eye. Within the film, Einar's half-blindness can be read as a trope for a number of ways of seeing, not seeing, and mis-seeing. In the fluctuating space between the inside/outside of *The Vikings*, Einar's hampered vision contrasts with the audience's unfettered indulgence in a full and greedy gaze (as A. S. Byatt would say) that takes its enjoyment in the magnificent scenery of the film. And outside of the film, yet contributing to and/or constraining how we view it, hover two other narratives: the story of the making of the film and the story of the Production Code Association's interference with and influence on the film. Regulating spectatorship, of course, pertains not only to what and how one sees and is seen, but to what one has been prevented from seeing.

First, a summary of the plot of *The Vikings* is in order: Viking leader Ragnar (Ernest Borgnine) kills Edwin, the king of Northumbria, and rapes Enid (Maxine Audley), his queen, who is made pregnant. She sends their son Eric away to avoid any threats from the new king, Aella (Frank Thring), cousin to the former king. However, Eric is captured by Ragnar's men and made a slave. Ragnar's son Einar (Kirk Douglas) has a hostile encounter with the adult Eric (Tony Curtis), who flies his hawk at Einar. Neither Einar nor Eric know that they are half-brothers. The bird claws out Einar's left eye. Eric is condemned to death by drowning. Eric calls upon Odin, who sends a wind to drive back the tide, thus saving Eric's life.

Lord Egbert (James Donald), an English exile at Ragnar's court who is helping Ragnar harry Northumbria by furnishing maps of the coast, has recognized the stone that Eric wears around his neck, which, unbeknownst to Eric, is from the pommel of the royal sword of Northumbria (Eric is an example of the *bel inconnu* in medieval literature). Einar then captures Morgana (Janet Leigh), a Welsh princess betrothed to Aella, and plans to ransom her. However he, as well as Eric, falls in love with her. Eric rescues Morgana from Einar, they pledge their love to each other, and escape to England — with Ragnar, now their prisoner. Ragnar is condemned to death by Aella, who orders Eric to push Ragnar into a pit of wolves. Eric instead cuts Ragnar's bonds and gives him a sword so that he may die honorably and reach Valhalla. Ragnar jumps into the pit. Aella plans on sending Eric in after Ragnar, but Morgana promises to marry Aella if he allows Eric to live. Aella instead cuts off Eric's hand and sets him adrift.

Eric reaches Einar's camp, and makes common cause with Einar. They go to England and overrun Aella's castle. Eric pushes Aella into the wolf pit while Einar seeks out Morgana, who is praying in the chapel with Father Godwin (Alexander Knox). Einar declares that Morgana will be his queen; she rejects him, and Einar, in his rage, goes in search of Eric. Morgan tells Einar that Eric is his half brother, but he refuses to listen. Eric and Einar fight on the castle battlements, and Einar, when given a chance to kill Eric, hesitates just long enough to give Eric the advantage. Eric kills Einar, and then arranges a Viking funeral for Einar.

Let me begin my discussion of the film with what seems to be the most transparently accessible part of *The Vikings*: its natural setting, the Hardangerfjord in Hordaland, Norway. The 111-mile Hardangerfjord, while sparsely populated (it was made a national park in 2005), is home to thirteen towns and villages, not one of which intrude upon what we see in *The Vikings*.[7] Thus the moviegoer enters into a suspended, unreal space and time, a glass snowball of a world. When we take our own photographs and videos of a beautiful scene, do we not maneuver to exclude telephone wires and even other tourists? We become *metteurs en scène* in small, specialists in fantasies in which we alone figure. "Nature" itself is a fantasy, for how we perceive it is a construction of a given culture's desires — and a common American desire is to see nature "as it is" — that is, unspoiled, untouched, magnificent on its own terms. The fraught and overdetermined term, "virgin territory," comes too readily to mind. "The visual is essentially pornographic," declares Fredric Jameson, "it has its end in rapt, mindless fascination ... [films] ask us to stare at the world as though it were a naked body" (1).

The Vikings puts nature on lascivious display, generating a desire to look, and to look again, at that which, we may be lulled into believing, has not been looked at before. And surely the Hardangerfjord has never been seen as we see it in the film: we should not forget that each unfolding vista is controlled by the camera — and, to boot, a camera often positioned at impossible angles and heights, unlimited in its potential compared to the limited scope of the human eye. And let us also not forget the revelation that Technicolor was for mid-twentieth-century audiences. Known and exploited for its saturated colors, Technicolor was primarily used for musicals, costume adventures, and animated films — fantasies all, the most famous of which is *The Wizard of Oz* (Victor Fleming, 1939). The highly-saturated colors have the effect of emphasizing the difference between the real world and the reel world; the latter, of course, infinitely preferable; we are indeed made rapt, as Jameson says. And the Technirama camera, an unwieldy monster of a machine, produced sweeping, panoramic views, perfect for capturing the mountains, sky, and sea of Hardangerfjord.[7]

Reviewers universally praise the splendid backdrop that is foregrounded in *The Vikings*; these reviews, as does the trailer for the film, feed already-existing expectations and create new expectations for visual pleasure. A moviegoer, after all, *looks forward to*. In fact, in his commentary that accompanies the DVD, Fleischer recalls that "the audience applauded the scenery" at the premiere of the film. In this respect, audiences may be responding to what Jean Baudrillard, in his controversial and often opaque *Seduction*, calls "seduction by means of visibility." He writes that film

> gives you so much — colour, lustre, sex, all in high fidelity, and with all the accents (that's life!) — that you have nothing to add, that is to say, nothing to give in exchange. Absolute repression: by giving you a little too much one takes away everything. Beware of what has been so well "rendered," when it is being returned to you without you ever having given it! [30].

Beware, says Baudrillard, for acceding to the idea of a there there has serious consequences. Looking at scenery in *The Vikings* may well be a passive pleasure, one in which nature is naturalized, made into a consumable object.

But nature becomes narrativized, and we are mobilized, at the point at which the Vikings first appear in their ship under full sail. Nature begins to speak only in relation to Ragnar, Einar, and others. Nature has no time; men (Fleischer, Vikings) tell the time, and it is the tenth century, in Technicolor. Consider the famous scene in which Einar "runs the oars" — that is, jumps from one oar held horizontally to the next all around the ship. The audience's gaze is propelled from the monumental scenery behind the ship to the scale of the human; the mountains recede as our vision contracts to one man who wears a crazy, exultant grin as he leaps from one oar to another.

No one doubts that the grin belongs not to Einar, but to Kirk Douglas, who insisted on doing the stunt himself — and insisted that Fleischer film him at close enough range so that moviegoers would recognize that he, not a stuntman, was running the oars. Diegetically, such a feat testifies to Einar's daring and to the Vikings' collective courage and strength; it also testifies to the Vikings' triumph over nature as their story begins to crowd out mountains, sky, and sea. Yet the Vikings' victory over nature is only temporary, as the staging of the Viking funeral suggests at the end of the film. Einar and his ship, set alight by hundreds of flaming arrows, sail slowly out of view and sink into the sea, memorialized not by a saga, but by a film. "Nobody had seen the running of the oars in the past thousand years," says Fleischer, marveling at the power of the camera to capture the past. Thus the filming of the running of the oars might also attest to an extra-diegetic desire that the camera function as a time machine.

Sometimes, however, a devotion to recreating the past has its repercussions. For example, using blueprints for the Gokstad and Oseberg ships in the *Vikingskipshuset* (Viking Ship House) in Oslo, Norway, Fleischer and production designer Harper Goff built three ships for the film. Fleischer stresses that they were "exact duplicates" of real ships. Yet there was an unexpected problem in reproducing the ships with such attention to detail, for the original ships were built by and for much smaller men. Fleischer relates that

> the oar holes were too close together, which meant that the rowers of these ships couldn't use the oars properly because their hands were hitting the backs of the man sitting in front of him

so they couldn't really row the boats properly ... we had to plug up every other oar hole and cut down the number of rowers.[9]

Sometimes history requires a retrofit. And Kirk Douglas, writing as a producer, is just the one to do it:

I employed experts from Norway, Sweden, and Denmark to give me an exact historical feeling about the period of the Vikings, the exact dimensions of the boats that they used, how the houses and the mead hall were built, etc. The experts disagreed, and finally I had to make the decisions myself [283].[10]

Thus the film as well as its paratexts (that is, publicity releases and DVD commentary), attest to its creators' commitment to verisimilitude of place and time in *The Vikings*, however expedient such a commitment might be. Fleischer is proud to say that "Kirk Douglas ... and I decided ... to make this the most authentic picture about the Vikings that had ever been made or could be made."

However, Fleischer and Douglas' concomitant dedication to verisimilitude of action, as it were, turned out to be subject to a force external to the film; that is, dependent on the Production Code Administration (PCA), the system of self-censorship to which Hollywood directors submitted for almost forty years, from the early 30s until the late 60s. While in production, *The Vikings* generated a good deal of correspondence between Geoffrey M. Shurlock, then director of the PCA, and Jerry Bresler, producer of the film. Shurlock objected to several proposed scenes on a number of counts. He had the following PCA guidelines in mind: "Brutal killings are not to be presented in detail" (Section I.1.a); "Repellent Subjects ... must be treated within the careful limits of good taste," including "Brutality and possible gruesomeness.... Apparent cruelty to ... animals" (XII.3, 5)[11]; "Scenes of Passion ... should not be introduced when not essential to the plot.... Excessive and lustful kissing, lustful embraces, suggestive postures and gestures, are not to be shown" (II.2.a, b); and "Seduction or Rape ... should never be more than suggested, and only when essential for the plot, and even then never shown by explicit method" (II.3.a).

Shurlock judged the initial screenplay for *The Vikings* as "unacceptable by reason of an improper treatment of illicit sex, and a great deal of excessive and unacceptable violence and brutality" (Letter, 28 January 1957). As the final version of *The Vikings* attests, Bresler agreed to cut out or modify many of the scenes that Shurlock objected to. It appears that a series of trade-offs were made: we have the scene in which Eric loses his hand, but we do not have the scene in which, apparently, Morgana was to lose a finger, or the scene in which Aella was to be mutilated. The rape of Enid is not shown, as originally called for, but is only suggested; the love scene between Eric and Morgana progresses only so far before a dissolve. Instead of subjecting Father Godwin to death by fire, he is merely pushed to the floor. (The PCA, which had strong ties to the Catholic Legion of Decency, included guidelines for the respectful treatment of religion and religious.) The PCA objected to the expressions "dilly-dong-dangle" and "jig her dizzy"—hardly Old Norse—as "unacceptably sex suggestive"; these phrases were removed (Letter, 28 January 1957).

An ongoing point of contention for the PCA was the depiction of Einar's blinding by the hawk—not only because of its "excessive gruesomeness," as Shurlock writes, but also out of a concern for the treatment of the bird (Letter, 28 January and 5 June 1957; Letter, 31 July 1958). The scene remains in the film—and it is indeed stomach-churning. Shurlock also writes that the scene in which Eric's hand is cut off and cauterized is "completely overboard on brutality, and could not be approved in the finished picture," yet this scene also remains as we watch the sweep of the sword and then see Eric bandaging his cauterized stump (Letter, 28 January 1957, Letter, 21 June 1957).

Bresler was following standard practice, for studios routinely negotiated with PCA Director Breen and then Spurlock after him. Leonard J. Leff has argued that, while producers, directors, and actors often reviled the PCA for its interference, many studios collaborated with the PCA because its involvement actually contributed to Hollywood's status as a legitimate entertainment industry, and because the PCA centralized censorship, so to speak, freeing studios up from dealing with distributors state by state.[14] While some studios might choose to submit scripts that did not generate any criticisms or suggestions from the PCA — a form of teaching to the test — others pushed back in varying degrees, depending on the film.[15] It seems that including numerous scenes that were known in advance to be in violation of the Code is one way to challenge the authority of the Code, since, theoretically, the more one has to give up, the more one might be able to negotiate to keep. Studios could also gamble on something slipping past the censor's eye.

Moreover, the PCA actually modulated its many proscriptions by conceding that a given scene may well be "necessary plot material," or "essential for the plot," and thus a producer, if persistent and persuasive enough, was often inspired to take full advantage of what often proved to be a loophole. The Spurlock-Bresler correspondence suggests strategic compromising on both sides; in fact, it is worth speculating that various depictions of violence found in the original screenplay which are not found in the final version were simply offered as red herrings to the PCA. (I find it hard to believe that "jig her dizzy" was seriously meant.) Bresler seems to have operated by capitulating on some scenes while ignoring Shurlock's objections to others.

In the middle of Bresler's correspondence with the PCA, the Supreme Court heard *Roth v. United States*, the case that, while it affirmed that obscenity is not protected under the First Amendment, also insured that the definition of obscenity was to be decided locally:

> The standard for judging obscenity ... is whether, to the average person, applying contemporary community standards, the dominant theme of the material, taken as a whole, appeals to prurient interest [4.c].[16]

Spurlock, now with six out of nine Supreme Court judges behind him, sent Bresler a copy of Motion Picture Association of America President Eric Johnston's letter to the Board of Directors of the PCA lauding the Supreme Court decision. The resulting correspondence between Bresler and Shurlock must be reproduced here at length to be fully appreciated. Bresler responds:

> It has always been my policy to keep you apprised of any new sequences, additions or deletions prior to shooting so that I could gain your advice and blessings. However, we did one sequence about which I did not have time to write you ... In order to strengthen [Einar] as a rough, violent Viking and emphasize the intensity and lust of his desire for Morgana ... we developed a sequence of Einar bathing ... in a large barrel of beer with [six] youthful, attractive Viking girls during a festive orgy. This sequence occurs just before his scene with Morgana in which she is rescued by Eric. Our research indicated this to be rather mild behavior for Viking warriors accustomed to taking what they wanted. They obviously did not resort to modern social graces. The scene is lush, exciting and could easily be considered sexy [Letter, 20 August 1957].

Now that he has shot the scene — and therefore paid for it — Bresler is worried that Shurlock is going to demand that it be deleted. Shurlock replies:

While it undoubtedly would be good news to audiences generally to learn that the Vikings never took a bath of any kind whatsoever, I am afraid that this sequence ... would have to be considered in violation of the Code.... Would there be any point in trying to trick this scene so as to suggest that the girls and Kirk are not nude in the beer barrel? [Letter, 26 August 1957].

Bresler is indeed disingenuous in his three-pronged argument: the hectic pace of filming, dramatic development of the plot, and historical verisimilitude. Bresler's strategy is not lost on Spurlock; note that Spurlock, disingenuous himself, suggests a way to save the scene. They collude in tongue-in-cheekiness. The scene was deleted. The exchange offers evidence for how the censor's Panopticon in Hollywood was able to function; both Bresler and Spurlock acquiesce in, if not embrace, their respective roles. And the more Bresler and Spurlock (or anyone else in Hollywood) participated in such back-and-forths, the more their positions began to harden into established discursive nodes. It is the many accretions of such moments that made film censorship the discursive practice that it was, in a space that had not existed before Bresler, Spurlock, et al., helped to create it. Judge Potter Stewart's famous description of pornography, "I know it when I see it," ought to be reversed: "I see it when I know it." In other words, one's seeing (a common enough metaphor for understanding) is controlled by the discourse in which one is situated.

While the above exchange certainly hints at economic forces at work in the operations of the Panopticon, I am more interested in Bresler's insistence on his commitment to historical accuracy. It is necessary, he says, to depict hacking and hewing and drinking and wenching. "Our research indicated." Being faithful to the Age of the Vikings collaterally and conveniently licenses representations of violence and sex, for such representations, are, as the Code allows Bresler to argue, "essential for the plot."

As does many another student of movie medievalism, Nickolas Haydock argues that the "very alterity of the Middle Ages works to make it an especially potent preserve of fantasy" (7). While medieval scholars are very much engaged in debates about the degree to which the Middle Ages is Other to us (Jauss, Eco, Spiegel), pop cultural appropriations of the medieval often depend upon the assumption of, or the desire for, alterity. In this case, the alterity of the Viking Age furnishes the pretext for representations of violence and sex, and this very alterity serves as the discursive grounds for testing the limits of the PCA Code. Still, this alterity is both historical and fantasized, and, if at any point the historical is found lacking, fantasy will supply.

For example, Fleischer relates with relish the story behind the scene in which the young married woman with whom Einar had been having an affair loses her braids. Fleischer says proudly, "We invented this game," thus contradicting all that he has said before about how meticulously authentic *The Vikings* was. "The character girl, 'Pigtails,'"[17] as Fleischer refers to her, is subjected to a fidelity test — she is put in stocks and her braids are fastened to the boards; her husband, quite drunk, is loudly encouraged to throw axes at her; if faithful, she would lose only her braids; if unfaithful, her husband would miss the braids, with dire but, according to the rules of this game, just consequences. As the husband loses his balance, it looks like he may indeed miss the last throw, but Einar steps forward and throws the axe, cutting off the last braid, and, as the partner in infidelity, subverting the test entirely.

Twenty-first century viewers may wonder at the PCA reaction to violence in *The Vikings*, especially since the Vikings hack and hew with so much glee that there is nothing really frightening about them.[18] *The Vikings* is far less bloody and violent than anything that we might see today, and certainly less violent than what we see on network television. If a claim to historicity enables the representation of violence in *The Vikings*, what does that violence in turn enable? It is almost meaningless in the film except to register the oth-erness of the Vikings. However, what the violence means outside of the film, in 1950s Holly-wood, has some significance. Just as reviewers raved about the scenery in the film, they almost always commented on the violence. By doing so, reviewers reproduce the violence as violence, foregrounding it as a subject in itself. Almost all reviewers are complicit in Bresler's anti–PCA project by granting that such violence was to be expected, given that *The Vikings* was set in the barbaric past. Such reviews helped to further, I would argue, both an appetite and a justification for the scopic un/pleasures of violence in the film. The 1953 Marlon Brando vehicle, *The Wild One* (Laslo Benedek), to make a comparison, though less violent, was much more shocking than *The Vikings* because of its contemporary setting. A motorcycle gang just might invade one's town; a Viking ship is not going to sail into one's harbor. By exploiting precisely this distinction between past and present, *The Vikings* was able to push the limits of violence that were hitherto accepted in Hollywood, expanding what might be seen on the screen in the name of historicity.

So far, I have been discussing the violence in *The Vikings* as it occurs in various battle scenes — and one could also include various carousing and drinking scenes, for Ragnar's men are represented as playing awfully hard. Such violence in both contexts is offered as homosocial good sport. However, there is another kind of violence that is enacted on the individual body, and that is the depiction, respectively, of Einar's losing his eye and Eric's losing his hand.[19] Because less abstract, this violence is more visceral. There is a greater pos-sibility for audience identification with a singular body than with plural bodies, making the mutilations more horrific. United Artists, exasperated with the PCA impositions on the film, circulated a publicity handout that mocks the censors for caring more about the treat-ment of the hawk than the depiction of Einar's blinding (*Variety*, 3 July 1957). This handout suggests that the studio knew full well that the scene in which Einar is blinded is tough to watch. And most reviewers reacted strongly to the scene as well, proving that the PCA's sense was correct.

The scene is indeed gruesome — more so because the weapon in Eric's hand is a bird. There is something cowardly, not manly, not human, even perverted, about a man grating out the command "Kill!" and setting a hawk at another man. Such an attack is nature (under the control of a slave, no less) gone wrong, made into a prosthesis to carry out Eric's mur-derous intentions. Based on a much more gratuitous episode in *Viking*, the book by Edison Marshall on which the film is based, the scene is not well integrated into the film, which demands that Einar be blinded, though the means by which matter not at all. What is important is that Einar displays outwardly his flawed, even fatal, perspective; his vision is invariably self-serving, narrow, cruel, and hubristic.

In his commentary on the DVD, Fleischer says of the hawk scene:

> The hawk sequence in the picture was much talked about and actually not a very difficult shot to make, because the trick of doing that kind of thing was in the editing ... we have a trained hawk fly toward the camera and then have a shot of the hawk's legs that were between his [Kirk's] fingers so he could control ... we taped the hawk's beak so that it wouldn't actually take Kirk's eye out and all he needed to do was move his arm with the hawk on it up to his face fairly quickly.

Directors who perform tricks are not bound by the prestidigitator's code, apparently. Fleis-cher proudly advertises the *techne* that contributes to *telos*. Fleischer continues:

> You know this film has a reputation of being a very bloody film, lots of blood, lots of fighting, and it's just not true; there is in fact no blood shown in this picture except in this one shot

where Kirk has his hand up holding the hawk and you see a small stream of blood trickling down between his fingers ... but everybody talks about how bloody it was because of the impression you get.

Fleischer is correct; there is very little blood in the film, though much hammy violence. Einar crouches on the ground, blood indeed trickling through his fingers — very red Technicolor blood. And yes, "everybody talks about how bloody it was because of the impression you get" — a more marvelous tautology to convey the power of the camera could not have been invented by a film critic.

Still, however much the PCA sought to limit what it considered to be unnecessary violence and sexual explicitness in *The Vikings*, one shockingly laughable scene remains in the film. What is included in the final film was not in the screenplay — all dialogue and only a few directions, keep in mind — that the PCA so assiduously examined. This scene is, in fact, quite "sex suggestive," as the Code puts it, and is entirely dependent upon looking, and looking in a certain way.

When the Vikings storm Aella's castle, they bring up a huge battering ram on wheels. The drawbridge over the moat is closed, and the scene of the battering of the main gate is shot from below, from the moat, so that what one sees appears to be the shaft of a huge penis (the tree trunk) and two equally huge testicles (the wheels) crashing into the gate. Cut to the interior: a lone guard, pike in hand, stands to the side of the gate, which bursts violently inward. Cut to the gate bursting inward; cut to the outside as Vikings swarm over the battering ram and enter. These cuts alternate with shots in which a terrified Aella watches the assault on the gate through a very narrow arrowslit — yes — in the castle wall. Is that really a brutal phallic ramming? Is that guard a kind of hymeneal sentry? Is the viewer retrieving some embarrassing connection between siege warfare and sexual intercourse from a stock of visual memories — now perhaps to be distrusted and certainly disavowed? Is the viewer reading too much into the scene?

And to compound this image is another visual penetration, this one bordering on the sacrilegious. After the castle has been so breached, Einar goes in search of Morgana, who is praying in the castle's small chapel with Father Godwin. What might the viewer make of Einar's crashing through the stained glass window to gain entry? The window, a shattered aperture from which red and blue shards of stained glass hang inward, dominates the frame as Einar presses his lustful suit upon Morgana. "The chapel is a sanctuary!" exclaims the priest, protector of chastity.

Fleischer, in his DVD commentary, may offer a clue to why we see what the PCA didn't see, refused to see, or declined to see. (Film reviewers are silent on both scenes.) At one point, Fleischer discusses a photograph of himself and cinematographer Jack Cardiff clowning around in wigs. He says: "Jack and I ... always do a gag picture [when we work on a film together] ... just kidding around, it became a tradition." Fleischer and Cardiff obviously have a sense of humor. It is tempting to think that Fleischer and Cardiff set up both scenes deliberately and thus were able to flout the following part of the PCA Code: "Obscenity in word, gesture, reference, song, joke, or by suggestion (even when likely to be understood only by part of the audience) is forbidden" (IV).[20] Spurlock had required that the single "damn" in the film be excised; this was something unequivocal, readable and viewable on the page (Letter, 28 January 1957). However, the visual obscenity that is the siege engine must be witnessed, and witnessed *to* in such a way that advertises something rather embarrassing, perhaps, about the viewer's own ways of seeing.

I would like to employ another way of seeing to the PCA file on *The Vikings* in order

The one-handed Tony Curtis (left) as Eric and the one-eyed Kirk Douglas as Einar, the Viking half-brothers, in Richard Fleischer's 1958 film *The Vikings* (editor's collection).

to consider how medievalists might view this material, for what emerges from the correspondence and the newspaper clippings is a cinematic version of a situation familiar to scholars, and that is the vagaries of manuscript production, reproduction, and circulation that we usually discuss under the rubric of *mouvance*.[21] In 1958, there was no single version of *The Vikings*, but multiple ones, for different countries employed different censorship standards, resulting in different cuts of the film. One simply did not see the same film in Los Angeles, in London, or in Berlin. German censors, for example, objected to Einar's boast about Morgana, "I will make her scream so that she will be heard as far as Wales" and to the "Pigtails" scene, and to other scenes that they considered excessively violent (Letter 1, 28 November 1958); Australian censors wanted the scene in which Father Godwin is thrown to the floor deleted (Letter 2, 28 November 1958). In these cases, it is not a single author (a James Joyce who wrote a novel called *Ulysses*, for example) who is being censored, but a corporate product; the film has long since left the director's hands (who, for a variety of reasons, has already introduced *mouvance* into the screenplay, whether his own or another's altogether).

If we think of films (keeping in mind the death of *auteur* theory, if not of *auteurs* themselves, *pace* Indiewood), as having no single author; more radically, if we think of films as "authorless," then a thick description of the history of production of a given movie might be viewed as a study in the cinematic parallels to textual mobility and variability and as a collaborative, social artifact[22] which resides in an extremely complex, intertextual space.[23]

This Venn diagram-like space includes, but is not limited to, the finished film — itself a notion destabilized by the director's cut, for we must now distinguish between the initial release of a film in theatres and different DVD versions. This space also includes the oeuvre of a given actor. Walter Metz writes of the star persona as itself a generator of intertextuality (31).

The cult of the celebrity at mid-twentieth century makes it difficult to see (with emphasis on "to appraise") *The Vikings* as anything but a palimpsest of the pseudo-medieval and of faux Hollywood: Kirk Douglas, Tony Curtis, and Janet Leigh are much too present as stars to suspend our belief with respect to the characters that they play — not that the makers of *The Vikings* intend for us to forget Douglas, Curtis, and Leigh. (And the powers behind the film do not mind if we know that Ernest Borgnine, who plays Ragnar, father to Einar, is one year older than Douglas in real life. It serves as a humorous talking point.) Intertextual associations between and among films are not necessarily made diachronically, but synchronically: because of DVDs, films exist in a kind of super-time — Bakhtin's great time, in which chronology no longer matters.

For example, it may be impossible to see Janet Leigh in *The Vikings* as anyone but a glamorously blonde star wearing a tight bodice and having impossibly pointy breasts; this branding was integral to the creation of her star persona. Thus it is difficult to see Leigh as Morgana in *The Vikings* without reference to her other roles in other films (eighty-three altogether, including television roles); consider Leigh as the pointy-breasted Princess Aleta in *Prince Valiant* (Henry Hathaway, 1954); the abducted and abused pointy-breasted newlywed Susan Vargas in *A Touch of Evil* (Orson Welles, 1958); and of course most famously, as the doomed pointy-breasted Marion Crane in *Psycho* (Alfred Hitchcock, 1960), a role that not only haunts all of Leigh's work after 1960, but also travels backward to interfere in one's viewing of any film that she had made previously.

For another example, Kirk Douglas the actor keeps breaking through the character Einar, resulting in a kind of double vision for the spectator. Thus part of the shock of the hawk scene is that it is Kirk Douglas, not Einar the Viking, whom we see ("identify") crouching on the ground. If one knows Douglas in his role as Vincent van Gogh in *Lust for Life* (Vincente Minnelli, 1956), how could one watch the hawk scene in *The Vikings* and not think of the earlier film? Van Gogh's/Douglas' self-mutilation is carried out offscreen to the sound of a crashing 50s score. We hear a scream, and Douglas rises up, bloody hand clasped to bloody head. This may not be a welcome intertext as one watches *The Vikings*.

Lust for Life was intended to be serious, historical drama. Therefore Douglas had no qualms about growing a beard for the film. As self-portraits of van Gogh placed strategically *mise-en-scène* suggest, Douglas actually bore enough of a resemblance to the painter to pull off the role. But *The Vikings* is a "star vehicle." Richard Dyer observes:

> In certain respects, a set of star vehicles is rather like a film genre such as the Western, the musical or the gangster film. As with genres proper, one can discern across a star's vehicles continuities of iconography (e.g., how they are dressed, made-up and coiffed, performance mannerisms, the setting with which they are associated), visual style (e.g. how they are lit, photographed, placed within the frame) and structure (e.g. their role in the plot, the function in the film's symbolic pattern) [62].

In *The Vikings*, Douglas is not interested in bearded verisimilitude (there never was an "Einar"), even if Vikings customarily wore beards. In fact, Tony Curtis relates in his memoir that Douglas offered a two-hundred-dollar bonus to all the men acting in the film to grow beards (187). Douglas is the only clean-shaven Viking in the film. Surely the fact that *The*

Vikings is an action adventure picture dictated Douglas' decision to foreground his own handsome, craggy face. In an interesting, perhaps anxious, meta-moment, the film offers an explanation for Einar's lack of a beard. Ragnar says of Einar that: "He is so vain of his beauty he won't let a man's beard hide it. He scrapes his face like an Englishman." And Ragnar's jibe sets us up for Ragnar's later taunt in which he declares that Einar is worried that his "pretty dainty face [could be] spoiled."

After his blinding, Einar is usually filmed from the right so that his scarred face and milky blue eye are highlighted. But Douglas is obviously playing at Einar. We know that it is makeup and a contact lens. However, the stare of that cloudy blue eye remains unsettling, serving to distance us from the character and figuring as a sign of swaggering bombastic masculinity. It is established early on that Einar is an enthusiastic wencher. After his blinding, Einar's already peculiar notions about love as a battlefield turn darker: "Look at me," he says to Ragnar. "Do you think with this face I want the kind of wife who would let me touch her? I want her to fight me tooth and nail the first time I take her and the last." (The PCA objected to this dialogue—as well as to his boast that "I'll show [Morgana] what forging can be done when fire meets fire! I'll make her howl till they hear her in Wales!") Einar forces his will on everyone that he has dealings with. The ruined face and vision of Einar functions chiastically: he is difficult to look at and he has difficulty looking. He is at his most self-delusional with Morgana:

> EINAR: "You will be my queen. I knew it the first moment I saw you. You knew it too. You knew it that night on my ship."
> MORGANA: "It's not true."
> EINAR: "Yes ... it is true."
> MORGANA: "I don't love you."
> EINAR: "You must love me exactly as I love you."

Einar's end is located in the moment that his perception betrays him.

I conclude by relating an anecdote about Jacques Derrida at one of his lectures:

> An audience member stood up and recounted the scene from *The Wizard of Oz* in which Dorothy and her friends finally meet the wizard, who is powerful and overwhelming until Toto pulls away the curtain to reveal a very small man. "Professor Derrida, are you like that?" the audience member asked. Derrida paused before replying, "You mean like the dog?"[24]

The story is a brilliant enactment of Derrida's critical and philosophical project, for not only does it hinge upon an ambiguous first referent, but it also may not be true. The anecdote's *mouvance* suggests that it is apocryphal: it is set in either Nebraska or, perhaps out of a desire for narrative felicitousness, Kansas.

In addition, the story offers a tantalizing occasion for one to identify as a dog, or at the very least, as a poststructuralist literary or film critic invested in exposing the workings of the ideologies that organize textual and cinematic fantasies. In the context of this essay, however, I am particularly interested in the fact that Toto's pulling back of the curtain is a diegetic event. It has very real consequences for those pilgrims who have reached the Emerald City. Diegetically, Toto's action replaces one fantasy (an omnipotent wizard) so that another, more ideologically satisfying one ("there's no place like home") may supplant it. Yet extra-diegetically, and keeping in mind the fable that Derrida has enabled, the wizard and the dog also play parts in an allegory about the *techne* and *telos* of cinema in which *techne* is the more privileged term.

As we have seen with respect to *The Vikings*, those involved in making a film, no matter how much they desire us to suspend our disbelief, also often desire for us to see how a film is created. Let me return to the fidelity test in which Einar axes Pigtails's braids. Fleischer tells us that the scene was actually shot in reverse, which depended upon a number of judicious cuts between the woman in the stocks and the men throwing the axes. "It looks absolutely convincing," he says. Almut Berg, who plays Pigtails, had to learn to grimace backward, which doesn't quite work. Moreover, there is a slight shimmer to the film at the point at which the axes quiver in the wood next to Pigtails's head. Thus the technology behind the trick has a way of revealing itself; it becomes part of the viewer's experience of the film, as in the *Wizard of Oz,* where one can see where the scenery ends at the studio wall. Such glitches (I hesitate to call them failures) function as small admonishments to Jameson's "rapt" viewer: the shimmer or the obvious studio wall invites investigations into how film constructs fantasy, and this way of seeing has its pleasures (consider the delights of continuity errors) comparable to the suspension of disbelief—and, I would argue, this is not an either/or proposition.

The scene in which Einar is blinded can be compared to that uncurtaining in the *Wizard of Oz* if we read both scenes as diegetic commentary on the power of the scopic with extra-diegetic implications. We who have consented to giving the control of our gaze over to the camera willingly watch as another loses control over his vision. Einar will never look the same, transitively and intransitively. But the compelling force that is Kirk Douglas is able to reassure us that it is just an illusion. We are grateful for the cut, the gap, between the hawk attack and the result, a man kneeling on the ground, raising one blue eye while covering the other, now bloody. Perhaps in Lacanian terms, the foregrounding of *techne* is one of the ways a film might manifest its unconscious. And perhaps every film could be said to contain its own Toto pulling back the curtain so that we may see, and take pleasure in, the wizard working his levers.

Notes

PCA correspondence courtesy of Special Collections, Margaret Herrick Library. Dialogue is transcribed from the film.

1. Released on DVD in 2002; based on *Viking,* a novel by Edison Marshall (New York: Farrar, Straus and Young, 1951). Fleischer had previously directed Kirk Douglas in *20,000 Leagues Under the Sea* (1954), and then went on to direct a number of popular film across several genres, including *Barabbas* (1961), *Fantastic Voyage* (1966), and *Soylent Green* (1973).

2. Another set of graphics worth noting is found in the initial backstory and the final credits: the use of The Bayeux Tapestry in animated cartoon form. See Richard Burt, "Re-embroidering the Bayeux Tapestry in Film and Media: The Flip Side of History in Opening and End Title Sequences." And it is also worth noting that Orson Welles furnishes the opening voice-over:

> The Vikings in Europe of the 8th and 9th century were dedicated to a pagan god of war, Odin. Cramped by the confines of their barren, icebound northlands, they exploited their skill as shipbuilders to spread a reign of terror then unequaled in violence and brutality in all the records of history. The greatest wish of every Viking was to die sword in hand, and enter Valhalla where a hero's welcome awaited them from the god Odin. The compass was unknown and they could steer only by the sun and the stars. Once fog closed in, they were left helpless and blind. After all, the earth was flat. Sail too far off course and the black wind would blow them across the Poison Sea that lay to the west and over the edge of the world into limbo. Their abiding aim was to conquer England, then a series of petty kingdoms, each one the jealous rival of the next. Thus, when the Vikings set forth to rob and plunder England, they never sailed out of sight of land. They confined their attacks to swift, overnight raids. It was no accident that the English Book of Prayer contained this sentence: "Protect us, Oh Lord, from the wrath of the Northmen."

3. Mario Nascimbene (1913–2002) also scored such films as *The Barefoot Contessa* (Joseph L. Mankiewicz, 1954), *Alexander the Great* (Robert Rossen, 1956), and *Solomon and Sheba* (King Vidor, 1959). The entire soundtrack for *The Vikings* can be heard on YouTube.

4. While mainly filmed in Norway, interiors for *The Vikings* were shot at Geiselgasteig Studios, Munich.

And the climactic scene of the battle between Einar and Eric on the parapets of a castle was filmed not on the coast of England, but at Fort de la Latte in Brittany. The studio, Kirk Douglas, and several reviewers seem to have lost their memories, claiming that a film about the Vikings had never been made before — for a quick counter claim, simply see the filmography at the end of this collection of essays.

5. Cardiff worked on *The Red Shoes* (Michael Powell and Ermeric Pressburger, 1948) and *The African Queen* (John Huston, 1951); he also directed his own Viking film, *The Long Ships* (1963).

6. What follows is a select group of reviews in the Herrick clippings file of *The Vikings* which specifically praise the scenery, admire its historicity, comment on the violence, or all three; I quote bits: "seascapes ... mystically beautiful," Jack Moffitt, "'Vikings' Biggest," *Hollywood Reporter* 20 May 1958: 3; "terror of the times is communicated," "The Vikings," *Variety* 21 May 1958: 6; "pretty gamey stuff for the kiddies," "breathtaking long shots," Vincent Canby, "The Vikings," *Motion Picture Herald* 24 May 1958: Product Digest Section 840; Bosley Crowther, "Norse Opera," *New York Times* 12 June 1958: 35; my favorite comment: "[*The Vikings*] seems extraordinarily faithful to its sources and research (except for a few armorial details)," "Rip-Roaring Seagoing Adventure," *Cue* 14 June 1958; "authentic scenery," Philip K. Scheuer, "'Vikings' Filled with Violent Action Scenes," *Los Angeles Times* 20 June 1958; "views of the fiords are impressive," *New Yorker* 21 June 1958; "gore is the keynote," Kay Proctor, *Los Angeles Examiner* 20 June 1958: [in Herrick clippings file]; "gore ... for the kiddie trade," ships are "memorable," Dick Williams, "'Vikings' Brawling, Lusty and Savage," *Mirror News* 20 June 1958; Hazel Flynn, "'Vikings' is Epic in Heroic Mood!" *Beverly Hills Citizen* 20 June 1958; "one of the bloodier bores ... the only good things to be said for it are that the scenery is nice, and the book ... was worse" *Time* 30 June 1958.

7. Production Designer Harper Goff built a medieval Viking village on the high cliffs of the fjord.

8. For a discussion of Technirama, see Martin Hart, "The American Widescreen Museum," http://www.widescreenmuseum.com/widescreen/wingtrl.htm.

9. For an account of the experienced local rowers that Fleischer and Douglas hired, see Göran R. Buckhorn, "Nordic Rowing Goes Hollywood," http://www.rowinghistory.net/vikings.htm.

10. Ernest Borgnine tells the story this way: "Kirk Douglas got fed up with these so-called experts.... [H]e measured a section of hull ... and told his production people to make it 'that big'" (123).

11. According to the original script (which followed the book more closely), it was called for Einar to cut the legs off the hawk ("Synopsis"). The killing of animals has been represented on screen since Thomas Edison's first forays into film at the end of the nineteenth century; after the public outcry over the filming of a horse being ridden off a cliff to its death in *Jesse James* (Henry King, 1939), the American Humane Society established a Film and Television Unit in 1940. See http://www.americanhumane.org/protecting-animals/programs/no-animals-were-harmed/ and http://www.cbc.ca/fifth/cruelcamera/cruelty.html.

12. The Motion Picture Production Code of 1930 (also known as the Hays Code) can be found conveniently at *ArtsReformation* <http://www.artsreformation.com/a001/hays-code.html> as well as in Leff and Simmons.

13. The original screenplay also called for Morgana to become a nun, to which the PCA objected, given her role as love/lust interest.

14. Leff, "Breening of America." Also see Jerold Simmons, "Violent Youth: The Censoring and Public Reception of *The Wild One* and *The Blackboard Jungle*."

15. See my "Hollywood Simulacrum: *The Knights of the Round Table* (1953)," in which I discuss how the director and screenwriters avoid a confrontation with the PCA by rewriting the Arthurian legend so that no adultery or incest surfaces in the narrative.

16. Conveniently at http://www.bc.edu/bc_org/avp/cas/comm/free_speech/roth.html.

17. Almut Berg, uncredited in the film, but credited on the Internet Movie Database (IMDb).

18. Though it could be argued, and perhaps should, that such a lack of seriousness makes the Vikings look like psychopaths.

19. These mutilations have their parallels in Norse mythology, and may well be the only real point of contact between *The Vikings* and medieval literature. Odin, father of the gods, sacrificed an eye in order to gain wisdom; that is, the ability to see the past, present, and future, through drinking at Mimir's Well. And the Norse god Týr, the god of victory and glory, lost his hand to the wolf Fenrir, who had been bound by a magical thread by the other gods frightened of his power. Fenrir had agreed to be bound only if one of the gods put his hand in his mouth. Once bound, realizing that he could not escape, Fenrir bit off Týr's hand. The film makes nothing of what a medievalist identifies as a literary allusion.

20. Spurlock was paying attention to the filming of the siege of Aella's castle, urging Bresler to "avoid as much as possible any detailed scenes of slaughter that might be unduly brutal or horrifying" (Letter, 21 June 1957).

21. See Joseph M. Sullivan, in "MGM's 1953 *Knights of the Round Table* in its Manuscript Context,"

who reads *Knights* in the context of other spectacle films produced by MGM in the 50s. Jonathan Stubbs, in "Hollywood's Middle Ages: The Development of *Knights of the Round Table* and *Ivanhoe*, 1935–53," makes an argument for reading screenplays as "crucial historical documents" (399). A stunning example of filmic *mouvance* is Orson Welles' 1958 *A Touch of Evil*, no longer extant as a rough cut, released in 1958, and revised and restored in 1976, and then reassembled in 1998, in accordance with a newly-discovered memo written by Welles.

22. See Jerome McGann, *A Critique of Modern Textual Criticism* (Chicago: University of Chicago Press, 1983).

23. In addition, it is possible to "see" a film that in fact exists only in the archives, as it were. For example, Douglas originally wanted Charlton Heston to play Eric: it would have been quite a different film if he had accepted the role. For another example, the beer-barrel scene that I discuss above is not extant in any copy of the film—compared to the famous case of *Spartacus* (Stanley Kubrick, 1960), to which the "snails and oysters" scene was restored in 1991. Yet the PCA correspondence offers a "restoration" of a sort in its documentation of the scene. In fact, the PCA correspondence might be said to offer a hypothetical, other film entirely. Given that Einar is blinded and Eric has his hand amputated, what sort of film would *The Vikings* have been if Morgana had lost a finger and Aella had been mutilated in some grisly way? This film, if it had been made, might then lend itself to a reading in which body parts and bodily boundaries figure. A prototypical slasher film? As it stands, the film that exists in the interstices between the various projections or even drafts of the film and the film that was actually made offers an opportunity for another small allegory, this time to be spun out of things cut off, cut short, and cut out.

24. Leland de la Durantaye, who relates this story and places it in Kansas, goes on to comment: "Appearances notwithstanding, this was no joke—or at least not merely one. The image of Derrida that readers often had was that of a wizard—wonderful or not—booming from behind an imposing curtain of works and words. But to himself, he was far more like the dog. The philosophical vocation that he adopted and advocated was a classical one—that of tugging at the loose ends of accepted truths, of taking hold of the curtains of metaphysical, linguistic, and political certainty, and pulling" ("Of Spirit"). But see Nass, who tells the story and places it in Nebraska (229).

Works Cited

Baudrillard, Jean. *Seduction*. 1979; trans. Brian Singer. Montreal: New World Perspectives, 1990.

Borgnine, Ernest. *Ernie: The Autobiography*. New York: Citadel, 2008.

Burt, Richard. "Re-embroidering the Bayeux Tapestry in Film and Media: The Flip Side of History in Opening and End Title Sequences." *Exemplaria* 19 (2007): 327–350.

Curtis, Tony, and Peter Golenbock. *American Prince: A Memoir*. New York: Harmony Books, 2008.

Douglas, Kirk. *The Ragman's Son: An Autobiography*. New York: Simon & Schuster, 1988.

Dyer, Richard. *Stars*. London: British Film Institute, 1998.

Haydock, Nickolas. *Movie Medievalism: The Imaginary Middle Ages*. Jefferson, NC: McFarland, 2008.

Kelly, Kathleen. "Hollywood Simulacrum: *The Knights of the Round Table* (1953)." *Exemplaria* 19 (2007): 270–289.

Leff, Leonard J. "The Breening of America." *PMLA* 106.3 (1991): 432–445.

_____, and Jerold L. Simmons. *The Dame in the Kimono: Hollywood, Censorship, and the Production Code*. Lexington: University Press of Kentucky, 2001.

Metz, Christian. *The Imaginary Signifier*. 1977; rpt. Bloomington: Indiana University Press, 1984.

Metz, Walter. *Engaging Film Criticism: Film History and Contemporary American Cinema*. New York: Peter Lang, 2004.

Nass, Michael. *Derrida from Now On*. New York: Fordham University Press, 2008.

Simmons, Jerold. "Violent Youth: The Censoring and Public Reception of *The Wild One* and *The Blackboard Jungle*." *Film History* 20 (2008): 381–391.

"UA 'Viking' Handout Kids Hollywood Censors." *Variety* 3 July 1957 [in Herrick clippings file].

Guess Who's Coming to Plunder?
Or, Disorientation and Desire
in *The Long Ships* (1964)

DONALD L. HOFFMAN

In the small but luminous galaxy that extends from Greta Garbo to Ann-Margret, from the Bergmans (Ingrid and Ingmar) to the Swedish Chef, inspired Swedes have lent their talents to popular culture in general and the Hollywood film in particular. One of the lesser lights in this galaxy is the genial journalist and garrulous essayist, novelist, and historian Frans Gunnar Bengtsson, whose epic novel, *Red Orm*, provided the origin of Jack Cardiff's remarkable and remarkably odd film, *The Long Ships*.

Born in 1894, Bengtsson brought more than a little of a late Romantic aesthetic into the twentieth century, an aesthetic that may well account both for his early popularity and his near total obscurity (except in the annals of Swedish *belles lettres*) today. A major ingredient in his Romantic sensibility is a susceptibility to hero worship, most particularly for the undeniably great (and, yes, romantic) Swedish king Charles XII, whose full title was "Charles, by the Grace of God King of Sweden, the Goths and the Vends, Grand Duke of Finland, Duke of Estonia and Karelia, Lord of Ingria, Duke of Bremen, Verden and Pommerania, Prince of Rügen and Lord of Wismar, and also Count Palatine by the Rhine, Duke of Bavaria, Count of Zweibrücken-Kleeburg, as well as Duke of Jülich, Cleve and Berg, Count of Waldenz, Spanheim and Ravensberg and Lord of Ravenstein."

This heroic king was famous as a military leader, ravaging most of the northern hemisphere from Denmark to Russia and Helsinki to Constantinople. Like Lawrence of Arabia, he was captured by the Turks and, after an extended imprisonment, managed to escape without having suffered the indignities apparently wreaked upon the dramatically costumed body of the enigmatic Englishman.

Back in Sweden, Charles barely survived his remarkable adventures and died not long before the final collapse of the barely viable Swedish empire. To moral historians, he is well known for having sworn off the vices of alcohol and women, as a consequence of which he was succeeded by his own elderly mother, and the ruling house of Palatinate-Zweibrücken came to an end. It was a kind of repetition of the end of the previous dynasty, when Queen Christina (known to Hollywood as Greta Garbo), who displayed as little interest in men as Charles did in women, retired to a convent in Rome unwedded and unbedded, and thus brought the House of Vasa to a dramatic and impolitic end.

In his essays, collected under the English title *A Walk to an Ant Hill*, Bengtsson continues his love affair with heroes, writing enthusiastically about such men of action as Wellington (which allows him to indulge in his reluctant admiration of his "anti-heroes," Napoleon and Masséna), Stonewall Jackson, Robert Monro (the Scottish hero who fought in the Thirty Years' War under the command of the Swedish king Gustavus Adolphus), and, yet again, an appreciation of Charles XII. Reflecting his love of letters, he does manage to include one writer in his catalogue of heroes, the scandalous, adventurous poet Villon, whom Bengtsson particularly admires for his equanimity in facing his own death, a quality that links him with Bengtsson's more conventional catalogue of military men. Other essays, however, remind us that this gentle man (at least that is the impression created by the persona of the essayist) mostly admired heroes from the comfort of his book-lined study where he turned the lives of heroes into the meditations of a literary man, transforming life into literature and barely suspecting that there might have been a difference.[2]

Bengtsson's major work, however, was the story of Red Orm, a rather clever Viking, whose first voyage took him to Leon in Spain where he recovered the bells of Santiago from the Caliph of Cordova, sojourned in the England of King Ethelred, where he participated in the Battle of Maldon and witnessed the beginning of the conversion of the North in the fateful year 1000. He settled down in Sweden, converted to Christianity, and became a powerful leader in his area. He undertook a last voyage to seek the Bulgar gold, which took him to Constantinople.

Bengtsson tells this story with an attention to detail that one might expect from a bookish part-time medievalist, who was devoted to the scholarly works of August Müller and W. P. Ker. Less expected, however, is the impish sense of humor that erupts in the book surprisingly and frequently. Much of this humor is at the expense of Christians. Indeed, within the first two pages of the novel, Bengtsson distinguishes between the sensible monks who are sold as slaves and become decent servants to their masters, while lamenting that "the majority continued to denounce the gods and to spend their time baptizing women and children instead of breaking stones and grinding corn, and made such a nuisance of themselves that soon it became impossible for the Göings to obtain, as hitherto, a yoke of three-year-old oxen for a sturdy priest without giving a measure of salt or cloth into the bargain, So feeling increased against the shaven men in the border country."[3] Things are hardly more pious after the conversion when Orm, now a Christian himself, hosts an enormous party for his neighbors, a great majority of whom are still pagan. As his guests lie strewn upon the ground in a drunken stupor, Orm suggests to the visiting English priest Father Willibald that this would be a great opportunity for a mass baptism. Willibald gives an extended response the essence of which is that the Pope has reluctantly decided that forced baptisms of the unconscious are invalid. Orm is sad, but feels obliged to defer to the opinion of the Holy Father. Willibald sympathizes with him, but suggests that "our task would be rendered too simple if we could enlist the assistance of ale in our endeavors to baptize the heathens" (291).

It is not surprising, perhaps, that Vikings are not particularly adept at theology nor that they are somewhat deficient in cross-cultural awareness. The first cross-cultural exchange occurs when on his first voyage Orm's men discover a disheveled figure floating in the sea, apparently having been thrown overboard from the passing Jutish ship. The men have a great deal of difficulty understanding him, but think that he is explaining most perplexingly that he is a Jute, disliked rowing on Saturday, and refused to eat salt pork. The Vikings are quite puzzled by this peculiar man, but finally work out that he is Jewish, not Jutish, and find him quite useful as a guide to the location and customs of the kingdoms of Spain, particularly Leon, Castile, and Cordova. Bengtsson manages a somewhat wittier Islamic joke when Toke suggests to Father Willibald "that we three shall sit down together in friendship, Bismillahi er-rahmani, er-rahimi! as we used to say when we served my lord Almansur" (348). Father Willibald is appalled. Orm, apparently having learned the art of exegesis from Father Willibald, launches into a charming explanation. "I can tell you the meaning of what he said," said Orm. It is: "In the name of God, the Merciful, the Compassionate. The Merciful One is Christ, as everybody knows; and the Compassionate One evidently refers to the Holy Ghost, for who could be more compassionate than He? You can see that Toke is practically a Christian already, though he pretends otherwise" (348). In his sweetly blasphemous exegesis, Orm, with all good intentions, transforms one of Islam's holiest invocations of the Divine into a justification of the Trinity, a tenet that more than any other Christian doctrine violently offends the rigorously monotheistic sensibility of the Muslim.[4] It is an example of a cross-cultural collision that is merely charming in an old-fashioned and unexamined Western context, but that might excite less acculturated readers of Viking, that is, Danish, cartoons.

The occasional reference to Islam aside, Bengtsson's novel is firmly rooted in Nordic traditions. The routes his Vikings travel are well documented,[5] and Bengtsson is careful with historical details in his renderings of the Norsemen and their culture, as well as the English in the Age of Maldon and missionaries, and the kingdoms of Spain under Muslim rule. While some of his set pieces may seem a bit frivolous, particularly the religious ones, his attitudes reflect the skepticism of an early twentieth-century Romantic humanist and are an attempt to capture the pose of the objective and not always reverent narrators of the sagas. On the other hand, despite his twentieth-century skepticism, he is, perhaps, closer to the spirit of his originals than, for example, John Erskine in his witty and urbane reconstructions (deconstructions?) of much of the Arthurian corpus. Unlike Erskine, however, Bengtsson is still widely read. Widely read, that is, in Sweden and in Swedish. To the Anglophone, he is virtually unknown, except for his surprising contribution to Hollywood's Viking period. Somewhere between the first publication of *Röde Orm* in 1941, and its English translation in 1954, the year Bengtsson died, and 1964, he became the first of three authors receiving credit for the 1964 Viking epic *The Long Ships*, surely one of the oddest Viking films ever made.[6]

The script was sent to the cinematographer and director Jack Cardiff. As a cinematographer, Cardiff worked with nearly all of the important directors of the twentieth century from Norman Walker in 1929[7] to Paul Merton in 2000.[8] These relatively unknown directors bracket a career in which he worked with Arthur Robison (*The Informer*, 1928), Alfred Hitchcock (*The Skin Game*, 1931; *Under Capricorn*,[9] 1949), René Clair (*The Ghost Goes West*, 1935), Zoltan Korda (*The Four Feathers*, 1939), Gabriel Pascal (*Caesar and Cleopatra*, 1945), Charles Friend (*Scott of the Antarctic*, 1948), Henry Hathaway (*The Black Rose*, 1950), John Huston (*The African Queen*, 1951), Joseph I. Mankiewicz (*The Barefoot Contessa*, 1954), King Vidor (*War and Peace*, 1956), Laurence Olivier (*The Prince and the Showgirl*, 1957), Joshua Logan (*Fanny*, 1960), and numerous others.

Cardiff is probably best known, however, for his extraordinary collaboration with Michael Powell and Emeric Pressburger on the amazing series of films *The Life and Death of Colonel Blimp* (1943),[10] *A Matter of Life and Death* (U.S. title: *Stairway to Heaven*, 1946), *Black Narcissus* (1947), and *The Red Shoes* (1948). Although Cardiff went on to have a more than respectable career as a director (his version of *Sons and Lovers* [1960], in particular, was a great success), his reputation ultimately rests on his magnificent and unforgettable Technicolor experiments in *Black Narcissus* and *Red Shoes*.

He was also, in 1958, the cinematographer on *The Vikings*. It is undoubtedly the success of this film that led to his being contacted to direct *The Long Ships* a few years later. It was a natural choice, since the film was not only successful, but Cardiff's attention to detail created, at least for Hollywood, a vivid recreation of Viking settlements; his fearlessness and his work ethic allowed him to create in daunting circumstances brilliant images of sea voyages in a blustery Norwegian winter, and, most of all, scenes of gorgeously detailed Viking ships sailing swiftly and silently through the majestic fjords. Despite the follies of the plot, the film leaves an indelible impression of Viking grandeur and Arabian splendor.

In any case, in his progress towards becoming a director (what he has called his "path to purgatory"[11]), he received, after the difficulties of filming *The Lion* (1962), the greatest success of which was that he managed to complete it "without anyone getting torn to pieces" (*Magic Hour* 240), the script of *The Long Ships*; he sent it back without reading it, because he "had worked on *The Vikings* and had no desire whatever to direct a similar project" (*Magic Hour* 240). For reasons he does not quite recall, when he returned to England from Switzerland, he was persuaded to read the script, thought it was "an interesting story," and was, as he says, "conned into doing it," adding enigmatically, "I really didn't realize the kind of picture it was going to turn out to be" (*Conversations* 183). There is apparently no record of the script that Cardiff liked, but it might not be too wild a guess to suggest that it might well have been an epic very much in the style of Bengtsson's novel. Shortly afterward, however, Richard Widmark arrived and the script Cardiff thought "very good" was pronounced "lousy" (*Conversations* 184). The script was totally revised by a friend of Widmark's, who, Cardiff notes, "arrived in a large white Stetson" (*Magic Hour* 240). Whatever this version was, it was not Bengtsson. Cardiff thought it was "pure Abbott and Costello" and walked off the set, for what he points out was "the first time" (*Magic Hour* 240). Widmark agreed and the story went off for a third rewrite, this time to Beverly Cross, whose primary film credit up to this point had been *Jason and the Argonauts* (1963).[12] Since Argonauts and Vikings are both sea-going peoples, it seemed, I suppose, like a natural choice. Thus, in a kind of Goldilocks process, a script was chosen, eliminating the one that was a little too Bengtsson, the one that was a little too Abbott and Costello, and settling on something in between that was deemed to be "just right." In this farrago of scripts running the gamut from too serious to too silly, the resulting amalgam of saga and slapstick may well have caused Cardiff to wonder what kind of picture this was going to turn out to be.

As if a disorientation of style was not already embedded in the transformation of the pre-shooting scripts, it was exacerbated when Richard Widmark decided to make improvements. Probably reflecting his original distaste for the script, he made a few textual changes, but then chose to "play it for fun, almost like a comedy" (*Conversations* 186). Cardiff believes that this choice "actually turned out very successfully for him and really lifted his part" (*Conversations* 186). On the other hand, Sidney Poitier gave a Shakespearean, not to say Othellian, seriousness to his role, which "didn't turn out so well for him," according to Cardiff (*Conversations* 186) and most viewers and reviewers. With these crucially diverse approaches in place, the cast prepared to sail away and film their Viking epic in the fjords of Yugoslavia[13] with Belgrade and Budapest providing "authentic" locations for Norseman and Arabs. Lest there be any remaining shreds of ethnic verisimilitude, a cast was assembled involving Vikings with German, Scots, Irish and Welsh accents, North Africans played with equal gusto by Italians, African Americans, and the occasional Arab, and a local girl, the Yugoslavian Beba Lončar, as the Viking princess, Gerda. With a background such as this, the film could have become the "sordid story" (*Conversations* 183) Cardiff once referred to it as. On the other hand, it seems to celebrate (if not quite deconstruct) ethnic diversity in a carnivalesque and multicultural masquerade that is both a disaster and a delight.

It begins, as every Viking film should, in Byzantium. Well, actually, it does begin on the sea in the midst of a violent storm. But, once the credits have rolled, we are in Constantinople, or, at least, some monastic sort of complex east of Mt. Athos, and slightly west of Lhasa, where Rolfe, the lone survivor, has been cast ashore.[14] He is rescued by monks and taken to their monastery, where he is surprised by their fondness for tiny colored stones, then dazzled by the mosaics the monks create with them, and even more enchanted by their lavish use of gold *tesserae* (not a word that would have occurred to Rolfe) in the pictures made of stones that cover the monastery wall and tell the fantastic story of the Golden Bell of Byzantium, "the mother of voices." As one might expect of a film directed by the genius of Technicolor, Jack Cardiff, the mosaics flame in brilliant reds and blues, and the bell revealed at last glistens with delicately incised gold. It is visually amazing bell. Somewhat disappointingly, though, the "Mother of Voices" peals with an underwhelming rumble that seems almost designed to illustrate the gulf between a whimper and a bang. Still, it is remarkable that it sounds at all, since a bell cast from gold would be dishearteningly soundless. It is then something of a miracle that the Mother of Voices bongs at all.

In a remarkably cut sequence, as the story of the bell, related initially by an anonymous narrator over images of the mosaics and of the casting the bell, is surprisingly completed by Richard Widmark, who is revealed in the square of an unnamed city that could be almost anywhere between Marrakech and Samarkand, but is probably meant to be somewhere in North Africa, where Rolfe the Viking is dressed in a *djellaba* telling the magical *Arabian Nights*ish tale of the bell surrounded by querulous Arabs listening to the blue-eyed *hakawati*. It is almost impossible to imagine in what language the Viking must have addressed his Arab/Berber audience, although what we hear is pure Widmarkian American English, a dialect which the North Africans seem to have mastered as they respond in their native West End stage dialect (which makes them sound a bit like most of the Vikings).

The opening scenes then present a binary: grimy, soggy, rugged Vikings going down in a storm; Byzantine monks surrounded by splendor and gold. Conventional East-West conflict, one might think. But, then, the apparent binary is resolved in a peculiar hybrid, the Africanized, Asianized, Orientalized Viking entertaining as a traditional Moroccan storyteller with traditional (almost) tales and techniques (the audience interaction and the pauses at high points in the narrative to ask for money or pique the audience's interest for the next day's story). No sooner is this apparent binary resolved than Rolfe is captured and taken to the Caliph for a new kind of binary: Richard Widmark vs. Sidney Poitier.

Although not developed with any complexity, this Viking-Moor, (quasi-proto) Christian-Muslim, sea-desert, West-East, barbarianism-civilization, white-black binary recurs like a minor theme with major resonance throughout the film. Oddly, it is only in that early shot of Rolfe as a *hakawati* that for a brief moment seems to reconcile the opposites; thus, it is the only moment of the multicultural masquerade that seems to suggest a resolution of ethnicities in one harmonious hybrid body. This idea of a reconciliation is, however, cast off almost as soon as Widmark casts off his faded Tuareg turban, which he does when arrested by Moroccan spies, who have overheard his narrative of the bell, an artifact in which the Caliph has more than passing interest.

Of more than passing interest as well is this original confrontation of Rolfe and the Caliph. In the first place, neither of these characters exists in Bengtsson's novel.[15] Nor does the Barbary Coast. There is, however, in Bengtsson's novel an account of Orm's first voyage

Sidney Poitier (left) as El Mansuh and Richard Widmark as Rolfe in Jack Cardiff's 1963 film *The Long Ships* (editor's collection).

which does involve a stop in Spain in which Solomon, the rescued Jew, proves invaluable. Orm for a time serves Ramiro, King of Leon, a vassal of the Caliph of Cordoba, al-Mansur, who is clearly the model for Poitier's far different character with the most peculiarly altered name, Aly Mansuh.[16] A comparison of the description of al-Mansur in the novel and in the film serves to illustrate the distance the script has traveled from the novel. Aly Mansuh owes almost as little to the novel as does Rolfe, who has no Bengtssonian origin at all.

> The first occasion on which Orm and his men entered Almansur's presence, to be shown to him by the commander of the guard, they were surprised at his appearance, for they had imagined him to be of the proportions of a hero. He was, in fact, an unprepossessing man, pinched and half-bald, with a yellow-green face and heavy eyebrows. He was seated on a broad bed among a heap of cushions, and tugged meditatively at his beard as he addressed rapid commands to two secretaries seated on the floor before him, who took down everything he said [90].

This unprepossessing figure plays distractedly with a brace of monkeys, before he finally turns to address the assembled Vikings. In Hollywood terms, this half-bald, yellow-green, character is clearly not leading man material. Replacing him with Sidney Poitier would surely boost the box office and enhance the visual appeal of the movie's poster.[17]

As a consequence of this choice, the power dynamic of the novel is reversed. While the book presents a confrontation between a virile young Viking and a sallow satrap, the film confronts a lithe, if aging, Viking with a young, passionate, dark and emphatically potent potentate. While our sympathies may lie with the witty and reckless Viking, our eyes are drawn to the compelling figure of the Caliph, who, whether bare-chested or clothed in white or black or purple robes, is an icon of Oriental splendor with the radiance of billowing Asian textiles complementing his skin tone. In the scene in which Aly Mansuh prepares to torture Rolfe so he will reveal the location of the bell, there is a two-shot that concretizes the visual resonances of the two men, and subtly establishes a subtext of erotic tension, a tension that is underscored by the primary prop of the scene, the whip Aly Mansuh is preparing to use on Rolfe. In the iconic two-shot, Rolfe is to the left and behind Aly Mansuh who is in the foreground on the right. The Viking is diminished by his position and the lighting emphasizes his paleness and frailness, presenting him as the victim awaiting the whip. Aly Mansuh, on the other hand, dominates the screen. Although Cardiff made his reputation photographing the most fabulous blondes in Hollywood history, from Marlene to Marilyn, and on to Marianne Faithful, here the master of white women exercises his mastery lighting a black man, and does so with great success.

The confrontation here clearly embodies the Orientalist aesthetic critiqued by Said[18] and Kathleen Kelly's analysis of Hollywood's fascination with the "Arab" body.[19] The Caliph dominates the image and, at the moment, the Viking. But, while the black body seems to possess power and position, it is also a position subject to the gaze.[20] Thus, while the image at first seems to diminish the Viking to promote the Moor, as the action continues with Aly Mansuh's whipping of Rolfe, the dynamic shifts and the Caliph becomes again an Orientalist stereotype of effeminized, tyrannical fury. (Lawrence's Turkish tormentors may come to mind again.) Any desire provoked is condemned as seductive, deceitful and treacherous. Thus, the beauty becomes the beast and the Viking is promoted as a figure of resistance and courage and even athleticism and improvisation as he escapes from the Caliph (in the great tradition of Tristan) by leaping from the palace window into the sea below. The Moor may win the beauty contest, but, when it comes to action, the Viking shows himself to be brave and resourceful and, in a word, masculine. With his leap through the window, the Viking also prevents any further acting out of the erotic tension between the fair Westerner and the exotic Oriental.[21] So much depends upon an open window, and, once again, the film sets up artificial images of destabilized ethnicities and sexualities, only to reaffirm traditional cultural, ethnic, gender and racial presumptions of superiority. The film allows the audience to feel for a moment the thrill of subversion only to allay its anxiety by reverting to conventional expectations without delay.

After his escape, Rolfe (once again he alone seems to have survived) returns to his people and to Viking lands, which sets up a reprise (with a difference) to his solitary arrival in a Byzantine monastery. There is a dramatic contrast between the sobriety, silence and glitter of his first refuge and the drunkenness, boisterousness and grimness of his Viking village. With the addition of his Maghrebian sojourn, there are also the cultural and topographical contrasts of palaces as opposed to huts, court ritual as opposed to drunken rowdiness, desert and sand as opposed to mountains and sea. Even returning home, however, Rolfe arrives as a stranger.

If Rolfe the Viking is alien in Byzantium and North Africa, he is hardly less so among the Vikings he returns to. Among the Norsemen, actual Scandinavians are about as rare as actual North Africans are in the lands of the Caliph. It seems little more than a coincidence that Rolfe and his brother Orm are both Americans (and, therefore, at least have a country in common), but their father, Krok (Oscar Homolka), is Austrian, while their king, Harald (Clifford Evans), is Welsh, and their tribe is made up of Scots (Gordon Jackson as Vahlin), Northern Irish (Colin Blakely as Rhykka), and English (David Lodge as Olla and Edward Judd, who counts as English, even though he was actually born in Shanghai). While to a contemporary audience this peculiar assemblage of peoples might pass muster, to an actual Viking it would be no less bizarre than Lionel Jeffries trying to pass himself off as Aly Mansuh's grand vizier, Aziz. There is no way to tell if this polyethnic mélange is the consequence of laziness (and the belief that ethnicity depends not on birth but on Max Factor) or insensitivity or an intriguingly advanced view of ethnicity as performance rather than nativity. In the latter case, this bizarre multicultural masquerade moves from comedy to deconstruction (which does not rule out the comic). It is impossible in a Hollywood entertainment of this sort to rule out simple sloppiness, but from the unforgettable image of Richard Widmark as a Viking *hakawati* to the racial conglomerates impersonating Vikings and Moors there seems to be a consistent questioning, although it remains at a fairly superficial level, of an innate national identity, replacing it with a sense of ethnicity as an aspect of conscious self-fashioning.

With the shift to Skandia, the story focuses for a time on Orm, as the hero of Bengtsson's novel finally makes an appearance. Needless to say, the Viking setting does nothing to restore the narrative to Bengtsson, as an elaborate and "unauthorized" plot develops involving Orm and Gerda (the Yugoslavian Viking princess), the treacherous King Harald and the exuberant Kroc, father of Orm and Rolfe. As Rolfe, once again, lands shipwrecked on an alien shore (despite the fact he is returning home), he is rescued by his brother Orm, who has left the mead hall to escape "the stink of treachery." Skandia may be home, but it is no less dangerous than the Barbary coast. Rolfe returns to his obsession with the Golden Bell.[22] Harald has no interested in providing him with a ship, since he has already wrecked one, but the sons of Orm plot with their father to steal the new ship he has just made for Harald, who has cheated him on the deal. After a great deal of often gratuitous fighting, the Kroclings take off in the ship, having taken the princess as a hostage, and head towards the bell, somewhere near the Pillar of Hercules. As they journey on, they encounter the maelstrom and in the turbulence and fog hear the sound of the bell in the distance.

As they approach the bell, however, a storm comes up, overwhelms the ship, and for the third time in slightly under an hour, Rolfe is shipwrecked. "Where are we?" asks one of the crew, and Rolfe replies, "Somewhere on the Moorish coast." As the sailors look around, they see the Moorish host in the far distance riding towards them. The impressive army rides on horseback to encounter the Vikings,[23] and, surprisingly, is routed. Rolfe points out that "they don't like giving up," and, as if on cue, they return, led by a beautifully-plumed Aly Mansuh, who pulls up short in front of Rolfe, with the greeting, "Welcome again, Norseman." Dragged from the shore to the main square before the palace, one of the Vikings repeats his earlier question, "Where are we now?" This time, Rolfe replies, simply, "Civilization," adding, "You wouldn't understand."

This intriguing exchange seems to have its origin in *The Vikings*, which, as DP, Cardiff certainly knew. In that film, a Viking and an Englishman are discussing torture, as they consider how to dispose of Ernest Borgnine's character. The Englishman recommends one of his favorite homegrown methods: throwing the offender into a pit where he is torn apart by wolves. The Viking listens approvingly, adding, "Then you *are* civilized." When this theme recurs in *The Long Ships*, it is with an ambivalence that goes beyond the ironic cruelty of its first iteration. At first hearing Rolfe's comment would seem to contrast the ignorant

Viking ("you wouldn't understand") from a barbarian land with the splendor of the Moorish palace and the rituals of an Oriental court. In this reading, there is an implied (and, from a post–9/11 perspective, surprising) recognition of the intellectual and artistic superiority of the Muslim world. For a moment, this interpretation is probably true, but with the lingering resonance of the line from the previous film, there is a suggestion that Rolfe's Viking sense of "civilization" includes an appreciation of sophisticated cruelty and advances in techniques of torture.[24] Read in this way, the valence shifts, and, if the Vikings cannot claim to be superior, they need no longer feel inferior. As we discover that barbarism and civilization both rest on foundations of cruelty, we are left not with values, but empathy, and we can approve of a "civilization" not because it is better but only because it is ours.

When we last saw Rolfe and the Caliph, we witnessed a scene of subtextual sex and sadomasochism, the implications of which were avoided only by a timely leap into the sea. The Caliph has learned his lesson. When we return to the scene of torture, he points out that the window is now barred. Unable to escape, Rolfe attempts to persuade the Caliph that, even if he knew where the bell was, he could not get there in his leaky Moorish boats. The Caliph, master of the desert, is incompetent on the sea. Thus, Rolfe escapes with the promise of a very fragile Moorish-Viking alliance.

Meanwhile, back in the harem, erotic themes come close to shattering the often tested sexual decorum of the narrative. Aly Mansuh begins to express an interest in the Viking girl in a kind of oriental "Occidentalism," while threatening to have his protesting consort, Amina, whipped and sold in the slave market. That, she replies, "would be better than weeks or months without a sign of affection," as she whiningly recalls when she and aly-Mansuh were young lovers and dreamed of flying on a magic carpet to Damascus. That never happened. Now, starved for the occasional hug, she seems to define a court that is structured around erotic spectacle, while actually denying Eros. Appearances to the contrary, aly-Mansuh's carpet does not fly.

Amina's thwarted desires play out in a different key, when she meets with Rolfe, who asks suggestively, "What can I do for you, Lady?" to which she replies, equally suggestively, "I would like to do something for you." Then she, like her husband, replaces sexuality with a different desire: "I only want the bell." In this little bait and switch moment, the film comes as close as it ever does to defining its structure of desire. Desire begins with Eros and is quickly sidetracked into acquisition. Desire becomes focused on the bell, as an acquirable object, while Eros circulates freely and aimlessly among and between Aly Mansuh, Rolfe, Amina. Without the bell, desire might have liberated itself and made the world safe for anarchy, disrupting the competing hegemonies of Moors and Vikings, and, most dangerous of all, possibly provoking the desires of the adolescents (of all ages) to whom the film appeals, desires the film provokes, but never addresses and never satisfies. A polymorphous perversity is evoked, provoked, then neutralized, and sublimated into a capitalist ethic of acquisition.

As if to illustrate the danger of rampant desire, Russ Tamblyn (Orm) breaks into the harem to rescue Gerda and, without quite breaking into a musical number from *Seven Brides for Seven Brothers,* gives over to fighting, leaping, and cavorting in tiny little Viking hot pants in a gymnastics *cum* chorus line mode that sort of leads us to imagine the paradoxical figure of a Viking metrosexual. It is a peculiar little moment in a film that is littered with peculiar little moments.

And then the rumble (Tamblyn was also in *West Side Story*) breaks out, as the Vikings invade the harem, and run wild amongst the Moorish women. Rather than a sudden outbreak of heterosexuality, the scene collapses into comedy rooted in adolescent fears of women and unthinkable fears of men. In three episodes, a Viking assault on the women is oddly transformed into a barely averted homosexual encounter. In the first instance, a Viking seems to be caressed by a Moorish maid and turns his head to place his puckered lips on hers; instead, he finds himself smooching a eunuch. Awkward Viking moment number one.

Awkward Viking moment number two: two Vikings and a Moorish lady seem poised for a three-way. On either side of the lady, a Viking is poised to move in for a kiss. At the last moment, the lady moves away and the Vikings find themselves in liplock.

Awkward Viking moment number three: in order to escape the melee, the eunuch dives into a giant ornamental pot. Shortly afterward, a Viking also dives into the pot. When the ruckus dies down, the camera focuses on the pot. A Moorish head and a Viking head pop out simultaneously and there is a puzzled look on both their faces as they jump out of the pot and run in opposite directions. Considering the size of the pot and the respective sizes of the Viking and the Moor, neither could possibly have been unaware of the presence of the other. The question arises, then, since they had spent a not inconsiderable amount of time in the pot, what had they been doing?

Hollywood traditionally portrays homosexual desire as comic (when not threatening), and, clearly, the point is to diminish the intensity or even the reality of such desires by ridiculing them. But to do this three times in a row seems something like overkill, perhaps reflecting a kind of a return of the repressed in the imagined Viking community of men without women. But, if homosexuality is ridiculed, heterosexuality is consistently thwarted. The film seems insistently interested in provoking then denying sexual desires of all sorts, thus making it safe and suitable for the adolescents of its probable audience.[25]

As the (non-)sexual riot ends, traditional triangulated desire returns.[26] Rolfe and Amina are discovered *in flagrante non delicto*. Rolfe's most erotic line to Amina is, "If we ever had children, what princely liars they would be, my lady." The stress is on the "if," but what Rolfe reveals is the importance of lying in their relationship, underscoring the theme he introduced in his first appearance in native costume on the shores of Babary. In this film, all is performance. Ethicity, sexuality, desire, all is imitation, narrative, masquerade, illusion, and lies. All identities are merely masks.

And the masquerade gets stranger as the Caliph plays his role as vengeful, jealous Moor. Sidney Poitier is well aware of the *locus classicus* for that character and plays his Moor with Shakespearean passion, although with nothing approaching Shakespearean language. Thus, with a passion just barely avoiding a headlong tilt into absurdity, he threatens Rolfe: "You shall pay for this insult to me. You shall ride the Mare of Steel!"

And so we are introduced to the grandest invention of the film, the outrageous, impossible, torture device, the Mare of Steel. There is much that is amazing about the Mare of Steel; foremost is that this elaborate invention is almost totally gratuitous. Aly Mansuh threatens Rolfe with the device, provides a demonstration, Rolfe reminds the Caliph that he needs the long ships, and so they form a temporary alliance and go to seek the bell. Nothing more is heard of the Mare. But, despite its irrelevance, the Mare provides the most unforgettable image of the film, and one certainly designed to provoke deep-seated psychic fears in a presumably adolescent and presumably male audience.

What is the Mare of Steel?[27] First of all, it is immense. Its size alone reinforces the sense that it is totally gratuitous. It looms over the city like a nightmare version of Chicago's Picasso. Its shape echoes that of a giant, somewhat sway-backed mare; its head is a cartoonish evocation of a horse's head, but bright with colors unknown to equine flesh. Its back is even sketchier than its head. It ends in an allusion to a tail. It is supported on risers that only suggest they belong to a quadruped. It is reached by an immense set of steps leading to a position between head and spine roughly where a horseman might sit astride it. The spine is a sloping blade. It lacks only a rider.

With techniques that might delight an Al-Qaeda recruiter, Amina surveys the troops before her, and asks the man she chooses with only a hint of the menace "Do you believe in Allah?" To the man who is brave enough (or foolish enough) to answer, "Yes," she says simply, "Go then." (There is, of course, an obvious trap in Amina's question, since anyone brave enough — or foolish enough — to answer "No" would undoubtedly suffer an identical fate.) The unhappy Moor ascends the terrible stairs, mounts the device, and seats himself where the saddle would have been. The sign is given, the executioner pulls the lever, and the soldier slides down the spine of the Mare to arrive at the tail neatly sliced in two. The only surprise (to me, at least) is that he is obliged to make the bloody journey prone rather than supine. While it is a mere matter of seconds before the Moor and all his organs are bisected, it may not be too significant to consider which bit of flesh first makes contact with blade. The way the device is set up, it seems to prepare for a punishment particularly apt in a *contrapasso*[28] sort of way to punish sodomy. (Recall the tale of Nicholas in Chaucer or the tragic end of Edward II.) The sudden forward flip of the subject, however, overturns the sodomitcal presumption and gives painful precedence to the organ of generation. The punishment implies then that the Mare punishes desire in itself; the mode and method in which desires may be actualized are irrelevant. The Mare of Steel is a monstrously memorable device, whose archetypal challenge to masculine desire overwhelms what is actually only a minor episode in the narrative.[29]

The Mare is ignored, the pact is made, and the allies build their ships and sail toward the maelstrom to find the bell at last. As they sail through the Pillars of Hercules, they see the bell in the distance, a tiny domed chapel high on a cliff over the sea.[30] When they finally get to the chapel, they find suspended from the ceiling a small, utterly unprepossessing, gilded bell.[31] When Rolfe slams the bell in disgust, the Mother of Voices rings out, this time with an impressive peal. The disappointing little bell was, in fact, merely the clapper for the giant golden bell concealed in and as the dome of the chapel, a large breast-like structure. There is a great deal of complex mechanics getting the bell off the cliff and into the boat, including a dramatic moment when the bell falls off the cliff and plunges into the sea to be rescued at last and towed back to "Civilization." ("You can keep it [i.e., civilization]," one of the Viking sailors remarks.)

On their arrival in "civilization," there is a major melee with Aly Mansuh's Moors and Rolfe's Vikings, along with the troops of King Harald, who arrive hoping to steal the bell for themselves. The Viking-Moorish alliance collapses almost instantly and the combined Viking forces defeat the Moors, largely because the bell is once again loosed from it moorings and tumbles through the court crushing the Caliph in its path.

In the end, the two (almost) archetypal images of the film, the Mare and the Mother, are set in opposition, and both seem set on killing Moors, just in case we thought all barbarians were equal. The Mare that slices its riders is clearly threatening, a terrible mother, if there ever was one. The bell is a bit more ambiguous, but, in the end, almost as deadly. Without getting too Freudian (i.e., too silly), the undeniable "breastliness" of the bell as well as the name it is given[32] compel a reading of the bell as some kind of maternal symbol. In its role as the killer of the Caliph, it seems almost to animate its own brief history as the creation of Christian monks in Byzantium stolen and imprisoned in an Islamic prison from where it is liberated by Rolfe, who had already been protected by the creators of the bell (and thus Rolfe is something like the foster-brother/son of the bell). The bell may be an inanimate object, but its position in the narrative comes close to animating it as the vengeful goddess coming to the rescue of her chosen hero. The bell (and with it the weight of symbolism it bears from its monastic, Byzantine origins) intervenes to save her devotee, save the Western (proto-) Christians, and resolve the deadlock between barbarism and civilization. The Vikings, we see at last, are civilized, not because they are wise or good or any other rational reason, but because they have been divinely chosen, a destiny that is given, not earned, and, certainly, not questioned. And that, of course, is what myths are for.

And so back to Rolfe, desire, and the adolescent devotees of adventure who have been entertained by the film. Rolfe ends not by exulting in his victory and the opportunity to return home and relax, but by trying to convince King Harald to underwrite an expedition to find the legendary Three Crowns of the Saxon kings, and a diamond as big as a gull's egg. There is no closure for this narrative, only respite in a sequence of never-ending quests. Having defeated the Moors, Rolfe returns, although dressed as a Viking, to his original role as a trickster and narrator, reciting the never-ending story. For Rolfe and the screenwriters, coherence and logic are irrelevant. The tale is a masquerade and identities and ideologies are mere morphemes to be played with; the only ethic is that the tale continue. The success of the film is entirely dependent on this ethic. Despite the apparent consolation of the Byzantine bell authorizing Nordic Christianity, there is no serious analysis or endorsement involved, merely the relentless flow of the story, which pauses to end the film, but does not cease to impel a further quest for crowns, or diamonds, or, simply, adventure.

And what is the message for our presumed early 1960s audience of adolescents in the early dawn of the sexual revolution? And how confusing it must have been with its destabilizing of ethnicities, its buxom Italian/Moorish and Yugoslavian/Swedish princesses, its men cavorting in pots, drunken northern courts and seductive southern ones. It seems almost a vision of anarchy. And it is. But then it's not. For, ultimately, normalcy is saved by the bell.

In his introduction to *The Pervert's Guide to the Cinema*, Slavoj Žižek presents the argument that "film is the ultimate pervert's art. It doesn't tell you what you desire. It tells you how to desire." *The Long Ships* may not tell you what to desire, but it does provide an extraordinary range of desirable objects. But, if it does also tell you how to desire, it tells you how to desire *things* and to desire them continually without a resolution or a climax. The occasional woman and the Caliph, the imaginary objects of desire, are abandoned by the vengeful Mother of Voices. All the play of difference, the play of desire is cancelled. All is questing, deferring and deflecting. For all its apparent carnivalesque excess, the message of the film is determined, perhaps overdetermined, by the punishing mechanical mothers and all deviance, and all desire, except for objects, is deviant, is sliced or crushed or forgotten. After a dizzying disorientation, we are Occidentalized and normalized at last. Desires that are not punished are ridiculed and there is no end, only a continuing desire to desire that continues beyond the borders of the film, propelled by the only approved desire, the desire to acquire things (bells, crowns, diamonds) as momentary stops along the journey to acquire more things. It is a lesson perfectly tailored to an audience of incipient capitalists: to seek, to acquire, and to never be satisfied. There is always more to plunder.

Notes

1. *http://en.wikipedia.org/wiki/Charles_XII_of_Sweden*. Accessed 7 January 2010. Bengtsson is not alone in his enthusiasm for the king. The Amazing Ben featured Charles as "Badass of the Week" for 2 December 2005 (at *www.amazingben.com/arf0080.html*). Accessed 7 January 2010.

2. In the essay entitled "In Front of My Bookcase" (*A Walk to an Anthill*, 40–41), Bengtsson discusses Carl Johan Tornberg's translation of the chronicles of Ibn-el-Athir. Bengtsson's interest in Arabic culture is reflected in his novel and takes a surprising twist in *The Long Ships*.

3. Frans Gunnar Bengtsson, *The Long Ships: A Saga of the Viking Age* (14).

4. Tim Mackintosh-Smith recounts an encounter with a similar good humor, but that also stresses absolute Muslim monotheism. Traveling in Northern Syria and speaking excellent Arabic, Mackintosh-Smith is, at first, assumed to be Muslim; when he points out that he is, in fact, *Masihi* (Christian), his interlocutor ("a plump lady with shopping bags") replies, "Of course, the main thing that separates us is that Trinity thing of yours. [...] You can't have three people running the same firm, you know. It just wouldn't work" (*Travels with a Tangerine* 189).

5. Bengtsson was aware, as noted above, of the works of Ibn an-Athir on the Crusades, but not, apparently, of the travels of Ibn Fadlan, who would have helped him enormously with his firsthand account of tenth-century Volga Vikings.

6. It cannot, however, hold a candle to the oddness and over-the-topness of the astonishing Turkish production *Tarkan the Viking* (1971), a tribute among other things to Turkey's cheerful disregard of copyright agreements.

7. *The Hate Ship*. Cardiff was assistant camera. (*Conversations* 237.)

8. *The Suicidal Dog*. Bowyer also lists *Untitled* in 2002 directed by Christopher Coppola, but there are no further references to it. It seems likely that this film was never completed. IMDB lists three more films: *The Other Side of the Screen* (2007), TV mini-series, *Lights 2* (2005), and *The Tell-Tale Heart* (2004). If to this list we add the 1918 *My Son* in which he played a bit part, Cardiff comes close to nine decades of serious activity in film from black and white to Technicolor (in which he was a brilliant pioneer and innovator) to digital.

9. In this film, Cardiff had to deal with Hitchcock's experiment in elaborate single takes, a technique he "invented" in *Rope*. *Rope*, however, had a single set; in *Under Capricorn*, Cardiff (and the actors) had to deal with tilting beds and collapsing furniture that, like the actors, had to manage to get out of the path of the advancing camera.

10. In an oft-told story, it was when he was working as second-unit photographer on this film that he impressed Michael Powell when he was given the tricky task of lighting the wall of the Colonel's den that was covered with the trophy heads of a large number of horned animals. The trick was to light the wall so that it was not inconveniently pattered with the shadows of horns. Powell, noting his success, hired him to photograph his next film. (See *Magic Hour* 83.)

11. *Magic Hour* 240.

12. Cross went on to win fame as the writer of similar scripts (*Sinbad and the Eye of the Tiger* [1977] and *Clash of the Titans* [1981]) and as the second husband of Dame Maggie Smith.

13. The fjords of Yugoslavia provided a particular problem for the film, since a previously assigned director had chosen the location, apparently with little more than a cursory glance. It turned out that the body of water meant to stand in for the Nordic seas and the Mediterranean was only about three inches deep. A canal had to be dredged in the middle of the river to allow the Viking ships to sail (*Conversations* 184–5).

14. Rolfe, a more typical sort of Viking hero, although given a rather sly interpretation by Richard Widmark, is an invention of the screenwriters. The original hero of the novel, Orm, is reduced to a minor role played by Russ Tamblyn.

15. It would become tedious to point out every deviation from the novel, since virtually nothing besides the long ships, not even the plot, is "authorized" by Bengtsson.

16. Why a perfectly good Arabic name is transformed into a name of no ethnicity whatever and with no resonance at all remains a mystery. Is it possibly simply a typo that never got itself erased?

17. The poster, at least the one on the cover of the DVD (the original poster, which can be accessed on *The Long Ships* page on *Wikipedia* and in the French press release, is more accurate and less conventional and features a large and impressive Viking ship and several Vikings; neither of the stars, surprisingly, perhaps, are prominent) highlights headshots of Widmark and Poitier facing in opposite directions dominating the upper half of the space. Widmark looks hard-edged and grizzled, while Poitier looks air-brushed and glamorous with impossibly seductive eyes. Below them is the title and below that in the bottom half

is a long shot of the Caliph's troops riding out from the city led by a heavily veiled Caliph. At the very bottom is the motto "Long Will You Remember These Mighty Viking Adventurers," which is surprising considering that except for the top left picture of Widmark, there are no Vikings in the poster, which places a heavy emphasis on the Orientalist, as opposed to Skandic, appeal of the film. The poster may also provide a clue to Poitier's peculiar make-up, especially his sort of bizarre James Brown hairdo. Considering how often the Caliph is shown in long shots (especially on horseback) or veiled, the makeup may have made it unnecessary for Poitier to actually show up for a good portion of the Caliph's scenes. Easily disguised, the Caliph and Poitier may have had only an infrequent congruence in those few scenes when the Caliph interacts in close-up or medium shot with Rolfe or Rosanna. He has, in fact, remarkably little screen time in any case, which may explain why he is made so strikingly dominant in those scenes in which he does appear.

18. Edward Said, *Orientalism*.

19. Kathleen Coyne Kelly, "Medieval Times," pp. 200–224.

20. See Mulvey's essay "Visual Pleasure and Narrative Cinema" in *Visual and Other Pleasures*. The image of the Caliph here seems to represent a masculine revision of the feminist dynamic analyzed famously by Laura Mulvey with the black man in the position of the white woman. It could almost be read as a riff on Cardiff's career as a photographer of blondes (summed up by the fact that his own autobiography features on the cover not the subject of the book but Marilyn Monroe, the photographic subject and notoriously subjected icon).

21. Aly Mansuh is undoubtedly Muslim, but the depiction of the Muslim world in this film is so imprecise that "Oriental" seems to be the only way to define the Muslim Otherness of the Caliph, whose kingdom may be anywhere between Fez and Isfahan; "Oriental," then, is chosen to cover this imagined space located imprecisely in Africa and/or Asia.

22. Intriguingly, we learn that Rolfe's obsession with the bell predates his sojourn in Byzantium. Apparently, in his youth, there was an Egyptian slave girl in the Viking Court who sang the story of the bell. Her exotic looks and her enchanting tale were imprinted on Rolfe from his childhood.

23. The long shots of the galloping Moorish troops (reminiscent of the great "Fantasias," which are a staple of Moroccan tourist entertainment) are exciting. From a contemporary perspective, however, the troops seem a little undermanned, reminding us, perhaps, that *The Long Ships* was created after the heady days of cheap labor (and/or massive government sponsorship) that enabled the astonishing spectacles of battle in Eisenstein's *Alexander Nevsky*, for example, but before the age when human insufficiencies can be remedied by computer graphics and infinite CGI armies.

24. It is a notion of civilization that seems remarkably congruent with the views of a recent vice-president of the United States.

25. The creative team may, in fact, have been playing games with the Hays Code in its final years of interference in the industry. By playing homosexual jokes, the team would provoke the interest of the committee, but neutralizing the possibility of realizing those desires would not have violated the code, however much it may have tweaked it. Jack Cardiff may have had a particular interest in testing the code after the grief it gave him in the final days of production on what is arguably his masterpiece as a director, *Sons and Lovers* (1960). See, for example, the extended discussion of the film in *Magic Hour* (pp. 219–32).

26. The phrase "triangulated desire" is, of course, derived from René Girard's *Deceit, Desire and the Novel*, a breakthrough study of the ways in which many novels figure the woman as a medium through which the desires of and between men are played out.

27. It may be unnecessary to point out that there is absolutely no hint of this device in the Bengtsson novel.

28. There is almost certainly no reference to Dante intended here (although since Cardiff was noted for his extensive reading in the classics of Western literature, it cannot be ruled out). Suggestively, however, the severing of the body achieved by the Mare of Steel recalls the punishment for heresy in Dante's *Inferno*, in which Mohammed is split from neck to navel and is accompanied by Ali split from crown to neck.

29. There is also, in fact, a peculiar feature of the episode on the diegetic level. The Caliph's plan to kill a Viking results only in the loss of one of his own men. Just as sexual desires in the film are turned inward and thwarted or denied, so the desire for vengeance turns inward and destroys only the destroyer's forces.

30. The view of the Moorish chapel on a cliff looks remarkably like the tomb of the Aga Khan as seen from Lake Nasser in the vicinity of the Aswan Dam. This is a view that Jack Cardiff was most likely familiar with from his visit to Abu Simbel (in its original location on the pre-dammed Nile) when he was filming *The Four Feathers* for Zoltan Korda (see *Magic Hour* 66).

31. Unlike the Mare of Steel, the bell does have a source in Bengtsson. There, however, it is an impressive

set of small bells that Orm and his companions rescue from Cordova to return to the cathedral at Santiago de Compostela. The little bell in this episode may recall the diminutive bells in the novel.

32. It may be unnecessary to point out that the name (Mother of Voices), like the object itself, is the creation of the screenwriter.

Works Cited

Bengtsson, Frans G[unnar]. *Karl XII's Levand*. Stockholm: P.A. Norstedt Söner, 1950.

_____. *The Long Ships: A Saga of the Viking Age*. Tr. Michael Meyer. Stockholm: P.A. Norstedt Söner, 1954.

_____. *Red Orm*. Tr. Barrows Mussey. New York: Charles Scribner's Sons, 1943.

_____. *Rhode Orm*. Vol. 1, *Sjhofarare i Vhasterled*; Vol. 2, *Hemma och i Osterled*. Stockholm : Vingfhorlaget, 1958–59.

_____. *A Walk to an Ant Hill and Other Essays*. Tr. Michael Roberts and Elspeth Schubert, née Harley. New York: The American Scandinavian Foundation, 1951.

Boyer, Justin. *Conversations with Jack Cardiff: Art, Life, and Direction in Cinema*. London: Batsford, 2003.

Cardiff, Jack. *Magic Hour*. London: Faber and Faber, 1997.

Girard, René. *Deceit, Desire, and the Novel: Self and Other in Literary Structure*. Baltimore: Johns Hopkins University Press, 1976.

Ibn al-Athir. *The Chronicle of Ibn al-Athir for the Crusading Period from al-Kamil fi'l-Ta'rikh*. 3 Parts (Crusade Texts in Translation). Tr. D.S. Richards. Farnham, Surrey: Ashgate, 2007.

Ibn Fadlan, Ahmad. *Ibn Fadlan's journey to Russia: a tenth-century traveler from Baghad to the Volga River*. Tr. with commentary by Richard N. Frye. Princeton: Markus Wiener, 2005.

Kelly, Kathleen Coyne. "Medieval Times: Bodily Temporalities in *The Thief of Bagdad* (1924), *The Thief of Bagdad* (1940), and *Aladdin* (1992)." In *Hollywood in the Holy Land: Essays on Film Depictions of the Crusades and Christian-Muslim Clashes*. Ed. Nickolas Haydock and E. L. Risden. Jefferson, NC: McFarland, 2009. 200–224.

Mulvey, Laura. "Visual Pleasure and Narrative Cinema." In *Visual and Other Pleasures*. Bloomington: Indiana University Press, 1989.

Said, Edward. *Orientalism*. London: Vintage, 1979.

Žižek, Slavoj. *The Pervert's Guide to the Cinema*. Dir. Sophie Fiennes. 2006.

Jack Cardiff Filmography

Clash of the Titans, dir. Desmond Davis, 1981.

Hate Ship, dir. Norman Walker, 1929.

Lights2, dir. Marcus Dillistone, 2005.

My Son, My Son, dir. Charles Vidor, 1918.

The Other Side of the Screen, dir. Stanley A. Long, 2007.

Rope, dir. Alfred Hitchcock, 1948.

Sinbad and the Eye of the Tiger, dir. Sam Wanamaker, 1977.

The Suicidal Dog, dir. Paul Merton, 2000.

Tarkan the Viking, Mehmet Aslan, 1971.

The Tell-Tale Heart, dir. Stephanie Sinclaire, 2004.

Under Capricorn, dir. Alfred Hitchcock, 1949.

Untitled, dir. Christopher Coppola, 2002.

For more complete information on Jack Cardiff as cinematographer and director, see the extended filmographies in *Magic Hour* (245–248) and *Conversations with Jack Cardiff* (229–249).

"To be, or not to be" — King:
Clive Donner's *Alfred the Great* (1969)

CHRISTOPHER A. SNYDER

In *Alfred the Great*, Clive Donner gives us lusty pagan Vikings, a beautiful Saxon princess, and a brooding young Alfred (played by David Hemmings) who is not quite sure whether he wants to become king and kill Vikings or whether 'tis nobler to become a learned but cynical priest. When all is said and done, no cakes are burnt but plenty of blood is spilt in this gloomy and quite loose adaptation of Asser's *Life of King Alfred*.

Alfred of Wessex, who reigned 871–99, is the first — and only — English monarch to have been given the epithet *Magnus*, "the Great." Indeed, he is perhaps more deserving of the description than those who bore it in antiquity — Alexander, Pompey, Cyrus — not because he was a more successful general, but because he combined martial and intellectual abilities to such an extent that even modern statesmen pale in comparison. The closest comparison would be with Charlemagne, a greater conqueror but only a sponsor of scholarship, not a scholar himself. If we are to believe his friend and biographer Asser — and some recent scholars have expressed reservations about the accuracy and veracity of Asser's biography — Alfred was not just a warrior but a military innovator, not just a scholar but a political philosopher and an inventor, and he brought all of these abilities together in the service of God, the state, and the law.

Now, the question is, what would Hollywood make of such a medieval monarch? Were we given a 1950s Technicolor Alfred, he would no doubt be a noble and devout figure, if not a man of much intellectual substance. An Alfred of the CGI age would be all brawn and grit, facing down steroid Vikings with swagger and inflicting high-definition wounds. As it stands, only one major biopic devoted to Alfred has reached the theaters, MGM's *Alfred the Great* (1969), directed by Clive Donner with a screenplay written by Ken Taylor and James R. Webb.[1] This all-but-forgotten film (it has yet to be released on DVD and a version released earlier on VHS is almost impossible to find) stars David Hemmings as a conflicted and brooding Alfred and Michael York as his less than buff Viking rival, Guthrum. Prunella Ransome is Alfred's unfaithful bride, Aelhswith, while Sir Ian McKellen makes his major motion picture debut here as a swamp fox who befriends Alfred in the Somerset fens. The result is not so much Alfred the Great as Alfred the Disillusioned, for Donner and Hemmings give us a monarch who reflects the skepticism and brutality of the age — not the Viking Age, but the age marked by student protests and televised images of the war in Vietnam and the assassinations of Robert Kennedy and Martin Luther King.

The anti-romanticism is made apparent from the beginning, as the film opens with two graphic images: two young English peasants coupling against a stone, undifferentiated from the sheep that surround them, and the arrival of Guthrum's Viking warband, who leap into action straight from their longships by slaying the rutting peasants. The scene nods in the direction of an historical event cited by Hall (72). Sometime between 789 and 802, the royal representatives in Dorchester who rode out to meet a party of Viking raiders, whom they mistook for traders, were promptly killed by the Vikings once they landed. Clearly, in the film's opening scenes, then, we are in an England in need of a strong king, a defender of the Christian faithful against the pagan onslaught. Well, there is a king, but he is the weak and wounded Anglo-Saxon monarch Ethelred (Alan Dobie), Alfred's older brother.

When we first meet Alfred himself, he is kneeling before a bishop, about to take his final vows for the priesthood. Reluctantly, and with much bitterness, he agrees to leave the Church behind and come to aid his brother in his war against the Danes. In his first battle scene, Alfred shows himself to be a brilliant tactician, with Hemmings nonetheless muttering such anti-war sentiment as "This is all folly" and praying that God will give him courage rather than raw battle-lust. While the Saxons are portrayed as brave and resourceful, the Danish army is robotic and violent, marching to an incessant Nordic chant, a mass of medieval storm troopers in black and iron.[2]

The battle scenes (filmed in County Galway, Ireland) appear primitive and minimalistic compared to those in today's big-budget epics, yet they are similar in their graphic portrayal of the brutality of war, with close-ups of swords plunging into abdomens and blood spurting from gashed limbs. Hemmings' Alfred, still sporting a tonsure, often looks small and confused among the bearded masses. He is the thinking man's hero, and yet, as Asher (the film's Asser, played by Colin Blakely) states early on in *Alfred the Great*, "He is ruled by his passions." (The real Asser certainly does not give us this impression in his *Life of Alfred*.)

The conflict between intellect and passion is played out in Alfred's seduction by the Mercian princess Aelhswith. Overcome with lust, Alfred, still in tonsure and habit, proposes to the princess whom he had known since childhood. "I thought you wanted to become a priest?" she asks Alfred as he paws her. "I did, but now I want you more." Things sour quickly as Alfred's brother dies shortly after the betrothal ceremony, and Alfred, feeling trapped by his barons and advisor, refuses the kingship and threatens to enter the priesthood and not consummate his marriage. Aelhswith's vows of love are met with violence, as Alfred relents only to rape his new wife on their wedding night. While she prays to understand and forgive him, Alfred is forced into the kingship by another attack of the Danes. Weak, Wessex must seek a treaty rather than fight the heathen, and the scene in which Alfred and Guthrum negotiate is one of the best in the film. It is clear in this scene that Hemming and York are more comfortable in dialog uncluttered by cinematic spectacle, the stage play, not the battlefield.

The plot turns here as Alfred begins to embrace duty and sacrifice, while Aelhswith agrees to be Guthrum's hostage, more to flee her cold husband than for honor. She gives birth to Alfred's son while living with Guthrum, and eventually gives in to the Dane's sexual advances. Whereas Alfred is afraid of his passion and cannot tame it, Guthrum embraces his and can play the part of the gentle lover. Aelhswith not only abandons her marital vows, but she falls in love with Guthrum, and he with her.

Meanwhile, Alfred is slow to learn the craft of the early medieval monarch. He desires both absolute obedience and egalitarianism, ordering a Saxon noble to be flogged for a perfectly reasonable protest. This scene fails in both regards, historically speaking, for royal

David Hemmings (center) in the title role in Clive Donner's 1969 film *Alfred the Great* (editor's collection).

absolutism did not exist in the ninth century and Alfred is famous for being the first to iterate the tripartite division that dominated medieval society: those who pray, those who fight, and those who work. No Anglo-Saxon monarch would have desired a dissolution of the distinction between noble and peasant, however much modern cinematic heroes continue to call for equality in the Middle Ages (see, for example, the more recent example of Orlando Bloom's character in Ridley Scott's 2005 film *Kingdom of Heaven*). "You are too proud," Asher warns him, and indeed Alfred meets defeat by the Danes and a humiliating retreat into the wild fens of Somerset, at the furthest western extremes of Wessex.

It is here that Alfred learns — well, it's not exactly clear what he learns. The bandits who take Alfred in, led by the good-hearted Roger (McKellen), prove more loyal than his barons, though inexplicably the nobles turn from their plans of regicide to stand by Alfred as he meets the Danes in the film's climactic battle at Athelney (i.e., the battle of Edington, in 878). Employing a wedge formation for his shield wall, Alfred meets with some success against Guthrum, but Roger realizes that Alfred needs help to achieve victory. In another great egalitarian moment, a motley band of monks, old men, and peasant women (!) arrive with clubs and pitchforks to lend Alfred a hand, and give Alfred the numerical advantage he needs to overcome the Danes. The English victory is mirrored by a single combat in which Alfred, on foot, somehow manages to unhorse Guthrum and knock him senseless in a fist-fight. In the end, he spares Guthrum, forgives Aelhswith, and laments the death of Roger. A closing chyron tells us that England is now united under Alfred the Great.

Hemmings' Alfred is, through much of this film, a Hamlet without friends. He is conflicted — priest or king? recluse or lover? — and he is tormented, unable to love without rage and violence. He has no real friends until he meets Roger, but then again, why should he have friends? In this film, the young Alfred is portrayed as a spoiled and petulant prince, enjoying the finer things — hunting, feasting, reading Ovid — and used to getting his own way. "You are the cruelest man I know," Aelhswith tells him after he has taken her son and had her imprisoned. We are inclined to agree with her. He does manage one non-ironic smile at the end of the film, but, despite Donner's interest in portraying Alfred's spiritual turmoil, it is not clear how he got there.

The casting is a bit strange. David Hemmings, though an accomplished stage actor, had just appeared as the wicked and cowardly Mordred in Joshua Logan's *Camelot* (Warner Bros., 1967). Despite all efforts, the diminutive Hemmings hardly strikes the viewer as a great warrior king.[3] Similarly, Michael York needs more than a bushy beard and fur tunic to convince us that he is a Viking warlord.[4] The bluster of both Hemmings and York is contrasted with the understated performance of Prunella Ransome. Her Aelhswith is believable and sympathetic, though her emotional return to Alfred at the end of the film seems forced. Several reviewers praised the performance of McKellen, and we are left wishing more from his Roger, who does not even get a death speech.

The musical score by Raymond Leppard is also mismatched with this film. Too often, we hear triumphant brass, yet all we see is a bored or sneering Hemmings. The cinematography leans toward grays, browns, and subdued colors, and exterior shots capture a windy landscape blanketed with rain, mist, and smoke. The bleakness mirrors the violence and psychological turmoil of the main characters, none of whom seem too merry in Olde England.

Production details are, historically speaking, hits and near misses. The Viking ships seen in the opening minutes of the film are replicas of the Gokstad Ship, discovered near Oslo in 1880. So well and accurately built were they that one was used to recreate the eleventh-century journey from Norway to Newfoundland described in the sagas.[5] Several of the Vikings wear helmets that are almost exact copies of the now iconic helmet found in Mound 1 at Sutton Hoo, which, though possibly of Scandinavian design, is three centuries too early. As the camera pulls away from one early battle scene, we see an aerial view of Alfred bravely fighting within the famous White Horse of Uffington, carved centuries earlier into the chalk of an Oxfordshire hillside. Although the scene and shot present a nice cinematic image, the battle was actually fought at Ashdown in Berkshire.[6]

Costuming and hair styles are very close to the medieval visual sources, and ornament in particular — brooches, crosses, pins — is quite accurate. Swords are mostly of the wide and flat shiny prop variety, rather than the modified spatha with deep fuller common among both Saxons and Vikings. Inexplicably, the Saxons adopt flimsy wicker shields at the battle of Edington, and somehow these shields withstand the assault of the Great Heathen Army. The uniform scale armor of the Vikings in this film may help audiences identify the enemy more easily, but historically only the richest Norse warrior could afford such armor, and never was it uniform.

There are also more serious breaches with the historical record. Portraying Alfred as desiring priesthood over kingship is a complete invention. The rape of Aelhswith on her wedding night would have been impossible, according to Asser, because Alfred was then suffering from a great malady and unable to consummate the union. It goes without saying that the historical Alfred would never have allowed his queen to be given to the Danes as a hostage, and their lengthy marriage and five children do not suggest that there was marital discord.

The film gives the impression that Alfred was the first to establish a unified law code in his kingdom. In reality, the *Law of Alfred* continues a Wessex tradition begun by King Ine two centuries before Alfred. Alfred's life in the marshes was not quite as primitive as depicted in the film, for Alfred was able to construct a fortress there on the island of Athelney that he used as a base for raiding. Guthrum, or rather Guthram, was *not* the leader of the Danes who attacked Æthelred and Alfred in 871, but only emerged later as Alfred's chief nemesis (and Æthelred was not an invalid languishing in his tent during the battle). Ivar the Boneless, in the film made Guthrum's cousin and subordinate, did not die at the battle of Edington in 878, for he was not there, nor was he ever, to our knowledge, part of Guthram's army. A king in his own right, Ivar conquered York and died most likely in the north sometime around 870 (or, if he is the same person as King Ivar of Dublin, in Ireland in 873).

Overall, the film's portrayal of the Vikings is fairly stereotypical. They are violent and lustful robbers, at one point raping a group of nuns and stealing their gold with equal gusto.[7] The ideological battle between pagan and Christian values brought up throughout the film seems anachronistic. Guthrum reminds his warriors at one point that they are "sons of Odin," while the Saxons have abandoned the old gods for a new. "They are afraid of life, and afraid of death," he sneers. The historical Guthram was baptized by Alfred after Edington, a practice common among the Norse as they sought integration in the Christian states of medieval Europe.

Can we know the historical Alfred, or should writers and directors be given free rein to invent or at least flesh out a character from the bare bones of history? Putting aside the issue of artistic freedom, the truth is that we *do* know more about Alfred of Wessex than just about any monarch of the early Middle Ages.[8] We have a great variety of written sources from and about Alfred, we have coins from his reign, and we have archaeological evidence for many settlements from this period. Asser's *Life of Alfred* is a detailed and fascinating account written by a learned Welshman who was very close to the king.[9] Alfred Smyth's argument that it is a forgery written a century later has not been generally accepted by Alfred scholars.[10]

King Alfred himself also sponsored a great historical project known as *The Anglo-Saxon Chronicle*, which is actually a series of chronicles (in both Latin and Old English) produced by Wessex scribes chronicling the deeds of the Anglo-Saxon kings (especially the Wessex dynasts) from the fifth to the twelfth centuries.[11] We have laws and charters attributed to Alfred. We have his will, but, most remarkable of all, are the works he is said to have translated himself, from Latin to Old English: Pope Gregory the Great's *Pastoral Care*, Boethius' *Consolation of Philosophy*, Augustine's *Soliloquies*, and the first fifty Psalms. In the case of Boethius, Alfred offers his own interpretation of political philosophy in his translation, perhaps the only such example from a statesman since Marcus Aurelius and unmatched by any medieval monarch.

The first remarkable fact about the historical Alfred is that he was the fifth son of King Æthelwulf of Wessex, which means that no one expected him ever to become king.[12] According to Asser, his mother introduced him to books and his father took him on trips to Rome and Gaul. Alfred's victory at Edington is justifiably famous, for it prevented a Viking conquest of Wessex and thus enabled Wessex to take the lead in the unification of Anglo-Saxon England. However, Alfred's accomplishments *after* Edington (the film's end point) are even more noteworthy. With the Danes held in check (for a while at least) under the peace treaty of Wedmore, Alfred launched several reforms. He converted the royal army — the *fyrd* — from an ad hoc warband to a mounted, standing army, and surrounded Wessex with thirty fortified towns called *burhs*, linked by a network of army roads called *hereweges* ("highways"). *Burhs* were also trading centers and housed the royal mints, providing Alfred with more wealth than any of his predecessors.

Complementing his in-depth strategy of land defense was Alfred's creation of a small fleet of longships, larger than their Norse counterparts, that could intercept Viking boats before they landed. Just before a second Viking onslaught, Alfred began his educational reformation by luring scholars from Mercia, Wales, and elsewhere to his court and monastic schools. The children of his nobles were expected to receive a vernacular education at his court (along with his own children), and Latin was mandated for all members of the clergy. As already mentioned, Alfred himself led a translation scheme in an effort to make what he deemed the most worthy Latin books available to his nobles in Old English. The vernacular, as well as Latin, was thus made to serve administrative purposes. When he died in 899, Alfred was "King of the Anglo-Saxons," a title signaling his transformation of kingship in England.

The accomplishments of the historical Alfred are perhaps too numerous and complex for a single commercial film. Donner chose to focus on the early years of Alfred's reign, but the problem is that he shows us an Alfred with hardly any sign of greater things to come. Historians are not alone in finding fault with this film. It opened to mixed criticism, and it has not aged well. Donner's Danes are "hippy flower-children turned on by draughts of blood," wrote one critic (Allen 187), while another lamented Hemmings' "weak face and lack of acting ability" (Hugesson 513–14). "A devoutly Christian Freud confronts the druid mentality," proclaimed *The New York Times*, "effective ... neither as conjecture nor as history" (Canby 70). For Pauline Kael in *The New Yorker*, "It is all so terrible that after a while one sits back and counts the money going by on its way to the furnace" (175) — reportedly $6.5 million.

Not surprisingly there were some film critics who appreciated the anti-heroic tone and gave Donner the benefit of the doubt because of his earlier and better work. But even those who praised *Alfred*'s "meaningful images" (Gow 59–60) and art direction cringed at its poor and anachronistic dialog, seeing the film as a poor imitation of *Lion in Winter* and *A Man for All Seasons*, and pandering to a youth market. Despite its sex, violence, and revolutionary sentiment, however, *Alfred the Great* failed to win over this demographic, alienated their elders, and was thus doomed to box-office failure and near oblivion.

Thus, Clive Donner's *Alfred the Great* gives its audience little appreciation of the historical Alfred and his Viking foes. Furthermore, clichéd dialog, stereotypes, and failures in casting and acting prevent the film from being an entertaining, let alone enlightening, viewing experience. Donner and Hemmings may have aimed for *Hamlet* or *A Man for All Seasons*, but what they have given us is a prince from 1969 who just needs to grow up.

Notes

1. The screenplay was based on Eleanor Shipley Duckett's popular history, *Alfred the Great: The King and His England* (Chicago: University of Chicago Press, 1956).

2. Aberth believes that Donner has attempted a Nazification of the Vikings in the film (52).

3. For an account of Hemmings' battle scene preparations, see *"Alfred the Great" Merchandising Manual* (MGM, 1969). As Billington points out in his review, Hemmings' Alfred is neither the "wild boar" described by Asser nor an introspective scholar (9).

4. Perhaps Michael York, an Oxford graduate who had read Old English at university, should have assisted the film's writers.

5. See William K. Stevens, "Norse Longship to Sail Vikings' Atlantic Route," *New York Times* 19 April 1969: 35.

6. The inspiration for this scene may be the local tradition commemorated in G.K. Chesterton's *The Ballad of the White Horse* (1911).

7. A group of revisionist historians has resuscitated the reputation of the Vikings somewhat by stressing their role as peaceful traders and by accusing the monastic chroniclers of grossly exaggerating the violence of Viking raids. See, for example, Gwyn Jones, *A History of the Vikings* (Oxford: Oxford University Press, 1968), and Peter Sawyer, *The Age of the Vikings*, 2d ed. (London: Edward Arnold, 1971). See now, however, R.T. Farrell, ed., *Viking Studies: Whence and Whither?* (London: Phillimore, 1982), Julian C. Richards, *Blood of the Vikings* (London: Hodder & Stoughton, 2001), and Benjamin T. Hudson, *Viking Pirates and Christian Princes* (Oxford: Oxford University Press, 2005).

8. The best modern study of Alfred is Richard Abels, *Alfred the Great: War, Kingship, and Culture in Anglo-Saxon England.*

9. *Alfred the Great*, trans. by Simon Keynes and Michael Lapidge. See also *The Medieval Life of King Alfred the Great.*

10. Smyth, *King Alfred the Great.* For a critique of Smyth's thesis, and a more balanced account of Alfred, see Abels, *Alfred the Great.* Asser did, however, model his biography on Einhard's *Life of Charlemagne.*

11. See *The Anglo-Saxon Chronicle*, ed. and trans. by Michael J. Swanton.

12. For a concise discussion of Alfred's accomplishments, see Richard Abels, "Alfred the Great," in *The Early Peoples of Britain and Ireland: An Encyclopedia*, I: 22–25.

13. Judith Crist, for instance, calls Hemmings' Alfred "a rather contemporary young man" in "an interesting film" with stark scenery, "the Dark Ages photographed darkly" (75).

Works Cited

Abels, Richard. "Alfred the Great." In *The Early Peoples of Britain and Ireland: An Encyclopedia.* Ed. Christopher A. Snyder. Oxford: Greenwood International, 2008. I: 22–25.

_____. *Alfred the Great: War, Kingship, and Culture in Anglo-Saxon England.* London: Longman, 1998.

Aberth, John. *Knight at the Movies: Medieval History on Film.* New York: Routledge, 2003.

Alfred the Great. Trans. Simon Keynes and Michael Lapidge. London: Penguin, 1983.

Allen, Don. Review of *Alfred the Great. Monthly Film Bulletin* 36 (September 1969): 187.

The Anglo-Saxon Chronicle. Ed. and trans. Michael J. Swanton. London: Routledge, 1998.

Billington, Michael. Review of *Alfred the Great. Times* [London] 17 July 1969: 9.

Canby, Vincent. Review of *Alfred the Great. New York Times* 4 December 1969:70.

Crist, Judith. Review of *Alfred the Great. New York Magazine* 2 (8 December 1969): 75.

Gow, Gordon. Review of *Alfred the Great. Films and Filming* 15 (September 1969): 59–60.

Hall, Richard. *The World of the Vikings.* London: Thames & Hudson, 2007.

Hugesson, Vivienne. Review of *Alfred the Great. Films in Review* 20 (October 1969): 513–14.

Kael, Pauline. Review of *Alfred the Great. New Yorker* 45 (13 December 1969): 175.

Smyth, Alfred P. *King Alfred the Great.* Oxford: Oxford University Press, 1995.

_____. *The Medieval Life of King Alfred the Great: A Translation and Commentary on the Text Attributed to Asser.* New York: Palgrave, 2002.

Valiant and Villainous Vikings

ALAN LUPACK

In his book on *The Vikings and the Victorians*, Andrew Wawn observes that, for the Victorians, "the ubiquity of the term 'Viking' masks a wide variety of constructions of Vikingism: the old northmen are variously buccaneering, triumphalist, defiant, confused, disillusioned, unbiddable, disciplined, elaborately pagan, austerely pious, relentlessly jolly, or self-destructively sybaritic. They are merchant adventurers, mercenary soldiers, pioneering colonists, pitiless raiders, self-sufficient farmers, cutting-edge naval technologists, primitive democrats, psychopathic berserks, ardent lovers and complicated poets" (Wawn 4). A similar variety of images can be found in cinematic representations of the Vikings.

How different depictions of Vikings can be in film might be demonstrated by comparing the Northmen in *The Vikings* (United Artists, 1958; directed by Richard Fleischer) with those in *Prince Valiant* (20th Century–Fox, 1954; directed by Henry Hathaway). As with many of the variations in the Victorian period, the source of the depictions is instructive and in some ways determinative of the general image presented. Intertextual relationships are as important in understanding the variety of "constructions of Vikingism" in film as they are for Victorian and other literary texts. *The Vikings* was based on the book *The Viking* by Edison Marshall. Marshall's book, in turn, draws from medieval sources such as *Ragnars saga loðbrókar (The Saga of Ragnar Hairy-breeches)*, a blend of historical fact, pseudo-history, and legend and folklore. The figure of Aella and an account of the slaying of Aella by the Vikings, as well as of the Viking attacks in Northumbria, appear in the *Anglo-Saxon Chronicle* and various other medieval chronicles, such as Asser's *Life of King Alfred*. Thus Marshall's book, like most historical novels, is grounded in historical people and events, even as it takes great liberties with the lives of those personages and the details of those events.

The film based on Marshall's book similarly takes liberties with its source, and yet it strives for a degree of historical credibility. The Vikings are not caricatures of the historical raiders. There is some attempt at realistic depiction of Viking life (though here too liberties are taken). They are seen feasting and drinking in a hall and not a castle. The film also tries to achieve authenticity in the depiction of their ships and arms and clothing. The Vikings do not, for example, wear the horned helmets of the Vikings in *Prince Valiant* (which will be discussed further below). A key object in the film is a compass and not a singing sword. In the attack on the stronghold of Aella (Frank Thring), a battering ram made from a tree, with roots still attached, is used to breach the castle, and the victory is not the result of the heroics of the main character alone — even though the leap of Einar (Kirk Douglas) across a moat to grab axes flung by other Vikings and then to climb to the top of the raised draw-bridge so he can lower it and allow access to his comrades does strain probability. And in contrast to Valiant, whose features appear unscathed despite his fighting much larger Viking opponents and being shot in the shoulder with an arrow, Einar has his faced scarred and an eye scratched out by a hawk, and Eric (Tony Curtis) has his hand cut off by Aella because he allowed Ragnar (Ernest Borgnine) to die holding a sword like a Viking in defiance of Aella's command to force Ragnar into a wolfpit without a weapon.

To be sure, the storyline of *The Vikings* has been transformed and significantly reshaped by its Hollywood interpreters. Such transformation and reshaping are particularly true of the romantic triangle: Ragnar's illegitimate son Eric and his legitimate son Einar both fall instantly in love with the beautiful Morgana, and much of the action revolves around their attempt to win her love. But there is, in the larger plot, at least a minimal attempt to depict Vikings and their surroundings with a modicum of authenticity.

By contrast, the story of Prince Valiant was based not on a real Viking who has taken on heroic, legendary, and folkloric traits but on the story and art created by Harold R. (Hal) Foster (1892–1982) and appearing in the weekly comic strip *Prince Valiant* since February 13, 1937. (In 1971, John Cullen Murphy began drawing the artwork for the strip; and in 1980 his son Cullen Murphy took over. Foster continued writing the strip until February 10, 1980, when Murphy's son Cullen Murphy assumed the writing of it. In 2004, Gary Gianni started drawing the strip.) The difference in source material in the film versions of *The Vikings* and the 1954 *Prince Valiant* is immediately obvious. The opening narration (by Orson Welles) of the former is heard over images of, or based on, the Bayeux Tapestry, while the latter begins with comic-strip images of knights and ladies, castles and Viking ships.

Prince Valiant was not Hal Foster's first attempt at depicting Vikings. He had previously illustrated a Viking sequence, written by Don Garden, for the *Tarzan* comic strip. Brian M. Kane has suggested that "the success of the [Viking] story-line [in *Tarzan*] may have encouraged Foster to pursue *Prince Valiant*" (Kane 74). Foster originally intended to call the hero of his comic strip Derek, Son of Thane; his second choice was Prince Arn. Fortunately, both names were rejected by Joseph V. Connolly, president of William Randolph Hearst's King Features Syndicate, who suggested Prince Valiant (Kane 80), a name that Foster originally disliked. Admittedly, "Valiant" sounded rather unmedieval (though in the *Alliterative Morte Arthure*, 1. 1982, there is a reference to Sir Valiant of Wales). In the muddled medieval time of the strip, however, readers neither looked for nor expected historical accuracy. Nor was Foster himself concerned with the chronology of history or even the kind of probability that a historical novel would require — even though Foster conducted considerable research into details of medieval clothing, armor, and castles so that he could draw them as accurately as possible. Yet the name "Valiant" now seems crucial to the success of the strip. It imparts a symbolic value to the courageous young hero, who has a Boy Scout–like preparedness for every misfortune and who no doubt contributes to the comic strip's enduring appeal.

Over the last seventy years, as Foster's character moved increasingly into the popular culture, he became the subject of numerous books, games and toys, including a *Prince Valiant* board game, and an animated television series, *The Legend of Prince Valiant* (1991), voiced by Robby Benson. "Prince Valiant" was even the theme of Mardi Gras parades in both 1955 and 1967 (Kane 170). Foster's comic strip also served as the basis for two movies, the popular *Prince Valiant* (Twentieth Century–Fox, 1954; directed by Henry Hathaway, with a screenplay by Dudley Nichols), which was adapted as a Dell comic book that same year, and the more recent *Prince Valiant* (Constantin Film, 1997; directed by Anthony Hickox), which was subsequently adapted into a novel by Martin Delrio.

Like its predecessor, the 1997 *Prince Valiant* claims Foster's strip as its source and utilizes comic strip panels "as introductions and segues to the live action" (Lupack, "Camelot on Camera" 280). It also contains some of the same plot elements, such as Valiant's (Stephen Moyer) fighting in place of Gawain (Anthony Hickox) and the storming of a castle so Valiant can defeat the wicked Vikings who have usurped the kingship of his native land. And it borrows elements from the original strip, such as the contention between Valiant and Arn (Ben Pullen) for the love of Princess Ilene (Katherine Heigl). But it contains plot elements that are far-fetched even in a film based on a comic strip: Morgan (Joanna Lumley) exhumes Merlin from his grave to obtain the book of enchantments that was buried with him; at Morgan's direction, wicked Vikings, posing as Scottish warriors to deceive Arthur about who the true enemy is, steal Excalibur; Ilene is killed but is brought back to life by Excalibur's power. And the film quickly dissolves into a series of unlikely and unintentionally comic special effects, so that "even young viewers fond of the comic strip would find this film adaptation unsatisfying" (Lupack, "Camelot on Camera" 280).

More engaging, and ultimately more faithful to Foster's vision, was the original 1954 adaptation. Using some of the same plot details, Henry Hathaway's film tells the story of the young Viking prince Valiant (Robert Wagner), whose family is driven into exile after his father Aguar (Donald Crisp), the king of Scandia, is overthrown by the evil Sligon (Primo Canera). After reaching manhood, Valiant journeys to Arthur's court, where he is befriended by Sir Gawain (Sterling Hayden), who trains him to be a knight; falls in love with a beautiful princess, Aleta of Ord (Janet Leigh); and faces the treachery of Round Table knight Sir Brack (James Mason), the illegitimate son of King Uther, who has assumed the guise of the Black Knight in order to betray Valiant's family and usurp Arthur's throne. By his brave acts (and without preposterous obstacles like the man-eating reptiles of Hickox's version to surmount), Valiant restores his father's kingship and receives his own knight-hood — and, of course, wins Aleta's hand in marriage.

In its emphasis on honor and individual achievement, Hathaway's *Prince Valiant* is certainly consistent with the spirit of Hal Foster's comic strip. Foster, in fact, was asked to make "sketches on which the settings of the film could be based," and he eventually "drew 23,980 of them" (McCarten 93). His influence and presence were also evident in the visual effect of the film, including the portrayal of the Vikings and particularly of the lead Viking Prince Valiant; and Foster's inspiration helped to shape the nature of the action and the straightforward presentation of the thematic confrontation between good and evil.

Both specific scenes and general motifs borrow directly from Foster's strip. In the early years of the strip (conveniently collected in the first volume of *Prince Valiant: In the Days of King Arthur*, published by Nostalgia Press in 1974), as in the film, Valiant is portrayed as a Viking in exile whose father Aguar's throne has been usurped by the villainous Sligon. Once he makes his way to Arthur's court, as squire to Sir Gawain, he must earn knighthood. In fact, in the strip as in the film, the knighting of Valiant after he has more than proven himself is a climactic event.[1]

In the early pages of the strip, however, in contrast to the film (in which he rescues his parents and his beloved), Valiant uses his wits and courage to free Sir Gawain, who is imprisoned in a castle. He saves the knight who is his master by using a ruse in which he makes his enemies believe he is a demon — though, like his counterpart in the film, he also swings around the parapets of the castle and fights fearsome warriors. Even the scene in which Valiant escapes his pursuers, the Vikings who are in league with the Black Knight (actually Sir Brack [James Mason] in disguise), by submerging himself in a river and breathing through a reed, is borrowed directly from an episode in the strip in which Valiant eludes his pursuers with the same trick.

But whereas the adventures of the film's Valiant were restricted to the old world, Foster's Valiant engaged in adventures all over the globe and even in the new world of the Americas. Such broad travels, though chronologically, geographically, and historically improbable, were required in order to continue Valiant's exploits over the long run of the comic strip. Yet even in the early years of the strip, Foster seemed less concerned with historical fact and more intent upon providing (at least initially) an example of a principled, valiant, resourceful young man who could serve as a model for young readers. In this way, Foster was consistent with other writers and educators of the first half of the twentieth century, who focused much of their attention on the activities and development of the young, especially young boys. Chivalry, and specifically the Arthurian stories, provided good sources for those models, as evidenced by the Arthurian youth groups that abounded in the early twentieth century, and in retellings of Arthurian tales by Howard Pyle and other adapters of the Arthurian legends, whose works were often read by the members of those groups as examples of virtuous living. In his study of *America's Great Comic-Strip Artists*, Richard Marschall has observed that "the work of illustrator Howard Pyle was [Hal] Foster's inspiration as he created *Prince Valiant*, and as a matter of fact many panels are visual references to illustrations of the King Arthur and Robin Hood stories by Pyle. Like Pyle, Foster discovered that nobility is not found just within the nobility; that the everyday can be as important, as interesting — and as noble — as participation in epic battles for romantic causes" (189). This transformation of nobility into a matter of character rather than of birth — a pervasive theme in the Arthurian youth groups, in Pyle's works, and in the writing of many other contemporary authors and educators — is an idea that seems to be at the heart of Foster's strip. His Valiant is a prince, but a Viking prince who quickly learns that his status will not automatically qualify him for knighthood and that he must earn that honor. This notion that one must prove himself by his deeds and that birth alone is not enough to merit knighthood is at the heart of the film as well.

The film *Prince Valiant* had a large budget ($3 million) and an impressive cast; and it incorporated such innovations as Cinemascope, a technique used so effectively in another Arthurian film, *The Black Knight* (Warwick-Columbia, 1954; directed by Tay Garnett). But contemporary and current critical opinion has generally held that the actors played down to their material; and the film itself has been treated as little more than juvenile adventure. The review in *Film Daily*, for instance, considered *Prince Valiant* "escapist fare" that would appeal to children and to adults "seeking cleverly fashioned escapism" (6). *Time* magazine agreed, noting that *Prince Valiant* was "all a small boy could ask for. His parents," the reviewer added, "might as well relax and enjoy the fun too" (106). Bosley Crowther, writing in the *New York Times*, called the film a "transcript of the funnies" (40). John McCarten, reviewing it for the *New Yorker*, was even more mocking of the film, which he said was "hardly up to the cerebral standards of 'Orphan Annie'" (93–94). Adding to the impression that *Prince Valiant* was hardly worth serious consideration was the admission of the film's director, Henry Hathaway, that he made the picture "as a personal favor to Darryl [Zanuck]. I didn't particularly care one way or the other and the picture looked it" (Eyman 11).

The *Times* of London review was also harsh in its criticism. Hollywood, it asserted, "has a way of presenting the past in a *genre* which can only be described as pantomime-historical" (4). The *Times* reviewer also decried "the absurdities, the anachronisms, the vulgarities, the disconcerting accents, and the even more disconcerting dialogue" but allowed that the landscapes and the action, particularly the storming and the burning of the castle occupied by Sligon, were well done (4). The review in *Film Daily* similarly singled out the "lollapaloosa of a battle," in which the castle occupied by the wicked Vikings is taken when it is burned in "a blaze that is a conflagration" (6).

The siege sequence and the burning of the castle, which occupied "one-fourth of Dudley Nichols' script, [and] cost around $250,000," were indeed among the visual highlights of the film. The castle itself, constructed of plaster and wood on the Fox lot, cost nearly $88,000 to build, and in "eight nights the whole structure was burned and charred with 2,500 gallons of a secret formula inflammable fluid which was tested and retested before being pronounced photogenic for the Technicolor cameras" (Brownell 2.7). Commenting on the spectacular destruction of the castle, Philip T. Hartung, in a review in *Commonweal*, called it "the biggest conflagration since Nero burned Rome in 'Quo Vadis'" (41). And *New York Times* reviewer Bosley Crowther, despite his other objections to the film, found "the best part of the picture" to be the "bigslam-bang rowdy-dow that occurs when two armies of Vikings put on a fight in and around a castle's walls. With Val ... inside the enemy's stronghold, spreading fire and destruction, while his friends come battering in from outside. It all makes a fearsome conflagration of human passions and burning oil" (40). Significantly, in Crowther's analysis, the notion of conflagration, so central to the plot and vital to the visual effect of the film, becomes a metaphor for the emotions of the characters in a tale of loyalty and treachery, faithlessness and love.

Yet if, as Hartung observed, the film succeeds "as lively entertainment" because it "never takes itself too seriously" (41), then much of the liveliness comes from this conflagration of emotions, from Valiant's rollicking adventures, and from the literal conflagration in the siege scene. No doubt other contemporary reviewers must have enjoyed that liveliness, even if their critical reputations or their sense of what constitutes a serious film kept them from admitting their feelings in print. Their almost uniform praise for the conflagration and siege scenes, however, suggests that at least some of them appreciated the film, even if only as an adventure story — a guilty pleasure perhaps, but a pleasure nonetheless. In fact, they probably enjoyed it the same way that audiences enjoyed many Middle English romances — for the fast pace, the wild exploits, the wit and valor of the hero, the ultimate triumph of love, and the simple presentation of right and wrong.[2] And as in Middle English romances, the narrative liveliness obviated many of the questions of historical and geographic probability, "the absurdities, the anachronisms, the vulgarities, ... and the ... disconcerting dialogue."

Another reason that the siege scene and the conflagration of the castle resonated with critics may be because the film, like all texts, is intertextual, in the most expansive sense of that word. It interacts with cinematic and literary traditions, other texts, the comic strip, and society — just as Foster's comic strip had. Yet even as critics recognized the intertextual forces at play in the film (even when they did not call them intertextual), they continued to point to certain historical inaccuracies in *Prince Valiant* (and many other films set in the Middle Ages) to suggest that the film is less than serious.

One such detail in *Prince Valiant* is the Vikings' distinctive headgear. Like Crowther, who referred to the "top-heavy Viking horns" (40), the *Motion Picture Herald's* reviewer specifically commented on the horned helmets of the Vikings, noting that the villains "in this period, actually wore horns." But he went on to observe that such helmets were not an adequate signifier of villainy since Valiant and his family and friends are also Vikings. Thus he concluded that telling the valiant from the villainous Vikings by their helmets is more difficult than telling the good cowboys from the bad by the color of their hats in the Western films that influenced *Prince Valiant* (2255).

It was not only the contemporary reviewers who scoffed at the familiar helmets worn in the film. Helmut Nickel has observed that "unfortunately, no archaeologist so far has unearthed a Viking helmet with horns, let alone [the] wings" (237) that also appear on some of the film's helmets. But while judgments such as Nickel's are useful in demonstrating the lack of historicity in *Prince Valiant*, they are little more than academic quibbles to the audiences who view the film. Those audiences accept the film's depiction of the Middle Ages, which incorporates the very trappings commonly associated with that time — Vikings, knights, castles, tournaments, values, and so on. In fact, for many people, and certainly in the popular consciousness, the Middle Ages has become such a muddle of historical periods and motifs that they do not even recognize the historical inaccuracy of Vikings living in the age of Arthur. So why, then, is there such interest in the horned helmets? Perhaps it is because of their omnipresence in the scenes in which the Vikings appear. They seem to define Vikingness, at least the type of Vikingness that connotes barbarianism and paganism in the film.

Laurie A. Finke and Martin B. Shichtman have commented perceptively on the use of signs in historical films: "Viewers accept a Caesar haircut, for instance, as a sign of Roman-ness not because they are (or are not) unsophisticated or naïve but because they have become competent readers of the cinematic shorthand that allows a two-hour visit to a remediated ancient Rome. The systems of signification that make up this shorthand resonate across any number of disparate films, triggering a willing suspension of disbelief that enables us to enter into the worlds these films create (at least momentarily), even when, as historians, we might be suspicious of the film's representation of the past" (36). Finke and Shichtman's analysis not only helps to explain the ongoing fascination with details such as the horned helmets, but it also reinforces the way that those details serve as a sign of Vikingism — on the screen and in popular culture (cf. the cartoon *Hagar the Horrible*, not to mention Minnesota Vikings fans). Moreover, in *Prince Valiant*, the helmets have an even more specific significance; they come to represent perceptions, such as the image that the father (Barry Jones) of Aleta and Ilene (Debra Paget) have of Vikings. When Valiant is recuperating in his castle and Aleta shows affection for him, her father observes that "he's a Viking, bar-barians, pirates, uncivilized pagans all of them."

Yet, despite the concerned king's prejudice, not all Vikings are alike. Some, like the fresh-faced, clean-shaven Valiant, do not physically fit the stereotype. And even some of those who do look the part — like Valiant's friend Boltar (Victor McLaglen), who is as heavily-bearded and elaborately horned as some of the worst of the Northmen (Review, *Motion Picture Herald* 2255), and his comrades — wear the familiar horns but are secretly Christian and oppose the tyranny of Sligon. Boltar's horned helmet, in fact, provides an excellent disguise for him as he acts as a spy among the wicked Vikings.

Although Valiant himself never wears a horned helmet, Aleta's worried father nonethe-less warns her, even before he arrives at Arthur's court, that they need to learn more about Valiant, because "all that we know about the Viking is that he is a Viking." He is openly contemptuous of Valiant's origins. After the squire fights in Gawain's armor to win the hand of Aleta for Gawain, who loves her, and his identity is revealed, Aleta's father says disdain-fully, "It's the Viking. Impostor." Even Sir Gawain is concerned about curbing Valiant's Vikingness. When Valiant berates himself for running off and getting himself into trouble with the treacherous Vikings, Gawain calls him a "Viking fool." And when Valiant suspects

Sir Brack, Gawain tells him to "control that knavish Viking imagination of yours." Like Aleta's father, Gawain apparently believes that Vikings have different values from those of Arthur's knights. In fact, at the tournament to win Aleta's hand, Gawain has Valiant guard his armor so that "maybe I'll get a few ideas of chivalry into my Viking head."

The contrast between chivalric and Viking values is suggestive of another important level of intertextuality in the film. *Prince Valiant* draws its meaning — and the audience draws its fullest understanding of it — not just from cinematic and literary traditions, other Arthurian texts, and Foster's comic strip, but also from the conditions of the age in which it was created. The fact that the film offers a lively narrative and a commonly accepted if ahistorical picture of its Viking hero and of the Arthurian age does not preclude it from commenting in some way on important social, political, or religious issues, as popular Middle English romances often did. Just as the 1954 film *The Black Knight* (which I have analyzed at greater length elsewhere) is not only a tale of Arthur's knights discovering a threat to the very existence of Camelot and Christian Britain and defeating traitors but also a thinly disguised exploration of the Communist threat so feared in the McCarthy era, so too are there contemporary political overtones to *Prince Valiant*. Susan Aronstein has argued that the film similarly depicts "a national Christian Self threatened by a pagan Other aided in its ambitions for invasion by an enemy within." Aronstein goes on to state that it is surprising that, given other films they collaborated on, producer Daryl Zanuck and screenwriter Dudley Nichols would produce such an anti–Communist film; but she suggests that "working on an anticommunism film was often seen as a test case, akin to taking the Loyalty Oath and perhaps *Valiant* functioned in this way for its producer and writer" (73).

Aronstein is right in her assessment that *Prince Valiant* should be viewed in the context of the political concerns of its day. The threat to Christian civilization that was perceived as a significant aspect of the Communist threat is apparent in the film. Even the trailer observed that the film treats "the Christians' revolt against the Infidels" — a strange way to advertise a film that otherwise is presented as offering the medieval pageantry of tournaments and sieges and swordfights, the kidnapping of lovers, and the knighting of Prince Valiant. And it is especially strange in a film that, as reviewers suggested, was largely a juvenile adventure. The villainous Vikings, as a voice-over informs the audience, have overthrown "the Christian king of Scandia" and wish to exterminate all of the Christians in the realm. Later in the film, as Boltar says when rallying the Christian Vikings, "Once Aguar's dead, Sligon won't rest till he's crucified every Christian in Scandia." The heathen Vikings are also a threat to Arthur's realm and to chivalry, which the film defines as a Christian code. When Valiant is about to leave for the court of Arthur, whom he calls the "most Christian king of the Britains," he pledges "to restore the cross of Christ to all our Vikings." He thus sets up even more explicitly the conflict between Christian and pagan. The contrast is highlighted again when Valiant promises to regain the singing sword, which Sligon "has sullied with pagan hands." Before Valiant rescues his parents and Aleta, the priest who is imprisoned with them and who consoles them holds up a cross and says, "By this sign you shall conquer." The line is echoed by another priest who addresses a council of Christian Vikings by announcing that "by this sign [the cross] shall ye conquer"; and they repeat the line — even though Boltar objects that "signs won't conquer Sligon" and advises that "the Lord helps those who help themselves." When Sligon tells Valiant that he will talk or die on the cross, Valiant replies, "the cross is our salvation; you'll burn in hell." When Valiant finally kills Brack with the singing sword, he does so in front of a prie-dieu surmounted by a disproportionately large cross, a piece of furniture that seems out of place in the hall that houses the Round Table but that is obviously there for its symbolic value. And after the trial by combat, Arthur knights Valiant as a member of "our most Christian order" of the Knights of the Round Table.

When Valiant is captured and brought before Sligon, the threat to Christianity is combined with unmistakable links to the McCarthy era. But this scene actually suggests that the movie is more than what Aronstein calls "an anticommunism film," the making of which was "akin to taking the Loyalty Oath" (73). It provides a more blatant analogue of Senator Joseph McCarthy's Communist witchhunts. One of Sligon's henchman, appearing particularly crazed, asks Valiant to name the other Christians in their company, a command that is echoed by Sligon. At first, the henchman asks simply for the names of those whom he contemptuously calls "cross worshipers"; then he unrolls a scroll wrapped, significantly, around a set of horns and says, "Call out the names of the conspirators; I'll check them on this list." He continues the ruse of pretending to know who the Christians are by asking Valiant merely to "confirm this list." He then compounds the lie by telling the young prince, "Your father named them all." The tactics of the wicked Vikings and their association with the attempt to ferret out the "conspirators" by forcing those being interrogated to name names, or merely to confirm names that the inquisitors pretend to know, align the villainous, pagan Vikings with the Communist hunters. The film thus casts the McCarthy-like tactics in a very negative light, and even implies that such conduct is antithetical to the Christian values represented by Arthurian chivalry and the Christian Vikings. The contrast of values and tactics can be seen most dramatically when Valiant suspects Sir Brack of coveting Arthur's throne, but Sir Gawain defends Brack. He tells Valiant that his is a base suspicion because Brack, though "born on the wrong side of the blanket," is a knight of the Round Table "sworn to lay down his life in defense of our king and to defend truth, the weak and the helpless." Assuming that a knight will always be loyal, Gawain exhibits too much trust. But at the same time, his actions are in stark opposition to those of Sligon and his followers.

Valiant and the Christian Vikings are staunch allies of the Christian court at Camelot. In the symbolism of the film, the real threat to the realm of both Arthur and Valiant — and a real threat certainly exists — is from Sligon and his pagan Vikings, who resort to despicable tactics to force their prisoners to inform on friends and family. Since they are also the ones who burn their enemies on the cross, a cross that functions throughout the film as a sign of faith and faithfulness, the symbolic Communist hunters are the ones who are vilified. *Prince Valiant* is thus more than a simple "loyalty oath." It is a social commentary that actually calls into question the values and tactics of those who would demand such oaths and implies that they and their supporters are the true enemy of the people and a threat to the culture. The very symbolism of having pagan and Christian, treacherous and faithful, valiant and villainous Vikings, moreover, implies that it is not always easy to recognize the enemy within.

Admittedly, the motif of betrayal is not unique to *Prince Valiant*. It is also one of the plot devices in *The Vikings*, in which the lord Egbert betrays the English by providing maps to the Vikings. But Egbert's disloyalty lacks the political implications of Brack's treason. So therefore, while *The Vikings* tends to be more historical in its presentation of the Vikings and somewhat truer to its literary sources, it lacks the blatant dialogic interaction with its own times displayed by *Prince Valiant*, which offers a kind of political engagement with the issues of its day.

Such a reading of the film is not to argue that *Prince Valiant* is a great work of art. It

Prince Valiant (Robert Wagner) defeats Sir Brack (James Mason) in Henry Hathaway's 1954 film *Prince Valiant* (editor's collection).

is not. But it is an entertaining and often exciting film, one that evokes some of the spirit — if not always with historical accuracy — of the medieval, and especially the Arthurian, world. As the *Times* of London reviewer noted, "it would clearly be ridiculous to snub *Prince Valiant* on the score that it would give Malory, and Tennyson for that matter, several fits" (4). Yet while it is true that the liberties taken by the film might have disturbed Malory and Tennyson, I would suggest that a later author, novelist T. H. White, would have understood that even a juvenile tale could, like his own *Sword in the Stone*, make a comment on values and contemporary events. Ultimately, that is how the 1954 film of *Prince Valiant* should be viewed: as a kind of "buried treasure of the comic strip film genre" (Hofstede 138) that has some interesting intertextual connections to Hal Foster's comic strip, to Arthurian literature, to Viking films, and to the concerns of its age.

Notes

1. The panel in which Valiant is knighted by King Arthur was later reproduced in a large lithograph, limited to one hundred and fifty copies.

2. Larry Benson has noted that "the typical English romance remained a relatively brief and simple narrative ... the emphasis was on action rather than description and reflection. Brevity remained a virtue, and simplicity of setting and characterization and the dominance of action remained the guiding principles of most native romancers" (47).

Works Cited

Aronstein, Susan. *Hollywood Knights: Arthurian Cinema and the Politics of Nostalgia*. New York: Palgrave Macmillan, 2005.

Benson, Larry D. *Malory's Morte Darthur*. Cambridge: Harvard University Press, 1976.

Brownell, William H., Jr. "Comics Come Alive." *New York Times* (1 Nov. 1953): 2.7.

"A Comic-Strip Camelot: American Film Curiosity." *Times* [London] (3 May 1954): 4.

Crowther, Bosley. "The Screen in Review: 'Prince Valiant' Comes to the Roxy Theatre." *New York Times* (7 April 1954): 40.

Eyman, Scott. "An Interview with Henry Hathaway." *Take One* 5.1 (February 1976): 6–12.

Finke, Laurie A., and Martin B. Shichtman. *Cinematic Illuminations: The Middle Ages on Film*. Baltimore: The Johns Hopkins University Press, 2010.

Hartung, Philip T. "I'm Calling Yoo-Hoo-Hoo-Hoo." *Commonweal* 60 (16 April 1954): 41.

Hofstede, David. *Hollywood and the Comics: Film Adaptations of Comic Books & Strips*. N.p.: Zanne-3, 1991.

Kane, Brian M. *Hal Foster: Prince of Illustrators, Father of the Adventure Strip*. Lebanon, NJ: Vanguard Productions, 2001.

Lupack, Alan. "An Enemy in Our Midst: *The Black Knight* and the American Dream." In *Cinema Arthuriana: Essays on Arthurian Film*. Ed. Kevin J. Harty. New York: Garland, 1991. 29–39. [Rpt. in *Cinema Arthuriana: Twenty Essays*. Rev. ed. Ed. Kevin J. Harty. Jefferson, NC: McFarland, 2002. 64–70.]

Lupack, Barbara Tepa. "Camelot on Camera: The Arthurian Legends and Children's Film." In *Adapting the Arthurian Legends for Children: Essays on Arthurian Juvenilia*. Ed. Barbara Tepa Lupack. New York: Palgrave Macmillan, 2004. 263–94.

Marschall, Richard. *America's Great Comic-Strip Artists: From the Yellow Kid to Peanuts*. New York: Stewart, Tabori & Chang, 1997.

McCarten, John. "Glorifying the Scandian Boy." *New Yorker* 30 (10 April 1954): 93–94.

Nickel, Helmut. "Arms and Armor in Arthurian Films." In *Cinema Arthuriana: Twenty Essays*. Rev. ed. Ed. Kevin J. Harty. Jefferson, NC: McFarland, 2002. 235–51.

Review of *Prince Valiant*. *Film Daily* 2 April 1954: 6.

Review of *Prince Valiant*. *Motion Picture Herald* 10 April 1954: Product Digest Section 2254–55.

Review of *Prince Valiant*. *Time* 63 (12 April 1954): 106.

Wawn, Andrew. *The Vikings and the Victorians: Inventing the Old North in Nineteenth-Century Britain*. Cambridge: D. S. Brewer, 2000.

Silly Vikings: Eichinger, Hickox, and Lorenz's Anglo-German-Irish Production of Hal Foster's *Prince Valiant* (1997)

Joseph M. Sullivan

In two short months, between May and June 1997, the German production and distribution company Neue Constantin Film completed major photography on its medium-budget production of *Prince Valiant*. Starring newcomers Stephen Moyer as Valiant and a teenage Katherine Heigl as his love interest, and featuring known German actors as their Viking adversaries, the film received general release in the United Kingdom, Canada, France, and Germany (as *Prinz Eisenherz*).[1] Like the other film version of *Prince Valiant*, namely, Henry Hathaway's 1954 picture of the same name starring Robert Wagner, the movie is based on the weekly comic strip *Prince Valiant in the Days of King Arthur* created by Harold R. Foster.[2] Drawn and scripted by Foster from its inception in 1937 until 1971, and continued by other artists and writers to this day, the strip begins with the youth of Valiant, whose Viking father has been unlawfully deposed from his throne in the Scandinavian kingdom of Thule and has sought refuge in England, where his son eventually becomes a member of King Arthur's Round Table. While the strip would eventually track the adventures of Valiant's family members, including his own children, over a period of decades and across vast swaths of the world, this conflation of the Viking and the Arthurian has remained the thematic heart of the comic throughout its run.[3] It is the purpose of this essay to show how the filmmakers of the 1997 *Prince Valiant* modify this coming together of the Arthurian and the Viking to create a very non-traditional notion of Vikings and Vikingness, one that is unfortunately characterized by a pronounced silliness.

Despite the temporal oddity of the conflation of the Viking and the Arthurian — an historical Arthur would have died several centuries before the rise of the Vikings — the comic strip's fans have long prized its presentation of medieval history and the highly detailed realism of its illustrations. Indeed, such qualities have made the strip popular world-wide. In Europe, for instance, generations of children from the United Kingdom to Germany to Iceland had, by the mid–1970s, grown up with the strip as a primary source of knowledge about the Arthurian legend, the Vikings, and the Middle Ages, having read the comic translated into their own languages as a regular periodical feature or, more recently, in the form of novel-length compilation volumes.[4]

Neue Constantin's decision to make *Prince Valiant/Prinz Eisenherz* can be seen as a recognition of the international bankability that such widespread familiarity with the strip had created. Thus in areas as diverse as casting, filming, marketing, and financing, the firm would act in a manner distinctly international, or, perhaps more accurately, European. Indeed, *Prince Valiant* is a prime example of the "Europudding," that is, a film that draws on resources from several European countries to produce pictures that might also be shown in a variety of countries.

In *Prince Valiant*'s case, the key countries involved were the United Kingdom and Germany. Thus one of the three important creative personnel behind the film was an Englishman, director Anthony Hickox, who also co-wrote the script with the film's second important creative force, the German Carsten Lorenz. And it was a German, Bernd Eichinger, the producer and largest stakeholder in Constantin, who in the early 1990s developed the idea to film *Prince Valiant* and recruited Hickox and Lorenz. Further, both Germany and the United Kingdom provided filming locations, with exteriors shot in Wales and interiors in Berlin studios. Lastly, financing was international, obviously to take advantage of favorable tax regimes for film production in countries like Ireland and the United Kingdom, and European Union incentives for co-productions.[5] For *Valiant*, Eichinger's Constantin put together the Irish Legacy Film Productions and British Celtridge production companies, which apparently ceased to exist once filming was completed and their usefulness exhausted. Although with such international productions it is difficult to determine where the influence of one particular national film culture on a picture stops and another begins, I will attempt below to provide some suggestions of how *Valiant* partakes in both British and German film cultures.

In scriptwriters' Hickox and Lorenz's version of the tale, Morgan Le Fey teams with Viking brothers Thagnar and Sligon the Usurper—who had seized unlawfully the throne of Thule from Valiant's father—to steal Excalibur from Camelot. With Excalibur, the three believe, they can dominate Arthur and the world. Meanwhile at Camelot, Valiant, who is serving as Gawain's squire, receives an assignment from Arthur to escort back to her father in Wales the beautiful Princess Ilene, with whom he falls in love. (In the script's most significant departure from Foster's strip, Valiant's love interest is thus not Queen Aleta.) Having succeeded in taking Excalibur, but believing they need Gawain (played by Anthony Hickox) to make it functional, the Vikings kidnap Gawain and bring him along with a captured Ilene back to their stronghold in Thule. Valiant therefore ventures to Thule, links up with a band of indigenous freedom fighters trying to liberate the land from Sligon, and together with them storms the stronghold. While Sligon, Thagnar, and Morgan perish, Princess Ilene also receives a mortal wound only to be brought back to life by Valiant's prayers and the magic of Excalibur.

As with most comic strip adaptations for the screen, scriptwriters Hickox and Lorenz thus have taken some substantial, but by no means untypical number of, liberties with the basic storyline inherited from the original material. But what makes the film so distinctive is not its modification of story elements but rather its unusual tone. While the comic strip is certainly not dour, it is rarely downright funny, and among its international fans "humor is not generally regarded as its strongest point."[6] By contrast, the film exhibits an unmistakable "joking tone."[7] Although Hickox has claimed that "'we didn't want it played for laughs'" (Jones, "The Arthurian comic strip" 6), as reviewers noted the film exhibits "a voracious appetite for sight gags ... and anachronistic wise-cracks" (Spencer 9). For instance, when the little person Pechet—played by Warwick Davis—is humorously catapulted into the Viking stronghold, he stumbles upon a bottle anachronistically identified as "Quaeludium," and quips that "one should never leave drugs around" before using the soporific medication to aid Ilene and Valiant. And when the Viking Thagnar asks him how he would like to die, Valiant retorts, in tongue-in-cheek fashion and before being tossed over a cliff, "Old age." As Stephen Moyer observed, he regarded his Valiant character "as a mixture of Dudley Moore and Sir Lancelot."[8]

Such silliness, in ample supply here, is a hallmark of the films that the then–thirty-three-year-old Anthony Hickox had directed prior to *Prince Valiant*. The reputation of Hickox, a true working director with more than a dozen cinema and television credits already to his name, at the time rested primarily on a string of films including *Waxwork* (1988), *Hellraiser III: Hell on Earth* (1992), and *Warlock: The Armageddon* (1993). The signature of these small-budget pictures of the "video bin" variety (Brown, "Ma's out" 34) is their parody of traditional horror genres and the injection of a heavy dose of over-the-top, sometimes downright ridiculous humor. That very same humor finds its way also into *Prince Valiant*, leading to both a very non-serious take on the Arthurian legend as well as to a highly silly notion of what this essay calls Vikingness.

The Arthurian in Advance

As the film opens on a rocky outcrop, Morgan Le Fay and a small band of ambiguously-clad barbarian warriors disinter the body of Merlin and remove a magic book with the label "Merlin" upon it from his clutching hands. Merlin's well-preserved corpse wears the metallic skullcap that John Boorman's 1981 *Excalibur* had made an iconic element of his dress.[9] Thus from the very beginning of the picture, the filmmakers pursue a strategy to present viewers with characterological and visual cues that place their narrative centrally within the Arthurian tradition. In highlighting the Arthurian, and doing so at the expense of the Viking, the filmmakers choose to depart from Foster's original vision. While the strip has involved its characters in adventures across the Old World and even in North America, its central geographic focus has always been Britain and Scandinavia, with elaborate treatment, and more or less equally detailed discussion, of the two cultures it associates with those places, the Arthurian-British and the Viking.

In contrast, the film eschews elements clearly identifiable as Viking and instead structures its narrative around icons that would be easily recognizable as Arthurian by competent readers of what Finke and Shichtman term "cinematic shorthand" (36). For example, Morgan — cinema arthuriana's arch-villainess — is here ubiquitous, both guiding the actions of the film's two principal Vikings, Sligon and Thagnar, and thus integrating their home base of Thule more closely into the Arthurian ambit, as well as devising the plan that drives the entire storyline. That plan itself, to seize Excalibur, is significant not just because Excalibur is arguably the most identifiable Arthurian icon. Rather, in choosing Excalibur, the filmmakers forego using that most important sword of the original comic strip, namely, the Singing Sword, or *Flamberge*, which the strip associates with Valiant's Viking heritage. Valiant, too, is made more clearly Arthurian than in the strip, where he had been raised by his Viking father in Britain with full knowledge of his Nordic heritage. By comparison, Valiant goes through most of the film fully unaware of his Viking origins, learning of his parentage — and thus stepping outside the Arthurian sphere, albeit very slightly — only after he has ventured to Thule to free Gawain and Ilene.

Costuming also seems intended to signal viewers to the most familiar Arthurian. In a departure from the strip, whose Arthurian knights wear predominantly mail armor from "vaguely 'around 1200'" (Nickel 236), the film's Round Table warriors wear plate armor reminiscent of the fifteenth-century Late Gothic style. While Hickox in a promotional interview claimed "the Victorian idea of medieval movies," and elsewhere referred specifically to a certain pre–Raphaelite "'Waterhouse'" painting (Press Book 16), as the inspiration for that costuming, one is hard placed not to notice, as one reviewer did, that Hickox "unabashedly pilfers from John Boorman's *Excalibur*,"[10] and to surmise that with *Prince Valiant's* highly polished plate armor, Hickox was relying on audience familiarity with Boorman's iconic film and its own use of similarly shiny armor to trigger an immediate and strong recognition of the Arthurian.

Other less obvious choices the filmmakers made also work to highlight the Arthurian and medieval Britishness of *Prince Valiant*. Perhaps most important among these is location. As Boorman did with *Excalibur*, as Antoine Fuqua and Jerry Bruckheimer did with their 2004 *King Arthur*, and as directors and producers of medieval movies have done going back to MGM's 1952 *Ivanhoe* and before, our filmmakers likewise chose to film in the British Isles. In *Prince Valiant*, North Wales and Snowdonia provide the backdrop for the action that takes place in the film's fictional Arthurian realm. For all *Prince Valiant's* flaws, Hickox uses to full advantage the experience shooting in beautiful, remote locations that he had gained with his earlier films, like the low-budget *Sundown: The Vampire in Retreat* (1988), which he filmed in Moab, Utah. With *Valiant*, he achieves quite breathtaking shots of the mountains of Snowdonia in many types of weather. Arguably, however, it is the many shots in the foggy hills and woods that partake most in the "misty, moisty" (Whitaker 46) standard iconography of Arthurian films. By contrast, the relatively little amount of outdoor action that takes place in the Vikings' fictional homeland of Thule occurs almost entirely in the dark of night, prohibiting any kind of association between location and Vikingness.

The preference of the Arthurian over the Viking in *Prince Valiant* seems to have been entirely intentional. As co-writer Lorenz told *Cinefantastique*, "Naturally we decided to place our story against the backdrop of Camelot, Excalibur, King Arthur, and his Knights of the Round Table." Indeed, by invoking the familiar Arthurian as the backbone of the storyline, the writers relied upon the assumption that "we wouldn't have to explain too much to the audience about the background ... [since they] know these legendary characters and events already" (Jones, "An epic adaptation" 53). Thus the filmmakers aimed for, and achieved, a certain narrative economy by using standard icons of cinema arthuriana to suggest the Arthurian. Conversely, by avoiding the introduction of too many, perhaps to young audiences, unfamiliar Viking elements, they avoided the complexity that might have made their picture difficult to follow.

Largely, the filmmakers' strategy to anchor their *Prince Valiant* more firmly within the Arthurian milieu than had Foster's strip seems to have been successful, with the vast majority of reviewers at the time seeing it as belonging to those films "devoted to the Arthurian legend."[11] Or as one reviewer wrote in a rather negative treatment of the picture, *Prince Valiant* is a just a "cut-price jumble of Arthurian motifs" (Johnston 17). Interestingly, the lessened profile of Viking elements *vis-à-vis* the strip did not register as a concern among professional reviewers at the time of *Prince Valiant's* release nor has it surfaced as a major concern in the many reviews posted on the internet by individual users who have bought DVD copies of the film over the last several years.[12]

The Viking in Retreat

Although the Arthurian thus constitutes a more elaborated thematic focus than does the Viking in *Prince Valiant*, the creation of a certain kind of Vikingness is nevertheless critical to the overall development of the storyline and to the final feel that the film achieves. Such Vikingness is marked by the foreignness of the Vikings, by the existential evil they represent, and by a mode of behavior that, while suggesting ruthlessness, regularly crosses over to the ridiculous. To understand that Vikingness more fully, I will analyze it in terms of three major groupings of *dramatis personae* portraying Vikings, namely, the extras who appear as non-speaking Viking soldiers in larger battle scenes, the principals who have speaking parts and who are Valiant's primary adversaries, and the band of rebels who fight for the freedom of Thule.

While the filmmakers promoted to the public that "several members of Hell's Angels were recruited as Vikings,"[13] it was in fact another set of extras that spent much more time in front of the cameras. In the film's major battle scenes, the Viking principals are surrounded by extras from the United Kingdom's largest Dark Age reenactment society, "The Vikings," a group that on its website proudly claims a reputation for a "high standard of presentation, historical accuracy and attention to detail" in portraying Viking-age warfare. Thus, unlike the Vikings of the comic strip, who conform largely to the traditional Viking stereotype of the bare-chested, pig-tailed, shaggy-bearded warrior in a horned helmet, "The Vikings" extras wear the more authentic conical helmets of early medieval warfare and, generally, are fully clothed.

The filmmakers' motivation to engage daily up to forty members of "The Vikings" seems to have been wholly financial, conditioned by the limits of the film's relatively small, $20 million budget. As the group's site explains, "We are respected for the ability to turn out at any time" fully costumed and already trained in the use of period weapons, thus allowing "production companies ... [to] greatly reduce ... overheads." While the filmmakers admittedly did not, in Lorenz's words, "worry all too much about historical exactness,"[14] the presence of "The Vikings" extras nevertheless adds a noticeable level of authenticity, and hence a kind of dignity, to the film's notion of Vikingness.

Interestingly, this more accurate Dark Age warrior in conical helmet is also (with just one exception) carried over to the non–live-action sequences, that is, to the CGI-generated cartoon-panels that appear several times throughout the film and then fade neatly into live action. Perhaps the film's most skillfully executed and incorporated aspect, the panels bear a remarkable visual fidelity to Foster's strip. Despite the visual impact of the panels, however, they and their more authentic Dark Age warriors appear far too briefly to emerge as the film's definitive Viking image. Similarly, the realistically equipped extras from "The Vikings," because they do not speak enough to engage the audience, play only a secondary role in establishing the overall impression of what a Viking is. Rather, it is around those characters who are the principal Vikings that the film most greatly establishes its conception of Vikingness.

We get our first good taste of the dominant flavor of that Vikingness early on, specifically, in the scene that opens the film and which, as described above, also does so much to establish the Arthurian. As Morgan Le Fey looks onto Merlin's final resting place, the panning camera captures several men at arms, in the hands of a number of whom are what might best be described as totems: tall, crooked sticks festooned with bones, ragged fabric, and skulls, both animal and human. The warriors themselves are clad in furs and spikes and armored leathers, with none of the conventional cinematic cues to suggest their true Viking identity, save for their round shields. Indeed, the filmmakers have eschewed almost completely the Hagar the Horrible Viking stereotype of the light-haired Norseman in a helmet of upturned horns. Instead, both their weird totems and the Vikings' leathery, bondage-type garb suggest, as Kevin J. Harty has remarked, that the Viking aesthetic developed here is closer "to the cinematic tradition of *Conan the Barbarian*" (127–128) than to past depictions of Vikings on film. We might add that the Vikings' clothing as well as their accoutrements serve — as had similar clothing and equipment in *Conan*— to highlight otherness and their place outside civilized society. By forgoing features of more traditional Viking portrayals, the filmmakers likely intended their viewers to be unencumbered by preconceptions about Vikings and to accept *Prince Valiant*'s Vikings as standing for a more generalized idea of foreignness, barbarity, and evil.

Their Viking aesthetic, clearly part of the filmmakers' formula to update the material into, in Lorenz's words, "something kids will drag their parents along to" (Jones, "An epic adaptation" 53), can be glimpsed most clearly in the film's central Vikings, namely, Sligon the Usurper, his brother Thagnar, and the Viking helpers who assist them in their stronghold. For his part, Thomas Kretschmann's Thagnar, the most visible of the film's Viking principals, is as one reviewer noted a "Thonged ... ton of Teutonic muscle" (Sweet 2.8). Kretschmann, who admitted he "pumped up a bit," spent "two months in the gym" prior to filming to achieve the kind of highly muscular physique made attractive in 1980s and 1990s popular culture by actors like *Conan*'s Arnold Schwarzenegger before scares over steroid abuse and changing tastes made such body types less attractive.[15]

With his shaved head, Kretschmann's Thagnar also taps into a look made popular in the 1990s by the likes of internationally visible sports stars including the NBA's Michael Jordan and Charles Barkley. And while Udo Kier's villainous Sligon sports an arguably less attractive look than does Kretschmann's buff Thagnar, the filmmakers' attempt to make him contemporary is also evident. Thus he, too, is clothed in leather, and the wild long dark hair that falls far down his back vividly recalls the hairstyle of villain Thulsa Doom, whom James Earl Jones had played in *Conan*. Additionally, this Sligon has none of the graceful body language one might expect of a powerful ruler, but rather, as contemporary reviewers noted, hobbles about "like Rumpelstiltskin" or a "computer-animated monster."[16] The final effect is to render this key Viking figure a quite ridiculous, undignified character.

Both the rather silly Vikingness that Kier's Sligon epitomizes and an updated Viking aesthetic that disposes of past stereotypes of Vikings on film is echoed in the characters who surround Thagnar and Sligon in their stronghold. Thus the Hell's Angels extras who populate the interior scenes as Viking guards do indeed, as a critic for the *Times* remarked, "look like medieval bikers" (Brown, "Ma's out" 34). And their leather-bound, spike-bedecked costuming is carried over in the appearance of the film's only female Viking principal; with her skin-tight metallic leather outfit exposed at the arms, she reminds one of Jane Fonda's Barbarella updated with the type of backcombed, teased-out, big-hair coiffeur made popular by the hair bands of the 1970s through early 1990s. Clearly, the visual aesthetic evident in all the Viking characters samples from a broad spectrum of streams in 1960s to 1990s popular culture. Thus we may see, for instance, the influence of the body-building craze, clothing trends, music videos, films like *Conan*, and television programs with remarkably similar visual palettes, like *Xena: Warrior Princess* (1995–2001). The visual effect is to create a Viking who looks almost nothing like the earlier cinematic, or, for that matter, comic strip, Viking. Indeed, in their rather eclectic, non-specific nature, *Prince Valiant*'s Vikings become merely

"Eurobaddies" (Sweet 2.8), embodying what Udo Kier saw as a general "evil" and representing "uncivilized otherness."[17]

The filmmakers create that otherness not only through dress but also through the speech of the figures inhabiting the Viking stronghold. While English-speaking actors fill *Prince Valiant*'s Arthurian roles, German actors play Thagnar, Sligon, and most stronghold personnel. That Hickox apparently makes no attempt to soften their rather heavy German pronunciation of English adds positively to the impression that these Vikings are separate from the civilized figures of Arthur's Camelot. However, German-accented English also adds a shade of the ridiculous. Thus Thagnar and Sligon pronounce their homeland not as *Th*ule but as *T*ool. And in Sligon and Thagnar's harem — an element that further contributes to the exotic otherness the Vikings represent — the captured princesses who serve there also speak a rather silly-sounding German-accented English. Thus one of those princesses, whom a critic for the *Independent* cheekily labeled "pre–Reformation lap-dancers" (Sweet 2.8), announces the day of the week on which she pleasures her lords: "I am *V*ensday." And another asks about Princess Ilene, whom Thagnar has just delivered to the harem, "I wonder if she is a *w*irgin."

It is this silliness, characterizing the Viking principals and those who serve them in their stronghold, which emerges as the most prominent trait of the film's notion of Vikingness. Indeed, the filmmakers even choose largely to exclude from the company of Vikings a last group that, arguably, would have added a significant degree of seriousness and dignity to the film's overall presentation of Vikingness. This latter group consists of a large band of rebels, addressed by their leader, King Thane, as the "free people of Thule," and who strive to remove Sligon the Usurper from the throne. In struggling for freedom, they fight for a serious, noble cause and the one value with which nearly all modern audiences can identify. While their rebel camp does harbor a large Vikingnesque rune stone, from which Valiant learns of his roots in Thule, other features of Vikingness are absent. Thus the rebels do not wear the costumes of stereotypical Vikings from earlier films, nor do their clothes resemble those of the movie's Viking principles, nor are they like the costumes of the extras furnished by "The Vikings" reenactment group or the Hell's Angels. Instead, they wear ragged textiles and, with the bowed weapons that they fire from trees in the darkened woods, their appearance and actions recall, more than anything else, cinematic depictions of Robin Hood and his band of sylvan outlaws.

Among other choices the filmmakers make that contribute to the rather unspecific notion of Vikingness that emerges in *Prince Valiant* is their decision to avoid treatment of religious ideology. Although the comic strip and, for example, Hathaway's 1954 film had foregrounded the Christianity of Valiant and Arthur's Britain and contrasted that with the cruel paganism of Thule's Viking usurpers, religion is virtually absent in our film. Thus while the picture does suggest on one occasion the existence of a God — Valiant cries out "Answer me, my God" when he wishes that his slain love, Ilene, be returned to life — and while Sligon sarcastically accuses Gawain of not exhibiting "the attitude of a Christian," mention of spiritual beliefs, Viking or otherwise, is conspicuously rare. Thus these Vikings stand for a generalized evil and not one that flows from denial of, or adherence to, a specific belief system.

Whose Film Is This Anyway?

While international co-productions like *Prince Valiant* challenge the very idea of national cinema, itself a useful but highly debated concept in film studies,[18] a closer look at the film cultures of the two countries most instrumental in getting *Prince Valiant* to the screen, namely, those of Germany and the United Kingdom, helps illuminate many of the decisions the filmmakers took to create their notion of Vikingness and to frame the overall movie.

Let us first, then, cast our focus on German film culture and the influence it exercised on *Prince Valiant*. Any discussion of the German film industry over the past quarter-century must include the name of *Prince Valiant*'s producer, Bernd Eichinger, of the production and distribution firm Neue Constantin Film. More than any other individual, Eichinger is responsible for the resurrection of a popular and commercially viable German film industry since the early 1980s. Once a robust producer of popular small- and medium-budget features for the domestic market, the German film industry had, by 1970, become moribund, unable to compete in a rapidly evolving media market increasingly dominated by Hollywood. The original Constantin Film, the leading German production and distribution company of the 1960s, managed to live on into the early 1970s on profits mainly derived from ventures into the soft-porn market. In 1977, it declared bankruptcy only be revived two years later by Eichinger as the Neue Constantin Film.[19] By the mid–1980s, Eichinger was pursuing a highly successful "twin-track strategy," putting together large-budget co-productions for the international market, like *The Name of the Rose* (1984), and a string of smaller-budget products for domestic consumption (Wedel 74).

The preference evident across Eichinger's oeuvre for mostly light-hearted fare with mass appeal may be seen legitimately as a direct reaction to those films most associated with German 1970s film culture, that is, with the films of New German Cinema. New German Cinema's star *auteurs* like Rainer Werner Fassbinder, Wim Wenders, and Werner Herzog looked down upon popular movies as shallow, and instead produced complex, introspective, and highly challenging works that defied traditional generic categories and often probed the questions of German identity and the recent German past. While critically acclaimed especially outside Germany, these often pessimistic films remained "an otherwise unpopular minor cinema" within the country, never finding a large viewing public (Rentschler 261). Bernd Eichinger's films, however, return to the formulas of German popular cinema of the 1950s and 1960s, before the heyday of New German Cinema (Baer 279–80).

Eichinger's preferences for a film culture with ideals opposed to those of New German Cinema are especially visible in those pictures that he and fellow German filmmakers produced for the domestic market in the 1990's after the fall of the Berlin Wall. These films, of what Eric Rentschler has aptly termed "the Post-Wall Cinema of Consensus" (260), fall into standard generic categories and have similar contours. The most successful are comedies, like Constantin's smash 1994 domestic hit *Der bewegte Mann* (*Maybe … Maybe Not*). Additionally, they "skirt the 'large' topics and hot issues," avoiding serious discussion of sensitive areas like religion or the German past (Rentschler 262). Although Eichinger conceived *Prince Valiant* for an international audience, he seems to have imposed upon it this same formula for making financially successful domestic films. Thus *Prince Valiant* falls more or less into a common generic category, the "adventure spectacle."[20] Moreover, recognizing how well humor was selling, at least in the very large box-office of Germany, Eichinger allowed director Hickox to "do it your way" (Jones, "An epic adaptation" 52), in other words, with a great deal of over-the-top comedy. And in stark contrast to the program of New German Cinema, *Prince Valiant* conspicuously avoids treatment of hot button topics, like the German past.

Such non-engagement with recent history is especially apparent in *Prince Valiant*'s

Valiant (Stephen Moyer) prays that the slain Ilene (Katherine Heigl) be restored to life in Anthony Hickox's 1997 film _Prinz Eisenherz_ (British Film Institute).

portrayal of Vikings. Indeed, representing Vikings is an enterprise fraught with potential danger for Germans, whose countrymen during the period of National Socialism saw the blue-eyed, blond-haired, stoic Viking warrior as an epitome of the Aryan and Germanic ideal. *Prince Valiant*'s principal Vikings, however, are not blond but rather bald (Thagnar) and dark-haired (Sligon). Further, their bondage-style manner of dress, not to mention their often ludicrous comportment, does little to recall the more traditional image of the proud Viking in helmet of upturned horns or wings, itself intimately connected in the popular imagination with the Germanic heroes of that most nationalistic of German composers, Richard Wagner. We might also mention that the soundtrack itself does little to conjure up a troubled German past. While Hathaway's 1954 version, for instance, featured an unmistakably Wagnerian-sounding score by Franz Waxman, Frenchman David Bergeaud's quite good score for Hickox, Lorenz, and Eichinger's *Prince Valiant*, though stately in tone, has none of the familiar sound signatures or unique pathos of Wagnerian composition.

That *Prince Valiant* contains virtually no mention of religion is also in harmony with Eichinger's very German notion of a successful popular film. Indeed, Eichinger apparently had the film re-cut, removing almost all references to religion, without the director's knowledge.[21]

In addition to the film's content reflecting preferences typical of 1990s German film culture, the choice of personnel also is in line with German practices of the decade. For instance, Eichinger's selection of director Anthony Hickox — an individual with a long record of completing television and film projects on time, with limited budgets, and with little fuss — conforms to his, and the 1990s German film industry's, aversion to engaging *auteur* directors with strong independent visions, like the larger-than-life directors of New German Cinema. However, that Eichinger, once having chosen Anthony Hickox to direct, allowed him great freedom to mold the film, is also in line with Eichinger's "rather devolved approach to production ... [which] relies on external creative input" (Bergfelder 244). Moreover, the casting of the film's German actors is also in harmony with what Thomas Elsaesser has characterized as "a cockily mainstream, brazenly commercial" German cinema of the decade (3). Specifically, German films in the 1990s came to be used as "star-vehicles, featuring actors who have become bankable" both at the box office and as television stars (Elsaesser 4). Thus, *Prince Valiant* possessed in veteran actor Udo Kier a face well known to German audiences. And by engaging as *Valiant*'s central Viking, Thagnar, up-and-coming young actor Thomas Kretschmann — whom it advertised in the movie's official press book as "the German Tom Cruise" (22) and who had achieved widespread recognition for his performance in Joseph Vilsmaier's acclaimed *Stalingrad* (1993) — Constantin both hired an actor who would be a box-office draw in Germany as well as provided that actor a platform from which to expand his own fame and career possibilities.[22]

In terms of marketing, also, Eichinger and Constantin managed to have the domestic critics and audiences conceive of *Prince Valiant* as at least a *mostly* German production. One might first mention the obvious as likely contributing to that perception: in the German-speaking countries, films are rarely subtitled but rather almost exclusively dubbed into German, so that even English-speaking actors appear on screen with German voices. More importantly, however, are a number of other factors, including the use of German actors like Kretschmann and Kier. Thus reviews at the time, even the relatively few that treat the performances of non–German actors, focus predominantly on the German speakers, whom they tend also to praise. For instance, one reviewer noted that Stephen Moyer as Valiant "impressed me less than the *German* [my emphasis] Thomas Kretschmann."[23] Further,

Constantin fostered the impression among German audiences of the movie as national property by shooting interior shots at the venerable German studio facility Babelsberg in Potsdam outside Berlin. And just as one reviewer seemed to take national pride when noting, somewhat inaccurately, that the film "originated *primarily* [my emphasis] in the Babelsberg studios,"[24] so too did reviewers revel in giving German super-producer Eichinger the lion's share of credit for the film's creation. Constantin seeded that impression successfully among German reviewers with, for example, its German-language press book for *Valiant*, which begins "Bernd Eichinger presents."[25] Thus the daily *Süddeutsche Zeitung* speaks "of this little film from Bernd Eichinger's incubator."[26] And a *Welt am Sonntag* reviewer exhibited a nationalistically proprietary glee, seemingly parroting information that only could have come from Constantin itself, when he noted that with this "triumph of the *German* [my emphasis] company Constantin," Eichinger "snatched *Valiant* from right under the noses of the Americans and ... got the film on its feet."[27]

But Germans were not alone in justifiably seeing *Prince Valiant* as belonging, at least in part, to their nation's film culture; indeed, that United Kingdom audiences perceived the film as also British is unsurprising given some of choices that the filmmakers made. Most apparent among these is the language of production — that is, the language of the movie before dubbing for non–English-speaking audiences — namely, English. Secondly, we might mention the thematic concentration of the film, which downplays Vikingness, to the point that it represents little more than a general kind of unspecific foreignness and evil, and instead highlights the Arthurian, which the British, a large percentage of whom believe Arthur actually lived,[28] regard as patrimony. Next, the filmmakers cast British actors in the majority of speaking parts, and it is these actors who seem to have received the greatest attention from British audiences. Thus most British reviewers expressed their opinion regarding English newcomer Stephen Moyer's Valiant. However, it was particularly Joanna Lumley, so well known in the United Kingdom for her then recent portrayal of Patsy in the television series *Absolutely Fabulous* (1992–2005), who garnered a disproportional share of (mostly positive) film reviewer comments about the movie's actors. For example, *The Guardian* wrote, "But the best of all [in *Prince Valiant*] is Joanna Lumley as scheming Morgan Le Fey." It continued enthusiastically of Lumley, clad here in a black leather bodysuit and chainmail headdress, "see *AbFab*'s Patsy get medieval!" (Howlett 19). By contrast, several reviewers suggested along with *The Scotsman* the inappropriateness of the American "high-school accent" of Katherine Heigl's Welsh princess, Ilene, in a film that they evidently regarded as British (Johnston 17).

Several less obvious features also align *Prince Valiant* with British films of the 1990s. Just as in Germany, the United Kingdom in that decade witnessed a boom in domestic filmmaking after a long period of stagnation. And here, too, "market forces, or pragmatism" would largely govern what kind of pictures ultimately received wide release in a film culture with relatively little interest in serious debate or "Anything that smacks of elitism" (Brown, "Something for Everyone" 31). As in Germany, the boom was also characterized especially by the financial success of rather light-hearted comedies, like *The Full Monty* (1997) and *Four Weddings and a Funeral* (1994). While Hickox remarked of his intent with *Valiant* that "it is not a comedy" (Jones, "The Arthurian comic" 6), one is very hard-pressed — given *Valiant*'s overall ludic tone and the humorously depicted love relationship at its center between Valiant and Ilene — to take the director at his word. Furthermore, *Valiant* also partakes in a basic casting recipe and narrative strategy at the heart the decade's most successful British romantic comedies. Thus like *Four Weddings*, with its English male principal, Hugh

Grant's Charles, and his American love interest, Andie MacDowell's Carrie, *Valiant* also features in Stephen Moyer an Englishman as male principal and a woman with an American accent, Katherine Heigl, as his love interest.[29] And like *Four Wedding's* Charles, Valiant too bumbles in his pursuit of the girl.

By depicting, in co-writer Carsten Lorenz's words, "'Valiant as a typical Generation X idol ... [with] high-flying plans and ideals but hardly a clue about how to put them into action,'"[30] either in the realms of love or other adult pursuits, *Prince Valiant* shares with the 1990s' most successful British films what Claire Monk has identified as a problematization of traditional masculinity (156–58). Thus like *The Full Monty's* unemployed factory workers, *Four Weddings'* goalless and inarticulate Charles, or even the cross-dressing Jody of *The Crying Game* (1992), Valiant too, despite what Eichinger extolled as his "know-how" and "cleverness," is anything but a traditionally macho male hero.[31] However, the undermining of traditional masculinities is most evident in *Valiant's* Vikings. Thus Morgan Le Fey repeatedly bends to her will Kier's "mincing warlord Sligon the Usurper" (Wilner E7). For example, when she wishes to be given control of a captured Gawain, she cozies up to Sligon and gives him a rub under the chin as one might do a small child or pet. And *Valiant's* arch-villain, Thagnar, also falls victim to female domination. In a scene more comic than shocking, Ilene tricks him into drinking a goblet of molten wax, leaving his darting tongue encased in hard white goo.

In granting their female characters Morgan and Ilene a high degree of agency, the filmmakers are, of course, simply in harmony with overall trends in the international film industry across virtually all genres of film. While Morgan's active presence in Arthurian films as the epitome of "sexual wiles as well as ... deceit and jealously" was already established by the early 1950s (Fries 70), it is especially in recent medieval pictures that more positive female figures have acquired more equal roles *vis-à-vis* male characters. One need only think, for instance, of the fiercely independent Lady Jocelyn of *A Knight's Tale* (2001), or of the bikini-clad, weapon-wielding Guinevere whom Keira Knightley portrays in Fuqua's *King Arthur* (2004). For their part, *Eisenherz's* filmmakers participate in this gender democratization of film by making an aspiring warrior out of their Princess Ilene, whom they market as "wild,"[32] and whom reviewers labeled "feisty," "bodacious and resourceful" (Spencer 9 and Cuff C2). Thus she informs Valiant early on, "They say that the tribes in the North pray to powerful woman warriors," and announces "I want to be a knight, and I want you to teach me how." Subsequently — and in a show of girl power that arguably would have resonated with the same young female viewers that made a hit of 1997's *Spice World*— she skillfully wields a sword against Thagnar and aides Valiant in taking the Viking stronghold by casting a spear to slay its one female Viking warrior. And at the end of the film, she appears with Valiant before King Arthur not in the dress of a princess, but rather in a man's pants and a cape, and with a sword slung around her waist.

What Doesn't Work?

Perhaps it is worth speculating why *Prince Valiant*, despite being a "stridently contemporary" picture (Richards 52), and sharing so many features with financially successful mainstream films produced in the same time in the United Kingdom, Germany, and internationally, was received as only very average fare by reviewers at the time of its release and by more recent purchasers of the DVD versions. Probably the greatest contributing factor was economic. As Hickox has noted of Constantin's original plans, a "long period of developing the project ... with a huge budget, hadn't panned out and they had to get any *Prince Valiant* in front of the cameras" (Jones, "An epic adaptation" 52). The relatively small budget that resulted meant that a frustrated Hickox — whose ability to achieve quite good visual effects can be seen, for example, in *Hellraiser III* (1992) — was forced "to sacrifice loads of good ideas" (Jones, "An epic adaptation" 53), and apparently to spend less money on the visual effects he retained, such as the two rather inauthentic-looking mechanical alligators that inhabit a pit in the Viking stronghold. As reviewers noted, the resulting film was a real "25-watt affair" (Speelman 12), visually characterized by "cheapness" (Dass 4), marred "by pseudo-innovative effects," and "really messy."[33] We might also note that Constantin's stipulation, in Hickox's words, "that the film should be family-fare" and the consequent absence of any blood or strong violence made the picture's action scenes even less visually believable than they might have been.[34] Finally, one must consider the choice to make the film humorous and the execution of that decision. While some reviewers granted that *Prince Valiant* was "nice silly fun" (Dass 4), not many praised it for being actually funny. Indeed, *Prince Valiant*'s best jokes and gags arguably rise only to the level of the average television sitcom. Most often, and despite Hickox's assertion that "camp is a word that has been banned from our vocabulary" (Jones, "The Arthurian comic" 6), the attempts at humor are so over the top as to seem out of place in a movie that also strives at times to be serious and dignified. This led one reviewer to quip, "Whatever director Anthony Hickox is inhaling, we'll have some" (Braun 5).

In conclusion, then, why should students of medieval-themed films care about an admittedly average picture like *Prince Valiant*? First, *Valiant* is an example *par excellence* of "the so-called Europuddings of the 1990s" (Bergfelder 240). Indeed, with *Valiant* we have an excellent window through which to see how in that decade filmmakers and financiers from different national film cultures came together in compromise to design films intended for international, and especially pan–European, consumption. Further, in *Prince Valiant* we see a conscious choice to represent a staple of movies with medieval themes, namely, the Viking, in a different light. In the film's apolitical, religion-less, heavy metal-costumed, and rather silly Vikings, we glimpse the exhaustion of the traditional Viking stereotype of the blond, pig-tailed, stolid, pagan warrior in horned helmet. Since, as Laurie Finke and Martin Shichtman point out, most people get their view of the Middle Ages largely from popular films (3), it probably doesn't go too far to imagine that *Prince Valiant* will influence many viewers to develop an untraditional idea of Vikingness. Indeed, the number of viewers getting their notion of Vikingness from *Prince Valiant* is only likely to increase in the coming years. This development has little to do with the film's merit but rather rests upon the rising profile of two of its stars. While both Stephen Moyer and Katherine Heigl were relative unknowns in 1997, Heigl has become internationally famous through the airing in many countries of the NBC drama series *Grey's Anatomy* (2005–present), in which she plays Dr. Izzie Stevens. As one Swedish blogger recently conceded, this rather average film nevertheless holds great appeal "because it shows a very young Katherine Heigl."[35] (And, indeed, the distributors of the Danish/Norwegian/Swedish and Spanish DVD versions of the film,[36] for example, have capitalized on her familiarity by making her enlarged face the most prominent element on their respective DVD cases.) For his part, Moyer, too, seems poised to become a well known name in many countries around the world once HBO distributes internationally its highly popular series, *True Blood* (2008–present), in which Moyer plays the male lead, the Louisiana vampire Bill Compton — who, in a nice touch, has Viking vampire companions. Indeed, it seems that Bernd Eichinger and the 1990s German film industry's vision of movies as star vehicles that sell products at the box office and, in a kind of perpetuity, live on as television features and DVDs, has in the second decade of the twenty-first century come to full fruition.

Notes

1. Paramount, who held the U.S. distribution rights, chose not to release the picture in the United States. See Jones, "An Epic Adaptation" 52.
2. See Alan Lupack's essay in this volume for a discussion of Hathaway's very different *Prince Valiant*.
3. For a synopsis of the action and characters from the long-running strip, see Goldberg, Horak, and Cane 13–72, esp. 71.
4. Such compilation volumes began to appear, for example, in German as early as 1953, in Castilian Spanish in 1959, and in Icelandic in 1961.
5. On tax regimes and financial incentives, see, for instance, Baillieu 141 and Christie 73–75.
6. "humor wordt algemeen niet als het sterkste punt beschouwd" (*"Prinz Valiant," Wikipedia: de vrije encyclopedie* [i.e., Dutch *Wikipedia*]).
7. "ton vaguement blagueur" (Review, *Positif* 48).
8. "wie eine Mischung aus Dudley Moore und Sir Lancelot" (Press Book 12).
9. In preparing this essay, I have found particularly useful the discussion of signs, icons, and symbols on film in Finke and Shichtman, *Cinematic Illuminations* 36 and 47–48.
10. "klaut frech ... bei John Boormans *Excalibur*" (Eggebrecht 15).
11. "consacré à la légende arthurienne" (Hachand 82).
12. See, for example, the many reviews posted on *amazon.com* and its European affiliates, such as the German *amazon.de*.
13. In the how-it's-made promotional video for the film. See "Así se hizo."
14. "'mit der historischen Genauigkeit nicht allzu genau genommen'" (Press Book 12).
15. "Ich hab' ein bisschen gepumpt," "zwei Monate im Gym" (Kretschmann, Promotional Interview).
16. "rumpelstilzchenartig" (Arnold 46); "computeranimiertes Monster" ("Ritter der Kopfnuß").
17. "das Böse" (Kier, Interview 158).
18. See esp. the seminal essay by Higson, "The Concept of National Cinema."
19. About both Constantin's past and its more recent resurrection under Eichinger, see esp. Bergfelder 71–87 and 243–46.
20. "Abenteuer-Spetakel" (Press Book 4).
21. At least according to the article "*Prince Valiant*" on imdb.com.
22. Since *Prince Valiant*, Kretschmann has enjoyed a highly successful television and cinema career both inside and outside Germany, recently appearing, for example, alongside Tom Cruise as Major Otto Ernst Remer in *Valkyrie* (2008).
23. "der mich allerdings weniger beeindruckte ... als der deutsche Thomas Kretschmann" (Tremper, *Prinz Eisenherz* 65).
24. "zum großen Teil in den Babelsberger Studios entstanden" (Review, *taz* 21).
25. "Bernd Eichinger zeigt" (Press Book 1).
26. "dieses Filmchens aus Bernd Eichingers Brutkasten" (Eggebrecht 15).
27. "Triumph des deutschen Constantin-Verleihs" *and* Eichinger "hat 'Eisenherz' den Amerikanern vor der Nase weggeschnappt" (Tremper, "Rockladies" 23).
28. According to a 2004 survey 57 percent (Milmo 3).
29. A casting formula followed also in the British romantic comedies *Jack & Sarah* (1995), *Martha, Meet Frank, Daniel and Laurence* (1998), and *Notting Hill* (1999). See Murphy 357–65.
30. "Eisenherz ist ein typisches Idol der Generation X, ... [*with*] hochfliegende Pläne und Ideale, doch kaum eine Ahnung davon, wie er sie umsetzen kann" (Press Book 12).
31. "Wissen," "Cleverness" (Press Book 11).
32. "wilde" (Press Book 13).
33. "mit pseudo-innovativen Effekten" ("Ritter der Kopfnuß"); "recht schlampig" (Arnold 46).
34. "daß der Film ein Familievergnügen sein soll" (Press Book 12).
35. "fordi den viser en svært ung Katherine Heigl" (Songvoll "*Prins Valiant*").
36. Respectively, *Prins Valiant* and *Las Aventuras del Príncipe Valiente*.

Works Cited

Arnold, Frank. "*Prinz Eisenherz.*" *EPD Film* 14 (August 1997): 46.

"Así se hizo [How It's Made]." *Las Aventuras del Príncipe Valiente*. Dir. Anthony Hickox. 1997. DVD. Aurum Producciones, 2005.

Baer, Hester. *Dismantling the Dream Factory: Gender, German Cinema, and the Postwar Quest for a New Film Language*. New York: Berghahn, 2009.

Baillieu, Bill, and John Goodchild. *The British Film Business*. Chichester, UK: John Wiley & Sons, 2002.

Bergfelder, Tim. *International Adventures: German Popular Cinema and European Co-Productions in the 1960s*. New York: Berghahn, 2005.

Braun, Liz. "A brave yet foolhardy tale of Prince Valiant." *The Toronto Sun* 16 March 1998: Entertainment 5.

Brown, Geoff. "Ma's out, Pa's out, let's talk crude." *Times* [London] 18 December 1997: 34.

_____. "Something for Everyone: British Film Culture in the 1990s." In Robert Murphy, ed. *British Cinema of the 90s*. London: BFI Publishing, 2000.

Christie, Ian. "As Others See Us: British Film-making and Europe in the 90s." In Robert Murphy, ed. *British Cinema of the 90s*. London: BFI Publishing, 2000.

Cuff, John Haslett. Review of *Prince Valiant. The Globe and Mail* [Toronto] 14 March 1988: C2.

Dass, Francis. "Fun-filled sword-and-sorcery flick." *New Straits Times* [Malaysia] 28 November 1998: Arts Cinema 4.

Eggebrecht, Harald. "Topf auf dem Kopf: *Prinz Eisenherz.*" *Süddeutsche Zeitung* 24 July 1997: 15.

Elsaesser, Thomas. "Introduction: German Cinema in the 1990s." In Thomas Elsaesser, ed. *The BFI Companion to German Cinema*. London: BFI Publishing, 1999.

Finke, Laurie A., and Martin B. Shichtman. *Cinematic Illuminations: The Middle Ages on Film*. Baltimore: Johns Hopkins University Press, 2010.

Fries, Maureen. "How to Handle a Woman, or Morgan at the Movies." In Kevin J. Harty, ed. *King Arthur on Film: New Essays on Arthurian Cinema*. Jefferson, NC: McFarland, 1999.

Goldberg, Todd, Carl Horak, and Brian M. Kane. "A Prince Valient Story Index." In Brian M. Kane, ed. *The Definitive Prince Valiant Companion*. Rev. ed. Seattle: Fantagraphics, 2009.

Hachand, Gabrielle. Review of *Prince Valiant. Cahiers du cinéma* 516 (September1997): 82.

Harty, Kevin J. "Briefer Notices: Books, Films, and Videos." *Arthuriana* 8 (Fall 1998): 126–128.

Hickox, Anthony. Promotional Interview. *Las Aventuras del Príncipe Valiente*. Dir. Anthony Hickox. 1997. DVD. Aurum Producciones, 2005.

Higson, Andrew. "The Concept of National Cinema." *Screen* 30.4 (1989): 39–46.

Howlett, Paul. "Watch this." *The Guardian* 5 May 2000: 19.

Jones, Alan. "*Prince Valiant:* An epic adaptation of the Arthurian comic strip." *Cinefantastique* 29.11 (1998): 52–53.

_____. "*Prince Valiant:* The Arthurian comic strip fantasy of swords & sorcery comes to the screen." *Cinefantastique* 28.7 (1997): 6.

Johnston, Trevor. Review of *Prince Valiant. The Scotsman* [Edinburgh] 18 December 1997: 17.

Kier, Udo. Interview. "Ich hab' alles mal ausprobiert." *Focus* 43 (21 October 1996): 156–160.

Kretschmann, Thomas. Promotional Interview. *Las Aventuras del Príncipe Valiente*. Dir. Anthony Hickox. 1997. DVD. Aurum Producciones, 2005.

Las Aventuras del Príncipe Valiente. Dir. Anthony Hickox. 1997. DVD. Aurum Producciones, 2005.

Milmo, Cahal. "1066 and all that: how Hollywood is giving Britain a false sense of history." *The Independent* 5 April 2004: 3.

Monk, Claire. "Men in the 90s." In Robert Murphy, ed. *British Cinema of the 90s*. London: BFI Publishing, 2000.

Murphy, Robert. "Citylife: Urban Fairy-tales in Late 90s British Cinema." In Robert Murphy, ed. *The British Cinema Book*. 3d ed. London: British Film Institute, 2009.

Nickel, Helmut. "Arms and Armor in Arthurian Films." In Kevin J. Harty, ed. *Cinema Arthuriana: Twenty Essays*. Jefferson, NC: McFarland, 2002.

Press Book. *Prinz Eisenherz*. Munich: Neue Constantin Film GmbH, 1997.

"*Prince Valiant.*" *Internet Movie Data Base*. Accessed 14 January 2010 <http://www.imdb.com/title/tt0119947/>.

Prins Valiant [Danish/Swedish/Norwegian version]. Dir. Anthony Hickox. 1997. DVD. Atlantic Film, 2008.

"*Prinz Valiant.*" *Wikipedia: de vrije encyclopedie* [i.e., Dutch *Wikipedia*]. Accessed 12 January 2010 <*http://nl.wikipedia.org/wiki/Prins_Valiant*>.

Rentschler, Eric. "From New German Cinema to the Post-Wall Cinema of Consensus." In Mette Hjort and Scott MacKenzie, eds. *Cinema and Nation*. London: Routledge, 2000.

Review of *Prince Valiant*. *Positif* 439 (September 1997): 48.

_____. *taz, die tageszeitung* 24 July 1997: 21.

Richards, Andy. "*Prince Valiant/Prinz Eisenherz*." *Sight and Sound* 8.1 (1998): 52.

"Ritter der Kopfnuß." *Die Presse* 26 July 1997. Accessed using *factiva.com* 1 June 2009.

Songvoll, Jon. "*Prins Valiant*. Legenden om Kong Arthur forsetter...." *X6.no*. Accessed 12 January 2010 <*http://x6.no/omtaler.php?id=2260*>.

Speelman, Jon. "Sequel opportunities." *The Observer* 21 December 1997: 12.

Spencer, Liese. Review of *Prince Valiant*. *The Independent* 19 December 1997: 9.

Sweet, Matthew. "*Valiant*, prince of the Europuddings." *Independent on Sunday* 21 December 1997: 2.8.

Tremper, Will. "*Prinz Eisenherz*— In Babelsberg gedreht." *Welt am Sonntag* 3 August 1997: 65.

_____. "*Rockladie*s, *Prinz Eisenherz* und eine Scheidung im Dschungel." *Welt am Sonntag* 29 June 1997: 23.

The Vikings. Accessed 13 January 2009 <http://www.vikingsonline.org.uk/>.

Wedel, Michael. "Eichinger, Bernd." In Thomas Elsaesser, ed. *The BFI Companion to German Cinema*. London: BFI Publishing, 1999.

Whitaker, Muriel. "Fire, Water, Rock: Elements of Setting in John Boorman's *Excalibur* and Steve Barron's *Merlin*." In Kevin J. Harty, ed. *Cinema Arthuriana: Twenty Essays*. Jefferson, NC: McFarland, 2002.

Wilner, Norman. "Ye Olde England tale is not very valiant: *Prince Valiant*." *The Toronto Star* 16 March 1998: E7.

When Civilization Was Less Civilized:
Erik the ~~Viking~~ (1989)

SUSAN ARONSTEIN

From the pages of history, the missing chapter, *Erik the Viking*: a time when civilization was less civilized, dating was dangerous, and peace looked a lot like war, when travel was tough and the ocean was scary, a time of lust and confusion, and everything was going to pieces, the future of the world rested on one man. Unfortunately, it was Erik the Viking.

Orion Pictures, as this voice-over from *Erik the Viking*'s (1989) theatrical trailer illustrates, aggressively marketed this film as post–Python Python from Terry Jones, the man who had brought audiences *Monty Python and the Holy Grail* and *Life of Brian*. Both the trailer and the film's promotional poster promise audiences a parody of Viking and action-adventure films in the same vein as *The Holy Grail*'s send-up of medieval and Arthurian cinema and *Life of Brian*'s irreverent biblical epic. The trailer emphasizes a comically absurd, violent Viking past, cousin to the "dark ages" so famously chronicled in *Holy Grail*; it punctuates each look back into the film's less-civilized time with a Pythonesque scene, whetting the audience's appetite for a Viking *Holy Grail*. Its ending nod to the action-adventure genre — "the future of the world rested on one man" — immediately undermines that genre as it cuts to a scene of the film's hero laboriously scaling a wall, when he could have simply "taken the stairs," and concludes, "Unfortunately, it was Erik the Viking."

This promised send-up of the action-adventure blockbuster also informs the film's promotional poster, which invokes the iconic *Star Wars* art that features Luke on top of a hill — his companions grouped below him and Darth Vader's head filling the background — raising his light saber to the sky. Erik takes Luke's pose on top of the mountain, his various companions perched comically below and the Dragon of the North Sea occupying Vader's menacing position. All in good fun, as the poster's taglines assure us, with a quotation attributed to Erik (A.D. 790), "You can fight the Gods and still have a good time," substituted — in the same spot — for *Star Wars*' "A long time ago and in a galaxy far, far away," and the film's second tagline, "A fun trip through the dark ages," explicitly tying *Erik the Viking* to the Python's earlier romp through those ages. The preview ends with a Gilliam-style cut-out graphic firmly fixing the film within the Python brand.

The studio's attempt to brand his film as a Python-product gave, Jones argues, audiences and critics, "the wrong signals"; Jones insists that his film adaptation of the stories he had written for his young son is a fairy-story, not a Python riff. Explaining the difference between the two genres, he observes: "With Python you never let anyone suspend their disbelief, you're saying we're playing tricks, we're doing this and that, where this is a fairy story and it needs to suspend your disbelief in order to be able to sort of go along with the tale." However, in spite of Jones's insistence that *Erik the Viking* is a "fairy story"— that the studio's marketing got it wrong— the film suffers, like its hero, from a crisis of identity. Its fantasy narrative is constantly disrupted by the very comic distance — the insistence on disbelief— that Jones sought to avoid; as a result of this disconnect between the two modes, *Erik the Viking*, in its initial release, pleased no one. Python fans, lured in by the marketing campaign, were dissatisfied; critics, on the whole, were baffled, either complaining that the film's comic distance got in the way of its narrative or that its narrative got in the way of its comedy; not surprisingly, the film performed disappointingly at the box office.[1]

Neither good fairy story nor good Python, *Erik the Viking* flounders in its own earnestness, an earnestness captured by a very young Tim Robbins (who plays Erik), "It was an action-adventure film," he explains, "that worked within the milieu of action adventure and basically was advocating an end of violence and a more reasonable loving life ... which is rare for that kind of film ... I read ... lots of dramas, detective dramas, action-chase kind of scripts that are very hateful, very violent, filled with murder, filled with death, just so gratuitous, dangerous, ultimately, to anyone who sees it, especially children. But here you have an epic adventure about a Viking that believes in non-violence and ... respecting women. That's pretty rare." Robbins' explication of *Erik* as a Viking film that does not believe in violence — as incoherent as it is — correctly identifies the film's central premise and method. *Erik the Viking* explicitly invokes and then displaces key myths linked to our Vikings past: the myth of progressive history and the myth of regeneration through violence.

Since Jones himself identifies a Viking exhibit at the British Museum as the original inspiration for *The Saga of Erik the Viking*, it seems fitting to turn to a museum to examine the basis for these myths. In addition, the unearthing of a remarkably well-preserved tenth-century Viking village at the site on which the Jorvik Viking Centre in York (once a sweet factory, now a shopping center) is built, provides an apt metaphor for the relationship between the Modern West and its Viking past, a relationship that gives rise to these myths: the Vikings lurk under the layers of modern civilization, waiting to reemerge — a past identity, a repressed self, what lies beneath. When the York Archeological Trust opened the Viking Centre at Jorvik — a place visitors can, as their website promises, "Get Face to Face with Vikings"— it tapped into the progressive history version of the Viking myth. As visitors wound through the line for the attraction (a reconstructed Viking village), they encountered a series of posters: "The Vikings!"; "They came and they conquered"; "They raped and they pillaged"; "They sowed and they settled"; "The Vikings!" This tale both connects the modern visitor, as the descendents of those Vikings who, eventually "sowed and settled," with the past they are about to explore and distances them from those origins as it chronicles the "civilization" of the raiders who plundered England's shores, the domestication of warriors who move from raping and pillaging to building and farming.

Once through the line, modern visitors revisit their less-civilized past, a past clearly invoked in *Erik the Viking*'s "time when civilization was less civilized"; they travel in "time machines" back through the ages into a Disney-style attraction: a carefully reconstructed Viking Village that claims to re-embody (or re-member) the past, bringing what lies beneath to the surface. The Archeological Trust clearly committed itself to detail and accuracy in this attraction, using the Disney formula not only to provide entertainment (and, ultimately, to fund the dig) but also to bring the Vikings to hyperreal life. As the website promises: "You will journey through a reconstruction of the actual Viking-Age streets which once stood on this site, still with sounds and smells! The houses and shops are laid out in exactly the same pattern as they were at 5.30pm, 25th October, AD 975, and even the faces of the people you see have been reconstructed from Viking skulls." At the same time that the Trust promises complete accuracy, however, it also conforms to audience expectations; the village emphasizes the mud, muck and smells of the medieval/Viking past, showcasing a man using the cess-pit facilities and depicting Jorvik as "a city that is home to 10,000 people and is covered in filth and muck." Over and over again, visitors are invited to "smell" the past; to help them do so, the map of the site provides a "smell guide." At Jorvik, what Laurie Finke and Marty Shichtman dub "the Dirty Middle Ages" is brought to life in glorious, "accurate," smell-o-vision.

The progressive narrative of Jorvik — from raping and pillaging, through sowing and settling, to our world with all of its modern conveniences — emphasizes the mud and the muck of the Viking past in order to contrast it to a sanitized modern present. In this narrative, the reification of the past is, like the ride itself, meant to be a short journey to a time that we can look smugly back to and congratulate ourselves on having moved beyond. Other reenactments of the Viking past, rooted in nineteenth-century anti-modernism, function very differently, arguing against the progressive narrative offered at Jorvik.[2] Instead of looking smugly back at the dirty old days, this version of the myth advocates a return to our (masculine) Viking origins as an antidote to an over-civilized, feminized modern condition. Our Norse ancestors — for all their dirt — embody a time when men were men, when "violent lives," as T. J. Jackson Lears asserts, posed "a refreshing contrast to the blandness of modern comfort" and war provided a path to "social and personal regeneration" (57, 98). These Vikings may have been "butchers ... but they carved provinces and kingdoms" (101); their virile bodies displaced their effeminate counterparts — scholars and thinkers — to revitalize civilization; rather than asking questions about the meaning of life, they lived life. This is the Viking myth offered to us by the motion picture industry, from the *The Vikings* (1958), in which Erik, the half–Viking son of the English queen, saves England from a foppish and corrupt king, through *The 13th Warrior* (1999), in which an Arab poet's time with the Norse barbarians teaches him "how to be a man," to the announced Mel Gibson take on the subject, which, given Gibson's previous films, will almost certainly continue in the Viking tradition of hard-bodied men and regeneration through violence.

Erik the Viking situates itself within both of these popular versions of the Viking myth. In the Python tradition, it invokes the "dirty middle ages" to deconstruct the progressive view of history, collapsing the distance between a barbaric past and a supposedly civilized modernity.[3] As a fairy story, it seeks to displace the anti-modernist's (and Hollywood's) valorization of our violent past, rewriting our Viking origin myth — and the whole period — as not a starting point but an aberration. The film's first scene, which according to Jones, enabled him to adapt the loosely-connected stories he had written for his son into "a narrative structure for a film," establishes *Erik's* themes and concerns.[4] This scene invokes the cinematic myth of the Vikings only to undermine and — ultimately — to displace it.

The opening scene begins with a tight close shot of flames; the camera then draws slightly back to include fractured shots of a burning village and men in armor wielding axes and swords; on the soundtrack, masculine grunts, clanging weaponry and feminine screams join the crackling flames as the film follows the cinematic code for a Viking raid. As we might expect of raping and pillaging Vikings, a warrior bursts into a hut, advances, sword drawn, on a frightened woman (Samantha Bond), backs her into a wall and savagely rips off her bodice. Here the Python fun begins as the film stops to comment on the generic codes that it reenacts. The warrior spends several seconds fumbling with his belt, turning his chosen victim's fear into incredulous scorn. "Have you done this much before?" she queries. "Of course," her attacker replies indignantly, "I've been looting and pillaging up the coast!" "What about the raping?" she demands. "It's obvious you haven't raped anyone in your life." He frantically shushes her, his eyes going to the open doorway to make sure none of his companions, hacking away outside, have heard her accusation, and ineptly attempts to get on with it. His ineptitude leads her to question whether or not he "like(s) women" and forces him to defend his heterosexuality — "Of course I do; I love women" — while eliciting his confession that he "prefers it" if it's not rape. "I don't suppose that you do like me at all?" he finally manages to spit out. "What do you think!" she explodes, "You come in here, burn my village, kill my family and try to rape me!"

Now it is *she* who has the Viking backed against the wall; suddenly she realizes, in astonishment, "You don't like it, do you?" "I just think it's a little bit crude, that's all," he replies defensively. She points out that "killing and looting" is "just as crude," an observation that forces the bewildered boy to defend his entire economy: "You have to do them," he argues, "to pay for the next expedition." "That's a circular argument," she counters, "if the only reason for the expedition is the killing and looting and the only reason for the killing and looting is to pay for the next expedition, they cancel each other out." Exasperated, he glances nervously at his companions and asks her, nicely, to scream. She complies, and two of his comrades rush in to join the fun; he seeks to defend her from "a fate worse than death," but inadvertently kills her, running his sword through the man on top of her and into her heart; as she dies, each asks the question that motivates his future actions, "Why should you care?" He looks at the blood on his hands and, fighting tears, turns to stare hopelessly at the scene of looting and pillaging outside. The camera zooms in on his face, half-hidden in a curtain of hair, and the film's title appears on the screen, *Erik the Viking*, naming the hero at the very moment that his own sense of self has been destroyed.

In terms of narrative, this opening scene seems to be setting the stage for a Jorvik-style progressive history: they raped and they pillaged, they sowed and they settled. However, it also plays like a Python film, returning to past times and old genres to take apart the myths upon which we build the present. Like *Monty Python and the Holy Grail*, it first invokes the genre and codes that it will undermine — in this case the Hollywood Viking film. The flames, the hacking and screams, the threatened rape all mirror a standard cinematic raid such as the one found at the beginning of *The Vikings*. But, when Erik starts fumbling with his belt, the tone of the film changes, and *Erik the Viking* turns to a commentary on the genre; the Viking with a modern sensibility collapses the distance between the past and the present, and, by the time that Helga delivers her relentless explication of the "violence inherent in the system," the scene has become pure Python.

The next scene, however, switches from Python-style commentary to fairy tale quest, introducing a dissonance in *Erik*'s tone and genre that runs throughout its narrative.[5] The film cuts from Erik's desolate face as he observes the mayhem around him to his flight across snow-covered mountains, seeking Freya's counsel. "Has it always been like [this]? Since the beginning of time?" he asks. Freya takes him to the mouth of her cave to gaze upon the frozen wastes and the black sky beyond. "What do you see, Erik?" she demands. "I see the world," Erik answers; the world that Erik sees is all that he knows — a world in which "day" is dark, summer is icy, and the sun is "up beyond the clouds where it always is." Erik can conceive of no other. "Think back," Freya commands urgently; slowly, Eric replies, groping for the words, "I remember once as a child — a dream — it was if the whole sky were ... blue?" Erik clearly knows that his memory must have been a dream, that the sky cannot possibly be blue. Freya, however, looks deeply into his eyes, willing him to believe: "It *was* blue, Erik. The old stories tell of an age that would come such as this when Fenrir the wolf would swallow the sun and a great winter would settle on the world. It was to be an ax age, a storm age, when brother would turn against brother and men would fight each other until the world was finally destroyed."

Freya juxtaposes the Viking present and a lost past — a forgotten origin — asserting that the age in which Erik lives is an aberration; in this time of virile masculinity — of "young men interested only in fighting and killing" — the "gods are asleep" and men have forgotten themselves. This story disrupts the progressive narrative implied in the opening scene; Erik and Helga's puzzling empathy comes not from a nascent modern sensibility, but from their forgotten selves. Erik's quest, then, is one of anamnesis — of remembering — that will wake the gods and restore the world and the people who live in it to their true form. In order to remember, Erik must flee the masculine world of violence and return to a feminine world of stories. The film depicts Freya's dark cave — with its decidedly feminine imagery — as completely separate from the Viking village; her wisdom is not its wisdom as Freya herself observes. "Afraid," she challenges Erik, "they will make fun of you for listening to an old woman's stories?"

Freya's "old woman's story" introduces the film's fantasy quest. This scene is played absolutely straight. Instead of the expected shrill parody of an aged crone, such as the one who directs Arthur and his men to Tim the Enchanter in *Holy Grail*, Eartha Kitt portrays Freya (more or less successfully) with eerie dignity. Her description of a world turned to darkness and winter, a world in which the gods sleep, falls into fairy tale cadence with her formulaic triad of questions to Erik, as does her description of the quest she sends him on, with its perilous journey to an unknown land ("the land that men call Hy-Brasil"), its magical Horn Resounding, upon which Erik is to blow "three notes" (one to send him to Asgard, one to wake the gods, one to bring him home), and its many perils. This quest places *Erik the Viking* firmly within the fantasy genre: the wise enchanter sends the young and earnest hero on a perilous journey to save the world. As it does so, it switches the orientation of the film's commentary on "the violence inherent in the system" from the comic distance typically employed by the Python troupe — the various devices that pull the viewer out of the romance of the tale — to an attempt to envelope the audience within that very romance, to convince them to abandon their distance and "suspend their disbelief."

If *Erik the Viking* had maintained this shift in tone, these first two scenes could be seen as Jones's statement of purpose, announcing his reorientation from a member of Monty Python to a film-maker more in the Lucas-Spielberg mode (although even in its "best" fantasy moments, *Erik the Viking* makes it clear that Jones is neither Lucas nor Spielberg). However, it does not. The film consistently switches between the two modes; at one moment, the audience finds itself watching a semi–big-budget action film, in the next, a Monty Python sketch. The two styles work against each other. One depends upon myth and offers its audience narrative closure, the pleasures of the quest fulfilled; the other undermines myth and resists closure. One is premised on optimism; the other enshrines cynicism.[6]

Both the Python film and the fantasy romance work within the framework of the Viking myth. *Erik the Viking*'s narrative elements (the Viking raid, with its looting, pillaging and [attempted] rape and the sea voyage) and set scenes (a drunken party, building the long ship, the blacksmith's shop), and its characters (Sven the Berserk, Ivar the Boneless, Thorfinn Skullsplitter, Harald the Missionary) all invoke a long tradition of popular versions of the Viking tales, from comic books to Hollywood. The film also employs the iconic visual vocabulary associated with the Vikings, emphasizing the dirt and muck of our Nordic past. These are grimy Vikings — disheveled with greasy crow's-nest hair, smudged faces, and dull and tattered clothes augmented with animal furs — and the run-down, snow-swept village they live in seems to have used Jorvik as a model; you can almost whiff the smell-o-vision. From the matted fur, to the swords and axes and iron helmets, from the crowded hall and overflowing drinking cups, to the blood and gore, the film screams "Vikings!"— so much so that Graham Fuller, writing about the set, dwelled on "horned helmets," even though there is only one partial glimpse of such a helmet in the film (26). No matter — we all know Vikings wore horned-helmets, and *Erik the Viking* encourages viewers to experience its narrative in terms of what they know about the Vikings, supplying the gaps and using their knowledge of the myth both to give significance to Erik's fantasy quest and to produce the comedy of the Python sequences.

Erik's quest to find a "better way" and end the Age of Ragnarok, with its senseless violence, provides the narrative framework for the fantasy film, working within *Erik*'s Viking elements to displace them. His sea-voyaging quest is not based on the generic Viking conquest or revenge; rather it is a traditional fairy tale quest for renewal, to break the curse, to wake the princess, to bring peace and plenty to the land. In this narrative, Erik is not Viking, but fairy-tale hero. The film constructs him as such by consistently distancing Erik from his Viking compatriots, a technique that works both to identify him as the fantasy hero and, as we saw in the opening scene, to produce the comedy of the Python-style sketches.

Visually, Erik is clean; his clothes are actually white, he has flowing reddish locks (and apparently the only shampoo in the village), a baby face, and earnest eyes. In most of the Python-style sequences, he seems to have wandered into the wrong movie. Cinematically, the film emphasizes Erik's distance from his companions — situating him at the edge of the frame, showing him, sitting absolutely still in a swirl of drunken or violent activity, or having him leave the communal group altogether as it does in the scene following Erik's conversation with Freya. The film cross-cuts between a gang of drunken men hurling axes at the nailed-out braids of a distressed young woman (a scene borrowed from *The Vikings*) and close-ups of Erik's face. Erik sits apart from his companions — with the women and the old men; unlike the old men, he does not find what is happening amusing. His reaction is feminized — wincing, distressed. When a drunken brawl breaks out, rather than joining in, he leaves the smoke-filled hall, distancing himself from the community, to sit, musing on his own, in the frozen night.

Erik's physical separation mirrors his ideological separation. His scruples place him so far beyond the discourses of his village that he can only talk at cross-purposes with his fellow Vikings. When his grandfather (Mickey Rooney) follows him into the snow, protesting that Erik is "missing all the fun," Erik replies, "What's it all about? ... We toil and labor, we loot and pillage, we rape and kill, and yet ... where does it get us?" In a Viking world, Erik's musings are, as Grandpa is quick to points out, "piffle." A Viking who wants to know what it all means, Erik reverses the terms of the late nineteenth-century Viking revival's interaction between the Viking and modern worlds, which stemmed, as Lears argues, from a desire to infuse a generation "more interested in questions about life than in living" with manly fortitude and determination.[7] Erik, as we see in the next scene, wants to stop the action, ask what it means, and change its direction. He breaks up a fight. His grandfather demands, "What are you doing? Thorfinn ... just said that Finn's grandfather died of old age. They must fight to the death." This plan of action makes perfect sense to both the combatants and their audience, but not to Erik, who questions the entire basis of the Viking way of life: "There is another way," he insists; "Who gets killed?" Grandpa demands. "Nobody gets killed," Erik replies.

Erik's "other way" is the way of the fairy tale — the quest to wake the gods, with all of its fairy tale motifs: the sea voyage to the other/underworld, the Horn Resounding with its magical notes, the Rainbow Bridge, prohibitions and warnings — even a beautiful princess to be won. In this way, a hero crosses the bridge to the Halls of Valhalla not dead but alive, challenging a Viking system that rewards those who die in battle — and only those who die in battle — with eternal life in the realm of the gods. It changes the end-point of the narrative: "nobody gets killed." Not death, but life. The scenes which invoke this narrative and move the film's fairy tale forward are played, mostly, straight. Here Jones uses his big (for the man who co-directed *Monty Python and the Holy Grail,* anyway) budget for the film's special effects, which, although clumsy by today's standards, were not terrible in 1989 (certainly they are no worse than those in 1984's *Never Ending Story*). The companions' encounter with the Dragon of the North Sea, the sounding of the Magical Horn, the sparkling sequence in which the ship and its crew sail off the edge of the world and land at the base of Valhalla, and the Hall of the Gods itself, all use special effects to endow the film with an atmosphere of awe and wonder — of fantasy. These sequences also fall into fantasy cadence — hushed anticipation followed by quick action, somber voices, limited dialogue, panicked screams as the action speeds up: the calm before the storm, the storm, the calm after the storm. Taken together, they move the fairy-tale hero's quest through the narrative laid out for him by Freya — from beginning to conclusion, from first note to last, through danger and betrayal, despair and hope, to a miraculous rescue, triumphant return and the dawn of a new day — the end of the Age of Ragnarok, the "ax age," the Viking age.

This fairy-tale, however, is punctuated by a series of Python-style sketches — many of them starring John Cleese and Jones himself — that disrupt both its narrative and tone, pulling us out of the fantasy and into the postmodern world. If *Erik*'s fantasy narrative seeks to displace one myth with another, its sketches seek to employ the Python technique of burlesquing the past to comment on the present and dismantle myths. The script is littered with these sketches — comic sequences such as the group bickering like schoolboys over who sits where in the boat and Erik's rallying speech to his troops (in which he sounds more like Sir Robin's blood-thirsty minstrels than an inspiring leader). For my purposes here, however, I want to focus on two sketches that are also integral to the film's fairy-tale plot: the scene between Loki and Halfdan the Black, which introduces the villains who will hinder our hero and his companions, and the sojourn at Hy-Brasil, a land that functions both as one of the objects of Erik's quest and as a manifestation of the fairy otherworld.

Like all good fairy tales, *Erik the Viking*, presents its hero with multiple obstacles and antagonists, from the Dragon of the North Sea to the god Thor himself. His main antagonists, however, are the blacksmith's assistant Loki (Antony Sher) and the local warlord, Halfdan the Black (John Cleese). Realizing that the end of Ragnarok will be bad for business because it will seriously affect the market value of swords and axes, Loki scurries off to warn Halfdan and beg him to put a stop to Erik's non-profitable plans for peace. He creeps through a dark hall filled with the sound of whips and screams and twisted bodies and corpses. We expect the man who presides over all of this violence to be a man of startling Viking barbarity. Instead, we find John Cleese, acting, as Cleese himself indicates, "like an English merchant banker," calmly explaining why he, "not an unreasonable man," needs to behead, garrot, and flay alive the poor men who have failed to pay back their debts. Very

Tim Robbins as the title character in Terry Jones's 1989 film *Erik the Viking* (editor's collection).

calm, unfailingly polite, he sits in the midst of death and despair, sighing, "I really do wish they'd think ahead" and explaining that he "could really do with a holiday. All this financial work, the stress really gets you." In addition to this sequence's explicit commentary on the connection between a valorization of martial masculinity and corporate profit, the contrast between Cleese's calm businessmen and the violence he perpetuates is pure Python in its implication that, in spite of all of our progressive myths about the disjunction between an civilized present and a barbaric past, the past is very much with us.

Helmed by Terry Jones, in Python-mode, the sequence on Hy-Brasil also disrupts the fairy tale narrative at the same time that it fulfills it. The Vikings' arrival at this magical land marks their successful completion of the first task in Erik's fantasy quest; they find themselves in apparent paradise: a land of sun and blue skies, of flowers, and scantily-clad women, a land completely committed to non-violence. The Princess Aud (Imogene Stubbs), the first person the Vikings encounter, astounds them with her lack of clothes and weapons. They cannot conceive of such a thing, "maybe they've got weapons we haven't even dreamed of." Quickly the gang concludes, "Let's hack her to pieces," and — when Erik protests — demands, "What else could we do?" In response to Erik's suggestion, "How about making friends?" they fall back on Viking philosophy: "You don't go through all of the hardships of an ocean voyage to make friends. We can make friends at home." At this point, Hy-Brasil could still go either way: it could represent a utopic, sun-soaked, non-violent alternative to the Viking Village, or it could serve as the basis of a Pythonesque lampooning of such ideals (a sort of Castle Anthrax). It does the latter. Although Hy-Brasil lives under a fairy-tale prohibition (if one drop of human blood is spilled, the whole kingdom will sink), this prohibition has given rise not to a pastoral utopia but to a Pythonesque land full of practically-cross-dressed fops, ruled by the impotent and incompetent King Arnulf (Terry Jones in a white toga, opulent curled wig, and flowers in his hair). Since violence is unthinkable, Arnulf explains, "we are all terribly nice to each other."

Hy-Brasil lampoons modern utopic visions of a better world — hippies, with flowers in their hair — as impractical and willfully blind, portraying its citizens as effeminate, mindless sheep. The people of Hy-Brasil are a pretty, chanting, clueless mass, addicted to their own bad singing. Their king is obtusely blind, comically groping for the man (right in front of his face) he suspects is in his daughter's room, and insisting, after Loki's plotting against Erik's quest spills blood on the land and the ocean pours in, "whatever else is happening, Hy-Brasil is not sinking." Standing waist-deep in water, King Arnulf exhorts his people to "stick to the facts." He assures them that an inquiry into what actually *is* happening is underway, and suggests "a sing-song," insisting "it's not happening," even as the water closes over their heads.

This dismissal of Hy-Brasil as a viable alternative foreshadows *Erik the Viking's* portrayal of Valhalla, the land at the end of the quest, where, in fairy tales, the hero achieves his goals. Valhalla, although it visually invokes the fairy tale as it appears in a shimmer of light, is, like the Grail Castle in *Monty Python and the Holy Grail*, a dead end. Awakening the gods does not solve anything, for the gods are spoiled children at play, not the powerful saviors of a literally and figuratively benighted human race. Since Erik has indeed fulfilled the terms of the quest, Thor does release the sun, but he also condemns them all to the pit of hell, sending Erik and his companions helter-skelter into the flames. If this scene had been the ending of the tale, the Python side of *Erik the Viking* would have prevailed; the heroes' slide into the abyss would break the flow of the fairy-tale narrative just as surely as the hand over the camera in the final frame of *Holy Grail*, denying the audience the satisfactions of a quest-fulfilled and a happy ending. Instead of displacing the Viking legend with a new myth, it would have merely disrupted myth.

But the film does not end here. It turns to the fairy tale to rescue its hero and his crew, providing what Tolkien, in his famous essay, "On Faerie Stories," identifies as the genre's essential "eucatastrophe," the unexpected good catastrophe, the sudden joyous turning. Harald the Missionary sneaks out of Valhalla, sounds the third note, and brings the heroes home. What the film gives, however, it also takes away, inflecting its fairy tale structure with another common Python theme that runs through *Erik the Viking*: the exposure of myths, ideologies and beliefs as tools of the powerful, fictions that blind people to what is really there, a theme most famously exemplified in the coconut-steeds that open *Monty Python and the Holy Grail*. I have already discussed a typically Python version of this motif in the sinking of Hy-Brasil, and there are many other examples of discourse dictating perception and reaction throughout the film — from Erik and Aud's cross-purpose conversation on love, through the Japanese oar-master's rant against "horizontal-eyed," "rice-pudding" eating, western trouser-wearers, to the Viking's insistence that their fear is caused by magic and Erik's spectacular performance of derring-do when he believes himself concealed by the Cloak Invisible. The most persistent use of this motif, however, is in the portrayal of Harald, who, because he does not believe in Asgard, Valhalla or the gods, cannot see them — nor can they see him. His lack of belief, in the end, saves the whole crew; because he does not believe in the gods or their power, he alone is free from them; they cannot cast him into the pit of hell. This twist allows him — despite his own skepticism about the Horn Resounding and Freya's fairy-tale narrative — to sound the third note and save the day. Because he agrees to "believe" in the story, the story comes true.

The fact that Harald's belief saves the day reverses the Pythons' take on stories. One of the critiques of the troupe is that it takes apart myths and institutions but offers nothing in their place — only a symbolic hand over the camera. *Erik the Viking*, on the other hand, urges us to adopt a myth, even if it is not "real." Belief in stories, in myths, has the power to vanquish evil and change the world. Harald's note institutes a new order, restoring the erstwhile Vikings to their loved ones, and destroying Halfdan the Black (the longboat, in a nod to *The Wizard of Oz*, falls from the sky to crush him). The final frames of the film dwell on the rising sun, as it illuminates the faces of the awe-struck villagers, warming the ice and snow, promising a new dawn. In the end, the point of Terry Jones's fractured fairy tale seems to be that we choose what to believe. We can believe that violence is the answer — that "men fighting and killing each other" is the way that it has always been — or we can believe that there is "another way." Here Jones finds a new use for history; he does not return to the past to burlesque it, but to renew it — to give us a new past: "the missing chapter, *Erik the Viking*," a history that advocates, in Robbins' words, "an end of violence ... and a more loving life."

Notes

1. The titles of some of the reviews say it all: "'Viking' Film goes from bad to Norse" (Roger Ebert, *New York Daily News* 28 October 1989: 48); "'Viking's' Seasick Sensibility" (Rita Kempley, *Washington Post* 28 October 1989: C9); "A Viking Antihero runs Amok with Idealism" (Vincent Canby, *New York Times* 28 October 1989: 13); "Valhalla Vulgarity" (Jami Bernard, *New York Post* 28 October 1989: 15); "'Erik the Viking': A Voyage with Pythonic Norse Play" (Terry Kelleher, *Newsday* 28 October 1989: 37); "This Erik is a pretty bland Viking" (Johanna Steinmetz, *Chicago Tribune,* 1 November 1989: 3.2).

2. My discussion of the Vikings in late nineteenth-century anti-modernism is informed by T.J. Jackson Lears, *No Place of Grace: Anti-modernism and the Transformation of American Culture, 1880–1920* (New York: Pantheon Books, 1981).

3. Many critics have discussed the Python's use of this technique; for examples see Laurie Finke and Martin Shichtman, *Cinematic Illuminations*; Susan Aronstein, *Hollywood Knights: Arthurian Cinema and the Politics of Nostalgia* (New York: Palgrave, 2005) and "In My Own Idiom: Social Critique, Campy Gender, and Queen Performance in *Monty Python and the Holy Grail*" in *Queer Movie Medievalisms*, ed. Kathleen Coyne Kelly and Tison Pugh (Surrey: Ashgate, 2009), pp. 115–128; Wlad Godzich, "*The Holy Grail*: The End of the Quest," *North Dakota Quarterly* 51 (Winter 1983): 74–81; David Day, "*Monty Python and the Holy Grail*: Madness with a Definite Method" in *Cinema Arthuriana: Twenty Essays*, rev. ed., ed. Kevin J. Harty (Jefferson, NC: McFarland, 2002), pp. 127–135; Raymond Thompson, "The Ironic Tradition in

Arthurian Films Since 1960," in *Cinema Arthuriana*, pp. 110–117; Elizabeth Murrell, "History Revenged: Monty Python Translates Chrétien de Troyes *Perceval or the Story of the Grail* (again)," *Journal of Film and Video* 50 (Spring 1998): 50–63; and Donald Hoffman, "Not Dead Yet: *Monty Python and the Holy Grail* in the Twenty-first Century," in *Cinema Arthuriana, Twenty Essays*, pp, 136–148.

4. "I was about to give the whole thing up," Jones explains, "when I discovered a scene, which has now become the first in the film, enabling me to throw out everything else except the Dragon and the falling over the edge of the world" (Fuller 26).

5. This discussion of *Erik the Viking* analyzes the version of the film in the "Director's Son's Cut" as that is the version that Jones identifies as the one closest to his original vision: "With all the Python movies, I'd always been a hands-on editor ... for this film I was somehow persuaded by my editor to keep out of the editing and I actually only got my hands on the film about two weeks before we were due to start showing it" (Jones interview, "Behind the Director's Son's Cut").

6. For a discussion of the Python's techniques in *Monty Python's Flying Circus,* see Marcia Landy, *Monty Python's Flying Circus* (Detroit: Wayne State University Press, 2005) and Robert Hewison, *Irreverence, Scurrility, Profanity, Vilification and Licentious Abuse: The Case Against Monty Python* (New York: Grove, 1981).

7 *Scribner's* 20 (September 1896): 387; quoted in Lears, 48.

Works Cited

Cleese, John. "Interview." "The Making of *Erik the Viking*, 1989." On *Erik the Viking: The Director's Son's Cut.* MGM Home Video, 2001.

Erik the Viking. Dir. Terry Jones, perf. Tim Robbins, John Cleese, Antony Sher, Terry Jones, Mickey Rooney, Samantha Bond, and Imogene Stubbs. 1989. DVD, *Erik the Viking: The Director's Son's Cut*, MGM Home Video, 2001.

Finke, Laurie, and Martin Shichtman. *Cinematic Illuminations: The Middle Ages on Film.* Baltimore: Johns Hopkins University Press, 2009.

Fuller, Graham. "Having Heroic Fun on Way to Valhalla." *Los Angeles Times* 12 March 1989: Calendar 26.

Jones, Terry. "Interview." "Behind the Director's Son's Cut." On *Erik the Viking: The Director's Son's Cut.* MGM Home Video, 2001.

Mel Gibson Reinventing English with His Viking Movie." *http://www.cinemablend.com/new/Mel-Gibson-Reinventing-English-With-His-Viking-Movie-16625.html.* Accessed 1/19/2010.

Robbins, Tim. "Interview." "The Making of *Erik the Viking,* 1989." On *Erik the Viking: The Director's Son's Cut.* MGM Home Video, 2001.

Tolkien, J.R.R. "On Faerie Stories." In *Tree and Leaf.* Boston: Houghton Mifflin, 1965.

York Archeological Trust. *Jorvik Viking Centre Website. http://www.jorvik-viking-centre.co.uk/.* Accessed 1/06/2010.

"The Love of All Mankind but Also the Love of One Woman Alone": Hrafn Gunnlaugsson's *Shadow of the Raven* (1988)

JOAN TASKER GRIMBERT *and* CLAUDIA BORNHOLDT

Í skugga hrafnsins (*The Shadow of the Raven*, 1988) — the second film in Hrafn Gunnlaugsson's Viking trilogy, which also includes *Hrafninn flýgur* (*When the Raven Flies*, 1984) and *Hvíti víkingurinn* (*The White Viking*, 1991) — is set in the days of post-conversion Iceland (1077) and inspired by the imported legend of Tristan and Iseult, and the indigenous Icelandic mythology and *Íslendingarsögur* (its tradition of the sagas of Icelanders or family sagas).

This essay explores the film from these two distinctive and yet closely intermingled traditions: Joan Grimbert examines the film from the viewpoint of selected versions of the Tristan legend, especially the Norwegian and the Icelandic *Tristrams saga* and their continental sources. Claudia Bornholdt reads the film in the context of the eleventh-century Icelandic culture as presented in the Icelandic sagas (especially *Njáls saga*). She focuses on the tensions between the new and the old religion and their respective values and virtues, which are symbolically represented in the film by the use of the motifs of the white veil and the black raven.

The Legend of Tristan and Iseult[1] (Grimbert)

Hrafn Gunnlaugsson has said that the plot of *The Shadow of the Raven*, like that of the first film in his Viking trilogy, was based on sagas that his grandmother used to tell him when he was a child. He situated the film (which begins in 1077) in the period directly after the most fertile period in Icelandic history (873–1050), a kind of golden age immortalized by the Icelandic sagas of the twelfth and thirteenth centuries, which celebrated not only the native culture, but also the elements of other cultures with which the Icelanders came into contact, thus enriching their own (see Kupchik 61).

Since the two main characters are called Trausti and Ísold, the film promises in part a cinematic retelling of the story of Tristan and Iseult,[2] but it bears scant resemblance to the twelfth- and thirteenth-century versions of the legend preserved in Old French (Béroul and Thomas of Britain) and Middle High German (Eilhart von Oberg and Gottfried von

Straßburg), and only slightly more to Brother Robert's Norwegian *Tristrams saga ok Ísöndar,*[3] which was based on Thomas's poem, and to the mid-fourteenth-century Icelandic *Saga af Tristram ok Ísodd,* which followed the lines of the Norwegian saga but made some surprising changes.[4] The few elements from the legend that were incorporated into the film are bizarrely transformed.

Gunnlaugsson has said that he does not to know what version(s) of the legend his grandmother was following, and since the legend has for many years been extremely well-known throughout Scandinavia, we would need to examine at least the Norwegian and Icelandic *Tristram* sagas in order to see what they might have contributed to the film's romantic plot. Given limitations of space, I will concentrate in the following discussion on two intertwining aspects: the role of religion and the love binding Trausti and Ísold. I will also speak briefly about what the strong female characters (Trausti's mother Edda, the Bishop's wife Sigrídur, and Ísold) may owe to the Tristan legend.

What most sets the Scandinavian *Tristram* sagas apart from their earlier counterparts is the role played by religion. The most shocking aspect of the earlier versions is the way the lovers blithely flout the tenets of Christianity. The love that binds the protagonists obliges Tristan to betray Marc (his liege lord, king, and maternal uncle) and Iseult to engage in a relationship that is adulterous and even — given the importance of the maternal uncle — arguably incestuous. But God, in the rare instances when his presence is invoked, seems to be on the lovers' side, presumably because King Marc's barons denounce his nephew and wife out of spite and envy and especially because the force of the love potion, consumed accidentally by the protagonists is such that it effectively overrides all feudal and blood ties. Defiant to the end, the lovers refuse to recognize that they have sinned.

In the Norwegian saga, however, when Isönd, having arrived too late to save Tristram, sees him dead, she prays to God for forgiveness. She reminds Him that He saved all mankind, including Maria Magdalena, and begs him to be merciful and forgive sinners like her. Although Tristram's jealous wife has them buried on separate sides of the church in order to keep them apart, trees spring up from the two graves and intertwine above the gable of the church to show "how great the love between them had been" (Jorgensen 223).[5]

The same scene is described, somewhat magnified, in the Icelandic version, where the lovers are actually buried in the greatest cathedral in "Jakobsland" (Galicia) — doubtless that of Santiago de Compostela — and the intertwined trees are seen as "a sign that Tristram did not beguile Ísodd the Fair out of malice towards his kinsman Mórodd [Marc] but rather because God Himself in His wisdom had destined them for each other" (Jorgensen and Hill 289).

In Gunnlaugsson's film, religion plays a much more substantial role, since one of the main themes concerns the clash between the old and the new ways, between the indigenous religion and Christianity. As the film begins, Trausti is returning home to Iceland from Norway, where he studied theology and trained to be a priest; he has brought the artist Leonardo with him to paint an altarpiece for the church of his mother, a former heathen slave, who has become a devout Christian. His message of peace and love for all mankind is tested immediately when his clan, of which he is now the head, becomes embroiled with Ísold's over claims made by each family to a beached whale. In the ensuing battle, Ísold's family farm is set afire, and when Trausti tries to prevent blood vengeance by throwing down his sword, the knife of one of his men, Grímur, strikes and kills Ísold's father, Eiríkur.

Because Ísold mistakenly believes that Trausti killed Eiríkur, she conceives a hatred for him reminiscent of that felt by the heroine of the Tristan legend upon learning that Tristan had murdered her uncle. However, as is the case in all the literary versions of the legend, her feelings for Trausti — and his for her — are complicated by the consumption of a love potion. In the legend, it has been brewed by Iseult's mother to ensure that her daughter will love her (much older) husband. But the young people accidentally consume it on board the ship en route for Cornwall.

In the film, the potion is also brewed by Ísold's mother, but it is entrusted to her daughter to give to the man whom she will choose to love. Initially, of course, Ísold does not intend it for Trausti who, after rescuing her from her burning farmhouse, calls for water to revive her and is handed the potion. Regaining consciousness just after Trausti has put the liquid to her mouth and then drunk of it himself, she furiously tries to spit out what she has unwittingly consumed, screaming, "Murderer!" Later, when the two meet in Edda's church, where Trausti hopes to make peace with Ísold, she, grabbing a knife, attempts to kill him, and he, after wrestling her to the ground in an effort to disarm her, is suddenly overcome with passion and covers her with kisses. Eventually, he regains control of himself, only to be mocked by Ísold, who assures him that he will not have her by force or affection and asserts her duty to kill him. Trausti, as if in a trance, murmurs, "A thousand year...."[6]

Ísold changes her mind after witnessing with approval how Trausti responds when challenged to a duel by the Bishop's son Hjörleifur to whom her father had promised her. (Trausti had at first refused to fight, but when forced to defend himself managed to defeat his opponent — without, however, killing him.) Drawing Trausti back into Edda's church directly after, Ísold hands him the potion and commands him to drink, saying that her mother told her: "You shall drink this with the man you will love for a thousand years." She explains that, because he had drunk of it earlier without her bidding, she had tried to kill him. "I feared I'd have to love my father's murderer. But now I know who you are." She makes a cut in both of their hands so as to seal their mutual love with a blood pact. "I want you as my husband," she tells him: "You'll be the most powerful man in the land." When Tristan agrees publicly, at the Althing, the summer general assembly, to hand over all of his land to Ísold in reparation for her father's death, the bishop's family is thrilled. But when Ísold announces that she will marry Trausti (and not Hjörleifur), their joy turns to dismay. The protracted process by which the potion is consumed differs considerably from the literary versions where the consumption is accidental and irreversible and the lovers make love immediately. Here Ísold tries to maintain control over the potion, and, even when she gives it to Trausti, she does not allow him even to kiss her. The last step in the rapprochement between the couple occurs on their wedding night. As they are about to make love, Ísold tells her enthralled husband: "Every great deed a man does is merely a dream of love. And now you have me and I have you. Can we wish more than that love seals peace upon the whole land?" (See Chance and Weinstein 433.)

The dream of love to which Ísold alludes is more encompassing than it at first appears, for Trausti associates it with Christ's love for mankind. When his dying mother warns her son to stay away from Ísold, whose mother was a witch, Trausti shows her the preliminary picture that Leonardo has painted to use for her church's altarpiece. To Christ's lower right, in the place usually reserved in Crucifixion scenes for the Virgin Mary, Leonardo has depicted a woman in red whom Trausti identifies as "Mary Magdalene, the woman who loved Christ." He goes on to explain: "The sacred work of Christ was a single dream of love. The love of all mankind, but also the love of one woman alone." The connection between the former prostitute and the witch's daughter is crystal clear. Indeed, in the very next scene, when Ísold visits Edda's church for the first time and finds Leonardo sketching out his altarpiece, the artist drapes her head with a white silk cloth and then views it through a little frame. Ísold's sudden appearance in the church clearly inspires him to use her as his model for the figure of Mary Magdalene, and her image does indeed appear (with the white drape) on the final altarpiece when it is completed.

It is the explicit integration of the couple's passionate love into the Christian message of universal love that most sets *The Shadow of the Raven* apart from its literary antecedents. In the early poems, the lovers' passion, though somewhat excused by the potion, is seen as clearly opposed to the tenets of the Church. It is true as well of the Norwegian saga, since Isönd begs God's forgiveness just before she expires. But in the Icelandic version, the lovers' death is treated in such a way as virtually to ensure God's forgiveness. Gunnlaugsson's film goes one dramatic step farther.

Every version of the Tristan legend includes a love triangle. The hero must first overcome the heroine's hatred for his having slain a close relative of hers — her maternal uncle in the literary versions and her father in Gunnlaugsson's film. After the couple becomes united in an eternal love by virtue of the love potion, they must deal with the man who seeks an alliance with the female protagonist for social, political, or economic reasons. In all the literary versions, that man is the King of Cornwall, whose marriage to the Irish princess is designed in part to make peace between the two warring kingdoms. After the wedding, the lovers are condemned to live a double life, fulfilling their normal roles in society while meeting secretly whenever possible. In nearly all the versions, the king is deeply in love with his bride. However, the Icelandic saga offers a bizarre variant in that the king actually tells Tristram that he and Ísodd "would be a more auspicious match on account of her age" and proposes to grant him both the lady and the kingdom, but Tristram tells him he does not want to be king as long as his uncle is able.[7]

As we have seen, Gunnlaugsson replaces the Cornish king with the bishop's son Hjörleifur, to whom Eiríkur had betrothed his daughter, in part no doubt because she is in some sense "damaged goods": her mother was a witch (whom her father had burned at the stake), and she had had her daughter, Sól, out of wedlock. [8] (When Eiríkur discovered the identity of that father — a thrall — he had all his limbs cut off.) Thus, once Trausti's union with Ísold has been consecrated by their secret blood pact, Trausti must negotiate with the bishop's family so that he and Ísold can marry in a proper Christian ceremony witnessed by the entire community. By promising to hand over his land to Ísold and marrying her, he hopes to achieve peace and reconciliation among the warring clans. Although the bishop's family agrees to the marriage, they have no intention of letting the two live together in peace. Losing no time, they set fire to the couple's house on their wedding night, and right after Ísold has spoken to Trausti of their dream of love, which will seal peace upon the land, the dream is shattered. Once Ísold ascertains that Sól was removed from the burning house beforehand, she rushes out the door in a cloud of smoke. Hjörleifur, misled by his mother into thinking she is Trausti, hurls a knife at her heart, killing her instantly. Although Trausti manages to escape, Hjörleifur tries once more to kill him (in the bathhouse), sorely testing the hero's characteristic determination to avoid resorting to the violence of blood feuds. When the bishop's frustrated son proves untrustworthy on the third try at reconciliation, Trausti no longer has any choice but to kill him.[9]

In the Tristan legend, the love triangle pits passionate love against the law, and, although the lovers struggle to maintain their places in society while continuing to nurture their love affair, this untenable position leads them both to an early grave. Not so at the close of *The Shadow of the Raven* where Trausti and Sól are seen to have survived the carnage that killed

Ísold.[10] The two clearly represent the endurance of the lovers' "dream of love," which is symbolized in part by the altarpiece completed by Leonardo for Edda's church, where Ísold's face shines through in the figure of Mary Magdalene, who appears in blue[11] under the Cross, depicted in the place and color traditionally reserved for the Virgin Mary. The figure is holding Christ's hand lovingly.[12] The fusion or confusion of these two women so closely associated with Christ is telling. For "the woman who loved Jesus Christ" (Mary Magdalene) and the one who loved Trausti (Ísold) are assimilated to Jesus's mother — and, by implication, to

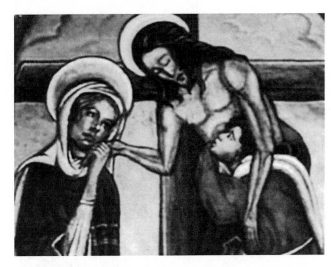

Leonardo's altarpiece in which the face of Ísold shines through in the figure of Mary Magdalene in Hrafn Gunnlaugsson's 1988 film *The Shadow of the Raven.*

Trausti's. When we recall that Maria Magdalena is the sinner mentioned by Ísodd in her prayer at the end of the Icelandic *Tristrams* saga, we see that Trausti's dream of love does indeed encompass not just his passion for Ísold, but also the entire community, which he hopes can now live in peace. Moreover, if Trausti is a Christ-figure, it makes sense for him to love a woman who bears some similarity to Mary Magdalene.

The presence of Sól may seem anomalous in a retelling of a legend whose protagonists are traditionally childless, and Gunnlaugsson has said that he recast the heroine as an unwed mother "to get away from the frustrating virginity and make her a woman with her own will."[13] However, already in the Icelandic version, Ísodd the Dark, the wife Tristram takes when he goes into exile in Spain, gives birth to a baby son, Kalegras Tristramsson. He becomes King of England and eventually marries Lilja, daughter of the emperor of Saxland; together, they have two sons (about which there is supposedly a great saga) and a daughter. Clearly, this version of the legend has been influenced by the Icelandic family sagas, which traditionally end with the genealogical outlook of the sagas' heroes.[14]

Should we attribute to the same influence the depiction of such strong female characters as we see in Ísold, Edda, and Sigrídur (who most seems to have at heart the interests of her family)? The family sagas undoubtedly had a role to play here, but it should be emphasized that Iseult is hardly a shrinking violet in the early versions of the legend, nor is she "the passive object of courtly love" evoked by some (cf. Chance and Weinstein 429). She is by far more clever and resourceful than her beloved, as one troubadour, Raimbaut d'Aurenga, recognized in his song *Non chant per auzel*. In an allusion extending over three strophes, he praises her for giving the "gift" of her virginity to Tristan and cleverly concealing her deceit from Marc. The portrait of the powerful woman who appears in all the literary versions of the legend may have come initially from the pre-literate versions, for in the Irish analogues the heroine, who lives in a matriarchal society, chooses and seduces the object of her desire by casting a spell on him.[15]

Tristan's mother is also depicted traditionally as a powerful figure, for she indulges in a secret relationship that mirrors to some extent that of her son with whom she becomes

From left to right, Isold (Tinna Gunnlaugsdottir), Hjörleif (Egil Oladsson) and Trausti (Reine Brynolfsson) in Hrafn Gunnlaugsson's *The Shadow of the Raven* (Pacific Film Archive).

pregnant out of wedlock. The mother appears particularly strong-willed in the Icelandic version where Blenzibly falls madly in love with Kalegras after witnessing his great prowess. She summons him to her bower where they make love and remain for three years, oblivious to anything other than their mutual passion!

The Raven and the Veil (Bornholdt)

We have shown in part one how Gunnlaugsson's film transfigures elements of the Tristan legend, and we have focused on the special love between Trausti and Ísold and the role played by religion, as well as the presence of strong female characters. In this part, we will look at the borrowings from the indigenous medieval Icelandic sagas and from pagan mythology. I will show first how the film uses several recurrent motifs, most importantly the raven and the white veil, which are deliberately placed in key scenes to guide us through our overall reading of the film. I will then more explicitly discuss the influences from the Icelandic literary tradition.

The repeated placement of ravens in carefully selected scenes visually underscores the film's title, *Í skugga hrafnsins* (*The Shadow of the Raven*).[16] The raven symbolizes Óðinn and hence the religion, society, culture, and values dominant in Iceland in pre–Christian times. As Snorri Sturluson tells us, another name for Óðinn is Hrafnaguð (Raven-god) because of his two messenger ravens, Huginn and Muninn, that sit on his shoulders.[17] In the film, the raven embodies the shadow of Óðinn that places itself over Trausti's efforts to live by the morals and values of the new, Christian, religion. On many occasions, the film's Christian protagonists and their Christian values and ways of dealing with conflict and confrontation quite literally clash with an indigenous Icelandic culture that is grounded in pagan Germanic concepts of kinship and honor. In this pre–Christian society, revenge and thus blood feud were considered the means to uphold the family's and the individual's honor and position in society. As I shall argue below, this basic conflict between the new and the old religion and their respective values and morals, which is a central theme in most of the *Íslendingarsögur*, is also a dominant theme in the film.

"I can't let down my name-sakes," joked Hrafn Gunnlaugsson when asked about the ubiquitous presence of the raven in this film and in his earlier *Hrafninn flýgur* (*When the Raven Flies*, 1984).[18] Undeniably, ravens appear in central scenes in *The Shadow of the Raven*. They function as a symbol of the pagan religion and the "old" way of conflict resolution by force as well as a portent of bad things to come, for the raven is not only Óðinn's messenger but, as a bird of carrion, well attested in Germanic poetry in *kennings* (poetic circumlocutions) and as *heiti* (single-word metaphor) for battle, death, and destruction. The raven appears in its messenger function in the film's opening sequence. Here the ravens that are sent out to guide the sailors on their way to Iceland are an obvious borrowing from the account of Hrafna-Flóki's (Raven-Floki's) settlement of Iceland in *Landnámabók*.[19] When one of the sailors recommends to "put your trust in the raven; if they can see Iceland we are saved," we have the first example in the film where faith and trust in the pagan gods supersedes that in the Christian God.

The next ravens we see sit in front of the beached whale. One of them lands on top of the whale when Grímur announces, under the cawing of the ravens: "Now Kross will be the richest farm in Iceland." In a slightly later shot that immediately precedes Grímur's announcement of the whale at Kross (Trausti's farm), the cawing ravens are again in front and on top of the whale. Clearly, their presence is a bad portent as they symbolize the coming bloodshed and feud. The beached whale marks the beginning of the end of Trausti's peaceful re-entry into Icelandic society and his resolve to be guided in his actions by Christian values. He expresses this resolve in his short speech to Ísold when they meet in the church at Kross shortly after Ísold's father, Eiríkur, has been killed by Grímur. Trausti explains to her that he is innocent in the murder, that he studied theology in Norway, was ordained a priest, brought a painter from Italy for an altarpiece, "but because of a stranded whale...." He does not finish his sentence, but it has already become clear that the conflict over the whale has given rise to a full blown blood feud.

A dead raven hangs from the wall in the pagan burial cave of Trausti's father, and, just like the sword that is covered in cobwebs and stuck in a large stone, it is a symbol of the pagan faith in which the sword rules. Accordingly, Trausti explains to the stunned Leonardo: "a raven is Óðinn's bird" and "even the gods become a little dusty sometimes." He goes on to explain that his father "believed in the raven," and he then puts his hand on the dusty sword and declares that "he who lives by the sword shall die by the sword." By quoting the words spoken by Christ in the garden of Gethsemane (Matthew 26:52), Trausti expresses his resolve to follow Christ, and not the raven, that is, he relinquishes the "old way" of settling conflicts with the sword. He stays true to this oath, because he only raises the sword in self defense and does not kill until after Ísold has been murdered by Hjörleifur on their wedding night. It is probably also no coincidence that Hjörleifur, Trausti's rival, wears black feathers (that are reminiscent of the raven) on the back of his head covering during the wedding scene.

The ravens appear again when Trausti returns to Kross after Ísold's death. In this scene, we see how Grímur is standing in the farmhouse he now considers his own. He becomes visibly shaken when a woman's voice announces that Trausti has returned. The eerie announcement of the return of the rightful owner of Kross, whom Grímur thinks has burned to death, is underscored by the crowing and cackling of ravens which can be seen when Grímur exits the house to look for Trausti. Grímur must think that a ghost has appeared. He enters the church with his drawn sword in hand, and, as is well attested in the sagas, he rings the church bell to drive out the presumed demon.[20] Trausti is located in his father's burial cave, which he has set on fire. Surrounded by wooden statues depicting Óðinn, the one-eyed god, he demands from Grímur that he swear loyalty to him and help him avenge Ísold's death. At this point, Trausti has returned to the old ways of blood feud. Trausti removes his mask, looks into the raging fire, gazes at one of the wooden statues of Óðinn, and reopens the wound on his palm, a wound he had obtained earlier when he had sealed his betrothal to Ísold with a blood pact. Standing in the temple of Óðinn, Trausti licks the blood from his wound and addresses a black raven that hangs over his right shoulder: "You gave my father strength. Now you shall help Jesus Christ."

This statement can be read in two ways; either as a call for help to place all the support that is possible — even that of the pagan gods and their followers — into aiding his cause, or literally as the request to help Trausti, who has been transformed into a Christ figure. The latter reading is supported by the fact that the wound Trausti receives in his side while hiding in the vat of curdled milk is an unmistakable allusion to Christ's side wound on the cross. The camera zooms in on the wound to make clear its location. The wound on his palm can also be seen as a reference to the stigmata. After the burning and the wound he obtained while submerged in the milk vat, everybody believes Trausti to be dead. There-fore, when he climbs out of the vat and is entirely covered in white milk, Gunnlaugs-son seems to suggest this emergence as a new birth or possibly (Christ-like?) rebirth of the hero. This idea finds further support when Trausti appears to Egill, one of the bishop's henchmen. Egill stands in front of the beached whale, which is now reduced to its skele-ton, and he is horror-struck when he recognizes Trausti, whom he believes to be dead. Trausti announces, "You see a dead man. Now you will follow him ... into hell," and then kills him (off-screen). He then rides off to the bishop's farm, kills the bishop, and, after yet another attempt to seek a peaceful resolution to the feud fails, beheads Hjörleifur. In the end, Trausti has been driven to revert to the way of the raven and to shed blood, because he could not leave the death of Ísold unavenged. He is unable to escape the shadow of the raven.

The foreigner Leonardo puts the contradictions he observes in the Icelandic society quite bluntly: "Your father lies in a heathen temple and your mother builds a church. I don't understand." This hopelessly intertwined relationship of the old and the new faith is a recurrent and central theme in the film. Trausti's mother formulates this conflict in a way that foreshadows the film's ending where the significantly named Sól represents a certain hope of future tolerance: "The God who created the sun has always been my God. And he has listened to my prayers. Whether he is called Christ or Óðinn is of no importance." The theme recurs in the scene immediately following Leonardo and Trausti's visit to the heathen temple. In that scene we find Ísold and Sigríður sitting in the bathhouse, when the bishop scolds his wife: "you follow Christ's example and again use heathen practices?" That the bishop is far from being a saint is evident throughout the film. Already at his first appearance, Grímur explains that in the retinue of Sigríður and Hjörleifur "there are no angels, but rather the bishop Hordur and all his devils." The bishop's hypocrisy is depicted most vividly when he uses his bishop staff, which conceals a sharp blade, to stab an innocent woman, who is kneeling in front of him, begging for mercy. Trausti's words to Leonardo ring true: "Most of us are still completely heathen. We are only Christian when it is necessary." Trausti finds himself in the opposite situation. He reverts to pagan customs when there is no other way out, for example when he is forced to participate in the *holmganga* (single combat) with Hjörleifur, or when he revenges Ísold's death with the sword.

While the raven is used to symbolically represent the pagan faith and the idea of justice achieved by the sword, the white, silken veil symbolizes the new Christian religion and values, for just like Christianity, the veil was imported to Iceland from abroad. Leonardo, who brought the veil, places it on Ísold's head the first time she enters the church at Kross. Ísold lets him do so, and she sits still and quite Madonna-like with the veil wrapped around her head, an image that will return in the altarpiece at the end of the film. Once Trausti enters the church, she tears the veil off and becomes visibly aggravated. In accordance with the "old" ways, she seeks blood revenge for her father's death and attempts to stab Trausti. After he has wrestled with her, and, overcome by the effect of the potion he had drunk earlier, covered her in passionate kisses, Trausti, in a display of unwavering trust in his Christian God, tells her: "If your father's death may be avenged by killing me, then kill me." Instead of stabbing Trausti however, Ísold begins to slice the silken veil, announcing: "I shall kill you." At the moment she raises the dagger to stab Trausti, the church bells ring to announce the arrival of the bishop and his retinue.

Trausti then engages in a *holmganga* with Hjörleifur, and, after he has defeated Hjörleifur and spared his life, he returns to the church and uses the veil to wipe the blood from his wound. The veil is used again to clean away blood in the very next scene. Ísold enters the church, offers the potion to Trausti because now she knows who he is and wants to be bound in love to him, and then slices open his and her palms to seal their love in blood. She then uses the veil to bind the wound. The blood oath underscores the fact that the older, pagan ways are still active, but the veil (as a symbol of Christianity) is applied to stop the bleeding. These two scenes show how the two religions are intertwined, and they foreshadow how Trausti's Christian faith and pure intentions increasingly become stained by blood.

The gown Isold wears as an undergarment at her wedding and on her wedding night is made of the same material as the veil. It is a white silken fabric through which thin silver threads are woven. We see how Ísold is sown into the gown before the wedding feast, and, at this moment, it seem that all conflicts have been laid aside. Ísold has been handed over to Trausti by the bishop and his wife, and, as the commentary of the law speaker indicates, by this ritualistic handing-over of the bride, the treaty between the two families has been sealed. The church ceremony, the wedding feast, and the departure of the guests follow, and then, in a long and dramatic montage, we alternately see Trausti and Ísold in their wedding chamber and the bishop's preparations to set the house on fire.

The most remarkable and dramatic scene in the film is the murder of Ísold. Believing that she can negotiate a peaceful resolution to the attack by the bishop's family, Ísold wraps herself in a white shawl and runs toward the door of the burning house. Hjörleifur's dagger hits her right in the heart, and, in a close-up, we see how her red blood runs down her white silken wedding gown while the (hellish?) fire rages in the background. Ísold dies and with her Trausti's hope that the blood feud has ended and peace returned to the land.

The veil once more returns in the final scene, after peace and calm finally seem to have returned to Iceland. Trausti has avenged Ísold's death and ended the blood feud (the bishop, his wife, and Hjörleifur are dead) and now returns to Kross with Ísold's daughter, Sól. They look at Leonardo's altarpiece, and, in the place where Mary Magdalene was located in the earlier smaller painting, we now find Ísold wearing the white veil. This final image of the loving Ísold/Mary Magdalene at the foot of Christ's cross suggests that she had to give her life, just as Trausti had to sacrifice his love for her, for the greater good. The future is now represented by Sól, and this future seems hopeful.

Every Icelander is familiar with the sagas, and Gunnlaugsson is no exception. As he himself stated: "...my way to the Icelandic sagas is not that of a professor of Old Norse, but working as a catalyst" (Jónsdóttir, p. 9). A professor of Old Norse will find many similarities and allusions to the Icelandic sagas. The obvious allusion to the account of Hrafna-Flóki's settlement of Iceland in *Landnámabók* has already been discussed, and Chance and Weinstein mention several of the similarities the film shares with *Laxdæla saga*, such as the strong female characters (Unn, Guðrún, Þorgerður), the love triangle (Guðrún — Kjartan — Bolli), and the "tainted" ancestry of some of the characters.[21]

Many other sagas suggest themselves as parallels, but none more so than *Njáls saga*, which is also known as *Brennu-Njáls saga* (*The Saga of the Burning of Njáll*), because the saga's eponymous hero, his wife, and many of the members of his household are burned to death in their home. This "burning of Njáll" comes as the end to the hero's futile attempts to abolish blood vengeance in favor of legal settlements and, connected with his enlightened attitude, his promotion of Christianity in pagan Iceland. *Njáls saga* is also famous for its willful and powerful women who give rise to many of the conflicts and incite the men to engage in blood feuds.[22] The presence of strong female characters and a gendered attribution of roles is familiar from the literary tradition, where we encounter "notably stereotyped portrayals of women [...], particularly in *Njal's saga*, where wives, sisters, and mothers incite men to vengeance despite male attempts to impose the judgments of the Althing as resolutions of blood feud" (Anderson 422).[23]

In Gunnlaugsson's film, we can observe a similar binary approach toward conflict resolution. However, the two approaches are not divided along gender but along familial divisions. Bishop Hordur, his wife Sigríður (notably called "the black"), and their son Hjörleifur rely on blood vengeance, whereas Trausti and his mother, Edda, are proponents of the legal system.[24] It is of course ironic, that it is the bishop, from whom a modern audience would expect adherence to the Christian values of mercy, compassion, and justice, is depicted as a ruthless murderer. But the bishop is also an Icelander living in the eleventh century, and, unlike Trausti, who comes freshly trained and ordained from abroad, the bishop is part of a culture that just recently (77 years before) had converted to the new Christian faith.

As has been mentioned in conjunction with the discussion of the raven and the veil, Gunnlaugsson's film makes ample use of the well-established dichotomy between the "native," Icelandic idea of blood vengeance on the one hand and the "foreign" idea of Christianity, a dichotomy that is well known from the sagas and undoubtedly borrowed from there.[25] This "foreign" Christianity, though superficially already established in Iceland as evidenced by the existence of the bishop and the churches at Kross and at Eiríkur's farmstead, is represented by Trausti and his travel companion Leonardo, the Italian painter to whom the Icelandic culture seems thoroughly barbarian and lacking in Christian values and virtues. It is Leonardo who brings the white veil to Iceland, and it is Leonardo who explicitly sets Trausti apart from the other Icelanders, when he tells him "you are not a barbarian," once Trausti's men set out to seek blood vengeance from Eiríkur's men.

Trausti's struggle to uphold the values of Christianity, to achieve justice and strive for peaceful conflict resolution, equals Njal's ultimately futile struggle to promote the conversion to Christianity and to abolish the feud system in favor of the law.[26] Just as is announced in the saga: "er ok illu korni sáit orðit, enda mun illt af gróa," "when evil seed has been sown, evil will grow," Trausti recognizes in his words to Ísold that the stranded whale is just such an evil seed that has shattered his hopes for a new, Christian, Iceland.[27] It comes as little surprise that the ravens seem to have settled comfortably on the whale's back.

Trausti has not only lost his dream of living peacefully a Christian life in Iceland, he has also lost his great love, Ísold. Yet, just as a former prostitute can be embraced by the love of Christ — as the altarpiece unmistakably tells us — there is hope for Iceland, and this hope is embodied in Ísold's daughter Sól. Trausti survives the mayhem, so it seems, to be a father to Sól and to guide Iceland on its path to true Christianity. After the bloody showdown at the bishop's farm, Sól and Trausti sit together quietly. Sól asks whether Trausti had a mother too, and he summarizes for her the basic story of the film: "I brought an Italian painter home with me to Iceland. I had promised my mother an altarpiece. When we were riding home, we found a grounded whale. And in the quarrel that arose over the whale, I lost my mother. Leonardo came here to paint a picture for her." Sól then asks Trausti "what picture?" and this question pulls him out of the pagan world and prompts him to visit the church at Kross. There, with the help of Sól's questions, he reflects on his Christian beliefs and once more embraces the idea of all encompassing love when he tells Sól with the final words uttered in the film: "You shall let the dream of love become a light in the darkness."

Notes

1. "Iseult" is the English spelling of the heroine's name, which appears in many guises, depending on the language ("Yseut" or "Ysolt" in Old French, "Isolde" in German, "Ísönd" in Old Norse, "Ísodd" in the Icelandic saga, and "Ísold" in Gunnlaugsson's film). The hero's name varies less, from "Tristran" in Old French to "Tristram" in most other versions, but Gunnlaugsson calls him "Trausti," perhaps to reflect his trustworthiness. (See Chance and Weinstein 429.)

2. For the evolution of the legend from the Middle Ages to the present, see Grimbert, *Tristan and Isolde*, xiii–ci.

3. Composed in 1226 for King Hákon Hákonarson the Old of Norway (1217–1263). See Jorgensen.

4. Presumably composed in the mid-fourteenth century, complete versions exist only in late seventeenth-century paper manuscripts, although there are several fifteenth-century fragments. See Jorgensen and Hill.

5. The religious element is also underscored in the late medieval Icelandic ballad *Tristrams Kvæði*, which describes the lovers' very Christian burial, attended by priests with candles, hymns, and bells. The bodies are carried into the church, placed in a holy cell, and lowered into stone sepulchers from which spring two trees that are joined in the middle of the church. See Cook.

6. On the possible meaning of this phrase, see Chance and Weinstein 437.

7. Jorgensen and Hill 277. On Tristram's unusually close ties with his uncle, see Kalinke, "Female Desire."

8. In the literary versions, both Iseult and her mother have knowledge of magical potions, but they are both of royal blood.

9. See Chance and Weinstein 435, and also 424, for the many times Trausti has resisted "justifiable" violence.

10. Nearly everyone else is dead. Trausti, before killing Hjörleifur, invokes Óðinn's help to avenge Ísold's death by killing the Bishop in his wife's church, and Sigrídur herself, upon seeing her son slain, sets fire to her church and to herself.

11. We recall that she was in red in the original design that Trausti showed his mother.

12. For a contemporary rendering (1906) of this image, see *http://www.sacredconnections.co.uk/holyland/Kilmorechurch.htm*.

13. In an e-mail to Weinstein (cited in Chance and Weinstein 429).

14. In other late medieval versions of the legend, especially in Spain, the lovers marry and are survived by children and grandchildren. See Grimbert, "The Matter of Britain."

15. See Rabine's description of how the patriarchal system undermined the power that women enjoyed in a matriarchal society.

16. See Chance and Weinstein 432.

17. See the account in Snorri Sturluson's *Edda* in Jónsson 39.

18. Jónsdóttir 9.

19. For *Landnámabók*, see the edition by Benediktsson and the translation by Pálsson and Edwards. See Chance and Weinstein 418, for the reference to the *Landnámabók* parallel. The film even includes the detail of the first raven returning to the ship (the first two return to the ship in Hrafna-Flóki's story), whereas the second raven leads the way to Iceland.

20. Ghosts and demons are common in the Icelandic sagas. A story that tells about the appearance of a demon that is driven out once the church bells are rung is "þorsteins þáttur skelks" ("The Tale of Thorstein Shiver") from *Flateyjarbók*.

21. Chance and Weinstein 430–31. See also the discussion in part one of this essay.

22. Njal's and Gunnar's wives (Bergþóra and Hallgerður) are engaged in a similar competition for might and influence as the women in the film.

23. See also Clover's important articles on the topic of gender roles in Old Norse–Icelandic literature.

24. As the head of his family, Trausti accepts full responsibility for Grímur's killing of Eiríkur, and he is willing to go to the Althing for the legal proceedings. He avoids bloodshed wherever he can and only engages in battle when he is provoked and must defend his life. Likewise, Edda advises her son not to seek blood vengeance for the injury she obtained and Eiríkur's theft of the whale but instead seek the bishop's judgment. See Chance and Weinstein 421.

25. For discussions of this distinction, see Lönnroth ch. 4; Sveinsson; and, for the references, Anderson, n. 10. See Chance and Weinstein *passim*.

26. See Lönnroth 29. Njal's sentiment is expressed in his actions and in many of his statements throughout the saga, such as: "Eigi er þat sættarrof," segir Njáll, "at hverr hafi lög við annan, því at með lögum skal land várt byggja, en eigi með ólögum eyða" ("It's not breaking a settlement," said Njal, "if a man deals lawfully with another — with law our land shall rise, but it will perish with lawlessness.") See the edition in Sveinsson 70. 172 and the translation in Cook, tr., *Njal's Saga* 80.

27. For the Icelandic, see Sveinsson 115. 288. Translation from Cook 115. See also Harris.

Works Cited

Anderson, Carolyn. "No Fixed Point: Gender and Blood Feuds in Njal's Saga." *Philological Quarterly* 81.4 (2002): 421–440.

Benediktsson, Jakob, ed. *Íslendingabók, Landnámabók*. Íslenzk Fornrit 1. Reykjavík: Hið Íslenzka fornritafélag, 1968.

Chance, Jane, and Jessica Weinstein. "National Identity and Conversion Through Medieval Romance: The Case of Hrafn Gunnlaugsson's Film *Í Skugga Hrafnsins*." *Scandinavian Studies* 75 (2003): 417–38.

Clover, Carol. "Hildigunnr's Lament: Women in Bloodfeud." In *Structure and Meaning in Old Norse Literature: New Approaches to Textual Analysis and Literary Criticism*. Ed. John Lindow, et al. Odense: Odense University Press, 1987. 141–183.

_____. "Regardless of Sex: Men, Women, and Power in Early Northern Europe." *Speculum* 68 (1993): 363–387.

Cook, Robert, tr. "Njal's Saga." In *The Complete Sagas of Icelanders (Including 49 Tales)*. Ed. Viðar Hreinsson, et al. Reykjavík: Leifur Eiríksson, 1997. III, 1–220.

Cook, Robert, ed. and tr. *Tristrams Kvæði*. In *Norse Romance.I. The Tristan Legend*. Ed. Marianne E. Kalinke. Cambridge UK: D. S. Brewer, 1999. 227–239.

Grimbert, Joan Tasker. "The Matter of Britain on the Continent and the Legend of Tristan and Iseult in France, Italy, and Spain." In *A Companion to Arthurian Literature*. Ed. Helen Fulton. Oxford: Wiley-Blackwell, 2009. 145–159.

_____, ed. *Tristan and Isolde: A Casebook*. 1995; rpt. New York: Routledge, 2002.

Gunnlaugsson, Hrafn, dir. *Í skugga hrafnsins* [The Shadow of the Raven]. Reykjavik: FILM, 1988.

Harris, Richard L. "'The Hand's Pleasure in the Blow Is Brief': Proverbs Escalating Danger in the Revenge Pattern of Njálssaga." *Proverbium: Yearbook of International Proverb Scholarship* 18 (2001): 149–66.

Jónsdóttir, Solveig K. "When the Raven Flies: Once Upon a Time in the North." *Icelandic Review* 25.4 (1987): 4–11.

Jónsson, Finnur, ed. *Snorri Sturluson. Edda*. Copenhagen: Forlagt af Universitetsboghandler G. E. C. Gad, 1900.

Jorgensen, Peter, ed. and tr. *Tristrams saga ok Ísöndar*. In *Norse Romance.I. The Tristan Legend*. Ed. Marianne E. Kalinke. Cambridge, UK: D. S. Brewer, 1999. 23–226.

Jorgensen, Peter, ed. and Joyce Hill, tr. *Saga of Tristrams ok Ísodd*. In *Norse Romance.I. The Tristan Legend*. Ed. Marianne E. Kalinke. Cambridge, UK: D. S. Brewer, 1999. 241–92.

Kalinke, Marianne E. "Female Desire and the Quest in the Icelandic Legend of Tristram and Ísodd." In *The Grail Quest and the World of Arthur*. Ed. Norris J. Lacy. Cambridge,UK: D. S. Brewer, 2008. 76–91.

———, ed. *Norse Romance. I. The Tristan Legend*. Cambridge, UK: D. S. Brewer, 1999.

Kupchik, Christian. "'Todos fuimos vikingos.' Entrevista a Hrafn Gunnlaugsson." *El Amante Cine* 6 (July 1992): 60–61.

Lönnroth, Lars. *Njálssaga: A Critical Introduction*. Berkeley: University of California Press, 1976.

Pálsson, Hermann, and Paul Edwards, tr. *The Book of Settlements: "Landnámabók."* Winnipeg: University of Manitoba Press, 2007.

Rabine, Leslie W. "Love and the New Patriarchy: *Tristan and Isolde*." In *Tristan and Isolde: A Casebook*. Ed. Joan Tasker Grimbert. 1995 rpt. New York: Routledge, 2002. 37–74.

Sveinsson, Einar Ólafur. *Njáls Saga: A Literary Masterpiece*. Ed. and tr. Paul Schach. Lincoln: University of Nebraska Press, 1971.

———, ed. *Brennu-Njáls saga*. Íslenzk Fornrit 12. Reykjavík: Hið Íslenzka fornritafélag, 1954.

Different Pathfinders, Different Destinations

ROBERTA DAVIDSON

From frozen north to North America, bull reindeer to white horse, and innocence to experience, the story of the Pathfinder, a boy who saves his people by tricking a band of marauders to their deaths, is quite different by the end of its journey than its initial form and content. Originally a folktale, it inspired a twentieth-century Norwegian film, which, in turn, was remade as a twenty-first century American film. The films' differences are due not only to dissimilar directorial visions, but also to the way that each director faces the challenge of realistically embodying folktale, and giving it a "local habitation and a name."

As reproduced by Thomas A. Dubois in "Folklore, Boundaries and Audience in *The Pathfinder*," the original folktale is a common type in which a Sami hero uses the natural landscape, quick thinking, and his ability to speak the Tchudes' language to lure them to their death.[1] Although there is more than one variant, in essence, all tell the same story: The Tchude, a band of raiders from what is now northern Russia and Finland, travel the world ravaging wherever they go. They come upon a small village and kill all the people in it except for one boy, whom they save to act as their guide to the other villages. The boy tells the Tchude to follow the light of his torch and persuades them to bind themselves together, intending all along to lead them to the edge of a precipice and hurl the torch off the edge, tricking them into following it. In both versions, one or two canny Russians refuse to be bound, but the rest agree; when the boy throws the torch, most of the Tchude follow it to their deaths. The boy then pushes the remaining one or two Tchude over the edge as well, then goes down to the village below, where the people are celebrating a wedding. He tells them he's saved all their lives. They are initially skeptical, but, when he shows them the bodies, they believe him.

Nils Gaup, director of the 1987 film *Ofelaš* (Pathfinder) which was nominated for a Best Foreign-Language film Oscar, claims that he first heard the tale from his grandfather, who in turn had heard it from a traditional storyteller, and that it had been passed down from generation to generation "for nearly a thousand years."[2] However, while many of the folktale's plot elements are present in Gaup's film, the story as he presents it is significantly different.

Ofelaš, the film, is ostensibly a story about a sixteen-year-old Sami[3] boy, Aigin, who returns from a hunting trip to find his family murdered by the Tchude.[4] He is discovered by them and wounded, but escapes. The film then introduces a different group of Sami villagers. We see their "Noaidi," or Pathfinder, Raste, hunt and kill a bear, whose spirit is respectfully thanked for its sacrifice on behalf of the people. Raste himself must stay away from the villagers for three days, lest the power of the bear, which he has absorbed, sear their eyes. Meanwhile, the wounded Aigin reaches Raste's village, and Raste returns, using magical precautions not to kill anyone, to heal him.

Raste leaves again, and the chief's daughter, Sahve, tends Aigin's wound. Despite Aigin's grief at the loss of his family, the shy attraction between the two young people is quickly evident. Meanwhile, the villagers have realized that Aigin's tracks will lead the Tchude to them, and they decide to relocate to the coast. Aigin remains behind, however, determined to avenge his family. During the ensuing night, he is visited by Raste, who teaches him what the Tchude have "forgotten," that every living being is attached to every other with invisible bonds. Then Raste disappears.

The next morning, a few of the Sami villagers, inspired by Aigin's determination to fight the Tchude rather than flee, return. All are killed, however, while Aigin, helpless to protect them because of the loss of his weapon, hides. He is found by Raste, who passes him the tribe's magical drum and distracts the Tchude so the boy can escape. However, when Aigin sees Raste tortured to reveal the location of the other villagers, he reveals himself and promises to lead the Tchude if they will spare the Noaidi. Nonetheless, unknown to Aigin, Raste is murdered.

Aigin leads the Tchude through a treacherous mountain pass to the coast, seemingly willing to fulfill his side of the bargain to save Raste at the expense of the rest of the village. The film cuts to the Sami women, left unprotected by most of the village men who have gone to find their male relatives, absent on a hunting trip. We see Sahve watching hopefully for Aigin, and the audience is impressed with the enormity of the boy's potential betrayal. During the journey, however, Aigin discovers that Raste is dead, and, while the film does not make it clear if this is the point at which he changes his intention, or if he had secretly planned to betray the Tchude all along, he then tricks the Tchude into linking themselves together with a rope, and leads them to a treacherous part of the mountain. He throws his torch over the side, and they follow it and fall, dragging one another to their deaths. Their violence toward others is now shown as turned against themselves, as they literally try to climb over one another to safety. Finally, an avalanche sweeps them all away while a group of the villagers, formerly suspicious of Aigin, watch from below, and realize that Aigin has tricked the Tchude to their deaths, and sacrificed his life to save theirs.

Aigin, however, survives the avalanche unharmed. On his way to rejoin the villagers, he experiences a vision of a bull-reindeer, a moment which mystically links him to the murdered Raste. Appropriately, when Aigin enters the tent where the villagers are gathered and returns the magic drum, he is recognized as their new "pathfinder."

Structurally as well as symbolically, the film tells a story of belonging — both to a specific ethnic community and to universal humanity. It reaches out to a non–Sami audience through the use of subtitles, realistic sets, and identifiable characters. Indeed, the visual signals of who is good and who is evil are literally dark and light. Other symbols are equally easy to comprehend without access to a specific cultural context. A reoccurring flying raven presages death. A bear dies so that the villagers might survive — this symbol of sacrifice does double-duty, for it is also by using strategy and the bear's violence against itself that Raste is able to kill the stronger animal. Similarly, Aigin will trick the Tchude into destroying themselves.

An equally powerful symbol is the circle. The film begins with natural images: a round moon, sea and snow, then Raste's face, and a circle of drawn figures. Raste's three sightings of the bull reindeer — youth, prime, and old age — close the circle of his life, even as Aigin's sighting begins a new circle, ensuring that the village "will always have a Pathfinder." After Raste kills the bear, the villagers must look at him through a camera-lens-like ring which "destroys the power of evil that is death, letting through the power of life." The tribe's dance around the bear is in a circle, and the people themselves sit in a circle, at the end of the film, until the image of the drum, the figures we saw at the beginning of the film is superimposed upon them, completing the film's circle.

Similarly, Raste's demonstration that oxygen, though unseen, is real, and his use of oxygen as a metaphor for the unseen connections between all living things, is explicit and highlighted as the film's central message. "Remember we are but parts of the whole," he tells Aigin, "parts of the infinite brotherhood.... No, my son. You cannot tear yourself apart from the whole. But you can lose sight of it; forget you're tied to it, and so become a Tchude.... Men who have lost the path, stumbling blindly on the path to self-destruction." Of course, this is literally what happens to the Tchude at the end of the film. Even the avalanche which rescues Aigin reinforces the impression that those who are in tune with natural law will survive, while those who "unnaturally" destroy fellow members of the human tribe will be rejected by the natural world.

Equally, however, *Ofelaš* creates a world instantly recognizable to an "insider" audience of Sami, presenting their lives and culture as givens, neither idealized nor voyeuristically depicted. The film's use of the Sami language, not even universally understood by the Sami themselves, was widely heralded. The bull reindeer is also particularly important to Sami culture, but its meaning is left mysterious for those unfamiliar with its exact symbolic meaning. Both the form and content of the film work together, therefore, to reflect the belief at the heart of the film, in which "belonging" is extended to every human being, but not at the expense of unique cultural identity.

Ofelaš has been identified as a part of the Sami revitalization movement (DuBois 255–277), and, as such, it celebrates not just Aigin's and the villagers' survival but the survival of the Sami themselves and their resistance to the linguistic and cultural hegemony of Norway. It positions itself in a larger philosophical framework, in which the uniqueness of a people's identity can be celebrated without diminishing their fellowship with others.

But the film, for all its claim to historic authenticity, is noteworthy for how much it adds to the original tale — Raste, the bear, Sahve, the drum, the men who return to fight, the avalanche, and the bull-reindeer; all elements that help shape the film's meaning. Also, present in the tale, but missing from the film, is the explicit mention of the boy's intention to deceive the Tchude all along, and his facility with their language. In fact, in the film, the language of the Tchude is unintelligible to the audience and the hero alike, making it all the more difficult for us to understand what motivates their relentless violence. DuBois notes:

> Wherever Sami Chude tales are told, the hero is always able to communicate with the enemy in their own language. Indeed, this ability is often cited as a reason for the hero's success in duping his dimwitted adversaries. Such a skill implies longterm contact between Sami and Chudes, contact understandable from the protracted history of Scandinavian, Finish, Karelian, and Russian intrusions on Sami populations from the Viking age onward. But by rendering his character Aigin incapable of understanding Chude speech, Gaup is able to turn the tale into one of initial intercultural contact, in which the suddenly beset Sami community must decide how to deal with a new and imminent danger. It becomes the familiar story but with a new twist (268).

Dubois further points out that, if the film was to be intelligible at all to a non–Sami audience, it was necessary to provide some explanation about Sami cultural practices. Gaup does so, for example, when Sami children are instructed by their elders about certain customs. For an insider Sami audience, on the other hand, Gaup added the suspense missing from, and unnecessary to, the folktale, by defamiliarizing parts of the story, and highlighting the young hero's naïveté:

> In fact, it is easy to suspect Aigin of the worst kind of folly in the scenes which take place on the mountain top. Such suspicions are largely impossible within the oral tradition, in which the genre of the Chude tale itself prepares the audience to expect an act of heroic trickery, not an act of foolish betrayal. Gaup's narrative alteration humanizes his character, rendering him unsure, untried, unpredictable, and rescuing the film's plot from the surety which would otherwise prevail for the inside audience (DuBois 267).

Max Lüthi, in his study of the formal aspects of folktale, notes, among its other features, the folktale's "one-dimensionality" (4), "depthlessness" (11), and impression of existing outside realistic time and space. Actors, however, are real, three-dimensional human beings, and, through acting, they tend to establish characters of greater or lesser degrees of depth. A natural background — and *Ofelaš* was shot on location, despite the unusually high degree of technical challenge involved in doing so (Background Notes 12–14) — is also perceived by an audience as a real place. "Reality," in other words, is different when a tale becomes a performance, and an audience interacts with a film's characters, narrative, and themes in such a way as to hold them accountable for what they are or appear to be saying on a different level. Not only is there the expectation of greater psychological and visual realism, but there is also the inevitable search for subtextual meanings. Accordingly, Bert Cardullo understands the final message of the film as one in which "what's left ... is the life of the tribe, which has been extended through the quasi-ritualistic sacrifice of one of its older members and the simultaneous maturation of one of its younger ones" (102), rather than as a story about a clever boy who uses his wits to overcome an enemy.

A second version of *Pathfinder*, directed by Marcus Nispel, was made in 2007. It is the inevitable fate of a remade film to be compared to the original, even as it was the fate of *Ofelaš* to be compared to the folktale that inspired it. Oddly, Nispel himself does not appear to have been very familiar with *Ofelaš* when he agreed to make the film, describing it vaguely as a Norwegian film resembling *First Blood* or *Rambo*.[5] One reviewer even suggested at the time that it was a mistake to engage with *Pathfinder* as a remake and rather to accept it "...as a piece of movie-going red meat, an adventurous, bloody, Vikings vs. Indians chase through the wilds..." (Moore E3). Indeed, had Nispel's film not been called *Pathfinder*, it is not certain many reviewers would have recognized it as a remake.

Mikkel Gaup as Aigin, the title character in Nils Gaup's 1987 film *The Pathfinder* (British Film Institute).

The film's script was written by Laeta Kalogridis, but it was artistically designed in collaboration with a graphic artist, Christopher Shy. This collaboration had a profound impact upon the way in which Nispel envisioned the film, and led to his inclusion of several graphic novel conventions, such as a quasi super-heroic main character (which Aigin is clearly not). Most noticeably, the Sami are transformed into Native Americans, and the location of the story changed from Norway to North America.

Not surprisingly, *Pathfinder* also has a different message than *Ofelaš*. In *Pathfinder*, ethnic identity is represented as self-constructed and artificial, suggesting it is the responsibility of an individual to choose his or her "real" culture. It is no longer a story about universal acceptance, therefore, so much as a morality play about the rejection of evil. "There are two wolves fighting in every man's heart," Ghost is told by Starfire, the Pathfinder's daughter. "One is love, one is hate." "Which one wins?" Ghost asks, and she replies, "The one who is fed the most."

Interestingly, Gaup himself had drawn an analogy between the Sami in mainstream Norwegian culture and Native Americans in the United States:

> What chances could an actor with no track record have? He even belonged to the lapp [sic] minority and wanted to shoot his film in the Lapp language which is incomprehensible to Norwegians. The situation could be compared to an American Indian who tries to mount a $20,000,000 production in Hollywood and insists on shooting it with no stars and in the Sioux or another Indian language [Background Notes 9].

However, the transformation of Norwegians to Native Americans by Nispel was due less to this association than to his own personal interest in the possibility that Vikings had visited the North American continent:

> When I first started to direct, I was always drawn to graphic novel material. Most of what I found was too over the top, but what about a real-life superhero stuck in a real-life predicament that is stranger than fiction in a war between Vikings and Indians?! ... I was fascinated with an American saga older than King Arthur or the *Niebelungenlied*— an imagined, untold history [Background Notes 9].

However, such a geographical transplantation cannot be effected neutrally.

The transformation of the Sami into the "People of the Dawn" places the story in a very different cultural and historical context, one with its own political and racial associations. No longer part of the cultural revitalist movement of an ethnic minority, the film appears to be a non–Native American director's commercial exploitation of Native American history. Indeed, the sense of cultural assimilation is only reinforced when the Native American characters speak English, the language of those whose ancestors eventually dispossessed them.

Nispel may have felt his use of an entirely Native Peoples cast to play the Native Americans in the film counteracted the danger of it being seen as a cultural appropriation. He acknowledged there was a risk of stereotyping the Native Americans, but felt the presence and advice of Russell Means, the founder of AIM and the actor playing the role of the Pathfinder, would enable him to avoid it. Means' advice to Nispel was to be careful not to portray the Native Americans in a "savage, primordial way." However, the charges of stereotyping in the film dealt more with the perceived passivity of the Native Americans (Director's Commentary). The familiar category of the enlightened hybrid hero — a man trained by the Anglo-European to oppress native peoples, but turning against "his own kind" to act as a savior — has frequently reflected thinly-veiled racism. Certainly this is the case in one model for the film which Nispel himself cites twice, *Tarzan*. It is not surprising, therefore, that an unintentionally racist message was perceived by more than one viewer. Along with the complaint that the film registered as cultural cliché when it showed native peoples hunting, fishing, and smiling with "the wisdom of the ages" (Dargis E7), there was a similar assessment that the "Vikings are apparently not from North Atlantic regions but the darkest depths of Mordor.... Native Americans may not wolf down the depiction of their forebears as helpless, cowardly and weak. So much for being in tune with nature: They can't detect a company of armored horsemen charging at them. Thank goodness there's a circa 900-A.D. Rambo to save them" (Ordoña E12).

Pathfinder's image problems were complicated further when it was decided that the hero should be a Viking. Ghost is a boy who was left behind during a Viking raid on the North American continent. He is raised by a kind Native American woman who finds him in a physically and emotionally tortured state. Adopted by her and raised as one of the tribe, he nonetheless retains the sword, the scars, and the awareness of his ancestry.

Years after the abandoned Viking boy's adoption, when he is a grown man, his village is attacked and his family destroyed by a new Viking expedition. Ghost warns a nearby tribe of the danger, showing them how technologically superior the enemy is by using his metal sword against their wooden weapons. The film thereafter incorporates many plot elements from *Ofelaš*, including killing a bear, the romance between Ghost and the Pathfinder's daughter, the spiritual teaching of the Pathfinder who dies, the escape of the tribe to a different location, the return of some of the men who die fighting, a rope-bound cliff-walk, and death-by-avalanche.

Nonetheless, it is hard to see this story as a narrative of a people's survival. Rather, it appears to be a prequel to the eventual fate of Native American tribes on the East Coast, and a suggestion that, if it hadn't been for Ghost crossing racial lines back then, conquest would have happened a lot earlier. For all the tribe's charm and spiritual wisdom, the film implies that these people really needed someone tougher to take over their dirty work for them. Moreover, Ghost's adopted identity is ultimately tenuous. He may be Native American in language, religion, and clothing, but these overlay his essential outsider identity and alien way of thought. Unlike Aigin, who is adopted fully into his new village, we see Ghost standing alone at the end of the film, albeit with his family near. "He had found his path of two peoples," the character of Starfire tells us in a voice-over. "He was neither, yet he was both."

In fact, Ghost's representation as an outsider reflects Nispel's personal circumstances. In the Director's Commentary to the film, he acknowledges his own identification with the character, as a German living in the United States. Moreover, Nispel reveals that the decision to make Starfire, and not Ghost, the tribe's new Pathfinder, was also personally motivated. His African American wife and father-in-law, Nispel suggested, would not have approved of a "honkey" running the tribe at the end (Director's Commentary).

Other narrative differences between the films are more reflective of the difference in their focuses. In *Ofelaš*, the bull reindeer represents spiritual wisdom and the survival skills of the Sami. In *Pathfinder*, the reindeer is replaced by a white horse, the signal the Vikings have arrived. The symbolic animal in *Pathfinder*, therefore, no longer represents the people, but the enemy. Indeed, as most reviewers agreed, more visual and textual attention is paid to the Vikings in the film, and Ghost's similarity to them, than to the people he is striving to save.

Another difference between the films is gender roles. The character of Starfire, the

Pathfinder's daughter, was the invention of Kalogridis, who thereby created not only a strong female character for the film but also a love interest for Ghost (Director's Commentary). Starfire's role is far more active than Sahve's was in *Ofelaš*. She fights alongside Ghost, is taken captive by the Vikings, and, at the end of the film, as already noted, it is she, not Ghost, who becomes the tribe's new Pathfinder. Nonetheless, it is Ghost, and his struggle against his demons, both inner and outer, who is at the heart of the film.

Like *Ofelaš*, *Pathfinder* uses language as a means of forging audience identification, but, unlike the Norwegian film, the language spoken by the indigenous population is unsubtitled English, highlighting the Native American characters as those with whom we are meant to identify. In the graphic novel version of *Pathfinder*, created in partnership with the film and published in 2006, Native Americans and Vikings alike "speak" English. A film's necessarily different standards of "realism" demanded the Vikings not sound just like the Native Americans, so they speak Icelandic. Only Ghost, who is bilingual, understands both the words we hear and the words we read on the screen. Language, like weaponry, represents blood inheritance. Ghost's blood makes him suspect to the tribe, in danger of reverting to his original ethnic identity. "Blood runs true," one tribal member suggests when he is first adopted. "He will turn into a monster like his fathers." Later in the film, when Ghost echoes this belief, telling Starfire, "They are beasts, not men.... It is in their blood. They live and die by the sword," Starfire understandably responds, "Is it in your blood?" Ghost's unwillingness to speak Icelandic reveals his own anxiety concerning the conflation of his language and his identity. The lead Viking makes the association between language and race obvious, gloating that he'd known Ghost must be able to speak "like a human being." When Ghost announces at the end of the film, "I know who I am," he speaks English — all the more noticeable for his previous speech, in Icelandic, denying kinship with the Vikings.

These are subtleties of characterization that might have been developed in such a way as to give Ghost's inner conflicts greater depth. However, Nispel's construction of character throughout the film was more visual than verbal. It is his self-admitted tendency to think of his characters as action figures. "I don't care about the Oscars," he writes, "I dream of plastic action figures with extendable lightsabers, model kits, and comic books...."[6] He describes his collaborative process with graphic artist Christopher Shy:

> As his artwork stacked up, it was clear what had to happen — we needed to fill in the blanks and I needed to fulfill my lifelong dream of putting together a graphic novel. This is Christopher's interpretation of our movie, and the movie is our interpretation of his artwork.... It was an extraordinarily inspirational situation — telling a story on paper and celluloid at the same time [Foreword 4].

However, Nispel's inspiration by images created by an artist steeped in the conventions of a comic book–like genre may have aggravated the film's problematic audience reception.

At one point, it is clear, Nispel made the conscious decision that authenticity was not his goal in the making of *Pathfinder*. Relaying a conversation with his script supervisor, he reveals he had initially hoped to begin and end the film with a scene in which a group of archeologists discovered a Viking sword, attracted by the idea that the premise of the film was grounded in reality. However, after his script supervisor suggested that bookending the fantasy film he was constructing with scenes of reality would cheapen both, he was convinced not to. Interestingly, in terms of what one genre can do that another cannot, the graphic novel version *does* begin in the present, with an archaeological discovery of a Viking sword.

From the start, the film, *as a film*, faced challenges which a graphic novel can largely elide. Once again, as in *Ofelaš*, the impact of living human beings playing the characters cannot be underestimated. Although the film is often monochromatic, the actor playing Ghost is and visibly remains Caucasian. Accordingly, the character's final declaration of self-knowledge is accepted as a denial of his racial identity, but does not erase it. In contrast, in the graphic novel, the colors of Ghost's, the Vikings', and the Native Americans' skins are all absorbed into an overall color scheme. Characters, regardless of race, appear blue and orange, their bodies blending into the cool tones of the forest, or radiating the ruddy heat of war. Ghost's visual difference from the members of the tribe is far less distinctive and, at times, forgettable. Accordingly, the question of with which group Ghost will identify is more about him as an

Ghost (Karl Urban) taunts the Vikings with the head of one of their compatriots in Marcus Nisepl's 2007 film *The Pathfinder* (editor's collection).

individual than as a member of a race, situated in his mind rather than in his body. There's no more suspense about the outcome than in the film, of course. The demonic characterization of the Vikings is also present in the graphic novel, but their two-dimensional characterization is an expectation of that genre. Moreover, the graphic novel version is self-identified as a "legend," to be passed on, like the folktale, from one generation to another, reinforcing our sense of its dreamlike quality of remembrance and our tolerance for a low level of realism. As the Pathfinder describes his role, "The People of the Dawn have always had a Pathfinder. He tells the tales that hold within them the heart of the People. He does not show you his path, but how to find your own" (84).

Graphic novels, like comic books, present a "soft reality." Robert Weiner, analyzing the way in which readers of comic books experience sequential narratives, suggests that "dreams, tales, stories, thoughts, and concepts are part of the real of ideas ... comic characters share this level of reality" (465). Conflict is the narrative's raison d'être, and action exists largely for its own sake. Whatever moral or philosophical position characters take is presented as a commentary on the action, rather than the motivation or meaning behind it. When sequential fiction is transformed into film, however, an audience's willing suspension of disbelief relies upon different visual and textual cues, and, as previously mentioned, it watches more analytically, particularly in evaluating the effectiveness of symbol and subtext. Virgil

Grillo and Bruce Kawin, in their study of the effect of subtitles on viewer experience in films, have noted that "sound film ... marshals all of the interpretive processes that we use in dealing with the roughly comparable experience of the real world," while "our most profound experience of a silent film"—and, by analogy sequential fiction—"begins nonverbally," and is related to the experience of dreaming (30–31). Films, therefore, for all their surface similarities to illustrated narratives, offer radically different experiences to their audiences, and require different directorial strategies to convince readers to suspend their disbelief (Becker 443–444). Peter DeBrudge's review of the film *Pathfinder*, in *Variety*, reflects how Nispel

> stacks every frame with layers of movement and texture from extreme foreground to deep, distant background. Yet the pic has difficulty carrying a thought from one shot to the next. Individual shots pack a strong emotional punch, but entire scenes ... unfold with numb, disorienting confusion.... Characters are exaggerated cartoons, hardly human at all [68].

Yet this critical commentary overlooks the fact that Nispel never intended to create a realistic film, but, rather, a graphic novel *on* film. In fact, once his desire to create a filmic graphic novel is recognized, by tapping into the two-dimensional, "soft" reality and narrative structures of sequential fiction, it is possible to see the flaws the audience perceived in his film as reflections of the conventions, even the strengths, of the graphic novel. Were *Pathfinder* not being judged, at least in part, by the same standards as, and in implicit comparison to, *Ofelaš*, we might perceive it differently. Not unproblematically, but not carrying the burdens of association with realism, or with a film of critical acclaim.

Adaptations from one genre or media to another have been done successfully many times, but they cannot succeed without an awareness of the challenges involved in taking a story from one form and embedding it in another. In this regard, Gaup, who consciously and extensively changed a folktale in order to re-embody it as a film, was critically praised and gave his audiences a sense of "authenticity." Nispel, who strove to be faithful to the vision of a graphic novel and recreate it on the screen, was not as successful. This difference in outcome may underline the message of the original folktale: when embarking on a challenging journey, it helps to know where you are going.

Notes

1. "Folklore, Boundaries and Audience in *The Pathfinder*," in *Sami Folkloristics,* ed. Juha Pentikäinen (Turku, Finland: Nordic Network of Folklore, 2000), p. 263.
2. "Background Notes," *Pathfinder* (International Film Exchange, Ltd., 2007), p. 8.
3. Juha Pentikäinen, in her Preface to *Sami Folkloristics,* notes that the Lapps are nowadays called *Sami,* "the ethnonym used by the people about themselves" (7).
4. There are multiple spellings of both Sami and Tchude. In the interest of consistency, I have chosen to use only one variant of each, unless quoting from another text.
5. "Director's Commentary," *Pathfinder,* Twentieth Century–Fox, 2007.
6. Laeta Kalogridis and Christopher Shy, "Foreword," *Pathfinder: An American Saga,* (Milwaukie, OR: Dark Horse Books, 2006).

Works Cited

Becker, Richard. "The Crisis of Confidence in Comic Adaptations: Why Comics Are So Rarely Faithfully Adapted to the Big Screen." *International Journal of Comic Art* 11 (April 2009): 436–456.
Cardullo, Bert. "Rites of Passage." *The Hudson Review* 44 (Spring 1991): 96–104.
Dargis, Manohla. Review of *Pathfinder. New York Times* 13 April 2007: E17.
DeBruge, Peter. Review of *Pathfinder. Variety* 13 April 2007: 68.

DuBois, Thomas A. "Folklore, Boundaries and Audience in *The Pathfinder*." In *Sami Folkloristics*. Ed. Juha Pentikäinen. Turku, Finland: Nordic Network of Folklore, 2000.

Gaup, Mikkel, dir. *Pathfinder*. International Film Exchange, Ltd./Carolco FilmInternational, 1987.

Grillo, Virgil, and Bruce Kawin. "Reading at the Movies: Subtitles, Silence, and the Structure of the Brain." *Postscript: Essays in Film and the Humanities* 1 (Fall 1981): 25–32.

International Film Exchange, Ltd. "Presents a Film by Nils Gaup, *Pathfinder*." 1987.

Kalogridis, Laeta, and Christopher Shy. *Pathfinder: An American Saga*. Milwaukie, OR: Dark Horse Books, 2006.

Lüthi, Max. *The European Folktale: Form and Nature*. Trans. John D. Niles. Philadelphia: The Institute for the Study of Human Issues, Inc., 1982.

Moore, Roger. "'Pathfinder' Follows Bloody Trail." *Pittsburgh Post-Gazette* 13 April 2007: E3.

Nispel, Marcus. Preface. In *Pathfinder: An American Saga*. Eds. Laeta Kalogridis and Christopher Shy. Milwaukie, OR: Dark Horse Books, 2006.

Nispel, Marcus, dir. *Pathfinder*. Twentieth Century–Fox, 2007.

Ordoña, Michael. "This is Sparta ... oh, wait, no it's not; There's gore galore and not much of a story in 'Pathfinder,' as native North Americans fend off some nasty Vikings." *Los Angeles Times* 13 April 2007: E12.

Weiner, Robert. "Sequential Art and Reality: Yes, Virginia, There Is a Spider-Man." *International Journal of Comic Art* 11 (April 2009): 457–477.

Who's Savage Now?!—
The Vikings in North America

KEVIN J. HARTY

The so-called *Vinland Sagas*—*The Saga of the Greenlanders* and *Eirik the Red's Saga*—offer at times overlapping, at times conflicting accounts of Viking explorers who set out from Greenland and went west landing at various spots in what is now North America some 500 years before Columbus "discovered" the Americas.[1] Principal among the explorers was Leif Eiriksson—dubbed "the Lucky" because of his rescue on one of his voyages west of compatriots earlier stranded on their own voyage to the to-them New World. These sagas also recount peaceful and less than peaceful encounters—the former for trade; the latter resulting in death for members of both parties—between the Vikings and the indigenous people—whom the Vikings dismissively called "Skrælings" (variously translated as "churls," "course fellows," or "weaklings" [Jones 92–93, note 16])—and the presence among the Vikings of Celtic slaves, who were first sent out as runners to assess the safety of landing in these new found regions.

The exact locations of the Viking landings—the sagas specifically mention landings by the Vikings at sites they named Helluland, Markland, and Vinland[2]—continue to be a matter of some debate, although Vinland is now generally identified with L'Anse aux Meadows on the northwestern tip of present-day Newfoundland, where ruins of a camp used by Vikings to weather the harsh winters of the region were discovered in the 1960s by Norwegian archaeologists Helge and Anne Stine Ingstad. While Viking settlements would flourish with varying degrees of success in Greenland for several hundred years from the late tenth century on, no evidence of similar long-term settlements has been found in Atlantic Canada or New England. Among the reasons offered for the lack of such settlements have been the harshness of the climate, the difficulties of maintaining supply lines from Iceland and Greenland to settlements further west, and the hostility of the native peoples, probably Paleo-eskimo people known as the Dorset, who were ancestors of the Innu of Labrador, the Beothuk of Newfoundland, and a number of Algonquian- and Iroquoian-speaking peoples living south and west of the mouth of the Saint Lawrence.[3]

While in the pages of history, Leif Eiriksson[4] came to the North American shores in 999 or 1000 C.E., he would first come to those shores on the silver screen in 1928, when MGM released its last silent film—in color no less—*The Viking*, directed by R. William Neill.[5] Neill's film would be the first of a series of films that would take decidedly different views about the encounters between Viking and Skræling. These films face a unique problem in constructing "the other." First they need to establish just who "the other" is. In the stan-

dard Viking film, the Viking is easily stereotyped as aggressive beserker — the savage, uncivilized other bent on marauding, pillaging, burning, raping, kidnapping, and killing.

In the standard Western, the Native American is just as easily stereotyped as savage —
often collectively referred to as "those or them Injun Savages"— the uncivilized other bent
upon scalping white men and kidnapping white women and children, whether their home-
lands be the great Plains or present-day upstate New York, New England, or Atlantic Canada.
Even worse, since "the only good Indian" was often "a dead Indian," tribal differences were
regularly blurred if not erased in films, and even ethnic distinctions between Native American
Indian peoples and the Innu and other first peoples of the north all but disappear.

> From the beginning Europeans have perceived Native Americans according to their own politi-
> cal and economic needs. Around the year 1000 Vikings from Greenland and Iceland met Native
> Americans in "Vinland" and described them as a "small and treacherous-looking"— and killed
> them. Five hundred years later Columbus found them gentle and physically strong — and
> helped enslave them. New England Puritans saw them as devil-worshippers or even children of
> Satan — and massacred them with the help of divine providence. Throughout Native Ameri-
> can–white history, as Francis Hennings put it, the myth of "an Indian menace" was "the
> boomerang effect of the European Menace to the Indians."
>
> At the same time, those people in Europe who were economically and emotionally less
> directly involved tended to idealize Native American life, ... and French Romanticism turned
> them into Noble Savages, these positive stereotypes being used to criticize the corruption of
> European society....
>
> Out of the French and British colonial wars, fought with Native allies, developed the first
> American literary genre, the captivity narrative. This soon developed into fictional gothic tales
> and frontier romances [Buscombe, ed., *The BFI Companion to the Western* 155].

On film, then, when Viking encounters Native American, the issue of whom the filmmaker
wants us to think of as other becomes, therefore, decidedly more complicated.[6]

Though one of the last silent films made, Neill's *The Viking* was released accompanied
by a soundtrack that included not only appropriately heroic Nordic sounding music, but
also voices singing, laughing, screaming in terror, and generally giving audible testimony
to the mayhem that goes on in any number of the film's scenes — and in Viking films in
general. The film's scenario is very loosely based on a 1902 novel, *The Thrall of Leif the
Lucky, a Story of Viking Days* by Otilla Adelina Liljencrantz.[7]

The film opens, as might be expected, with a series of intertitles, the most interesting
of which announces that the Vikings "were men of might, who laughed in the teeth of the
tempest, and leaped into battle with a song"— some of which song we hear on the soundtrack. The film then cuts from a scene of a typical Viking dragon ship plying unidentified
waters toward, we soon learn, the castle of Alwin, Earl of Northumbria. Alwin (Leroy
Mason) has just returned from the hunt and joins his mother and her ladies in waiting, one
of whom kneels to the side at a *prie-dieu* before a large crucifix praying that they might all
be delivered from "the sword and the chains of the Vikings,"[8] with whose savage reputation
the film assumes moviegoers will already be more than familiar.

As if on cue, the camera cuts to a shot of a Viking hiding in a tree who dispatches a
cross-bow toting Northumbrian coastal sentry with an arrow let loose from a long bow, as
his fellow Vikings murder a monk and defile the sacred manuscript that he is reading. Soon
enough the Vikings have overrun all of Northumbria and taken the castle, all the while
marauding, pillaging, and killing — and dragging back to Norway any survivors, including
Alwin, as slaves.

The tension within the film is then early and definitely established between pagan

Viking and Christian Northumbrian (or Anglo-Saxon), though curiously so. The raiders are clearly pagan, and the camp to which they take Alwin and the other slaves — one is inexplicably a Greek woman — resembles something out of Edgar Allan Poe more than it does anything medieval or Scandic — there are dwarfs, giants, and monkeys, and an emphasis on the grotesque and the macabre. But the camera's next cut is to the court of King (later Saint) Olaf of Norway, and the intertitles tell us that the monarch has been busily converting his subjects to Christianity. Indeed, King Olaf (Roy Stewart) later sends Leif Ericsson (Donald Crisp) off to discover a new world to the west of Greenland by bestowing his own crucifix on him.

But Neill's *The Viking* is primarily a love story involving what turns out to be a quadrangle rather than the typical love triangle: Leif, Egil the Black who is his master of sail (Harry Lewis Woods), Alwin, and Helga Nilsson (Pauline Starke), a now-grown woman who was orphaned as a child but reared under Leif's guardianship. Helga is equal parts Brunhilde, Calamity Jane, and stereotypical damsel in distress. Indeed, her costume changes throughout the film are frequent and radical, and she only appears in a dress when she is actually vamping or in distress, resorting to the stereotype of her being a member of the coquettish weaker sex when it is convenient for her to do so to advance the plot.

When we first meet Helga, she has just ridden in at the head of a troop of men, but falls from her horse and sprains her right arm. Never flinching as the sprain is set with a splint, she soon enough notices the dark-eyed and -tressed Alwin, who she is warned by

Donald Crisp as Leif Ericsson (center) in R. William Neill's 1928 film *The Viking* (British Film Institute).

the slave overseer has "the temper of a black devil." Helga buys Alwin, and this purchase sets in motion what is initially a love triangle involving Egil, Alwin, and herself. When Leif joins their company, affairs of the heart only become decidedly more complicated.

Leif respects Alwin for his bravery, and when Egil and Alwin duel, Alwin wins but spares Egil's life because, he says, the master of sail loves Helga. Soon enough Leif is off to Greenland for supplies in preparation for his voyage even further west. The film's religious tension or binary comes into play again though, since Greenland is ruled by Leif's father, Eric the Red (Anders Randolph), who takes great joy in killing Christians. In one scene, we see Eric handily dispatch a Viking Christian convert by throwing an axe through the convert's skull, and Eric seems intent upon wiping out any traces of Christianity in Greenland. When a disaffected slave jealous that he has been replaced by Alwin as Leif's principal servant tells Eric of his son's conversion, insurrection breaks out in Greenland, just as Eric is preparing to announce the betrothal of Leif and Helga. Leif loots his father's granaries, and sets sail for the western lands, as Helga, disguised as a man with an elaborate beard and the standard horned helmet that is wrongly the *de rigueur* headgear of choice in Viking films, stows away aboard Leif's ship.[9]

Those Vikings whom the original intertitles announced "laughed in the teeth of the tempest" soon enough prove cowardly as they sail further west fearful that they will be swallowed by great sea monsters or that they will fall off of an earth they are convinced is flat. Further fueling their uneasiness is their belief that Leif's embrace of the Christian God— the camera keeps cutting to a crucifix dangling over the doorway to the ship's hold and Leif's cabin—further dooms them.

Gender issues soon enough rear their head as well. Leif quickly makes it clear that he wants Alwin at his side, since, unlike the other Viking slaves, he is intelligent, brave, good at fighting, and loyal. When the two retire to Leif's cabin below deck to study the sailing charts and maps that Leif has brought with them, their moment of homo-social binding is spied through an open window by Helga, who returns moments later having shed her chain mail and horned helmet for a revealing dress and flattering hair veil. But any thoughts of bonding, homosocial or otherwise, quickly evaporate as Egil leads a mutiny only to be mortally wounded by Alwin who saves Leif's life in the process. Egil dies proclaiming that he did everything he did out of love for Helga.

Land is soon sighted, and Leif comes ashore planting a huge crucifix on the beach as he kneels in prayer to thank God—a scene more suggestive of a landing by one of the Spanish conquistadors in the Caribbean or in Central or South America than of one inspired by an episode in one of the sagas. At the same time, Leif has reconciled himself to the fact that Helga only loves Alwin, and blesses their marriage.

Then somewhat unexpectedly, an intertitle tells us that, as was Viking custom, Leif builds a great stone tower. The next scene shows the completed tower as Helga, still in her wedding dress, and her fellow Vikings exchange goods with a group of American natives sporting Mohawk hairstyles, whom Leif has converted to Christianity. Leif says that the tower and the crucifixes that the Mohawks now wear around their necks are symbols of the continuing peace between their two peoples.

Leif sets sail to return to Greenland, but leaves behind a small group of Vikings led by Helga and Alwin. The film's final intertitle tells us that no one knows what happened to this little Viking colony, but that the tower still stands today in Newport, Rhode Island. As the final shot of a Viking ship at sea slowly fades, "The Star Spangled Banner" can inexplicably be heard softly playing in the background.[10]

Leaving aside the seemingly gratuitous patriotic melodic ending of the film, the politics of Neill's *The Viking* are then mainly religious rather than cultural, with a dash of gender politics thrown in for good measure, though these latter issues are resolved in a fairly traditional way once Helga finally sheds her armor and helmet for a dress and veil. Native Americans make only one brief, docile appearance, and they have already been converted to Christianity. The film's plot is at best convoluted — the novel on which it is based is episodic and ends with the conversion of Eric and all the Greenlanders to Christianity, not with the conversion of the Native Americans and the building of the tower. The other here is then the Christian, and in the end the Christian triumphs over the pagan in both the film and in the novel, though in different ways — the final scene in the film depicting peaceful Native Americans intermingling with Vikings is at best a coda.

On screen, Vikings would not return to North American shores for almost another forty years. Beginning roughly in 1958 and continuing for at least a decade, the Italian film industry worked overtime to churn out "sword-and-sandal" epics set in (pseudo-) ancient and medieval worlds, in which often-overly muscled or ruggedly handsome heroes defeated an array of real and imaginary foes, sometimes moving peripatetically across recognizable historical divides to fight enemies medieval and ancient. Several of these film epics involved Vikings, most notably Mario Caiano's 1964 *Vengeance of the Vikings*, which took its cast of characters from the shores of Scandinavia to those of Vinland and back in search of a land where they could truly be free.[11]

Vengeance of the Vikings, originally released in Italy under the title *Erik il vichingo* (*Erik the Viking*), does indeed bring Vikings to the New World — although, since the film was shot in large part on Catalina Island, the flora and the fauna (lush jungle undergrowth, pineapple and palm trees, cacti, and an array of succulents), not to mention some of the indigenous birds and animals (flamingoes, pelicans, and an assortment of monkeys), are more times than not jarringly out of place in Northern Atlantic coastal Vinland. The film opens in 965 C.E. in Norway where the death of good King Thorvald leaves his treacherous son, Eylof (Erno Crisa), and noble nephew, Erik (Giuliano Gemma), as potential heirs to the throne. Thorvald's death had been preceded by a stock Viking raid elsewhere in Scandinavia involving rape, pillage, and murder in which Eylof proved cowardly and Erik valiant.

Erik willing pledges fealty to his cousin since he is intent upon sailing westward to find a new land where men can live free from fear and hatred. Erik specifically objects to Danish efforts to impose their ways and gods on the Vikings — the film's potential Cold War agenda at times comes heavily into play when Erik delivers several speeches about the hoped for freedom promised by the lands to the west and denied by the, albeit Scandinavian, lands in the east. Erik and his fellow Vikings are under the dictatorial rule of the King of Denmark who demands exorbitant percentages (50 percent) of tribute from and tax on any booty that Eric and his countrymen manage to accumulate, promising the harshest punishments will be doled out if they don't comply with his edicts.

Erik and the Vikings soon land in the new world — attempts by Eylof's spies to murder Erik having been thwarted by a Greek emissary, Angheropoulos (Aldo Bufi Landi), who has joined Erik's crew, and who later conveniently knows how to turn the fruits of the vines of Vinland into wine.[12] Just as there are good and bad Vikings in the film, so too there is a division among the Native peoples whom they encounter. Erik defends a Native American princess, Wa-ta-wa (Elisa Montés), saving her when she is attacked by a less-than-convincing-looking bear, and she soon enough falls head over heels in love with her blond savior. Potential language barriers in the film are easily overcome by having the Native

Americans speak a kind of infantilized pidgin English — a fairly standard cinematic way of stereotyping Native Americans (and other aboriginal or native peoples) as inferior to those who are, we are led to believe, clearly their European betters. Wa-ta-wa's favorite catch phrase becomes "me kissee," which she utters in both the declarative and the interrogative moods, and which she imploringly repeats incessantly to Erik every time that they meet.

But Viking films need conflict — in this case both in the old and in the new worlds — so Wa-ta-wa is, of course, betrothed to a member of another tribe, Winga (the actor playing the role is uncredited), whose jealousy of Erik leads to the formation of a group of "bad" Indians who are soon in league with the "bad" Vikings led by Bjarnik (Gordon Mitchell), Eyolf's agent, to eliminate Erik as a rival for Wa-ta-wa's affections — and Eyolf's throne — in exchange for gold from Winga. Winga and his co-conspirators attack as Wa-ta-wa is about to marry Erik. Incredibly, she is dressed in plumage from head to toe and carried aloft on a throne that seems more Polynesian than anything else; male Native costumes are equally out of place since all the Native men wear the hairpipe bead vests popular among Plains Indians in the nineteenth century, and used as a form of wampum in trade.[13] Attention to historical detail is not a hallmark of this film; earlier, the ambassadors of the Danish king, Christian the Brave, appeared in full armor more appropriate for twelfth or thirteenth century knights. Further, when Winga and his men briefly capture Erik, they tie him to a contraption made of pulleys and slowly lower him toward a fire around which they ritualistically dance while emitting war cries that are reminiscent of the stereotypical behavior found among Plains Indians in the movie Western.

At the wedding ceremony, Wa-ta-wa is killed by an arrow shot by Bjarnik and intended for Erik, dying in his arms while uttering her catch phrase "me kissee"— they are a pair of star-crossed lovers from beginning to end. The bad Vikings driven by greed are soon enough crushed in a cave which collapses on them as they try to pry out the veins of gold that the walls and ceilings of the cave contain. A saddened Erik returns home —

> Our voyage was useless and costly. We were betrayed here in the new land. Before our coming, these people were pure. We have been a bad influence, all of us. My dreams were too unrealistic. We'll never come back. Pray that our offspring are worthier men than we when they follow in our footsteps someday to find freedom here.

— settles his score with Eylof who dies as cowardly as he lived, marries a Viking princess, together with whom he ascends the throne promising that the land of the Vikings will be a bulwark for freedom in the north of Europe — the director twice again nodding less than subtly in the direction of contemporary Cold War realities. Caiano's film then wants to have it both ways in its construction of the other. There are both good and bad Vikings and good and bad Native Americans — the former further delineated because they are by and large blonde and blue eyed, while their bad Viking counterparts are not. And nicely, in a world engaged in a Cold War, the film has its heroes unflinchingly embrace democratic rather than autocratic ideals of government.

There is no question about who the savages are in Charles Pierce's 1978 film *The Norseman,* which brings Lee Majors as the Viking Prince Thorvald to the shores of North America — in *The Saga of the Greenlanders* Leif Eiriksson's brother, Thorvald, undertook his own voyage to Vinland in 1001 C.E. (9–12) — in search of his lost father, King Eurich, who along with the other members of his expedition came to the new world several years earlier, but who have since all vanished. Playing second fiddle to Majors is Cornel Wilde as Ragnar, who in a film notable for its outlandish costumes — the reviewer for *Variety* thought that the Viking cast looked "like 10th Century Hell's Angels" (2) — sports a horned helmet made from what appears to be the skull of a buffalo with an abundance of fur still intact. Majors himself wears a golden face masque *cum* helmet similar to that worn by Robert Addie's Mordred in John Boorman's *Excalibur*. With one exception, the Native Americans in *The Norseman* are clearly deceptive, brutal savages.

That exception is Susie Coelho's stock beautiful Indian maiden Winetta (film Vikings encounter any number of film Native Americans with names beginning with the letter *W*). Winetta betrays her people when she falls in love with the handsome Viking invader played by Majors. From Winetta, Thorvald learns that, under the ruse of having a celebration of the peaceful coexistence between the Native Iroquois and their European guests, the Iroquois chief, Kiwonga (Jacob Jerry Daniels), first drugged King Eurich and his men, and then blinded them. Ever since, he has imprisoned his Viking captives in an underground cave, where he has been forcing them to slave away running an underground corn grinding mill.

The Native Americans always seem in a bloodthirsty frenzy, egged on by an unnamed crazed woman shaman (Kathleen Freeman), who has a counterpart earlier in the film in the Viking Death Dreamer (Jack Elam) — and both actors really ham it up in their every on-screen appearance. But the Native Americans' costumes, their war paint, their dances, their war cries and whoops are all lifted from those of the stereotypical demonized Plains Indians of the Hollywood western. In typical Hollywood fashion, those responsible for the film, which was shot largely using Carolina locales (see the review in *Film Bulletin* Reviews G), chose to see one stereotyped savage Indian as good (or bad) as another — indeed Paul Taylor's review of the film labeled *The Norseman* as a "primitive, would–B Western" (49). In the end, the helpful Winetta must, of course, be killed, the Natives are for all practical purposes exterminated, and the Vikings sail home in victory having rescued their blind comrades. Eurich is restored to his throne, Thorvald will succeed him, and Thorvald's teenaged brother, young Eric (the director's son, Charles Pierce, Jr. — the only blonde, blued-eyed member in the film's cast), who has been in tow all along, has learned important lessons about his Viking heritage and about what it means to be a true Viking. Indeed, the conceit of the film's plot is that it is in reality a saga written by young Eric and handed down from generation to generation. Nobility is, in *The Norseman* and in young Eric's saga, clearly a European trait; savagery, a hallmark of the new world, home to an other whose lifestyle is clearly antithetical to that of the civilized Vikings from northern Europe.

The films discussed so far have made no attempt to reflect with any accuracy or authenticity real historical events or even the saga traditions, choosing instead to present cinematic narratives comprised of tropes easily found in any number of other films not related to the Vikings in general or to their visit to Vinland in particular. Easily more historically accurate is Pamela Berger's 1994 independent, low-budget film *Kilian's Chronicle*,[14] which recounts in English and Passamoquoddy the adventures of an Irish slave, the title character, who finds himself marooned when he jumps a Viking ship in the new world. Unlike her predecessor Viking filmmakers, Berger, who is a professor of medieval studies at Boston College, has done her homework.

The film's plot is based on multiple incidents recorded in a number of sagas, and Berger consulted Native American and linguistic experts and texts, including Roger Williams' 1643 *A Key into the Language of America*, to get things as "right" as possible in her film. The painstaking attention to detail that Berger and company paid to the saga traditions is spelled out in a booklet that accompanies the version of the film released on DVD.[15]

As Berger indicates in the booklet, *Kilian's Chronicle* was initially inspired by two inci-

Lee Majors as Thorvald and Susie Coelho as Winetta in Charles B. Pierce's 1978 film *The Norseman* (editor's collection).

dents recorded in the Vinland sagas, a battle between the Vikings and the Skrælings, in which the native peoples briefly held the upper hand —

> After that they [the Vikings] saw a large group of native boats approach from the south, as thick as a steady stream. They were waving poles counter-sunwise now and all of them were shrieking loudly. The men took up their red shields and went towards them. They met and began fighting. A hard barrage rained down and the natives also had catapults. Karlsefni and Snorri then saw the natives lift up on poles a large round object, about the size of a sheep's gut and black in colour, which came flying up on the land and made a threatening noise when it landed. It struck great fear into Karlsefni and his men, who decided their best course was to flee up river [*Eirik the Red's Saga* 45–46].

—and the presence on the Viking ship of two Celtic slaves (identified as Scots)—

> When Leif had served King Olaf Tryggvason and was told by him to convert Greenland to Christianity, the king had given him two Scots, a man named Haki and a woman called Kekya. The king told him to call upon them whenever he needed someone with speed, as they were fleeter of foot than any deer. Leif and Eirik had sent them to accompany Karlsefni.
>
> After sailing the length of Furdustrandir, they put the two Scots ashore and told them to run southwards to explore the country and return before three days' time had elapsed.... After three days had passed the two returned to the shore, one of them with grapes in hand and the other with self-sown wheat [*Eirik the Red's Saga* 41–42].

The resistance of the Skrælings and the presence of Europeans other than Vikings on the ship become the main plot points of Berger's film, which thus can present the encounter between the old and new worlds through the eyes of two very different kinds of Europeans as well as through those of the native peoples.

Kilian (Christopher Johnson) comes to the new world with his sister, also a slave, but she is killed almost immediately in the film by the Vikings when the two slaves attempt to escape once the Vikings land on the shores of North America. The new world into which Kilian escapes is at first idyllic if not almost Edenic, as Kilian is befriended and befriends a young Native American boy named Kitchi (Jonah Ming Lee) and eventually falls in love with his sister, Turtle (Eva Kim). But reality intrudes when a subsequent trading exchange between the generally peaceful Micmac—a branch of the Algonquian nation—the name *Algonquian* meaning "the People of the Other Shore"—who live in harmony with their surroundings and the Vikings goes horribly wrong because of a mutual misunderstanding about what is being traded for what—a misunderstanding recorded in the sagas (see *Eirik the Red's Saga* 45–47). In later battles in the film between the Micmac and other native tribes and between the Micmac and the Vikings, Kilian helps the Micmac, but the battles take their toll, and Kilian is once again left to his own devices as he prepares to set sail in hopes of returning to his native Ireland.

In Berger's film, Vikings are either mildly accommodating and begrudgingly adaptable to the new world in the hopes of trading with the native peoples or wide-eyed and berserk; indeed, when one of their number, Ivar (Robert McDonough), is wounded by a porcupine, he cauterizes his wound, and is then advised to eat some nearby mushrooms, which unknown to him have hallucinogenic properties. Soon enough Ivar turns into a Viking wildman, who spends the rest of the film intent upon killing Kilian and as many native people as he can. Unfortunately, the native people, almost hippie like in their passivity—Monder remarks on their "orderly, quasi-socialist utopia" (178–179)—seem doomed from the start, though Ivar does meet a fitting end, and Kilian abandons any desire to return home and decides to marry Turtle and live with her among the Micmac.

The Vikings in *Kilian's Chronicle* represent the other both to the title character, since they have enslaved him and his sister, and to the native peoples. As Berger points out in the booklet accompanying the DVD version of the film, Kilian's ability to read and to navigate using the "magic stone" as a directional instrument added to his value as a slave, just as his sister's beauty added immensely to hers. The film lays blame not at the feet of all Europeans for the first unsuccessful encounter between the old and the new worlds. It imagines instead an alternate accommodation between both worlds united against a common foe, a Viking culture whose standard response to any encounter is violent. Such accommodation is, as I say, imagined. The sagas do speak of the two Celtic slaves who accompanied the Vikings on their voyages to the North American shores but provides no further details about them. An earlier presence by the Irish on the shores of the American mainland before the Vikings is occasionally hinted at by historians and other scholars (see Fitzhugh and Ward, eds. 143), and Vikings do encounter two Irish monks living peacefully in the new world in Tony Stone's problematic 2007 film *Severed Ways*, which is discussed below.[16]

Marcus Nispel's *Pathfinder* pits even more peaceful Native Americans against even more-threatening marauding Vikings. A remake of Nils Gaup's 1987 film of the same name — though more accurately a total reworking with only a minimal connection to its predecessor — the later film decidedly suffers in comparison to the original.[17] Gaup's film has as its source a twelfth-century Sami folktale, "The Pathfinder and the Torch" (text in DuBois). It has the distinction of being the only film ever made in Sami nominated for an Academy Award, and the actors playing Sami parts were members of a Sami theatre group from Kautokeino, high above the Arctic Circle. The parts of their enemies, the Tchudes, were played by Icelandic and Norwegian actors.

According to the folk traditions from which the tale comes, the peaceful and docile nomadic Sami were often set upon by murderous bands of Tchudes (ethnic Rus descended from Vikings who sailed East and established settlements in present-day Russia), who killed for the pleasure of killing, and who would spare one member of a tribe as long as he led them to another tribe whose members they would then slaughter. This person was the so-called "pathfinder," a Judas-goat among his own people foolishly tricked into believing that his life would then be spared by the Tchudes.

Gaup's film recounts the adventures of sixteen-year-old Aigin, who having witnessed the slaughter of all the members of his tribe seemingly agrees to become the pathfinder for the Tchudes. Aigin, having in a dream been instructed by a Sami noiadi, or shaman, how to channel his thirst for revenge against the Tchudes into a powerful way to defeat them, tricks the Tcudes who fall to their death off a cliff when they think Aigin is leading them to yet another tribe of Sami. Nominated for an Academy Award for best foreign picture, Gaup's film celebrates the peaceful culture of the Sami and presents a startlingly beautiful travelogue of the lands that the nomadic Sami still inhabit today.

While Laeta Kalogridis claims to have based his screenplay for the 2007 film on Gaup's, the two films have little in common other than a title and a vaguely similar story arc. The later film's plot is not derived from a twelfth-century Sami folktale, but rather from a 2006 graphic novel called *The Pathfinder* with text by Kalogridis and illustrations by Christopher Shy. The film opening titles announce that, 600 years before Columbus, Europeans set foot on North American soil — the film, the titles further announce, will tell why they subsequently disappeared from the new world, and from the pages of history.

The opening scene of the 2007 film finds a lone Wampanoag woman (Michelle Thrush) stumbling upon a beached, wrecked Viking dragon ship of gigantic proportions. In the film, everything Viking, including the invaders themselves, is oversized, dwarfing everything Native American. Inside the ship, she finds dandling from chains any number of corpses, presumably of slaves who drowned when the dragon ship ran aground and broke up on the rocky shore, and a small boy of ten (Burkely Duffield) with blonde hair, a ripped jerkin, and lash marks on his back. We are clearly not in Newfoundland or elsewhere in Atlantic Canada, but rather somewhere in New England — though the film was shot in British Columbia. After some discussion, the boy, named Ghost in the credits, is adopted by the tribe and reared as one of their own.

Flash forward two decades, and a fresh crop of invaders arrives in the new world bent on obliterating the Native inhabitants for the pure joy of killing. Speaking Old Norse, they are clearly Vikings, but costume designer Renée April seems to have envisioned Vikings as a cross between Conan and the inhabitants of Mordor. Clad in chain mail and armor from head to toe, the Vikings are fairly indistinguishable from each other, except by the elaborate horned and tusked headgear that they wear. Indeed, more than one critic of the film saw *The Pathfinder* as *Conan, the Barbarian* meets *Apocalypto* meets *300*—other critics linked the film to the long-running television series *Xena*, to *Lord of the Rings*, and to *X-Men*, especially the character of Wolverine, and noted the director's previous efforts helming the 2003 remake of *The Texas Chainsaw Massacre*. Indeed, Nispel's Vikings are armed with everything but chainsaws.[18]

The Wampanoag are naively pacifist, and when they do finally rally against the Vikings, they further doom themselves by miscalculation after miscalculation. They are armed with wooden spears and flint arrows facing an enemy covered in chain mail and armed with swords, spears, maces, and shields — characters who seem to have stepped straight out of an *Alien vs. Predator* sequel. The Vikings here are clearly more than other — they are non-human. If the Native Americans are too good to be true, or almost patronizingly naïvely child-like, the Vikings are just plain "bad"!

The 2007 *Pathfinder* manages to lose the charm and clear cut ethos of its predecessor. The remake is little more than an exercise in testosterone gone wild. Here the title character is a shaman (Russell Means), not a Judas goat, and he instructs the adult Ghost (Karl Urban) how to defeat the invading Vikings who want to force Ghost to lead them to another tribe of Wampanoag, first by crossing a lake of ice where a fair number of the heavily-armor-clad Vikings drown when the ice gives way underneath them — the nod here is to both *Alexander Nevsky* and Bruckheimer's *King Arthur*. The remaining Vikings follow Ghost along a narrow avalanche-prone ledge where, after a series of near misadventures, they all fall to their deaths.

As in the original Sami legend, Ghost has convinced the Vikings to tie themselves together using ropes, so that they will not fall off the ledge. When one of their number does slip and fall, the others eventually fall after him. Ghost is united with the now dead shaman's daughter, Starfire (Moon Bloodgood), who in a nice touch of gender equity becomes the new pathfinder and marries Ghost, who we are told continued to live between two worlds. In a number of flashbacks in the film, we also learn that Ghost is the son of the leader of the original Viking raid and that he refused to behead a Wampanoag infant when he was ordered to do so by his father. Lashed and disowned by his father as a coward, Ghost was abandoned in the wrecked ship for acting un–Viking-like. In *Pathfinder*, to be Viking is to be destructive other, and while Ghost bridges the worlds of the Wampanoag and the Vikings, his mixed past makes him ineligible to inherit the title of pathfinder as shaman.

The 2009 *Severed Ways: The Norse Discovery of America* written and directed by, and starring, Tony Stone is almost without dialogue — substituting a deafening heavy-metal soundtrack with music ranging from the likes of Brian Eno to Judas Priest for all but a minimal number of verbal exchanges throughout most of the film. Stone's approach proves a blessing in disguise when one of the few lines of dialogue is one Viking's comment to another in Old Norse that "we're toast if we stay here." These two Vikings (Fiore Tedesco as Volnard and Stone as Orn), stranded they know not where in the new world, are, unlike their counterparts in the 2007 *Pathfinder*, not overly-testosteroned berserkers; they are simply uncouth boors, especially the blonde Orn. For no particular reason, Volnard and Orn brutally murder two Irish monks whom they stumble upon praying in a chapel — the presence of the monks in the new world is never explained. They murder native people at will, and Orn, whom we see ripping the heads off live chickens in a hunger-induced frenzy, earlier proves in a purely gratuitous instance of boorish behavior that it is not only bears who defecate in the woods. The film, if nothing else, points to one possible explanation of the failure of the real Vikings to establish permanent settlements in North America — their penchant for mindlessly killing everyone whom they encountered.

The film is set in 1007, and opens with a group of Vikings arriving on the shores of the Newfoundland in search of the fabled Vinland — in other words, after Leif Ericsson's voyages, when, according to the sagas, the Icelander Thorfinn Karlsefni, actually made such a voyage (see *The Saga of the Greenlanders* 15–17, 20–21; and *Eirik the Red's Saga* 38–50). As the film's Vikings await the return of two of their own number — not of two slaves — whom they have sent out to reconnoiter the territory, they are attacked by Skrælings and flee, leaving their fellow Viking scouts behind. The director's basic premise — to examine how other encounters other when ways (in any number of meanings of the term) are severed — could have led to an interesting film, but *Severed Ways* is at best a cinematic hodge-podge in terms of style, plot, characterization, and production. To be fair, *Severed Ways* is at times beautiful to look at — a travelogue of rural Vermont and Newfoundland where it was filmed — and Stone does seem at times to have

> loftier ambitions.... [And t]hough there's no doubt that ... Stone is as serious as a heart attack when it comes to creating an air of authenticity — hence the sloppily butchered chickens and authorial defecation — he never settles on a coherent tone for the movie. The idioms, excrement and heavy metal flourishes certainly goose up the gritty realism, but they also undermine the movie's moments of grandeur.... In one scene ... Stone manages to invoke Werner Herzog; in the next his characters are running around like costumed geeks at a comic book convention [Dargis C11].

And, in the end, the portrayals of both Viking and Native American suffer.

Viking films of all stripes are no strangers to violence — Christian Vikings have their skulls cloven in half by an ax in *The Viking*; Tony Curtis loses a hand, Kirk Douglas an eye in *The Vikings*; the title character in *The Viking Queen* is lashed to within an inch of her life by a Roman centurion; and there are all those overly-testosteroned berserkers in the 2007 *Pathfinder*. But violence reaches new levels in the most recent Viking film, Nicolas Winding Refn's 2009 *Valhalla Rising*.

The film opens in Scotland where highland clans keep Vikings tethered by chains or leashes in cages like animals and wager against them as they fight one another. The undefeated champion in these brutal and bloody fights to the death is simply known as One-Eye (Mads Mikkelsen), whose moniker is given to him by a young boy, Are (Maarten Stevenson), because he has lost an eye in one of his fights. One-Eye manages to escape from and then brutally kill his captors, at times by disemboweling them, and any number of other Scots. With Are at his side, he joins up with a troupe of Vikings intent upon going to the Holy Land on Crusade — though whether for reasons of faith or of personal gain is not always clear. Their leader is, however, clearly a deranged religious fanatic.

Setting sail for the east, the troupe soon find themselves lost in a dense fog and land on the shores of North America in what has to be one of cinema's most monumental wrong turns. In fighting among members of the troupe soon reduces their number, as One-Eye dispatches the rest of them, seemingly leaving Are and One-Eye marooned in the New World. They are, however, soon surrounded by Native Americans who club One-Eye to death — the dominant color throughout the film, red, becomes the only color in the last scene. A clearly bewildered Are stands on the shore all alone as the final credits roll. The film falls into five parts, each labeled by an intertitle — the fifth part appropriately labeled "Hell"[19] — might serve as a subtitle for the entire film. Refn has commented that he wanted to make "a mental science fiction movie" in which he could create his own myth (Huber 79). The Crusaders are bent on killing for Christ, an activity fraught with inherent contradictions; with One Eye in tow, they enter a Kurtz-like kind of heart of darkness from which only Are escapes.

In encounters between the old world and the new, whom a film chooses to demonize can tell us a great deal. This discussion of Viking films set in some version of the new world shows a decided lack of agreement about who's savage now. These films present Vikings, good and bad, and Native Americans, equally good and bad — often in the same film. As such, they challenge doubly some preconceptions that we may have about alterity. Perhaps, depending upon how we self-identify, we may be predisposed to see the dead Indian or Viking as the only good Indian or Viking — happily, at least some films are less willing to be so cut and dry in their characterization of either (or both) of these traditionally equally demonized groups.

Notes

1. The sagas were first written down in the early thirteenth century, some two hundred years after the events they recount. For the texts of the two sagas, see the translations by Keneva Kunz.

2. See the maps in Kunz's translation 63–64.

3. Of necessity, I have, in this brief paragraph, summarized, condensed, and even glossed over considerable anthropological, archeological, and historical materials, discussions, and disagreements about the activities of the Vikings in North America in the late tenth and early eleventh centuries. For fuller details, see, for a start, the essays in Fitzhugh and Ward, eds., *Vikings, The North Atlantic Sagas*; Jones, *The Norse Atlantic Saga*; Seaver, *The Last Vikings*; and Wiesner and others, *Discovering the Global Past, Volume 1: To 1650*, 3d ed., chap. 6.

4. The spellings of Viking names differ depending upon the text or film consulted. The texts of the sagas in translations use *Eirik the Red* and *Leif Eiriksson*. Films use a number of variations on these and other Viking names, and my practice throughout this essay is to use spellings peculiar to individual texts or films as I discuss them.

5. While the film still holds up today on most levels, it was a commercial failure, despite the previous box office successes and marquee appeal of a number of the principals members of the cast — most notably Donald Crisp as Leif and Pauline Starke as Helga — when it was released, in part because it was one of the last silent films and in part for the curious reason that Herbert T. Kalmus — one-time president of the Technicolor Motion Picture Corporation — alleges: film audiences in the late 1920s disapproved of bearded and mustached heroes (573). Published reviews, however, were generally favorable. See, for instance, *Bioscope* 3 July 1929: 43; *Film Spectator* 6 (17 November 1928): 7; *Harrison's Reports* 15 December 1928: 199; *Kinematograph Weekly* 4 July 1929: 65; and *New York Times* 29 November 1928: 32. *Variety* (5 December 1928): 12 was, however, more critical, also complaining about "too much whiskering."

6. The treatment — often ethnically and racially stereotyped — of Native Americans in film is beyond the scope of this essay, but it is clearly not a topic that has escaped extensive critical scrutiny. Again, the scholarship is complicated and voluminous, but for a start, see Buscombe, ed., *The BFI Companion to the Western*; Buscombe and Pearson, eds., *Back in the Saddle Again*; Kitses, *Horizons West*; Kitses and Rickman, eds., *The Western Reader*; Saunders, *The Western Genre*; Tuska, *The American Wild West in Film*; Walker, ed., *Westerns*.

7. Prints of the film are, alas, almost impossible to find. The plot is fully synopsized in print, accompanying or embedded in early reviews of the film, but with often conflicting details. See also Klepper 44–45. Happily, a version on VHS was briefly available, and it is on this version that the following discussion is based.

8. The prayer recalls that of Anglo-Saxon and Celtic monks in the eighth and ninth centuries, which they included in their litanies: "Save us, O Lord, from the fury of the Northmen."

9. On the fictive horned Viking helmets that seem so ubiquitous in literature, film and art, see Frank 199–208.

10. The structure still stands today in Touro Park at Bellevue Avenue and Mill Street in Newport, and the debate over its origins and history continues. In guides books to Newport and Rhode Island—see for instance the current American Automobile Association (AAA) *Tour Book for Connecticut, Massachusetts, and Rhode Island*—it is variously referred to as "a mill," "a windmill" (at times associated with Governor Benedict Arnold), and a tower—Viking or otherwise in origin. The earliest agreed upon date for the tower is currently the mid–17th century. The association with the Vikings was enhanced by Henry Wadsworth Longfellow's 19th-century poem "The Skeleton in Armor," about two tragic Viking lovers.

See also the excerpts from Manuel Luciano DaSilva's *Portuguese Pilgrims and Dighton Rock* at *http://www.redwoodlibrary.org/tower/hilgrims.htm (accessed* 13 August 2009) for a claim of a third, Portuguese, association with the origins of the structure.

The library of the Newport Historical Society holds boxes of materials related to the structure, which were last cataloged in a 1997 essay accompanied by multiple photographs by Hattendorf (98–111).

11. On Italian "sword and sandal" film efforts in general, see Luciano, *With Fire and Sword,* and Smith, *Epic Films.* On such films with (pseudo-) medieval settings, see Harty, *The Reel Middle Ages.* For details about other Viking films in the genre, see the concluding filmography to this collection of essays. Everyone involved in these films used a variety of pseudonyms and stage names, so the cast of stars and directors is actually smaller than it may seem, but their production output was truly voluminous.

12. Inexplicably, there had also been a Greek captive among the Viking slaves in Neill's *The Viking.*

13. See *http://twoelk2.tripod.com/BattleDressWeb/hpipinfo.htm* (accessed 23 March 2010).

14. For the original theatrical release, the film's title was spelled *Kilian's Chronicle*; the version of the film released on DVD spells the title *Killian's Chronicle.*

15. The unpaginated booklet—entitled *Killian's Chronicle, the Magic Stone*—contains two essays by Berger—"A Note on the Origin of *Killian's Chronicle: The Magic Stone*" and "Documenting the Sources for *Killian's Chronicle: The Magic Stone*"—as well as "A Recollection" by the film's executive producer, Barbara Hartwell Poirier. The booklet is also available electronically at http://www.bc.edu/school/cas/finearts/faculty/arthistory/berger_02.html.

16. Stories of westward voyages by the Irish St. Brendan, recorded in manuscripts as early as the tenth century though doubtless older, offer the teasing possibility of Irish monks sailing to a number of places including North America, perhaps as early as the sixth century. See Selmer's edition of the *Navigatio Sancti Brendani* xxi–xxii and 105, and Short and Merrilees's introduction to the Anglo-Norman poetic version of Brendan's travels (1–6). Irish hermits do seem to have settled on the Faroes prior to the arrival of the Vikings. See Richards 97–99.

17. For a more detailed comparison of the two films, see Roberta Davidson's essay earlier in this volume.

18. For representative reviews of the film, see the filmography below, pp. 203–04.

19. The six parts or chapters of the film are entitled "Wrath," "Silent Warrior," "Men of God," "The Holy Land," "Hell," and "The Sacrifice."

Works Cited

Buscombe, Edward, ed. *The BFI Companion to the Western.* 2d ed. London: Andre Deutsch/BFI Publications, 1993.

_____, and Roberta E. Pearson, eds. *Back in the Saddle Again: New Essays on the Western.* London: BFI, 1998.

Dargis, Manohla. Review of *Severed Ways. New York Times* 13 March 2009: C11.

DuBois, Thomas A. "Folklore, Boundaries and Audience in *The Pathfinder.*" In Juha Pentikäinen. *Sami Folkloristics.* Turku, Finland: Nordic Network of Folklore, 2000.

Fitzhugh, William W., and Elisabeth I. Ward, eds. *Vikings, The North Atlantic Saga.* Washington: Smithsonian Institution Press, 2000.

Frank, Roberta. "The Invention of the Viking Horned Helmet." In *International Scandinavian and Medieval Studies in Memory of Gerd Wolfgang Weber.* Ed. Michael Dallapiazza et al. Trieste: Edizioni Parnaso, 2000.

Harty, Kevin J. *The Reel Middle Ages: American, Western and Eastern European, Middle Eastern and Asian Films about Medieval Europe.* 1999; rpt. Jefferson, NC: McFarland, 2006.

Hattendorf, Ingrid M. "History and Mystery of the Old Stone Mill." *Newport History, The Bulletin of the Newport Historical Society* 68.2 (1997): 98–111.

Huber, Christoph. Review of *Valhalla Rising. Sight and Sound* 20 (April 2010): 79.

Jones, Gwyn. *The Norse Atlantic Saga.* 2d ed. Oxford: Oxford University Press, 1986.

Kalmus, H[erbert] T. "Technicolor Adventures in Cinemaland." *Journal of the Society of Motion Picture Engineers* 30 (December 1938): 564–85.

Kalogrdis, Laeta, and Christopher Shy. *Pathfinder: An American Saga*. Milwaukie, OR: Dark Horse Books, 2006.

Kilian's Chronicle, The Magic Stone. Cambridge, MA: Lara Productions, n.d.

Kitses, Jim. *Horizons West: Directing the Western from John Ford to Clint Eastwood*. London: BFI, 2004.

_____, and Gregg Rickman, eds. *The Western Reader*. New York: Limelight Editions, 1998.

Klepper, Robert K. *Silent Films on Video*. Jefferson, NC: McFarland, 1996.

Liljencrantz, Otilla Adelina. *The Thrall of Leif the Lucky, a Story of Viking Days*. Chicago: A. C. McClure, 1902.

Longfellow, Henry Wadsworth. *The Skeleton in Armor (Illustrated by Paul Kennedy)*. Englewood Cliffs, NJ: Prentice-Hall, 1963.

Luciano, Patrick. *With Fire and Sword, Italian Spectacles on American Screens 1958–1968*. Metuchen, NJ: Scarecrow, 1994.

Monder, Eric. "Kilian's Chronicle." In *The Motion Picture Guide: 1996 Annual (The Films of 1995)*. Ed. Jacob Levich. New York: CineBooks, 1996.

Review of *The Northman*. *Film Bulletin* October-November 1978: Reviews G.

Review of *The Northman*. *Variety* 5 July 1978: 2.

Richards, Julian D. *The Vikings: A Very Short Introduction*. Oxford: Oxford University Press, 2005.

Saunders, John. *The Western Genre*. London: Wallflower, 2001.

Seaver, Kirsten A. *The Last Vikings*. London Tauris, 2010.

Selmer, Carl, ed. *Navagatio Sancti Brendani Abbatus*. Dublin: Four Courts, 1989.

Short, Ian, and Brain Merrilees, eds. *The Anglo-Norman Voyage of St. Brendan*. Manchester: Manchester University Press, 1979.

Smith, Gary. *Epic Films*. Jefferson, NC: McFarland, 1991.

Taylor, Paul Review of *The Norseman*. *Monthly Film Bulletin* 46 (March 1979): 48–49.

Tuska, John. *The American West in Film: Critical Approaches to the Western*. Westport, CT: Greenwood, 1985.

The Vinland Sagas. Trans. Keneva Kunz. 1997; rpt. New York: Penguin, 2008.

Walker, Janet, ed. *Westerns: Films through History*. New York: Routledge, 2001.

Wiesner, Merry E., and others. *Discovering the Global Past, A Look at the Evidence, Volume 1: To 1650*. 3d ed. Boston: Houghton Mifflin, 2007.

Williams, Roger. *A Key into the Language of America*. Ed. John J. Teunissen and Evelyn J. Hinz. Detroit: Wayne State University Press, 1973.

Call of the Wild: Culture Shock and Viking Masculinities in *The 13th Warrior* (1999)

Elizabeth S. Sklar

As the Islamic protagonist of *The 13th Warrior* sails away from the land of the Viking Danes, where he has joined forces with his pagan hosts to defeat a terrifying enemy, he utters a prayer of thanks, invoking Allah's blessing "upon the pagan men ... who shared their food and lost their blood that Ahmed Ibn Fahalan might become a man and a useful servant to God." This prayer is a fitting conclusion to a film whose gestures — well-intentioned if sometimes naïve — towards cultural diversity and homosocial bonding set it apart from such Viking film classics as *The Vikings* (1958) and *The Long Ships* (1964).

Based on Michael Crichton's 1976 novel *Eaters of the Dead*, *The 13th Warrior* (1999, dir. John McTiernan) recounts the adventures of Ahmed Ibn Fahdlan (Antonio Banderas), a cultured, elegant, and socially well-placed Muslim poet whose impulsive dalliance with a wealthy merchant's daughter results in his banishment from Baghdad. Punitively appointed as diplomatic emissary to the fringes of civilization, Ahmed encounters a band of twelve Viking warriors led by one Buliwyf (Vladimir Kulich), en route to liberate Hrothgar (Sven Wollter), a Norse petty king, from an evil "so terrible that it must not be named," a "fire worm" that surges out of the mist and devours Hrothgar's people. Co-opted into the Viking company after an ancient, bone-savvy crone declares that they must be a party of thirteen to succeed in their mission, stipulating that the thirteenth warrior (hence the film's title) must be no Norseman, Ahmed reluctantly tags along. After a period of intercultural jostling, during the course of which Ahmed learns the language of his Norse companions and impresses them by his ability to "draw sounds," the Vikings and their alien ally gradually attain mutual respect and ultimately friendship facilitated in large part by Herger (Dennis Storhoi), who "adopts" Ahmed (affectionately referring to him as "little brother"), and serves as his mentor, schooling the poet in the tenets of Viking culture and Viking martial arts. Ahmed ultimately joins the Viking warriors in their stand against the monstrous fireworm, which, as it transpires, is a mounted host of torch-bearing, bearskin-clad, unspeakably savage primitives known as the Wendol, who dismember their victims, devour their flesh and abscond with their heads, presumably for some obscure religious purpose.[1] By the time the bloody dénouement rolls around, Ahmed, while never abandoning Islam or his Muslim identity, has become sufficiently acculturated to join the comitatus, proving a fierce and loyal warrior: in the film's terms, he has become a man.

Tribulations

Despite a lavish production budget for which estimates range from $100,000,000 to $160,000,000 with an additional $25,000 expenditure for marketing, a director whose 1988 *Die Hard* had garnered considerable acclaim, and a principal who had recently gained recognition currency from his lead role in *The Mask of Zorro* (1998) — not to mention a potentially engrossing plot, an exotic setting, manifold opportunities for action, decent performances all around, some classy cinematography, and a hunky protagonist — *13th Warrior* was neither a critical nor a box-office success. Its opening-day box-office take was only $10,694,788, and the highest take in the first month after its release was $8,477,149, a week following its debut.[2] The total losses for *Warrior* are estimated at $123,297,400 (imdb.com).

In a sense, the enterprise was doomed from the start. The lukewarm public reception may have had as much to do with the film's genre and the timing of its production and release as with any inherent weaknesses in the film itself. One need only to look at the blockbusters and award-winners for the three-year window prior to and including its release date in 1999 to understand why *Warrior* would have had little market appeal. The year 1996 saw *Fargo, The English Patient, The Birdcage,* and Branagh's *Hamlet*; in 1997 the big box-office draws included *Titanic, Good Will Hunting, L.A. Confidential,* and *The Full Monty; Saving Private Ryan, Shakespeare in Love,* and *Life Is Beautiful* hit the streets in 1998, and when it was released, *Warrior* went head-on with films like *The Sixth Sense, The Matrix, American Beauty,* and *Being John Malkovich.* Nary an adventure pic, epic or otherwise, on the horizon. Not a long-ship in sight. Clearly the time was out of joint: *The 13th Warrior,* which one critic dismissively compared to the "silly costume dramas" of the '50s and '60s (Bloom), simply did not play on the cusp of the new millennium. Indeed, it is probable that much of the film's target audience — presumably adolescent and young adult males — would not even have been born in the heyday of the Viking film, nor would they have been able to respond to the generic resonances and *hommage* upon which much of the film depends.

Also impeding the enterprise was the fact that adapting Crichton's *Eaters of the Dead* to cinematic format posed more than the usual challenges of such print-to-screen undertakings. *Eaters of the Dead* is a wickedly clever and surprisingly plausible re-telling of the *Beowulf* saga. Although the film follows Crichton's story-line fairly faithfully (*modulo* a couple of ill-judged directorial decisions), by its very generic constraints film cannot replicate one of the most crucial features of the novel: a type of verisimilitude that can be achieved only in a print text. *Eaters* is a first-person narrative based on the account of the historical Ibn Fadlan, an early tenth-century chronicler from Baghdad, whose *Risala* relates his travels as part of an embassy dispatched by the Caliph al-Muqtadir to the King of the Volga Bulgars in 921 C.E. In the course of his journey, he encounters a group of Norse traders, possibly of Swedish origin (although their ethnicity is a subject of debate), known as the Rusiyyah, or the Rus.[3] Extrapolating, perhaps, from Ibn Fadlan's description of the Northmen as "perfect physical specimens, tall as date palms, blonde and ruddy," Crichton hijacks the Rus and mischievously inserts them into the *Beowulf* master-narrative.

The first three chapters of the novel are verbatim extracts from Ibn Fadlan's text, establishing Crichton's historico/fictional traveler as the focalizer and determining the voice for the remainder of the narrative, as Crichton segues seamlessly into his own story without missing a stylistic or rhetorical beat — the entire narrative sounds as if it had been penned by Ibn Fadlan himself.[4] Verisimilitude is enhanced by Crichton's ehumerization of the clearly mythic elements of the poem — the monster Grendel is rationalized as "the Wendol," a savage tribe of cannibalistic Neanderthals, with the tribe's ancient matriarch standing in for Grendel's mother — and by his frame-narrative, a hilariously sober-sided and in his own words "extremely pedantic" parody of a scholarly introduction that so successfully fuses historical with fictive material that the University of Oslo library was besieged by requests to examine the entirely imaginary "Ahmad Tusi Manuscript," supposedly translated by one Per Frau Dolus. For some time after the publication of *Eaters*, Oslo librarians "on an annual basis had to send out letters telling enquirers that they have been the victim of a hoax" (imdb.com). As a result, Crichton was forced to add a disclaimer to the second edition of his novel ("A Factual Note" 283–291), in the course of which he revealed that the name he invented for the putative translator was his little private joke: "*frau*" and "*dolus*" are Latin synonyms for "deceit" or "trickery" (289). Parodic pedantry leaks out of the frame narrative and into the novel itself, as the bogus editor periodically and with deliberate tedium inserts himself into the narrative proper by means of occasional commentary and elaborate footnotes on stunningly marginal topics, such as a pointless retelling and analysis of "a very old Arabic joke" (188), a digression on Viking castration-anxiety that spins off the protagonist's report that "the loss of a nose they count equal to death itself, even to the loss of a piece of the fleshy tip" (206), a half-page discussion of the basilisk (164) and a discursus — complete with learned allusions to a spurious Icelandic saga, a dubious anatomy lesson, and a supercilious attack on a fictive nineteenth-century historian — on the *linea adeps*, or the "fat line" of an adversary towards which Vikings were purportedly taught to aim their spears (178–179).

All in all, *Eaters of the Dead* is a very tidy literary production. Which brings us to another difficulty in translating novel into screenplay: it is very much a *literary* production, the success of which depends not only on the skillful manipulation of voice (or rather voices) — a purely writerly strategy — but also on the reader's familiarity with Crichton's own pre-text, *Beowulf*. While it can be an entertaining read as a stand-alone narrative, *Eaters* is not about plot; the real pleasures of the novel reside in Crichton's re-versioning of his own literary source, and in the reader's gradual frisson of recognition thereof as pieces of the original narrative begin to seep into Ibn Fadlan's world, starting with transparently coded personal names from the source-text: Buliwyf, Rothgar, Herger, Rethel, Queen Weilew, Wygliff, Wulfgar, Helfdane, and the Wendol (read Grendel), among others, as well as paraphrases of portions of *Beowulf* itself. Now, in 1976, Crichton could count on a goodly number of readers who would have been exposed to *Beowulf* (or portions thereof) in high school English or college-level literary survey courses. Indeed, in his "Factual Note," Crichton ruefully confesses that his "playful version of *Beowulf* received a rather irritable reception from reviewers, as if I had desecrated a monument" (291). By 1999, this was no longer the case. Literary monuments were out of fashion, and since only a handful of the many reviewers (professional and amateur) between the film's release date and the present appear to have been aware at all that *13th Warrior* was a version of the Anglo-Saxon epic, it is reasonable to assume that the allusions to *Beowulf* would have been all but invisible to the majority of the viewing audience.

Still, had it not shot itself in the foot, *The 13th Warrior* might have proved a sleeper despite the less than propitious timing of its release and the challenges of adjusting its two pre-texts to the exigencies of cinema and the expectations of a pre-millennial audience. Unfortunately, the film's development was fraught with production problems. Accounts of the details vary, but the core narrative seems to be as follows.[5] The original version of the film was directed by John McTiernan, with a script co-written by William Wisher, Jr. and Michael Crichton. However early screenings of the original cut — at that point titled *Eaters of the Dead*— which ran for over two hours, are reported to have been disastrous: "the film was deemed unwatchable" (imdb.com). Following the failed test screenings and an apparently bitter disagreement with Crichton, McTiernan quit, and Crichton took over, stepping in as director, reshooting some scenes, adding others, and re-editing portions of the film as well.[6] Crichton also re-titled the film and fired the original composer, Graeme Revell, substituting a score by Jerry Goldsmith (a long-time Hollywood composer with some respectable credits to his name, including scores for *The Omen, Star Trek: The Motion Picture, Planet of the Apes*, and *Chinatown*). The running time was cut from 127 minutes to 103, a feat accomplished by excising some scenes altogether and severely pruning others, including the substance of two subplots, one to the point of near-incomprehensibility.[7] The end-product of this monumental flap, which delayed the film's release date by over a year,[8] was a cinematic patchwork, an astigmatic overlay of two very different directorial visions: as one reviewer opined, "*Warrior* is simply a mess" (Sanford).

Critical Reception

Although most viewers and reviewers agreed that the performances were strong across the board, critical reception of the film was not wildly enthusiastic. Roger Ebert panned it:

> To extract the story from the endless scenes of action and carnage is more effort than it's worth.... *The 13th Warrior* is another example of f/x run wild, lumbering from one expensive set-piece to the next without taking the time to tell a story that might make us care.

Similarly, McCarthy described *Warrior* as "underdeveloped and narrow in range, resulting in a tale more curious for its odd confluence of elements than for their edifying deployment.... In the end, the pic is an old-fashioned potboiler with half-baked serious intentions sprinkled about," while *New York Times* critic Stephen Holden dismissed it out of hand as "a slaughter-by-numbers swashbuckler." While responses to *Warrior* were not uniformly negative (McEwen declared it an "excellent Nordic war story," and the rare Viking film fans saw it as a welcome addition to the genre), complaints about *Warrior* were remarkably consistent. The script was deemed "skeletal," the plot confusing, the characters thinly-drawn. Jerry Goldsmith's score, when it was mentioned at all, was condemned as "insistently bombastic," and "blaring." Nor did the editorial gaucheries pass unnoticed, particularly in the case of the disappearing subplots: "[It] seems as if [the king's son] will be the warriors' other source of conflict, but after a two-man duel, he and his cronies disappear" (screenit.com). "Fahdlan's early career in Baghdad is dealt with in a perfunctory prologue, Banderas' narration obviously covering gaps created in the editing room.... There is talk of a treacherous Viking prince, but nothing happens with him" (Westhoff).

The strongest point of consensus seems to be that the film is unexpectedly flaccid, lacking in the type of dramatic tensions that could have made it an exciting, or at least a more interesting film: "McTiernan," says McCarthy, "shows no interest in maximizing the creepy tension" inherent in the plot. Viewers were surprised and disappointed that *Warrior*, unlike the typical guy-film, declines to serve up the generically anticipated hero-villain binary. Howe, among others, observes that "there's no major villain for our heroes to defeat," and more than one critic noted, quite correctly, that protagonist Banderas/Ahmed is not the hero of the piece: "[L]ead actor Antonio Banderas does not play the movie's chief heroic figure" serving as "more an observer than an instigator" (Berardinelli).[9] The battle scenes in particular were deemed "strangely devoid of tension" (Howe) and deficient in "nailbiting excitement" (Cavagna). Many experienced the final battle scene as anticlimactic: it was variously described as "perfunctory" and "oddly muted."

Complaints about the battle scenes also centered on the dark *mis-en-scène*: "It doesn't help that the eaters of the dead only attack under cover of darkness *and* mist, ensuring you spend most of [the] time squinting at the screen trying to work out who's wasting who [sic]" (Howe); or more succinctly "the fights are so chaotic and murky even the gore is a bore" (Sanford). Oddly, the battle scenes also took hits for excessive bloodshed and gross dismemberment: "much blood, much mud"; "an unrelenting celebration of blood and thunder"; "miles and miles of carnage"; "gobs of muck and mire"; "constant flow of blood and rain"; "gore is turned up to 11."

For the most part, the film is guilty as charged. With the exception of Ibn Fahdlan and, arguably, Buliwyf, the majority of the characters are so sketchily-drawn, including those who comprise what one critic dubbed "the dirty dozen" (Buliwyf's comitatus), that many of the film's credits read like the *dramatis personae* of a medieval morality play or a psychomachaea, where each character represents a single trait: "Herger (Joyous), Edgtho (Silent), Ragnar (Dour), Helfdane (Fat), Halga (Wise), Hyglak (Quarrelsome)." Strangely, most of the members of the comitatus remain anonymous throughout the film, with only Buliwyf and Herger gaining name-recognition."[10] The continuity *is* somewhat compromised by snips and emendations (the obligatory sex scene, as in most *Beowulf* films, is little more than an irrelevant passing gesture, and, as mentioned, the potential subplot of the prince seems like an afterthought); the battle scenes *are* murky and gory, and the final battle lacks the anticipated fanfare and hoopla. With the virtual elimination of the Unferth/Hrothulf figure, Wyglif, there *is* no bad guy — or at least no human bad guy — to create or enhance the film's dramatic tension. And beyond question, Banderas' Ibn Fahdlan, while clearly the protagonist, is not the hero of the piece, as heroes are generally defined, although he grows into heroism as the film progresses: this is the story of *Beowulf* after all. Ibn Fahdlan is merely the focalizer. The hero is Buliwyf.[11]

The Nature of the Beast

> "It's exciting to watch and it works as long as you aren't expecting it to be something other than what it is."
>
> Brian Webster, apolloguide.com

> "Here, at last, is a movie that is *exactly* what you expect it's going to be."
>
> Christopher Null, filmcritic.com

> "Is this an adventure film? Is it a sword and sorcery film? It's hard to tell...."
>
> Tony Toscano, Citidel Broadcasting

By far, the major source of audience discomfiture with *The 13th Warrior* is related to genre. One has a pervasive sense that one way or another, most viewers — regardless of professional status or film preferences — feel as if the film has somehow let them down, that it doesn't deliver the anticipated goods, fails to live up to its promises. The problem is that there is no consensus as to what those goods or promises might be, as viewers struggle to get a handle on the film's genre: the horizon of expectations is as murky as the mists from which the fireworm emerges. It is variously identified by reviewers as a "quasi-horror film," "a pseudo-historical adventure tale that falls squarely within the fantasy genre," an historical action film, an adventure-thriller, an action-adventure film, a "fairly standard sword and sorcery quest flick" (alternatively "sword and sorcery without the sorcery") an epic (a "swash-buckling epic," an "epic fantasy") or an epic-manqué ("a sword and anti-sorcery epic," a "wannabe-epic," "more fiasco than epic").[12] Because so few viewers recognized *Warrior* as a Viking film, they tried to shoehorn it into more familiar templates. *Braveheart, Seven Samurai,* and *The Magnificent Seven* led the pack, which also included *Excalibur, The Dirty Dozen, Conan* (or more whimsically *Conan* crossed with *Braveheart*), and even *The 7th Voyage of Sinbad.* Thus, *Warrior* is consistently judged and found wanting by what it is *not* and was never intended to be.

To be fair, this grasping at generic straws is honestly come by, in part because fidelity to the film's two pre-texts runs interference with its strict adherence to the formulas of the classic Viking flick, in part because the film couldn't make up its mind what it wanted to be when it grew up. Additionally, *Warrior* courted generic confusion with its muddled marketing strategies: the studio seems to have been as baffled on this score as the viewers. The promotional material is all over the place, emitting a barrage of mixed signals. The theatrical trailer advertised *Warrior* as an action/adventure/fantasy film, while poster tags promoted it variously as an action-adventure film ("Adventure Thriller," "Exhilarating Adventure Thriller") or as an adventure *cum* travelogue — one Italian poster promises "Un' Aventura ai Confini del Mondo" ("An Adventure to the Ends of the Earth") — and as a horror film ("Fear Reigns," or more explicitly "Fear Reigns August 13"; "Defy Fear Oct. 28"; "Prey for the Living"). The U.S. DVD cover blurb, a masterpiece of hyperbolic fudgery, may be taken as the apotheosis of this generic succotash:

> Antonio Banderas (*The Mask of Zorro*) brings huge star power to an immensely thrilling action-adventure from the hit-making director of *Die Hard* and *The Thomas Crown Affair!* ... Suspenseful and endlessly exciting, this exhilarating hit is sure to thrill anyone who enjoys action on an epic scale!

Tags include "An Ordinary Man ... An Extraordinary Journey!," "This Adventure Thriller Never Lets Up!" and "A Stunningly Effective Epic, the Best since *Braveheart*!" Action-adventure, suspense, epic, thriller, son of *Braveheart*: you name it, we have it. Polonius would have had a field day here.

Ironically, the one missing ingredient is the Viking connection. The only two instances that I've found that acknowledged this debt were film titles for the Portuguese and Czech releases, "O Último Viking" ("The Last Viking"), and "Vikingove" ("Vikings"), respectively. With few exceptions (one U.S. poster and a poster of unknown origin), the tags and poster art are all but devoid of Viking allusions or icons: indeed, with only minimal editing, one of the French promotional posters was able to take a head and upper-torso shot of Banderas, hair plastered to his forehead by rain, and give it a distinctively Napoleonic spin.

Is There a Viking in the House?

The sometimes desperate contradictions and radical miscues of both the critical reception and the promotional hype are revealing. For *The 13th Warrior* is, when we get right down to it, a generic anomaly, finding a comfortable fit with none of the standard taxonomies: it is easier to say what it is not, than to identify what it is. It is patently not a sword-and-sorcery flick, and is too historically-grounded to be considered a fantasy. If it "fails to achieve the rousing mood or narrative glory of a grand epic" (Garner), it is because it wasn't trying to do so in the first place. Despite the exotic setting, the blood, gore, and "bombastic" score, it is clearly not an epic (or what passes for an epic in film). Far from having the grandeur and sweeping scope of the Hollywood epic, *Warrior* is a deliberately claustrophobic, insular film, decking itself out in grunge, not glamour. Where adventure flicks and thrillers position a proactive central figure in an escalating series of challenges, preferably consisting in life-threatening situations from which the protagonist, through superior wit, strength, or martial skill manages to extricate himself, the protagonist of *Warrior* for much of the film is just along for the ride, more visiting anthropologist than adventurer. And while *Warrior* is richly-endowed with things that go bump in the night — and then some — it is not a horror film either: the Wendol are not, after all, supernatural presences, but merely a primitive tribe practicing an alternate religion in a particularly nasty way.

To complicate the issue still further, I would propose that *The 13th Warrior* simultaneously is and is not a Viking film. On the one hand, *Warrior* unquestionably pays homage to all the surface features of the classic Hollywood Viking film genre, dutifully marshalling the time-honored tropes and props that have become *de rigueur* since the paradigm was established by 1958's *The Vikings*; indeed, the opening scene of a dragon-prowed long ship plowing through a darkling sea sparks a distinct sense of déjà-vu.[13] *Warrior* offers up as well the obligatory gory violence of the battle scenes, the scruffy appearance, haberdashery insouciance, and questionable manners of the Odin-worshiping pagan Northmen, and a gloomy, dark-hued *mis-en-scène* backed by a musical score that vacillates between the martial and the nostalgic, all embedded in an overwhelmingly masculinist matrix. Even the oracle-crone is a Viking-film stock type. In fact, in some respects *Warrior* out–Vikings the classics: all of the major figures in *Warrior* save one are Vikings, the bulk of the film is set in the Viking homeland, and the Wendol are an exclusively Viking problem.

And yet, although this is a film very much about Vikings, it is not, strictly speaking, a "Viking" film. "This movie comes closer than any movie I have ever seen," remarked one blogger, "in depicting the Viking Norse as real people, much closer in depicting them as contemporary historians described them" (threerichs). The inherited tropes do not play out in the expected fashion. *Warrior* breaks faith with the classic Viking film paradigm and its successors by replacing its outmoded cold war assumptions, stereotypes, and clichés with something more congenial to contemporary understandings: if the genre itself is not timely, the ideologies are, or at least try to be, particularly with respect to representations of masculinity and the cultural other.

We're All Brothers

For all the disagreements about genre, critics are in complete accord about the gender-orientation of *The 13th Warrior*, the raging masculinities that define its human landscape.

Antonio Banderas as the title character, Ahmed Ibn Fahdlan, in John McTiernan's 1999 film *The 13th Warrior* (editor's collection).

This "story of he-men with broad swords and long ships" is "a macho thriller," a "testosterone-heavy epic," "action-movie man meat," "hairy-chested, testosterone-fueled filmmaking at its most bombastic," a "testosterone-laced guys' movie," aimed at a "target audience of chest-beating males." Or so the critical litany runs. And in terms of the physical presences of all the central characters save their Arabic visitor, this is true enough. Hefty, well-muscled, battle-hardy, and infinitely courageous, Buliwyf and his band of warriors care little about appearance, social refinements, or cleanliness. Bathing is scorned as a girly activity: they wash their hands and faces in a communal bowl, and use cow urine as a disinfectant. Clothed in whatever furs or rags happen to be lying about (except for the inevitably anachronistic battle gear), they are a noisy, rude, ribald, and rowdy bunch, whose drinking habits and table manners would give the frat boys of *Animal House* a run for their money. They are also quick to anger, with little regard for human life — they practice ritual human sacrifice and in one of the film's early sequences, while Ahmed recites a portion of the Koranic version of the creation to a Viking gathering, a mortal sword fight plays itself out in the background. They do not balk at risk-taking, nor do they fear death. In short, these Vikings are manly men doing manly things in a manly way.

With respect to their physical attributes and their socialization, *Warrior*'s Vikings conform plausibly enough to the film–Viking masculine paradigm, even down to the smallest genre details — evidently it is impossible for a film Viking to down a mug of beer without drenching his beard and baptizing his tunic. Where Buliwyf's warriors part company with the stereotype, however, is in their rejection of the masculine competitive imperative and in their performance of the affective component of masculinity. They are strangers, for example, to sexuality as a competitive sport, a key element in the classic Viking film (and in manly-man films in general): witness Eric and Einar (Tony Curtis and Kirk Douglas) going head-to-head over the glamorous English princess, Morgana (Janet Leigh, she of the improbably pyramidal bosoms), or Rolfe (Richard Widmark) seducing the nubile number-one-wife of his adversary, Caliph Ali-Mansuh (Sidney Poitier). In *Warrior*, womenfolk are a matter of complete indifference to the men (except as serviceable objects for the occasional momentary relief of sexual tension): the very concept of sexual posturing as a wooing maneuver is simply unavailable in their cultural lexicon.

As is competitiveness in any form. In the Viking culture of *The 13th Warrior*, masculinity is not about competition, but about teamwork and bonding. The homosocial masculinity of *Warrior* transcends its manly-man prototypes by envisioning a conflict-free configuration of entirely harmonious transactions amongst the men of the comitatus. Where male bonding, if it can be called that, in *The Vikings* and its successors entails competitive masculine display, usually of a physically violent variety, for which only grudging respect, not friendship, is accorded, in *Warrior* bonding is posited on mutual respect and mutual affection: the warmth of the relationship between Ahmed and Herger is exemplary of the latter. Buliwyf is clearly the leader of his band, but willingly accepts advice from his followers. None of the warriors disputes their leader's position or covets it, nor do they display envy or animosity towards each other: no mark of Cain here.

Additionally, each member is valued for the individual ability or talent he brings to the enterprise — Edgtho, for example has an infallible nose for the weather, and can always predict when the mist-monsters will appear. That is why Ibn Fahdlan, despite his foreign origins, strange appearance, and alien ways, is so readily absorbed into the company: far from feeling threatened by Ahmed's intellectual accomplishments — his ability to write and the ease with which he learns their language — the Vikings admire his facility, quickly perceiving that along with his equestrian skills and virtuosity with the scimitar, his intelligence bodes well for the collective good, and they welcome his contributions to their undertaking. These men like each other, they look after each other, quietly mourn their losses, and under stress, they operate as a single entity, a perfectly-running comitatus machine. It is *Beowulf* without the worm in the apple.

A Man Is Just a Man

Warrior's Vikings, then, refuse to act like proper film Vikings: "A few uncouth habits to the side ... the forest men behave in a remarkably rational and reasonable manner" (McCarthy). This film resists cultural stereotypes as strenuously as it rejects plug-and-play representations of masculinity:

> Devotees of such rowdy Viking epics from Hollywood's past as "The Vikings" and "The Long Ships" might take offense at what has to be the most politically correct band of Norsemen in movie history: no raping, no pillaging, complete tolerance of other races and creeds... [Arnold].

Indeed, Buliwyf and his warriors are remarkably free of ethnic prejudice and confrontational politics (this again in sharp contrast to the culture clashes — English/Viking or Viking/Arabic — that animate the prototypical Viking films). To the contrary, they appear to enjoy Ahmed's otherness.[14] There is some good-natured joshing about cultural differences — his small white horse inspires the observation that "only an Arab would bring a dog to war," and when he fashions a scimitar from a broadsword, one of the Vikings remarks, "Give a man a sword, he makes a knife." But they make no attempt to change his ways. Similarly, despite the fact that they are Odin-worshiping polytheists, they honor Ahmed's devotion to Islam: On the eve of the final Wendol attack, Herger respectfully listens to Ahmed's prayer to Allah, and their final exchange confirms their mutual religious tolerance. As Ahmed prepares to sail away, Herger calls from the shore, "In your land one god is enough, but we have need of many. I will pray to all of them for you. Do not be offended" to which Ahmed replies, "I'll be in your debt." Additionally, although pre-literate, they are fascinated by Ahmed's demonstrations of literacy and recognize the implications of his ability to write; at one point Buliwyf tries his own hand at "drawing sounds" in the sand — in Arabic — and at the moment of his death, he muses, "A man might be thought wealthy if someone were to — draw — the story of his deeds, that they might be remembered."

The Vikings' relaxed acceptance of cultural diversity is reciprocated by Ahmed Ibn Fahdlan, whose presence amongst the Northmen might, in other cinematic hands, have provided the perfect opportunity to develop a trite colonialist scenario: a cultured, educated, socially well-placed representative of an advanced civilization arrives amongst the primitives, exposes their ignorance, derides their retrograde social and religious practices, and attempts to "civilize" the savages: a sort of Muslim Yankee in King Hrothgar's Court. Quite the opposite pertains here, however. Playing the *vita contemplativa* to the Vikings' *vita activa*, Ahmed quietly observes, absorbs, and soon grows to respect and admire his host culture, using his linguistic facility to master their language; his initial dismay about their unsanitary habits and rude speech morphs into admiration for their values, which he internalizes to the point where he can reciprocate their hospitality by actively contributing to their collective mission, not only as a fighter but as a strategist: the poet discovers his inner warrior, as it were. He maintains his equanimity throughout.[15] Rather than responding defensively or confrontationally to the Vikings' ethnic jokes about his horse and his scimitar, he simply mounts displays of equestrian skill and swordsmanship, as much to represent his home culture as to impress his hosts. And like his hosts, he respects the rights of a different culture to practice a different set of religious beliefs. He retains his Islamic identity, regularly observing ritual prayer, but in appropriate situations (on the eve of the climactic battle and at the moment of Buliwyf's death), he joins in the communal invocation to Odin: "There do I see my sister and my brothers. Lo, there do I see the line of my people back to the beginning. Lo, they do call to me...." And once he has returned to his homeland, in a final gesture of respect, affection, and reciprocity towards his former comrades-in-arms, Ahmed, as per Buliwyf's final request, is seen "drawing the sounds" of his experiences amongst the Northmen.

It is worth noting that McTiernan and Crichton practice what they preach, starting with positioning a member of a currently demonized culture as the entirely *simpatico* protagonist of their film. They have assembled a multicultural cast, including a large component from Scandinavia — the film Norsemen are largely true-life Norsemen — as well as including representatives from Austria, Czechoslovakia (Buliwyf), Spain (Banderas), India, and Turkey. Aside from Banderas and a brief sequence featuring Omar Sharif, the actors are mostly unknowns to North American audiences, a transparency that works to the advantage of the film. The fact that the majority of players, including the two principals, speak accented English, enhances credibility considerably — a stark contrast to the Brooklynese of Tony Curtis, whose pretty legs far outshone his acting skills in *The Vikings*, or the flat Midwestern twang of an aging Richard Widmark in *The Long Ships*, who seemed to invoke the shade of Tommy Udo every time he opened his mouth.[16] Beyond that, the film demonstrates an unusual attention to language as a marker of cultural identity, making multiple gestures towards language variety and linguistic authenticity. Melchisidek (Omar Sharif), Ahmed's initial travel companion, establishes verbal communication with the Northerners by speaking Greek, and is answered in Latin by Ahmed's future mentor, Herger, thereby negotiating a nonce *lingua franca* between the Arabs and the Norsemen. Once Ahmed has been conscripted by the warriors, but before he has mastered their speech, the soundtrack is filled, sans subtitles, with what is apparently a potpourri of northern languages: a mélange of Danish and Norwegian, possibly with some Swedish and a little German thrown in for good measure.[17] Even the Wendol are allowed their own language.

None of the Above

The 13th Warrior is a curious production, and hardly a perfect one. Its surfaces are flawed, to be sure, and even its liberal ideologies slip from time to time into cinematic cliché. There are admittedly some retrograde masculinist moments in the film, particularly in the contempt expressed for men who do not conform to the macho paradigm: the perfumed herald who greets the warriors as they approach Hrothgar's compound is derided by one of the company as "a silk-swaddled messenger-boy," and Prince Wigliff is clearly marked as suspect by his effeminized appearance: short blonde carefully-coiffed locks, handsome (almost pretty) features, and upscale fashion choices. This reflexive queering sounds a false note, at odds with the more sophisticated representations of masculinity in the film. And it must be confessed that the gestures towards cultural diversity are somewhat compromised by the rendering of the Wendol, who, with their ritual chanting, their painted bodies, and their preservation of physical tokens from their enemies' corpses, are suspiciously reminiscent of Native Americans as imagined in movies from a bygone and less politically-correct era. Nonetheless, the film has much to offer if it is taken on its own terms.

Now, *Warrior* clearly doesn't fully fit the parameters of any available generic film templates, including, as I have argued, that of the Viking film: it doesn't rollick, it doesn't swash or buckle, it doesn't create tension-induced mangled cuticles or acid indigestion, it is non-confrontational (except when it comes to the Wendol), and the exotic locus to which it transports us is hardly Never-Never Land. But if we liberate it from the obvious paradigms and their associated generic expectations, *Warrior* comes into its own. It offers, amongst other things, a darkly utopian vision of human potential, and the "lack of tension" of which so many critics complained may in fact be the inevitable by-product of the elimination of interpersonal hostilities and intercultural conflict that are central to this vision. If we are not expecting a replica of *Braveheart* or *Excalibur* in the film's final battle sequence, we can see that despite the gruesome content, it is an effective, elegantly-choreographed slow-motion *a capella* ballet, accompanied only by the grim music of the battle-sounds themselves. Similarly, complaints about inadequate plot development and characterization may benefit from a shift of perspective: with its slender story-line, and its one-dimensional characters, *Warrior* functions like an ecumenical morality play, the very transparencies permitting the themes of fraternal bonding and communality to emerge without having recourse to overt didacticism.

From yet another angle, we may discover, embedded in the larger narrative, a coming-of-age story, which replicates with surprising fidelity the structural features and tropes not of the Viking or action-adventure film, but of the classic chivalric romance: a young, male, aristocratic protagonist, alienated from his home environment, ventures into unknown territory, where, through experiencing a series of adventures of escalating intensity, usually with the support of a mentor or a series of mentors, he confronts and transcends his personal vulnerabilities, ultimately returning to his home culture an improved individual and fully-functioning member of his society. *Warrior*, as much as anything, is the narrative of Ahmed Ibn Fahdlan's rite-of-passage, his development from poet into warrior under the good-natured tutelage of Herger, who ushers him into warrior-hood and pushes him to do his personal best. The film tracks his gradual metamorphosis from observer, to novice fighter, to fully-fledged warrior with considerable empathy and grace. His progress, as well as the phases of his acculturation, is encoded by a carefully-sequenced series of costume modifications that serve as visual markers of his internal development. Ahmed retains the garb of his home culture — a long robe and the traditional headgear, in this case a *ghutra* (silk scarf), held in place by an elegant band — from the moment of his departure from Baghdad through the first attack by the Wendol. Thereafter, however, we see him in increasingly relaxed dress, gradually shedding his outward symbols of cultural identity (and class) — first the headgear, then the robe — and ultimately donning the chainmail fitting for the seasoned warrior he has become. When he returns to his birthplace, although he resumes his native garb, he takes with him the enduring lessons he has learned during the course of his stay amongst the Northmen: the value of community, courage, commitment, and self-sacrifice.

The paradigms just adduced, of course, are literary rather than cinematic, and ancient ones at that. Whether or not viewers recognize these paradigms, however, is immaterial: these moves considerably enrich the film, and suggest what it might have been had the concept and vision of the filmmakers been less fragmented. In the end, if this is not a brilliant film, if it tries to do too many things at once and is unable to fuse them into a unitary vision, it is not a failed-potboiler or an epic-manqué either. At the very least, it bears re-watching and re-construing, warts and all.

Notes

1. In *Eaters of the Dead*, the Wendol are clearly Neanderthals. In the film, they become a more evolved, though admittedly still primitive, tribe, whose totem seems to be the bear: when they ride into battle, they don bearskins, head and all, and Ibn Fahdlan is able to deduce the location of their lair by suggesting that since the Wendol "think they're bears," they think like bears, and would take up residence accordingly.

2. That same year, *The Sixth Sense* netted $26,681,262 on its opening day; *The Matrix*, $27,788,331. Gross profits for *Sixth Sense* totaled $293,501,675; *Matrix* took in a total of $171,383,253,

3. For a brief introduction to Ibn Fadlan and a translation of his *Risala*, see *http://www.meganone.com/ nbulgaria/bulgaria/risala.htm*.

4. In his addendum to the second edition of his novel, "A Factual Note," Crichton writes: "I obtained the existing manuscript fragments and combined them, with only slight modifications, into the first three chapters of *Eaters of the Dead*. I then wrote the rest of the novel in the style of the manuscript to carry Ibn on the rest of his now-fictional journey" (*Eaters* 288).

5. My sources for this information include imdb.com and reviews by David Keyes and Wade Major.

6. One of the more dubious modifications made during the Crichton takeover was in the representation of the Wendol matriarch, Crichton's version of Grendel's mother: "In accordance with the book, John McTiernan's version of the Wendol's mother was an old woman.... When Michael Crichton took over and did the reshoots, it was decided that brutally killing off an old lady did not reflect very well on the heroes. Crichton decided after the fact to make her younger, sleeker and tougher" (imdb.com, Trivia). That it was

considered more acceptable for heroes to brutally murder a "younger, sleeker" woman raises some interesting questions.

7. Crichton's subplot concerning a character named Wiglif, a fusion of *Beowulf*'s Unferth and Hrothulf, was the chief victim of these cuts. Wiglif, son of Rothgar, is a devious, shifty-eyed fellow who is said to have murdered three of his brothers with an eye to taking over the throne once Rothgar dies. He makes an insulting speech to Buliwyf upon the latter's arrival at the king's hall (126), challenging his courage, and tries to persuade Rothgar that Buliwyf plans to murder the king and usurp his throne (163). In *Warrior*, this subplot is reduced to a one brief scene and a few quick shots of a Mordred-like character whose motives are murky at best, who has no apparent relation to the rest of the plot, and who subsequently disappears from the film as abruptly as he has appeared. He is named only once in the course of the film, in a whispered exchange considerably postdating his introduction.

8. The original release date was to have been some time during May 1998; the film did not hit the market until August 20, 1999.

9. To be fair to the puzzled viewers who could not see past the good guy/bad guy trope, the casting of Banderas was, albeit accidentally, somewhat deceptive: the only name-brand actor of the piece (aside from a bit part for Omar Sharif, who played Ahmed's travel companion, mentor, and translator in the opening chapters of the film), Banderas had the combination of dashing good looks, a strong screen presence, and a recent success as protagonist of an unabashed swashbuckler that would naturally create expectations that were at odds with his actual role.

10. We rarely even hear the names of all but a few members of the comitatus. Additionally, although in the credits the Beowulf-figure retains the name he is given in Crichton, in the film he is consistently referred to as "Bulvai." And although Ahmed's family name is represented as "Fahdlan" in the credits, it is pronounced "Fahalan" onscreen. Whether this is a deliberate move to "de–Beowulfize" the screenplay, or whether in all the directorial and editorial confusion no one noticed, is anybody's guess.

11. There is a lovely little irony in the name-form Crichton chose for his Beowulf figure. The second component of that name, *-wyf*, is the Old English word for "woman."

12. imdb.com classifies it as "Action/Thriller/Horror."

13. The ship itself is now a tourist attraction at Epcot (imdb.com, Trivia).

14. Amusingly, the only hint of snobbism, or rather classism, in the film is the visiting Vikings' reaction to their first sight of Hrothgar's hall: "No wall, no moat, not even a presentable fence ... couldn't keep a cow out of this place."

15. There's one exception here: In Ahmed's first full battle, he succumbs to a testosterone overload, becoming a veritable berserker, and continuing to strike even after the enemy has fled.

16. Tommy Udo was the name of Widmark's character in his film debut, *Kiss of Death* (1947).

17. A Norwegian blogger, attempting to sort through this Scandinavian Babel, wrote: "When it comes to the Vikings, I as a Norwegian couldn't get a complete hand on what they spoke, but took a guess it might have been some kind of Danish. However, when the King's son spoke, I could confirm that Norwegian was spoken in this movie" (Chewie-46, imdb.com). Given the mixed Scandinavian origins of cast, it seems likely that they were instructed to speak their own language, whatever it might be.

Works Cited

Anonymous. *www.screenit.com* (27 August 1999).

Arnold, William. *http://www.seattlepi.com* (27 August 1999).

Berardinelli, James. *http://www.reelviews.net* (n.m.1999).

Bloom, Bob. *Journal and Courier*, Lafayette, IN. Rev. pub. imdb.com (n.d.).

Cavagna, Carlo. *http://www.aboutfilm.com* (September 1999).

Chewie-46. *http://www.imdb.com/usercomments* (13 October 2008).

Ebert, Roger. *http://www.rogerebert.suntimes.com* (27 August 1999).

Garner, Jack. *Rochester Democrat and Chronicle*. Rev. pub. rottentomatoes.com (1 January 2000).

Holden, Stephen. *http://movies.nytimes.com* (27 August 1999).

Howe, Andrew. *http://efilmcritic.com* (24 April 2000).

Keyes, David. *http://www.cinemaphile.org*.

McCarthy, Todd. *http://www.variety.com* (27 August 1999).

McEwen, John R. *http://www.filmquipsonline.com* (n.m. 1999).

Major, Wade. *http://www.boxoffice.com* (1 August 2008).

Null, Christopher. *http://www.Filmcritic.com* (n.m. 1999).

Sanford, James. *http://www.imdb.com* (n.d.).

threerichs. *http://www.imdb.com/usercomments* (27 December 2005).

Toscano, Tony. *Citadel Broadcasting, Salt Lake Valley News & the Journals.* Rev. pub. rottentomatoes.com (1999).

Webster, Brian. *http://www.apolloguide.com* (n.d.).

Westhoff, Jeffrey. *http://www.rottentomatoes.com* (30 May 2003).

Harrying an Infinite Horizon:
The Ethics of Expansionism
in *Outlander* (2008)

DAVID W. MARSHALL

In 1975, NASA christened its two Mars missions after an image of medieval Scandinavian sailors as intrepid explorers. Since the Viking missions, those eponymous sailors have left a fairly small wake in science and science fiction, despite no loss of popularity and our increased awareness of just how far they actually sailed. The Vikings were, in fact, some of the most wide-ranging travelers of their day. Establishing trade routes and settlements, they extended their influence from Vinland to Persia. On the silver screen, their voyages have been just as extensive, ranging from Lapland to Newfoundland, from Russia to the African coast — with seemingly no space in between untouched. It is surprising, then, that Vikings have had so little exposure to the infinite horizon of space, with its countless potential planets to explore or ... pillage.[1]

Howard McCain's film *Outlander*, co-written with Dirk Blackman, moves Vikings towards space, even if it does not take them to the stars. It follows Kainan (Jim Caviezel), a space man who crashes with a monstrous alien aboard his ship into a Norwegian lake in A.D. 709. Kainan seeks out the monster — a Moorwen — and happens upon a ravaged village before encountering one of the local Vikings, who knocks him senseless and causes him to drop his laser blaster into a river. Captured by Wulfric (Jack Huston), a prince from Heorot, Kainan struggles to convince Hrothgar's people that a dragon has destroyed the village of a rival community. While Hrothgar (John Hurt) worries about the potential for retaliation growing from that rival's king, Gunnar (Ron Perlman), Wulfric bristles for just such a conflict. Kainan ultimately earns the trust of Hrothgar and his people by accompanying them on their hunt for the monster and killing the large bear they mistake for it. Later that night, Gunnar and his men attack Heorot and are repelled into the woods, where the Moorwen assaults them as they plan a subsequent raid. When Gunnar flees for the safety of Heorot, the Moorwen reveals itself, convincing them all of the real danger. To combat the Moorwen, Kainan suggests an oil-filled pit trap, which fails, though wounding it. In the ensuing action another, smaller Moorwen appears and flees with its burned mother back to nearby caves. In the conflict, Gunnar, Hrothgar, and several warriors are slain. As the people of Heorot flee to their ships, Kainan, Wulfric, and Hrothgar's daughter, Freya (Sophia Myles), salvage metal from Kainan's spaceship to forge stronger weapons. The film climaxes in a cave sequence in which Kainan, Wulfric, and three other Vikings seek out the lair of the Moorwen both to destroy the threat they pose and to save Freya, who was taken by the monster at the lake.

As this short synopsis indicates, *Outlander* is the product of a variety of genres: it is one part Sci-Fi story, one part monster movie, and one part historical epic. The meat of the script, however, adapts the story of *Beowulf,* consciously interpreting the Germanic figures of the poem as Vikings and setting them within the poem's concerns with feud. With aliens as analogs to the Grendel-kin, McCain's tale advances the Viking imagery by tapping a variety of texts and traditions that cast Vikings in two distinct roles. On the one hand, the Vikings of his movie are peaceful explorers and traders, noble in their idealism. On the other, they are fierce ravagers, slaughtering for land and power. Joining those images with the story of *Beowulf* ultimately produces a film that raises questions not just about violence, but about the ethics of expansionism, questions that the film is unable to resolve in the end.

Beowulf, Outlander, *and Feud*

As the above synopsis might suggest, *Outlander* is not an obvious adaptation of *Beowulf,* which may account for the fact that a majority of critics failed to notice it. Of more than fifteen substantive reviews, only seven made the observation, though to varying degrees. Kim Newman of *Empire* calls *Outlander* "a mutant adaptation of *Beowulf*" (par. 3) while Philip French of *The Observer* describes it as "an unfortunate meeting between *Alien* and *Beowulf*" (par. 1). Those reviews that did detect a hint of Anglo-Saxon epic in the film most often consider it to be "cribbing" or an "homage," but more often than not, Peter Jackson's *Lord of the Rings* trilogy is as likely to be noted for its influence as *Beowulf.* One significant reason for this oversight is the lack of a character named "Beowulf." Heorot in the movie features Hrothgar and includes Unferth, but no other character from the poem makes a clear appearance. Instead, the audience is presented with a self-identifying Viking community somewhere in Norway, a location not part of the poem either. Other than the monster-based structure of the film, what *Outlander* shares with its primary source is an interest in feud.

The poem *Beowulf,* even if structured around monsters or the titular hero's Danish and Geatish adventures, seems largely threaded together with stories of feud. Most notable is the story referred to as "The Finn episode" (ll. 1062–1159).[2] A poem recited after Beowulf's defeat of Grendel, it tells of the peace between Finn and Hengest that is violated a year later when Hengest seeks vengeance against Finn.[3] Yet, while this passage may be the most prominent example in the poem, the text is haunted by other references to feud. Hrothgar recalls that Beowulf's father, Ecgtheow, was brought to his hall as the result of a feud (ll. 456–72). The future strife between Hrothulf and Hrothgar's sons (ll. 1014b–19) is referenced less than 200 lines before Wealhtheow speaks positively of Hrothulf's potential guardianship of them (ll. 1180b–87). Beowulf predicts feud re-erupting between the Heathobards and Danes, despite the marriage of Hrothgar's daughter Freawaru to the Heathobard prince, Ingeld (ll. 2029b–69a). This list names only a few. The second half of the poem is littered with references to longstanding feuds between the Geats and the Swedes and Franks, feuds that lend the poem much of its gloom as the messenger to the Geats reminds them of the imminent attacks that will result from Beowulf's death (ll. 2999–3007a).

In part owing to the myriad feuds, critics have read the poem as concerned with questions of community and the violence that both preserves and threatens its security. As Nicholas Howe argues, one lesson the young Beowulf learns from Hrothgar is that conflict is inevitable among peoples because of their geographical proximity, and a strong leader is defense against them (153–56; 168). This comment echoes John M. Hill's suggestion that feud in the Anglo-Saxon cultural world worked as a sort of détente, with the threat of retribution staying aggressive impulses.[4] Running counter, perhaps, to Hill, David Day claims that the *Beowulf* poet "does not see the feud as a force for good, the sort of stabilizing social control described by Wallace-Hadrill for the Franks" (18). Feud, according to Day, is ideological; it structures the understanding of relationships between adversaries, sometimes to ironic effect. The varied explanations of feud in the poem convey the complex nature of the idea, yet these views share a sense of feud as a means of governing conflict, both the nature of its exchanges and the moral weight assigned to it. The violence used to found and perpetuate communities, Scyld's wrecking of mead benches and Hrothgar's success in battle, is opposed by the depredations inflicted by enemies and the ongoing strains of inevitable conflicts. Feud becomes the category by which violence is made comprehensible and given meaning.

For understanding *Outlander*, those terms are important, because the film uses feud as a structuring device to define the relationships among the various characters. McCain establishes this framework through expositional references that imply a backstory in which Hrothgar is a recently crowned king. His predecessor, Wulfric's father, was killed in an ongoing feud with the leader of a rival community, Gunnar. The effects of that conflict mark the continued actions of McCain's Vikings and divide them between those who embrace feud and those who reject it. Scene three begins to draw these lines when Wulfric interrupts an argument between Freya and Hrothgar to report the destruction of Gunnar's village. When Wulfric tells the king that Gunnar's village was attacked, leaving no bodies, Wulfric remarks, "It should have been us." He meets Hrothgar's alarmed "Was it?" with a long, smirking stare before denying it. The scene's establishing of Wulfric's desire for vengeance indicates that the feud ideology revolves around him within the walls of Heorot. The scene additionally lays the foundation for understanding the social dynamics among the film's Vikings by conveying the sense of obligation behind the impulse to feud. The challenging stare with which Wulfric meets Hrothgar's question conveys disapproval of what Wulfric deems cowardice. The "should" in his remark to Hrothgar implies the compulsory nature of feud, echoed by the compulsion Gunnar implies when he confronts Hrothgar in scene twelve and shouts, "Where's my wife? Where's my boy? You didn't even leave me their bodies! If it takes a thousand years, I'll carve your heart out of your rotting chest!"

The other half of this opposition gets voiced by Hrothgar and his daughter Freya, who represent a reticence to feud rooted in collective interests. The alarmed question "Was it?" with which Hrothgar replies to Wulfric's statement implies the king's fear over such a prospect, and his parting words perpetuate it. Upon commanding Wulfric to interrogate Kainan for any revealing information, he states, "If you don't it will mean war." The ominous ending to the scene bespeaks the threatening nature of feud, its potential for danger. Freya's earlier argument with her father, in hindsight, indicates the source of that fear. Freya rejects the idea of marrying Wulfric because he will be "just like his father, a tyrant and a butcher." Her description of Wulfric's father and prediction for Wulfric highlights the violence and destruction inherent in the feud ethos. *Outlander* subsequently develops Hrothgar as a king ever-cognizant of the safety of his people and Freya as an empowered woman intent on civilized values. By positioning them this way, the movie invites us early on to sympathize with their positions, effectively creating a moral rejection of the violence Wulfric embraces, and therefore a rejection of feud as a destructive system.

Having established the ideology of feud, *Outlander* uses that ideology as a structure for presenting the central conflict of the film, between Kainain and the Moorwen. As Day observes of *Beowulf*, "In the case of both the poet and his characters, describing the monsters as feuding with the human actors places their depredations within a well known model of interaction, serving both to make the monsters' depredations understandable and also to define the range of appropriate responses available to the human actors" (11). McCain's film functions similarly, though I would emphasize the way in which the feud idea structures subsequent relationships for audiences of the film. Whereas the poem *Beowulf* indicates early on the *fæhð* (feud) held by Grendel and his hatred for the sound of the harp in Heorot (ll. 86–89a), *Outlander* conceals the cause of the Moorwen's aggression until scenes sixteen and seventeen — more than half way through the movie. Instead, we see a smattering of hints and a sense of recognition by the Moorwen when it sees Kainan. When Kainan swims from his wrecked ship, for example, he drags the body of a crewman whose chest armor has been clawed open; in describing how the Moorwen came to be in Norway, Kainan tells a story of the monster stealing away on his ship and killing his crew; and when the Moorwen first attacks the people of Heorot, the camera lingers over the monster, when it stares at Kainan in recognition. The audience receives a general sense of a pre-existing conflict between Kainan and the Moorwen, but that general sense is elaborated for viewers by analogy to the feud with Gunnar. The conflict with the Moorwen emerges more fully for the audience because the terms of feud are present.

If there is a difference between Day's sense of feud in *Beowulf* and its narrative function in *Outlander*, it lies in the fact that McCain does not present a vague notion of vendetta. He displays an explicit series of wrongs against the Moorwen. Day suggests that the poet's use of the framework of feud facilitates for *himself* a comprehension of Grendel's actions. The poem mentions Grendel's hatred for the harp, but that seems an incongruous cause for mass murder. The poem seems not to reveal what grievance motivates his attacks on the hall, so feud becomes that explanation. *Outlander* conceals the Moorwen's motivation, but lays bare the origins in scene sixteen when Kainan flashes back to an attack on an alien planet. Spaceships create smoke trails in the sky over an alien landscape as a peaceful Moorwen grazes on some native species. Fire obliterates that landscape, and the film cuts to images of spaceships hunting and shooting panic-stricken Moorwens. McCain joins Robert Zemeckis (*Beowulf* 2007) and Sturla Gunnarsson (*Beowulf & Grendel* 2005) in presenting vivid cause for the attacks. In adapting *Beowulf* for the screen, McCain opens up the origins of the feud and explains what in *Beowulf* are mysterious causes.

His explanation, however, makes Kainan an odd hero. *Outlander* invites viewers to see Kainan as the hero with his isolated struggle and his flashbacks to a family killed by the last Moorwen. Yet the movie fails to realize that possibility fully, because he initiated the feud with it. The character to whom the audience attaches its sympathy is implicated in genocide, and, as a result, the audience must determine whether Kainan is heroic or not. This problem returns us to the fact that no character in the film is named "Beowulf," as if to consciously erase the obvious hero. Kainan's name, additionally, aligns him much more to the poem's explanation for Grendel's evil: he descends from the kin of Cain. Kainan, thus, is instigator of the feud and the cause of the monster, as well as its final solution. *Outlander* ultimately attempts to push through this conundrum with the two images of the Vikings that have dominated their remembrance.

A Tale of Two Vikings

Marijane Osborne has put the issue of feud in *Beowulf* into a broadly moral context by considering the poem's Christian narrative voice. According to Osborne, the various feuds dotting the text are framed by the "Great Feud, the cosmic battle between good and evil that controls the three main actions of the poem" (976) and which provides a scale by with to "estimate men's valor" (980). McCain's adaptation of the poem functions similarly, but alters the moral valence ascribed by Osborne. Whereas Howe highlights Beowulf's suitability to Christian Anglo-Saxons as a "warrior of peace rather than a killing machine," suggesting the potential benefit of feud-based violence, *Outlander* does leave space for such complex categories (174). As I have suggested, *Outlander* positions feud and its violence as bad, a destructive force that always threatens community. Those that abide by the feud ethos are therefore negative figures, potentially causing a problem for the heroism both of Wulfric and Kainan. The movie resolves this problem by recasting the poem as a story in which these two potentially heroic figures move between extreme positions. Their moral value is not a product of paralleling a Great Feud, but determined by the degree to which they resist the irrational compulsion to feud. This tension, the sense that our heroes are not entirely heroic, yields from a composite construction of the Vikings that leads us simultaneously to embrace and to condemn the values with which they are colored. The traditional depiction of Vikings as brutal pirates undergirds the emphasis on feud, while a Victorian fascination with the Vikings as precursors of civilized modern values unsettles it.

The tradition of Vikings as barbaric butchers and thieves, dates to at least A.D. 793, when, according to the Anglo-Saxon Chronicle, "the raiding of heathen men miserably devastated God's church in Lindisfarne island by looting and slaughter" (57).[5] A later, twelfth-century account in the Irish *Cogad Gaedel re Gallaib* attempts to convey the depredations of the Vikings by indicating its inability to do so adequately. A hundred steel heads with brazen tongues, it laments, "could not recount or narrate, or enumerate, or tell, what all the Ghaedhil suffered in common, both men and women, laity and clergy, old and young, noble and ignoble, of hardship, and of injury, and of oppression, in every house, from" the Viking attack.[6] The Viking age continued with many more such attacks and enough chronicle descriptions written by terrorized monks that the prayer "save us from the fury of the Northmen" began appearing in prayer books. The defining feature of the Vikings, according to these sources, is their propensity for violence as a means of advancing their own interests. The association with barbarity did not abate until the late Eighteenth Century, according to Andrew Wawn.[7] Movies have played on this idea of Vikings by depicting them as violent, drunken, sexist or some combination of those terms, all displayed in the 1958 classic *The Vikings*, with its mead-hindered tests of marital fidelity.[8]

Outlander appropriates the traditional image of the Vikings most clearly in Gunnar, whom McCain describes on the DVD commentary as "all about violence." Our introduction to him comes when he attacks Heorot in mistaken retribution for the slaughter of his people. With shots of charging forces popularized by *Braveheart*, we see the two bands clash in a fast-paced choreography of swinging swords and axes. That pacing shifts, however, when the slow-motion shots settle on Gunnar. Perlman plays him with a scowl of concentrated rage, and close-up shots reveal his shaved head, bushy beard, and tattooed face. McCain's slowed filming focuses attention on the might with which Gunnar swings two large hammers and the devastating effect they have on their victim, and the editing alternates our gaze between the two. Gunnar twirls the hammers about in tight, matching circles, then knocks the man to his knees. He swings them and the film cuts to an image of the hammers crushing the victim's skull from either side. The last shot in the sequence, another close-up, shows blood spattering Gunnar's face. The use of slow-motion aestheticizes the violence of his attack by allowing viewers to dwell on the musculature of his arms, the rage displayed in his face. The twirls of the hammers give the assault an individual flair that suggests pleasure taken in the act of vengeance. McCain's construction of Gunnar, thus, emphasizes the brutality associated with feud; it is an act driven by rage and aimed at destruction. Additionally, the "hack first, ask questions later" mentality of Gunnar's assault points to an irrationality that yields unjustified violence.

That barbarity of such violence, a significant feature of the Viking image from medieval descriptions, softened significantly in English depictions of subsequent ages. The gentler Viking emerged, according to Andrew Wawn, as a result of English national desires to separate themselves from their historical French connections. In *The Vikings and the Victorians* Wawn explains that a combination of factors drove this turn towards the North during Victoria's reign. Publication of saga translations, especially *Frithiof of Signofjord*, and their interpretation as Germanic romances by figures such as William Morris allowed the English to posit a Germanic source for their own cultural traditions, making them distinct from French sources that were being resisted by scholars of the day. That trend, coupled with the romanticizing works of Sir Walter Scott, whose *The Pirate* employed the Viking past of Orkney, initiated the imagining of a Viking identity in which the English could see the origins of their own cultural virtues. Thus, the *Thing*, or assembly meetings of Iceland (idealized in W. G. Collingwood's painting *Althing in Session*) were perceived as the origins of democracy in the North and part of England's own governmental lineage.[9] Vikings in the Victorian mind, therefore, were a noble sea-faring people ("Britannia rules the waves"), discovering other lands and bringing their civilized ideals of freedom and government with them.[10]

Outlander's Hrothgar opposes Gunnar in both the film's feud and in evincing an image of the Vikings that derives largely from the Victorian fascination with them as their own national forbearers. He is an idealizing of the mild-mannered Viking, an image of ourselves projected onto the past. While the film initially suggests Hrothgar to be a warrior — the film introduces him in a tense duel with Freya — rather than being associated with brutal carnage, as with Gunnar, McCain's Hrothgar is an even-tempered, wise ruler, traits attributed to the poem's sage old king. His bearing counters that of Gunnar in the handling of governance and conflict. For example, in a scene after the failed raid on Heorot, Gunnar lays down the plan for reengaging Wulfric. Gunnar's sole voice contrasts to Hrothgar's in scenes in which Hrothgar allows discussion among the men of Heorot. He functions as a moderator rather than a dictator. Scene fourteen concludes with a debate in which Kainan challenges Wulfric. When Hrothgar intervenes, he states to Kainan, "You're not one of us. The decision is ours; however, [turning to Wulfric] I'm still your king, and my judgment is the Outlander is correct." Rather than perpetuating conflict, Hrothgar resolves it with wisdom by acknowledging the correctness of each side before drawing the discussion to a close with his decision. His character works in a prioritized system that values the strength of community over individual interests, a fact manifested in his first appearance when he counsels a resistant Freya to marry Wulfric and serve as a restraint on his tendencies toward violence. *Outlander*'s Hrothgar, therefore, displays patient evaluation, careful planning, and slow anger. This Viking, despite his implicit self-identification as such, resembles modern sensibilities in his emphasis of diplomacy over warfare. He is a compassionate sort of Viking who defends the welfare of his people not with brutality, but with peace.[11]

With these traditional representations of Vikings behind them, Gunnar and Hrothgar function as opposing positions on a moral compass. McCain sets his two heroes, Wulfric and Kainan, between them, and, at least with Wulfric, uses them to promote an ideal of wise self-control modeled on Hrothgar.[12] Because the moral push of the film frowns upon feud and the destruction it creates, *Outlander*'s locating of heroism in that paradigm remains ambivalent. To some extent, that ambivalence is the product of McCain and Blackman's original conception of the Vikings as "like Seventh Century Hell's Angels: bad-ass and sexy and tough; just instead of choppers they were roaming the seas in their long ships."[13] McCain's idea of the Vikings taps Roberta Franks's impression of them as "terminally hip and incredibly cool," fashionable people admired as much as feared (23).[14] The hybrid of romantic cowboy outsider and counter-cultural renegade that undergirds McCain's image of bikers marks the heroes of *Outlander* with a troubled sense of their moral worth. They are figures that simultaneously strive to extricate themselves from feud while chasing to its ultimate end.

Wulfric best exemplifies the "bad-ass and sexy and tough" image of the Vikings, with Jack Huston's good looks and arrogant swagger. More like Gunnar than Hrothgar in the beginning, the film positions him as compelled towards feud by Gunnar's killing of his father, yet continually hampered by Hrothgar's efforts to stay him. Wulfric initially appears as indication that feud transcends generations in an ongoing cycle. We see it in scene three (discussed above), in which the young prince informs his king of the assault against Gunnar's village. In groping for information and strategies, Wulfric states that "it should have been" their attack, to which Hrothgar replies anxiously, "Was it?" Later in the scene, Hrothgar asks Wulfric to question the Outlander (Kainan), "or else it will mean war." The scene highlights the difference in the two men's perspectives, one the warlike disposition we will come to associate with Gunnar, the other diametrically opposed. Additionally, Hrothgar's ominous statement signals to the audience that war is an unappealing option, not to be

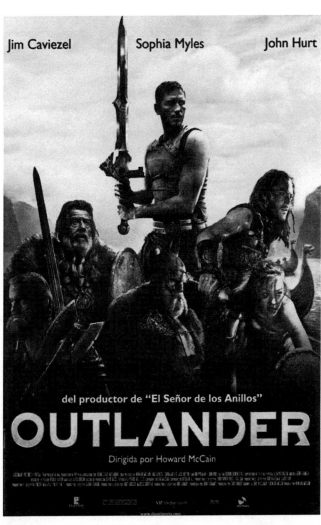

Poster for the release in Spanish of Howard McCain's 2008 film *Outlander* (editor's collection).

favored. Thus, Wulfric is not suited to the responsibilities of being king, because he thinks
more about the feud than the safety of his people. The film adds force to that opinion in
the sympathetic portrayal of Freya, who describes Wulfric as taking after his father, who
was "a tyrant and a butcher." Yet Wulfric has potential, the film suggests, since he works
towards the prevention of war by interrogating Kainan, and subsequently makes an overture
of peace to Freya.

A series of scenes, however, traces Wulfric's education by both Hrothgar and Kainan
and suggests that his vision grows beyond its initial shortsightedness and towards a more
sophisticated sense of leadership. When, in scene five, for example, Wulfric says, "My father's
dead because of Gunnar," Hrothgar retorts, "Your father's dead because he was a fool!"
Hrothgar continues, "It's not your sword that will make you king, nor shield hall; it's how
you rule your own head and heart." In scene fourteen, discussed above, after Wulfric
attempts to silence Kainan, the Outlander asserts, "You'll always be wrong, until you stop
thinking with this!" He grabs the pommel of Wulfric's sword, echoing in word and gesture
Hrothgar's advice. The king (appealing to modern sensibilities) and the Outlander (the
movie's focus) articulate a caution against Wulfric's tendencies towards violence that directs
Wulfric's development away from the barbarity of Gunnar. Together the scenes convey Wulfric's need to move beyond the feud ethos, driven as it is by egocentrism. *Outlander* presents
Wulfric as a work in progress; a future king who must grow into the wisdom voiced by
Hrothgar and confirmed by Kainan. He reaches that position after the failed attempt to
trap the Moorwen, when Kainan inquires what he will do now that he is king. Kainan
meets Wulfric's reply, "Of what?" with gestures to the remains of the village and its people.
Wulfric internalizes that responsibility and dies in the process of destroying the Moorwen
in defense of his people. The film develops the prince as a troubled young warrior torn
between desires for personal revenge and communal security, a combination the *Outlander*
suggests cannot coexist.

Kainan may be the best example of this shift from one moral position to the other,
but his development in *Outlander* recasts the narrative of the original poem. While *Beowulf*
articulates a theme of feud and violence that, as Osborne argues, valorizes the titular hero,
Kainan's story is one of troubled redemption, not moral greatness. Kainan is, no doubt, our
central hero, and *Outlander* encourages us to be sympathetic to his struggles. In addition
to our concern for him in scene one, when he discovers his crewmate is dead, the film goes
to lengths to reveal Kainan as a grief stricken husband and father when we see his memories
of his wife and child dead in the burning wreckage of their home. As a traumatized family
man, Kainan gains both audience sympathy and a patina of justification for his pursuit of
the Moorwen. Moreover, his invitation to have Freya join him in eating rather than waiting
until he is done signals his modern sensibilities and promotes an image of him as free of
primitive Viking patriarchal values. Add to all that several scenes in which he seems to begin
fostering an orphaned Viking boy, Eric, and his heroics in fighting the bear, Moorwen, and
Gunnar, and Kainan emerges as surpassing, perhaps, Beowulf himself. But the warrior with
a soft side ultimately undermines the seemingly moral structure that *Outlander* conveys in
Wulfric's growth. Despite any sense that Gunnar represents an appalling display of feud's
excessive brutality and that Hrothgar represents an admirable example of restraint in its
face, *Outlander*'s Kainan acts like a magnet on that moral compass and scrambles its sense
of direction, because the feud with the Moorwen was instigated by his participation in colonial genocide.

Science Fiction, Beowulf, and the Challenge to Expansionism

Outlander's interests in colonialism appear early in the film, when the stranded Kainan's survival computer informs him he is on "an abandoned seed colony." From that point, the film threads such concerns throughout the story. Post-Colonial encounters framed by feud are, in fact, a common theme in adaptations of *Beowulf*, especially the Sci-Fi versions — a fact not surprising, since issues of colonialism are not foreign to the original poem. Seth Lerer observes that Hrothgar himself is a sort of colonial conqueror. Highlighting the *fagne flore* on which Grendel stands in line 725, Lerer notes that *fag* refers to "patterned objects of the warrior's treasury" (77) and interprets the scene in relation to Roman mosaic floors found amidst Anglo-Saxon remains. That context sets up issues of post colonialism for Lerer, who situates Hrothgar within it. He explains, "The *pagus* on which Hrothgar builds his hall is already inhabited. There Grendel lurks — indeed, he more than lurks" (87). Lerer interprets the Danes as a colonizing force that takes over the land and makes it their own by building Heorot, an act that dispossesses the Grendel-kin, who held an earlier claim and who assert that claim in Grendel's ravages.[15] The Sci-Fi *Beowulf* adaptations reclaim the Grendel-kin in a similar fashion, though preserving the monstrosity of them to varying degrees. Each, however, uses them to trouble the noble image of the poem's virtuous characters, Beowulf and Hrothgar.

Star Trek: Voyager's "Heroes and Demons" approaches the story by self-consciously inverting the roles of *Beowulf*'s hero and villain and coating that inversion with the distinct patina of Star Trek's political correctness. In the episode, the Voyager crew sends their holographic doctor into a holodeck simulation of *Beowulf* after several crew members disappear into it. As the Doctor (Robert Picardo), who names himself Schweitzer, engages with the imaginary Danes and the luminous cloud that is their Grendel-like adversary, clues point to this inversion. First, a Dane attempts to strike the Doctor with a sword, only to have it pass through him. Second and most tellingly, in one attack by the amorphous light the Doctor is forced to flee back to Voyager's medical facilities, where he appears without one arm. These features of Grendel, transposed onto the supposed hero, indicate that the episode does not retell but rewrite the *Beowulf* story so that the actions of the Starfleet officers are implicitly called into question. Logically, if the Doctor demonstrates the qualities of Grendel (incapable of being wounded by weapons) and his penalty (the removal of an arm), then Starfleet, with the Doctor as its representative in the holographic Heorot, must be the enemy.

As the episode concludes, the audience learns that the light creature has been responding kind-for-kind in response to Voyager's collecting "photonic samples" from a nearby nebula. The capture of "photonic samples" — actually life-forms — transposes the Voyager crew as monsters that committed an act of aggression against a native being. Where the audience had understood the mead-hall/spaceship to stand in as Heorot, we learn that a peculiar light matrix a short distance from the ship was the real site of a ravaged community, since two of its inhabitants were torn away by the ship's transporters. The shiny, do-gooder personality of Starfleet proves to be flawed by its ignorance. Yet the writers do not allow that flaw to persist, instead putting into the mouth of Captain Janeway (Kate Mulgrew) a speech about unintentional harms and restored peace, a speech we might see as inspired by the real Dr. Schweitzer's philosophical treatise, *The Reverence for Life* and the pursuit of life affirming agendas it promotes. She says: "We had no idea that what we were doing, in essence, was capturing those life forms. We locked them in a containment field and began to experiment on them. If my people were taken like that, I know what my response would be. I would do whatever it takes to get them back." This short speech offers an encouraging world-view striving for mutual understanding. The show's politics, rooted as they are in Gene Rodenberry's idealism, preserves a romanticized view of the sorts of exploration that drove early colonialism by minimizing the trauma that such exploration can cause. Understanding one's mistakes remedies the trauma.

Graham Baker's abysmally bad adaptation, starring Christopher Lambert, takes a more pointed approach to conquest and domination than *Voyager*. While Lambert's Beowulf resembles Kainan, a mysterious man with a sketchy past, Baker's film does not center the back-story of violence around the hero; rather, Hrothgar (Oliver Cotton) becomes the morally suspect one. His Heorot, different from other versions, is not invaded from outside, but attacked from below and within. The first indications of this emerge in scenes of Grendel's mother slinking into Hrothgar's chambers and pleasuring herself on the sleeping leader. In the film's climactic scene, she defends Grendel's and her assaults, turning blame back onto Hrothgar. She says, "Long before the outpost was built this was my land and my home. My son has the older claim." She continues to explain that after Hrothgar had conquered the outpost he "took" her and fathered Grendel, "conceived at the height of victorious bloodshed." Revising the spatial binary of horizontal and vertically arranged rival communities observed by Franz Fanon in Algeria (38–39), the spatial relationship implicit in the source of the attacks and the above-quoted lines places the fortress on top of an earlier home. Human community and monstrous creatures share a space in this film, one layered over the other in a tumultuous relationship of bloodshed, with the feud instigated by Hrothgar himself. Baker's *Beowulf* shifts Hrothgar away from the innocent ruler or naïve explorer towards an image of colonial power rooted in violence. This *Beowulf* suggests that colonial or imperial conquest breeds resistance.

McCain follows Baker's *Beowulf* in this idea, yet *Outlander*'s flashback scenes of the Moorwen planet evoke colonization more explicitly. Subsequent to the scenes of conquest and extermination discussed above, Kainan's voice-over explains that in exchange for his service he received land. Shots of Kainan looking over a blasted landscape are replaced with images of burnt Moorwen bodies being bulldozed into a mass grave, below which is a valley now green and populated by Kainan's people. While *Voyager* plays with good intentions, *Outlander* implies guilt; whereas Baker's *Beowulf* hides the crime until the end, McCain announces a holocaust in which Kainan participated. Within the trend of post-colonial thinking, the three adaptations share the reclamation of the monsters—even if only in part—but *Outlander* alone displays the kind of transformation of the landscape that Lerer highlights. Colonial labor makes a world in the conqueror's image, as Kainan's people reshape the land to suit their own needs. As Ralph Waldo Emerson said of the British, "There is no Berserkir rage, no abandonment or ecstasy of will or intellect." He continues:

> But who would see the uncoiling of that tremendous spring, the explosion of their well-husbanded forces, must follow the swarms which pouring out now for two hundred years from the British islands, have sailed and rode and traded and planted through all climates, ... carrying the Saxon seed, with its instinct for liberty and law, for arts and for thought,—acquiring under some skies a more electric energy than the native air allows,—to the conquest of the globe [287].

Emerson's description of the Victorian spirit—the same spirit that imagined the noble, democratic Vikings—makes the civilizing mission of colonialism a living spring that brings life, the beauty of liberty, law, art, and thought, to an uncivilized space. Its survival in the "native air" is only possible because the British were capable of raising it up in such a space. Such is the obliteration of the Moorwen on its home planet, replaced by neat little grids of settler homes, akin perhaps to the "appropriation of nature for nation-building" detected by Alfred K. Siewers in the original poem in which the orderly self is set in contrast to the chaotic Other through transformation of the landscape (200).[16] But McCain acknowledges the naïve shortsightedness in this vision, with Kainan's misty-eyed recollection of obliterating the Moorwen in scene fourteen.

In another telling scene, Kainan's young son complains of having been stung by a strange alien flower growing by the bars of the backyard fence. Kainan kneels down, grasps it by the stem, causing it to reveal a luminous flower. When he blows into it, out pops a peculiar little flying lizard. The scene suggests something like an environmental version of Homi Bhabha's discussion of mimicry, which desires "a reformed, recognizable Other, *as a subject of a difference that is almost the same, but not quite*" (85). Here, the flower in the backyard presents a normalcy to the scene that conveys a reassuring sense of home and civilization, but the incubating creature inside reminds both Kainan and the audience of the plant's novelty, its difference from what we know flowers to be. That disruption seems more sinister with its foreshadowing of the "sting" the planet conceals in the final Moorwen. *Outlander*, therefore, recognizes the trauma of colonial expansion, but does not offer the reductive solution of *Voyager*'s Captain Janeway. McCain builds the thrust of his story from the action/reaction cycle of feud that, according to his film, is endemic to colonial expansion.

This troubling of the Victorian civilizing mission results from the way *Outlander* combines in Kainan the two images of the Viking that it separates in the film's Scandinavians. It does so by coloring the civilizing power of imperialism with the destructive brutality of pillage. McCain's correlating the colonizing Kainan to the Vikings produces the conflicted image. At times this connection is subtle, as with McCain's instructions to the production designers to model Kainan's spaceship (seen in numbers during the flashbacks to the conquest of the Moorwen planet) on the shape of Thor's Hammer. *Outlander* tightens the parallels explicitly, however, when, preceding the conquest flashback, Kainan tells Freya, "My people are just like yours. When we saw an island we wanted, we took it." McCain's efforts to link his hero to the Vikings suggest Kainan to be the future of the movie's Scandinavians (similar to the Victorians imagining the Vikings as their own past). The significance of that lay in how the conquest of the Moorwen planet is recontextualized within a traditional image of "going Viking," and how, as a result of that recontexualizing, Kainan's people are distinguished from the Vikings. Going viking for the norse people in the film involves bravery, might, and honor. The conquest of the Moorwen planet, in contrast, is simply might. The depersonalized destructive force of Thor's Hammer gunships removes any sense of heroism that we might associate with the Vikings. Kainan is not just a Viking, but a hyper-developed Viking in whom violence is distilled into a pure form. He and his people have so refined killing that it is sterilized slaughter, a technological Gunnar. As a result, the image of Kainan as noble warrior, Hrothgar-like in his instructive challenges to Wulfric, frays.

The only way *Outlander* can move audiences past this tension is to formulate Kainan's story as one of redemption, but that effort ignores implications laid out through the movie. We might look to Kainan's first words after having the Norse dialect implanted as the first clue that he is not initially all he seems; after an expletive, he picks up his laser, says "weapon" in his new tongue, and blasts a tree (à la James Caan in *Rollerball*). His stony glare is menacing, not noble. More significantly, when Kainan explains his people to Freya, we detect a hint of regret, but the object of that regret is unclear. Initially it seems to be sorrow over the extermination of the Moorwen, since the imagery shocks viewers in its destruction while Kainan's words offer a seemingly guilt-ridden justification of the act. He ends his story, however, with the death of his family, saying, "We thought they [the Moorwen] were all dead." His regret fails to attach clearly in the end, and the audience is left to wonder whether Kainan wishes he had not killed any of the Moorwen or had succeeded in killing the last one. That uncertainty seems to clear when, after the Moorwen attacks on Heorot, he counsels Wulfric, "Let's go kill this thing." This play back and forth between Kainan's lurking regret over genocide and his zeal for payback raises questions about his motivation: we know he seeks to defend Freya and Eric (a replacement family), but he seems equally driven by a personal vendetta, a vendetta problematic by virtue of the fact that he started the feud. Feud twists together the personal and the communal in a nihilistic struggle that, as Stanley J. Kahrl notes regarding the original poem, can only ever result in complete extinction of one side or the other (198)—and this is where the film's moral center seems to dissolve. Our admiration for Hrothgar and the sympathy we give Kainan, particularly in his attempts to stay Wulfric's violent impulses, promote a belief in peaceful resolution as the wise defense of the community. Yet the film climaxes with Kainan's defeat of the monster of Heorot, the alien Grendel-kin, and as such we are asked to rejoice at his completion of the genocide his race initiated. If redemption and a second chance are the theme of Kainan's story, they only emerge from completion of the trauma.

The challenge McCain's film struggles to overcome is the rejection of the colonial or imperial model of expansion being coupled with a valorization of a colonial soldier. One might try to read Kainan as the typical post-modern anti-hero, but *Outlander* lacks the irony that causes a figure like Sam Spade to succeed in the role. Humphrey Bogart's portrayal of Spade is marked by a nobility of character sometimes concealed by illicit maneuvering; he works towards good ends. Kainan's goals seem less clear-cut, and so his character never fully achieves the sort of noble development given to Wufric. Where Wulfric learns the burden of responsibility associated with leading a community, Kainan struggles to put the future behind himself so that he can start over in the past, and doing so requires completion of a monumentally grotesque task. Ultimately, therefore, what hinders Kainan from fully achieving the moral value of Wulfric is McCain's uncritical embracing of the genocidal imperialist—even a repentant one.

Outlander, thus, undercuts the peaceful ideal and allows Kainan to see his feud through to the end, a trajectory made inevitable by McCain and Blackman's equating the poem's Beowulf to Kainan. Use of *Beowulf* in this story, however, elevates the concerns with feud and ties it to concerns over territorial expansion and encounters with Otherness. Whereas the Viking feuds in the film (and the feuds noted in *Beowulf* above) are between like peoples, their conflicts derive from community differences. *Beowulf* extrapolates that sort of conflict by exaggerating differences into racial or even species terms. *Outlander*'s dependence on that story suggests that because the concept of feud can be used to structure understandings of conflict among peoples, it can structure understandings of expansionist politics. The destruction of Kainan's colony in the flashback sequences follows Lerer's sense that Grendel's attacks amount to a reassertion of territorial rights. Conquest creates resistance, *Outlander* demonstrates, and resistance is driven by revenge. The struggle against the colonial powers, thus, is interpreted within the context of feud, in which the tribal conflicts of *Beowulf* are transposed to the relationship between conqueror and conquered. Colonialism produces feud, the film seems to say.

Vikings are not associated with conquest, at least not in the popular imagination, and therein may lay a clue to the uncritical, morally righteous ending that McCain's sincere embracing of the tortured Techno-Viking presents. One of *Outlander*'s critics jabs, "Humanity has not yet devised more dispiriting words to flash at the start of a movie than these, found in the opening seconds of *Outlander*: 'Norway, year 709.' 'Norway, year 709'— you know, as opposed to 'Norway, year 708,' which was way before things got interesting, and 'Norway, year 710,' which was right after all the fun" (par. 1–2). The date is a confusing one for anyone familiar with the history of the Vikings, who appear in chronicles only in 793, since it locates Vikings — they call themselves such — in the pre–Viking age. *Outlander*, however, concludes with Kainan's choosing to remain among the people of Heorot as their king. If, we are led to assume, Kainan has learned of the self-perpetuating, feud-like tragedy incited by colonial conquest, then this is a band of Vikings who will refrain from such brutal action. Kainan's Vikings will be a kinder, gentler sort who will not become involved in violent rampages. Kainan's experientially-informed leadership will prevent the Viking terror of all those medieval chronicles and remove the need to pray "Save us from the fury of the Northmen."

Notes

1. Outside film, we find intrepid Astro-Vikings in a variety of media. In fiction, we find Henry Beam Piper's *Space Viking* (originally serialized in the journal *Analog* between November 1962 and February 1963) and David Drake's *Northworld* trilogy, which appropriates the Norse pantheon and its warrior ethos. The closest we come to Scandinavian spacemen in film is the animated web-toon titled *Space Vikings* (2007) or the Warner Brothers *Loonatics Unleashed* episode "Loonatics on Ice" (2005) which features techno–Vikings.

2. All references are from *Klaeber's Beowulf*, fourth edition.

3. Stefan Jurasinski argues that the idea of "bloodfeud" is an overstated one in *Beowulf* criticism, owing to a scholarly failure to read such references in light of early medieval laws.

4. John M. Hill argues in that feud was a stabilizing force in early Germanic cultures, a tool of mutual intimidation that preventing open conflict by shared fear of retaliation.

5. Quoted from the Peterborough Manuscript. *The Anglo-Saxon Chronicle*.

6. Quoted in Sawyer, "The Viking Legacy," 251.

7. Wawn's real interest is how Vikings were re-imagined after the Eighteenth Century, but he notes that images of Vikings drinking from the skulls of their victims lasted into the Victorian era. (See Wawn 21–23.) That barbarity has been a common feature in modern depictions. Perhaps at the extreme is the fantasy art of Frank Frazetta, whose Viking-inspired figures often feature horned or winged helmets, over-sized axes and swords (sometimes dripping blood), fur loincloths, and even demonic red eyes.

8. *The Pathfinder* (a remake of 1987's *Ofelaš*), which seems largely inspired by the fantasy images of painter Frank Frazetta, capitalizes on the extremes of this tradition.

9. This brief synopsis offers only the slightest overview of Wawn's thorough and wide-ranging study of the phenomenon. See Wawn 60–215 for the information distilled in this short paragraph.

10. While this image of Vikings is much more common to Victorian literature and art, we do find cinematic portrayals that invoke it in films such as *The Saga of the Viking Women and Their Voyage to the Waters of the Great Sea Serpent*, which portrays the Vikings as democratic in their decision-making and nearly pastoral in their love. The freedom of Ragnar's people in *The Vikings*, as contrasted against the tyrannical King Aella, may also owe its origins to this tradition.

11. Freya contributes to the modernizing of these Vikings. Germanic culture featured a notion of women as goads to action, such as the pregnant Freydis in the Vinland sagas, who, during a Skraeling attack, bared a breast and slapped it with a sword, sending the Skraelings running and shaming the Viking men into action. Freya, however, does not function in a behind-the-scenes way, as evinced by her dueling Hrothgar. That practice pays off for her later, when she kills one of Gunnar's men during their attack on Heorot. Later in the film, she refuses to let Kainan sideline her and asserts that she will accompany the five warriors into the caves, where McCain has her kill the young Moorwen and fight alongside Kainan in defeating the mother. Freya, thus, follows the Mia Hamm "anything you can do, I can do better" sense of woman as man's equal, confirming her place in society by her own actions rather than by association.

12. Most characters in the film slot between these poles, within an image defined by Kirk Douglas' *The Vikings* (1958). Those Vikings are pirates who harass the English coast. Their real barbarity is evinced more at home, where, in scenes set in their hall, they swill mead, letting it run down their chins before refilling their horns from a massive open-topped barrel. They test the fidelity of women by hurling axes at their braids (parodied by Terry Jones in *Eric the Viking*) and guffaw over their sexual exploits. That roughness is offset by the freedom of spirit that seems to define their lives. The hyper-masculine activity in *The Vikings* serves as the basis for subsequent Viking films, including another adaptation of *Beowulf*, that by Robert Zemeckis (2007), in which denizens of Heorot gather round a similar barrel and pursue the buxom women of that hall. *Outlander* similarly cribs from *The Vikings*, with its own massive barrel, though the lusty exploits are absent.

13. *Outlander*, DVD commentary.

14. In her salute to Carol Clover, Frank traces the way in which medieval accounts of Vikings depict them as threatening not just because of their violence, but, as declamations indicate, because the English were patterning themselves after their stylish adversaries.

15. We might extend Lerer's reading to read Grendel's depredations against the Danes as conveying anxieties of reverse colonization, along lines similar to those described by Stephen D. Arata in his discussions of Dracula. See Arata, 621–645.

16. Siewers' ecocritical approach leads him to argue that the Augustinian theology of corruption being writ in nature percolates in *Beowulf*. He claims that Heorot is the civilized spot in an chaotic waste, indicative of Anglo-Saxon identity forming in contrast to notions of the Celtic "Other."

Works Cited

The Anglo-Saxon Chronicle. Trans. and ed. Michael Swanton. London: J. M. Dent, 1996.

Arata, Stephen D. "The Occidental Tourist: 'Dracula' and the Anxiety of Reverse Colonization." *Victorian Studies* 33 (Summer 1990): 621–45.

Bhabha, Homi K. "Of Mimicry and Man: The ambivalence of Colonial Discourse." In *The Location of Culture*. New York: Routledge, 1994. 85–92.

Day, David. "Hwanan sio fæhð aras: Defining the Feud in Beowulf." *The Heroic Age* 5 (Summer/Autumn 2001). Rpt. from *Philological Quarterly* 78 (Winter 1999): 77–95.

Drake, David. *Northworld Trilogy*, Riverdale, NY: Baen Books, 1999.

Emerson, Ralph Waldo. *English Traits*. Boston: Houghton, Mifflin, 1883.

Fanon, Franz. *Wretched of the Earth*. New York: Grove Press, 1963.

Frank, Roberta. "Terminally Hip and Incredibly Cool: Carol, Vikings, and Anglo-Scandinavian England." *Representations* 100 (Fall 2007): 23–33.

French, Philip. *The Observer* (Sunday April 26, 2009). Accessed September 9, 2009 http://www.guardian.co.uk/film/2009/apr/26/outlander-film-review.

Hill, John M. *The Cultural World in Beowulf*. Toronto: University of Toronto Press, 1995.

Howe, Nicholas. *Migration and Mythmaking in Anglo-Saxon England*. South Bend: University of Notre Dame Press, 2001.

Jurasinski, Stefan. "The Ecstasy of Vengeance: Legal History, Old English Scholarship, and the 'Feud' of Hengest." *The Review of English Studies* NS 55 (November 2004): 641–61.

Kahrl, Stanley. "Feuds in *Beowulf*: A Tragic Necessity?" *Modern Philology* 69 (February 1972): 189–98.

Klaeber's Beowulf (4th ed.). Ed. R.D. Fulk, Robert E. Bjork, and John D. Niles. Toronto: University of Toronto Press, 2008.

Lasalle, Mick. "Vikings spaceship in 'Outlander'" SFGate.com (January 23, 2009). Accessed September 21, 2009. http://articles.sfgate.com/2009-0123/entertainment/17199254_1_outlander-king-rothgar-dental-floss.

Lerer, Seth. "'On fagne flore': the Postcolonial Beowulf, from Heorot to Heaney." In *Postcolonial Approaches to the European Middle Ages: Translating Cultures*. Ed. Ananya Jahanara Kabir and Deanne Williams. Cambridge Studies in Medieval Literature, vol. 54. Cambridge: Cambridge University Press, 2005. 77–104.

Newman, Kim. "Outlander." *Empire.com*. 2009. Accessed September 9, 2009. http://www.empireonline.com/reviews/reviewcomplete.asp?FID=135770.

Osborne, Marijane. "The Great Feud: Scriptural History and Strife in Beowulf." *PMLA* 93 (October 1978): 973–81.

Piper, Henry Beam. *Space Viking*. New York: Dorchester, 2008.

Sawyer, Peter. "The Viking Legacy." In *The Oxford Illustrated History of the Vikings*. Ed. Peter Sawyer. Oxford: Oxford University Press, 1997.

Siewers, Alfred K. "Landscapes of Conversion: Guthlac's Mound and Grendel's Mere as Expressions of Anglo-Saxon Nation Building." *Viator* 34 (2003): 1–29. Rpt. in *The Postmodern Beowulf*. Eds. Eileen A. Joy and Mary K. Ramsey. Morgantown: West Virginia University Press, 2006. 199–257.

Wawn, Andrew. *The Vikings and the Victorians*. Cambridge: D.S. Brewer, 2000.

Films and Television Programs Cited

Beowulf. Dir. Graham Baker. Dimension Films, 2000.

Eric the Viking. Dir. Terry Jones. Metro Goldwyn Mayer, 1989.

"Heroes and Demons." *Star Trek Voyager*. Paramount Television, 2005.

"Loonatics on Ice." *Loonatics Unleashed*. Warner Brothers Animation, 2005. Television.

"Space Vikings." *Loonatics Unleashed*. Warner Brothers Animation, 2007. Television.

Outlander. Dir. Howard McCain. The Weinstein Company, 2008.

The Pathfinder. Dir. Marcus Nispel, 2007.

The Saga of the Viking Women and Their Voyage to the Waters of the Great Sea Serpent. Dir. Roger Corman. Malibu Productions, 1957.

The Vikings. Dir. Richard Fleischer. United Artists, 1958.

Between Exploitation and Liberation: Viking Women and the Sexual Revolution

LAURIE A. FINKE *and* MARTIN B. SHICHTMAN

"SEE! Bladed chariots of death! Occult terrors of the druids! Men roasted alive in the cage of hell! Savage rites of the Icena!" scream the advertisements for Hammer Film's *The Viking Queen* (dir. Don Chaffey, 1967). "See the dance of desire, prelude to orgiastic revelries that only ancient civilizations knew," proclaims the trailer for Roger Corman's 1957 *The Saga of the Viking Women and Their Voyage to the Waters of the Great Sea Serpent* (hereafter shortened to *Viking Women*).[1] Released as Hollywood was beginning to relax its censorship of the movies, as the sexual revolution and the feminist movement were beginning to revolutionize cultural attitudes toward sexuality and women, often in contradictory ways, these two Viking movies illustrate the central promise of the exploitation film, that it will afford its audiences privileged glimpses of the forbidden, especially the sexually forbidden. As such, they offer an opportunity to explore the visual pleasures afforded by the cinema.

These pleasures were articulated by John Berger in his landmark 1973 essay on the nude: *"Men act and women appear.* Men look at women. Women watch themselves being looked at. Woman ... turns herself into an object — and most particularly an object of vision: a sight" (47; emphasis in original). Yet these films, ironically, offer up the pleasures of female objectification within narratives of political and feminist liberation. In this essay, we examine the ways in which these two Viking films display their sexual politics, drawing out the contradictions and connections between their proto-feminist narratives of liberation and a visual exhibitionism that relies on lurid sensationalism to attract and hold an audience comprised largely of adolescent males.

To do so, we return to the original premises of what Judith Mayne describes as the "bachelor machine" that characterized feminist theories of the gaze in the 1970s and 80s, in which men look and women position themselves to be looked at.[2] Exploitation films, with their promises of forbidden sights, seem cut to the measure of a cinematic apparatus that posits a male subject of desire engaged in the perversions of voyeurism and fetishism to master the potential threats posed by a female body that is at once fascinating and repulsive. We need, however, to complicate this apparatus in three ways:

1. by considering the relationship between the passive spectator of this early film theory, the "spectator-fish taking in everything with their eyes, ... a vacant spectator at once alienated and happy, acrobatically hooked up to himself by the invisible

150

thread of sight" and the social audiences, the historically situated individuals who patronized (and continue to patronize) these films[3];

2. by locating the gaps in a visual apparatus that props up the dominant ideologies of a hegemonic masculinity that seems to operate seamlessly but which is in fact rife with contradictions and incoherencies;

3. by taking into account the complex and troubled relationships between a feminist politics of liberation that in the 1960s challenged ideologies of male supremacy and a sexual politics of liberation that, at the same time, challenged ideologies of moral repression.

We understand the binary oppositions implicit in cinematic theories of the gaze — between male and female spectators, active and passive spectatorship, conformity and resistance — then, as mutually deconstructive terms, each term implicated in and complicating the other.

Furthermore, because exploitation films were video ephemera, quickly and cheaply made through an industrial process designed to feed a voracious appetite for cheap and accessible entertainment and intended to have the shelf life of about a week, before we can examine the fantasies of medievalism, both sexual and political, carried by the Viking themes of these two movies, a brief history of exploitation films will contextualize them within the history of filmmaking.

Exploitation films have existed since the beginning of the industry[4]; however, major shifts in the industrial structure of Hollywood in the 1950s and 60s brought the exploitation film out of the shadows and into the mainstream, in second-rate movie theaters that featured "sexploitation and gore-cinema" (Wood and Feaster 190). Although in 1945 motion picture revenues reached an all-time high, after the war, the major studios were beginning to feel economic pressures that would eventually bring an end to their stranglehold on film production and distribution. An anti-trust ruling in 1948 ended such economic practices as vertical integration (ownership of the means of production, distribution, and screening of motion pictures) and block booking (agreements extracted from theater owners to purchase all of a studio's product as a package; Turner 15). The studios were required to divest themselves of theater chains, making way for alternative systems of distribution that had the effect of making a wider range of films available (Nowell-Smith 509).

Exploitation filmmakers like Roger Corman, together with Samuel Z. Arkoff and James H. Nicholson, the founders of American International Pictures (AIP), the largest independent film company in the 1950s and 60s, created the model of independent filmmaking that would eventually break the studio monopoly. Arkoff notes, "The early 1950s was the worst time for the cinema because of TV, the breakup of the chains after the Consent Decree, and the fact that many of the old studio chiefs were dying or retired. Lots of exhibitors said there was no market for small pictures because TV would buy them up and show them to fill programming needs. Thousands of theaters went under — a downtime for the industry. That's exactly when we moved in" (Corman 26) with low budget movies like *The Viking Women*.

At the same time, the audience for movies was changing, and motion pictures were competing with television for a shrinking portion of entertainment dollars. During the heyday of the studio system, filmmakers produced films aimed at a family audience, which by the 1950s had been lost to television; audiences were becoming younger and better educated. A survey in 1957, the year *The Viking Women* was released, showed that 52 percent of the movie audience was under 20 and 72 percent was under 29 (Hillier 14; see also Harper 111).

The major studios' inability or unwillingness to change its formulae to appeal to this youth audience created a niche in which independent film makers could turn a profit by creating a cheaper product aimed at youth audiences. "The 1950s exploitation movies were aimed at teenagers exclusively, and were made only in established genres that might have youth appeal, such as science fiction and horror films, or in brand new genres that dealt with topics that had proven popularity with teens: rock music, hot rods, and motorcycles" (Clark 42).

Finally, the system of censorship that restrained what movies could show was beginning to break down during this period. The 1930 Production Code was designed to head off government censorship of the motion picture industry by creating a self-regulating standard. By 1934 any film that lacked the PCA seal of approval could not be shown in any MPPDA (Motion Picture Producers and Distributors of America) theater; a violation could result in a $25,000 fine (Walsh, *Sin and Censorship* 104). In 1953, when Otto Preminger's *The Moon Is Blue* opened despite being denied a Production Code seal of approval, the consensus that held the code together was already beginning to crack. By 1967, the year *The Viking Queen* was released, it was swept away, replaced by the current and much relaxed MPAA rating system. But exploitation films like *Viking Women* and *Viking Queen* worked outside of the Production Code entirely, even as they exploited their outsider status to increase ticket sales. Unable to obtain Code approval, exploitation filmmakers turned to alternative distribution systems, booking their movies into drive-in theaters, college theaters, repertory houses, and grindhouses (Nowell-Smith 513).[5] Drive-in theaters, suburban versions of the grindhouse, were especially fertile areas of expansion during this period. In 1947, there were only about 400 drive in theaters in the U.S.; by 1956, there were more than 5000. This rapid growth was occurring at the same time other theaters were closing (Clark 43).

American International Pictures (AIP), the largest and most influential of the independent film companies in the 1950s and 60s, which distributed most of Corman's pictures during this period, specialized in cheaply made 60–70 minute black and white movies geared to teenagers and usually shown as double features with other low budget films.[6] API style was marked by "monochrome, contemporary settings and functional techniques, and unknown performers" (Nowell-Smith 512). In the late 1950s and early 1960s, Hammer films improved on Corman's model, launching a series of horror exploitation films that combined "serious and spirited period style with color and quality performances" (Nowell-Smith 512). As Sue Harper suggests, their historical settings were part of these films' appeal (110).

If exploitation films seem most at home in contemporary settings, inhabited by science fiction monsters, gangsters, fast cars and motorcycles, we might well ask why the turn to the early Middle Ages at all — to ninth-century Scandinavia or, for that matter, Britain of the first century, pasts almost impossibly remote, and therefore presumably of little interest to a teen audience.[7] One, perhaps obvious, reason is that it allowed filmmakers to dress female casts in the skimpiest of outfits, offering variations on the performance of cheesecake. Corman's Viking women are attired in buckskin micro-minis and Chaffey's voluptuous Celtic princesses in flimsy diaphanous gowns and the occasional set of pasties. Despite the vacuity and evanescence of these films, the relationship between their historical frames and their appeal to an adolescent audience merits closer scrutiny. Sue Harper argues that Hammer Films' turn to costume drama in the 1960s provided a space in which to address "anxieties about the body (especially the female body)," but it also "permitted them to allude to hidden or forgotten elements in British popular culture." It "opened up a space in which notions of national identity could be examined in a new way." The very "Englishness" of these films, she argues, made them popular both at home and abroad.

We would argue that the medieval settings of both films function as a kind of fantasy space where young audiences can imagine things like sea serpents (even if, in the end, they look more like hand puppets).[8] The "fantastical materiality" of costume drama functions as a defamilarizing device, distancing viewers from their own worlds as a means of accessing that which civilization has thoroughly repressed; history becomes the "site of hideous yet fascinating acts" (Harper 115, 116). The historical frames of these films allow for the literal "staging" of desire. Judith Mayne quotes Laplanche and Pontalis who argue that "fantasy ... is not the object of desire, but its setting. In fantasy the subject does not pursue the object or its sign: he appears caught up himself in the sequence of images" (167). The conventions of the Viking film pit the civilization of modernity against the fantasy frame of the dark ages: the "savage rites of the Icena" and "orgiastic revelries that only ancient civilizations knew," "as barbarism and passion inflame a pagan empire."[9] Of course, the stereotype of Vikings as savages, outside the laws of propriety and property, raping and pillaging, has a long history and some basis in the documentary record. The *Anglo-Saxon Chronicle*, for instance, in its entry for 793, decries "the harrowing inroads of heathen men" creating "lamentable havoc in the church of God in Holy-island, by rapine and slaughter." The Viking exploitation films, set in the remote past, offer up the atavistic fantasy of barbarity, superstition, and violence from which civilization (modernity) is supposed to have rescued us.[10] Like more contemporary gangster and motorcycle genres, these movies allow audiences to explore the id, uncontaminated by the injunctions of the superego; this, finally, was what exploitation films sold, and they could get away with it — as long as by the end the superego returned, the guilty were punished, and conventional morality reestablished.

Roger Corman was undoubtedly the most important director of exploitation films in the 1950s. His sets served as an informal film school for an entire generation of filmmakers who would come of age in the 1970s (Ron Howard calls it the "Roger Corman University of Profitable Cinema"; see Rafferty). His protégés included Francis Ford Coppola, Robert Towne, Dennis Hopper, Jack Nicholson, Peter Bogdonovich, Martin Scorsese, Robert de Niro, Sylvester Stallone, Joe Dante, Jonathan Demme, Barry Levinson, Gail Anne Hurd, James Cameron, and Ron Howard (Rafferty, Nowell-Smith 513). *The Saga of the Viking Women and Their Voyage to the Waters of the Great Sea Serpent* was made for somewhere between $60,000 and $70,000; it was shot in ten days.[11] In the film, a group of women from the village of Stonjold venture out in search of their men, who have been gone for three years. Their voyage takes them to the waters of the great sea serpent and, after a perfunctory encounter with the eponymous "monster of the vortex," they are cast up on a strange shore and captured by Grimault warriors, who try to enslave them as they have enslaved the Viking men. It is up to the Viking women, led by Desir (Abby Dalton) and the "dark-haired" priestess Enger (Susan Cabot), to rescue the men and lead them safely back to Stonjold.

The film's narrative plays out not in the historical Viking Age, but in a fantasyland set in the canyons of the Hollywood Hills and perhaps most clearly illustrates the ways in which the medieval themed exploitation film could address itself to the fantasies of its adolescent audiences.[12] The Vikings — both men and women — of Corman's film appear to live in a world of perpetual adolescence. They hail from a village seemingly without adults or small children. The women spend their time hanging around the beach, waiting for their lovers to return and talking — or, more to the point, gossiping — about relationships. It is a wonder they can even survive. Who provides them with the food to nourish their models' bodies or with the clothes that cover them — albeit, just barely?

Both the men and the women stand at the intersection of virginity and sexual activity; they are simultaneously innocent and horny. Though played by actors and actresses well into their twenties — or beyond — they behave like teenagers, longing for absent lovers, afraid to "die unloved." The film's narrator may announce the bravery and fearlessness of Viking men, but the men themselves exhibit all the anxieties of love-struck high school boys; they have crushes. One of the men, Ottar, for instance, confides to his beloved Thyra, "I've always been afraid to talk to you." The women, for their part, obsess about marriage — dreaming of the time when "he'll give me a ring of betrothal and claim me forever as his own" — but never consider the responsibilities of domestic life: cooking, cleaning, childbirth. Corman re-imagines Vikings as the pampered children of California suburbs, and he directs a movie designed to appeal to those very children.

At the same time, the film offers up a proto-feminist narrative of empowerment and liberation. Corman himself notes that he tried to inject his liberal politics into his film-making, adding that he believed in the feminist movement and had "strong, assertive women leads" in several of his films, including *The Viking Women* (30, 34). The film's trailer enjoins viewers to "know the best elements of women and the worst appetites of men." It describes the Viking women as "beautiful, brave, and unbelievably courageous." Repeatedly, the film stresses the abilities that enable the women to survive captivity in the warrior culture of the Grimaults. A montage sequence shows them building a longboat and setting out to sea. They are able to withstand both the vortex and its sea monster without, unlike their male counterparts, losing any hands. Desir bests Senya, the effeminate son of Stark, leader of the Grimault warriors who capture the women, at both hunting and arm wrestling. Asmil, her sister, proves her mettle in an escape attempt thwarted only by Enger, the "dark priestess," a more powerful woman. Desir proves herself the equal of her captive lover when tested by Stark in the holy sacrificial fire to the storm god. They are saved only by the "dark priestess" who is able to call upon her priestly powers and "great Thor, god of the thunderbolt" to send rain and put out the fire before it can do much damage.

Poster for Roger Corman's 1957 film *The Viking Women and the Sea Serpent* (editor's collection).

The opening sequence of the film invokes positive images of Vikings as shipbuilders and democrats, creators

The young Viking Ottar (Jonathan Haze, right) confronts the Grimault leader Stark (Richard Devon) in Roger Corman's 1957 film *The Saga of the Viking Women and Their Voyage to the Waters of the Great Sea Serpent* (editor's collection).

of the first Parliament, extending these achievements to Viking women. We first encounter the women in Corman's version of an Althing, with the women voting "in typical Viking fashion" whether to stay or go, although Corman apparently thought it would be more cinematic if rather than vigorously debating the issue, weighing the dangers against the benefits, they chuck spears at a tree.

In fact, the film's politics play out in the most obvious and trite cinematic iconography contrasting freedom and slavery, civilization and savagery. The Vikings are for the most part pale blond Northerners; the blonder they are, the more leadership qualities they seem to possess (Desir and her lover are the blondest). They are depicted not only as shipbuilders, but as creators of civilization as well. When the Viking women are taken to the Grimaults' lair, it turns out to be a Romanesque-looking castle that we learn was actually built by the enslaved Viking men. The Grimault warriors, by contrast, are dark and swarthy, sporting hats reminiscent of Mongolians that give them a faintly oriental look (despite the entirely white and American cast). They are constantly described as savage, animalistic, and heathen (although technically so are the Vikings). The one dark Viking, Enger, is the traitor who betrays the escape attempt and must die for her treachery, although only after atoning for her crime by helping the others make good their escape.

Despite Corman's claim that cinematically he favored dense composition and a moving camera,[13] the film is ultimately static, lacking narrative depth. Corman is unable to keep more than two or three characters alive in any scene. Lacking a convincing backdrop (beyond the rocky canyons) of villages, people, buildings, and objects to suggest some kind of social world, actors and extras who are not speaking have little to do but stand around, and even those with speaking parts tend to deliver their lines statically. To understand why Corman's nod to feminism, while laudable, is ultimately ineffective (the action really is more reminiscent of children playing cowboys and Indians), it might be useful to think phenomenologically about the ways in which performers' interactions with the set create the "world" of a film.

Phenomenologists insist that our bodies are situated in space and time and that, as they interact with the world, turning toward some objects and away from others, they take shape and create paths carved out by repetition and habit. We call this response "orientation."[14] "If orientation is a matter of how we reside in space," as Sarah Ahmed argues, then acting might be described as "a matter of residence; of how [actors] inhabit spaces as well as 'who' or 'what' [they] inhabit spaces with" (Ahmed 1). In films, actors use the objects around them in this way, as extensions of their bodies, literally to create the fictional world of the film. In *Viking Women*, Corman fails to provide his cast with enough "stuff" to suggest a social world in which women's empowerment can matter, and the actors are not good enough to imply that they exist in an inhabited world. The drama plays out against a flat and featureless backdrop that can suggest neither depth or scale.

Best known for its signature horror films in the 1960s, Hammer Films improved on Corman's economic model of exploitation movie-making. They released films in almost as many different genres as AIP. The budgets were larger; *Viking Queen* went £61,000 over its £350,000 budget, but the films were still, by the standards of the day, relatively inexpensive, relying on talented but less well-known (and hence cheaper) British actors [15] and cleverly designed sets: "the actual creation process in Hammer was nearly always borrowing something from somewhere else," including apparently those sets (Harper 112). *The Viking Queen* has neither Vikings nor queens. Shot, like John Boorman's *Excalibur*, on location in County Wicklow Ireland, it tells a slightly altered version of the Bouddica story. Upon the death of her father, Salina (played by the Finnish actress Carita) must lead the Iceni people against their Roman conquerors. Selina falls in love with Justinian, the Roman governor of Britain (Don Murray), and it appears as if their union will lead to peaceful coexistence between conquered and conqueror. Predictably, the peace is broken by the machinations of both the druids and of Justinian's second in command, Octavian (Andrew Keir), forcing Selina to go to war against the Romans with tragic results. If the film's protagonist is Celtic rather than a Viking (her mother was a Viking), we might well wonder what historical capital the producers hoped to get from the association with Vikings? Perhaps they assumed their target audience would have more historical associations with Vikings than first century Britains.

Produced during a decade that spelled the end of the 1950s fantasy of domestic bliss and that saw the emergence of a new women's liberation movement, *Viking Queen* proclaims its feminist message most fully in its trailer: "She was made to be queen, this warrior woman who challenged men with her courage and taunted them with her flesh ... the Viking Queen, born to rule, love, fight."[16] While it cannot help but return obsessively to its promise of "orgiastic pleasures" (of which more below), the trailer exploits the language of feminism that was part of late 60s youth culture. The film itself talks less than Corman's about women's empowerment, although we are given a female protagonist who rules her people wisely and leads them into battle against what the trailer describes as "the Roman death legion."

In one of the first scenes in the film, the druid Maelgan prophesies on her father's deathbed that Salina will "wear armor and carry a sword." Alongside the Bouddica story, *Viking Queen* also alludes to the Lear story, as the dying King Priam must decide which of his three daughters should inherit his kingdom. Unlike Lear, Priam wisely chooses his middle daughter. The eldest, though the "natural choice," "would not be a wise one." Her "association with the druids would only end in disaster." The youngest, "little Talia" is simply too insipid to rule. Only Salina possesses the "level head" necessary to rule. "You will govern," Priam tells her, "with tolerance and understanding. Like your mother, you will be a Viking queen." Hammer scripts were known for the symmetry of their plots (Harper 113), and John Temple-Smith's and Clarke Reynolds's screenplay surrounds its Viking Queen with characters embodying the stark contrasts which she must negotiate to rule successfully. Her sisters represent a range of responses to Priam's and to the Roman's patriarchy.[17] The judicious Roman governor Justinian is contrasted with the vicious Octavian and the civilized Roman rulers with the atavistic druids.

Even if the writing is only marginally better than Lawrence Goldman's screenplay for *Viking Women*,[18] with its bigger budget, *Viking Queen* is able to create a more believable world in which we can accept that something important is at stake. Except for the lead, starring in her first and last English film, and the ingénue Talia (Nicola Pagett), the cast consisted of seasoned if not well known actors, many like Adrienne Corri (Beatrice, the elder sister) with more than 50 film credits or Wilfrid Lawson (Priam), at the end of a long

Carita as the title character Salina (center) and her princess sisters Beatrice (Adrienne Corri, right) and Talia (Nicola Pagett, left) in Don Chaffey's 1967 film *The Viking Queen* (editor's collection).

career (this was his final film). Don Chaffey, a prolific director who also directed Raquel Welch in *One Million Years B.C.*, creates believable spaces within which his actors can suggest a credible world. Exterior scenes are given depth because there are enough extras to suggest, for instance, the scale of the Roman legions. The chariot scenes, while hardly *Ben-Hur*, are convincing. Hammer Films was famous for its ability to borrow, manipulate, and light sets so that on film they achieved a depth and detail that belied their low budgets (Harper 117). Interior sequences, like the opening death scene that sets the film's various plots in motion, are given not only visual depth of field, but narrative depth by creating action in both the foreground and background. The opening shot of this sequence includes no less than nine characters that have to be kept alive. Later this busy scene will add Justinian, Octavian, Fergus, and his son Tristram, most of whom have speaking parts. The extras do not just stand around in the background; they are constantly interacting with objects within the frame.

Priam and his daughters initially occupy the foreground of the shot as well as the narrative focus; the druids in the background are performing the forbidden death rituals. The sounds of the women weeping and the chanting of the druids are layered over each other. The scene unfolds between these two groups with Beatrice and the druid Maelgan moving between the two and connecting them. When the action focuses on Priam and his daughters and the druids are out of frame, we are never allowed to forget their presence. The chanting continues over the dialogue. Coverage shots allow glimpses of the rituals in the background. External cutaways show villagers, merchants, and soldiers milling around, and servants cooking meals, suggesting a complex social organization within which Salina must define what kind of ruler she will be. Within its first ten minutes, the film has characterized the hierarchies, alliances, conflicts, and class[19] and ethnic statuses of this first century British tribe and its interactions with the conquering Romans. The threat that Salina's rule poses to both Roman and Celtic patriarchies (even if that threat is ultimately dispelled) matters in this world.[20]

Both films' gender politics, however, run quickly afoul of their sexual politics. Indeed, while the proto-feminist plots might offer a place from which to resist the films' sexual exploitation, finally, the more powerful the woman, the more titillating her sexual objectification. Exploitation films secured their desired audience by making explicit promises to *show* things that in the moral climate of the Production Code were prohibited, and, in doing so, even as they objectified women, they politically challenged the repressive mores of the period represented by the Code.[21] To examine the forms of spectatorship offered by these films, then, we need to look at the gap between what the advertising promises and what the film delivers.

More than mainstream films, exploitation films begin with their advertising.[22] The posters developed for both *Viking Queen* and *Viking Women* feature cartoon images of bikini-clad women in the style of the Vargas or Petty girl,[23] posed in the former wielding a sword and driving a chariot and in the latter fighting off an attack by a sea serpent. The images allude to the pin up girl popularized in men's magazines like *Playboy*. What action they might suggest is incidental, the implied battle skills all but annulled by the sexy poses that invite the viewer to gaze on perky cartoon breasts and shapely buttocks. The theatrical trailers, as we note above, are structured around the anaphoric repetition of the word "See," invitations to look, enticing viewers by promising glimpses of the forbidden, of orgiastic revelries that only ancient civilizations knew.

The chronotope of the exploitation film of the 1950s — where "spatial and temporal indicators are fused into one carefully thought-out, concrete whole" (Bakhtin 84) — is a space where delights are held out but never entirely granted, because the fulfillment of such pleasure would be, quite simply "too perilous." But perhaps the titillation is quite enough. Within the chronotope of the exploitation film, whether its genre be science fiction, horror, biker gang, or medieval fantasy, the promise of sex mixed with a bit of violence — of sexual power, sexual domination — is sufficient. Delivery of this promise would be excessive. While the prospect of sexual violence, including the fantasy of rape, might hold some attraction for the suburban male teenager — especially if the victims of the sexual violence seem somewhat complicit — the cinematic portrayal of its reality would be finally repulsive, horrific, at least by the standards of the time.

At the heart of *The Viking Women* is the sexual vulnerability of Corman's Viking teens, shipwrecked and enslaved by the Grimault warriors. The Viking women, according to the film's trailer, are doomed to be turned over "to men who take women in pursuit of violent pleasures, pleasures that must end in the thrust of the spear in the warm flesh." At the "orgiastic revelries" promised in the trailer, Viking women are groped by their Grimault captors, and the potential for rape hangs heavily over the scene. These anxieties are heightened by the suggestion of miscegenation carried by the Grimault's oriental dress, "false" gods, and heathen ways; they are "savages," "beasts," "infidels." Stark, the short, dark, curly-haired Grimault king attempts to seduce Desir with a line that vaguely echoes a racist commonplace: "Once you've known a Grimault warrior, you'll forget that pale Viking slave." As for the Viking women, they insist, "I would rather die than have one of those men touch me."

In many ways, however, the presentation of men's sexuality is more interesting, because it is, perhaps unintentionally, queerer. The Viking men, kept half-naked, are sent to labor in the mines. But they never get dirty. Despite a three-year incarceration, they remain remarkably fit, tan, and well-coifed. In fact, the Viking men are much cleaner and far better groomed than their Grimault masters. Rarely do these slaves actually work; they are shown listlessly pounding an occasional rock against another. What kind of slaves are they? What sorts of tasks do they really perform? For whose gaze are they on display? What is their relationship, say, to Senya, the effeminate son of the Grimault leader — who frequently breaks into tears, strikes preposterously dramatic poses, is a miserable hunter, an even more miserable arm-wrestler, and whose wardrobe choices seem to have been inspired by Richard Simmons? The film relies on connotation, suggesting taboos, but stopping just short of verifying them denotatively.[24] In the presence of their women, the Viking men vigorously proclaim their heteronormitivity, just as the Viking women always succeed in disengaging themselves from the clutching hands of Grimault warriors.

But no matter how many forms of penetration threaten the Vikings — spears, phalluses, fire — their bodies remain intact, inviolable. Throughout the film, there is the constant sound of a cracking whip, serving as a reminder of the master/slave, dominant/submissive relationship between the Grimaults and the Vikings. Rarely, however, is anyone actually struck by the whip; in the few cases when a blow does seem to land, it has no perceptible effect. Corman simultaneously provokes anxieties about rape even as he defuses them. The threat of sexual violence that permeates the film's narrative is never realized. Even the "orgiastic revelries" promised by the trailers involve little more than suggestive dancing and some light groping. Corman's exploitation film holds out the prospect of sexual transgression while delivering far less, a conclusion in which chaste lovebirds pair up and sail off to their home, return to their sandy beach apparently no worse for their adventure. The film takes place "in the days when the world was young, and the gods had not yet abandoned the race of man." In such a world, Corman assures his audiences, we can be excited by transgressive sexuality without having to deal with any of its consequences.

In the more relaxed environment of the late 1960s, years that saw the release of films like *The Pawnbroker, Blowup*, and *Midnight Cowboy, The Viking Queen* was able to deliver on more of its promises than *Viking Women* could in the more conformist 50s. *The Viking Queen* presents a normative heterosexual romance between its leading lady and man, Salina and Justinian, as the appropriate resolution to the conflict between the Romans and the Iceni; their marriage will cement the alliance Priam desires between colonizer and colonized and so create peace. But the Viking Queen does not just challenge men; she is a "temptress" who "taunts them with her flesh." The choice of words in the trailer is illuminating. Salina is marked not by her beauty or even her allure, but by a kind of animalistic sexuality. The trailer is built around the repetition of the word "SEE" splashed across the screen in giant capital red letters and repeated, with emphasis, by the voice-over. Each verb is followed by brief glimpses of the sex and violence we are invited to experience, including girls in togas so diaphanous that they barely cover anything, scenes of rape and torture, and of course the "pagan pleasure empire." "These and 1000 pleasures are yours to behold," the voice-over proclaims. The primary interest in exploitation films is not finally in its narratives, which, as in pornography, are almost always clichéd and thin, but in the visual apparatus they create, what they promise we will see: those pleasures — especially sexual ones — forbidden by normalizing narratives that have as their telos proper heterosexual marriage.

The visual pleasures afforded by *The Viking Queen* are established early on in a shot in which the villain Octavius engages in a brief discussion of the political situation of the Iceni with a traveling merchant. The dialogue is innocuous, even trite, exposition:

> You are a long way from London, Osiris. What does a rich merchant like you have to do here?
> I've come to pay my respects to the new queen of Iceni.
> Just how has your greedy brain worked out how to make gold out of her?
> I'm your obedient servant, governor-general.
> I'm not governor-general (beat) — not yet.

The mise-en-scène of this shot is remarkable for its gratuitous composition. The dominant position in the shot is taken up by the merchant's "Nubian girl slave" (a white starlet in blackface). She is sitting, apparently naked, on a horse, her back to the camera, one breast artfully exposed. At no point in the shot do the two men face each other as they speak. They are arrayed side by side in front of the horse, ogling the naked beauty in front of them. The viewer, positioned on exactly the other side of the horse, mirrors their position. The mirroring between these two points stabilizes the shot's representational logic, "producing its readability, which is coincident with the notions of unity, coherency, and mastery" (Doane 51). The gaze that emanates from this point is the possession of the camera and, through identification with that position, of the spectating subject. At this moment, the three cinematic gazes defined by Mulvey's classic 1975 article, "Visual Pleasures and Narrative Cinema," actually do line up; the gaze of the camera, the intradiegetic gaze of the characters, and the gaze of the spectator align making the viewer complicit in fetishizing the "Nubian girl slave." It seem likely that the film's producers created shots like this to appeal to its target audience of adolescent males, though we concede that the social gender and age of individual spectators might vary and might create either oppositional or conformist readings of the shot.

The Viking Queen is full of episodes that would have raised the hackles of the censors, even in 1967: orgies, premarital sex, rape, a decidedly S and M whipping, and frequent nakedness and near-nakedness, much of it gratuitous. Three scenes stand out, suggesting the shape of Hammer Films' exploitation machine, which takes the form, as Sue Harper suggests, of a kind of anxious confrontation with social taboo, an anxiety that needs to distinguish sexualities that pollute from those which will "ensure eventual freedom from defilement" (119).

Repeatedly, Chaffey handles scenes of plot exposition by decorating them with semi-naked, highly sexualized women who occupy the dominant position in the visual field. They neither say nor do anything; their sole function is to display their sexual availability not only to the men in the scene, but to the viewer as well. The scene in which Octavian and the merchant Osiris hatch a complicated plot to get rid of the "young upstart" Justinian, depose Salina, and claim Iceni exclusively for Rome and their own benefit is set in what appears to be a brothel and employs the conventions of the Roman orgy to suggest the sybaritic excesses of the evil Roman conquerors. Accompanied by the languorous sound of a single stringed instrument, suggesting a lyre, groups of beautiful semi-nude women suggestively drape themselves around men in various states of undress, their nakedness hidden by strategically placed towels and careful poses. The couples never embrace; instead there is lots of suggestive foreplay, primarily sexualized posing and massaging. Sexual stimulation is suggested by constant rubbing; the women rub the men's chests and legs, and occasionally the men rub themselves to signal their excitement. One shot in particular demonstrates the ways in which the sequence implicates the viewer in the pleasures of this glimpse into taboo sexualities.

The mise-en-scène is divided into thirds. Osiris, the speaker, occupies the left hand side and carries on with the plot exposition. He is balanced on the right by another couple in the background engaged in suggestive foreplay. But the dominant central position in the shot is occupied by the naked torso of a woman we cannot identify; her head has been cut off by the shot. Her exposed breasts are covered with brass pasties suggestive of a stripper. The shot is lit such that the torso is highlighted as the light reflects off the exposed skin. The viewer's eyes are inexorably drawn to this largely gratuitous and fetishized display of female sexuality.

If this scene offers up the pleasures of the brothel only to condemn them as excessive and corrupting, the sexual relation between the film's leads offers a more socially acceptable (because it can end in hetero-normative marriage), but no less doomed, sexuality. Separated from their companions during a hunt, the lovers make use of the opportunity to flirt by racing their chariots. When their recklessness results in broken wheels, the two are dumped into a river, where their wet clothing, especially Salina's, offers a tantalizing glimpse of what lies beneath. The lovers embrace and Justinian relieves Salina of her toga. The scene titillates the viewer with the promise that we will finally see all; we will be witness to the consummation of their love. But the shot dissolves into a shot of post-coital embrace. The actual sex is hidden from view by the dissolve; sex happens in the cut, as it were, stopping just short of fulfilling our desire to see it. Though doomed, Justinian's and Salina's sexuality is portrayed, in contrast to that of Octavian and Osiris, as innocent and romantic; its intended trajectory toward proper marriage forestalled only by the machinations of the two villains.

In the film's climactic scene, Viking themes of savage violence — of pillaging and burning, torture and rape — emerge with a vengeance (though they are all displaced onto the "civilized" Romans). Octavian has Salina flogged in a scene with obvious overtones of rape. The frenetic music builds as Octavian drags Salina from the building and strings her up on the back of a wagon. This scene involves several kinds of looking. There is a sexualized gaze that takes pleasure in watching the sadistic torture of a beautiful woman. The music abruptly stops as Octavian rips off Salina's gown in a gesture that mockingly recalls Justinian's earlier disrobing. He leers at her nakedness and very slowly repositions her hair to leave her back exposed. But the ensuing silence also suggests the shocked anticipation of the watching crowd — of Salina's subjects — and their fear.

At one point, Octavian forces the younger sister Talia to watch the beating, telling her, "You will be next." There is a two shot that economically condenses the various gazes — of sexual pleasure and fear — that converge in this scene. The viewer is poised between the smugly leering Osiris and a frightened male villager, who finally attempts to intervene to rescue Salina and sets in motion a riot that results in the rape of Talia. The ensuing violence of the Roman's pillaging of Iceni is represented by the soldiers' clutching and carrying off Iceni women with their breasts exposed. Octavian chases Talia back into the building, where he throws her on the bed. Viewers are then titillated with the possibility that we will witness the rape, but again the film stops short. The actual rape occurs, as the lover's sex did, in the cut; we only hear the victim's screams, and we must comprehend her pain through a surrogate, the wounded Tristram on whom the shot lingers. Viewers can enjoy the prospect of sex mixed with a bit of violence without having to confront the ugliness of the rape itself and the anguish of its victim.[25]

What did audiences really think about films like *Viking Women* and *The Viking Queen*? Certainly Roger Corman's cheap, nearly disposable, *Viking Women* served up the Middle Ages as a light aphrodisiac for young couples necking in the last row of the grindhouse (or the front seat of daddy's Chevrolet at the drive-in). *The Viking Queen*'s florid and overheated sexuality played hide and seek with its viewers, suggesting the possibility that all censorship had been swept away, that by witnessing the erotic excesses of the Middle Ages they were party to the sexual revolution of the 1960s. But the best evidence we have for the social audiences of these exploitation films may well be the films made by a generation of directors who came of age between 1970 and 1990, who began to translate the movies they had watched as teenagers into major blockbusters. Monty Python's *Holy Grail*, George Lucas' *Star Wars* films, James Cameron's *Terminator* series, Steven Spielberg's Indiana Jones franchise, and Antoine Fuqua's *King Arthur* with its blue-woaded warriors, pagan princesses, and military rivalries all look to this film genre for inspiration as they traverse the treacherous space between exploitation and liberation. In the late twentieth century, the exploitation film comes of age, supported by A-list directors, writers, and stars, backed by budgets running into the hundreds of millions. According to *Variety*, Sunday, December 13, 2009, Oscar-winning director Mel Gibson is gearing up to direct a new Viking movie, written by William Monahan, who won the Academy Award for *The Departed*, and starring three-time Academy Award nominee, Leonard DiCaprio. Gibson will deploy resources unimaginable to Roger Corman or to Don Chaffey; but in the end, he is making just another Viking movie.

Notes

1. The theatrical trailer for *The Viking Women* may be found at *http://www.youtube.com/watch?v=QXJ08m6u6ks* (accessed January 5, 2010).

2. Theories dependent upon the foundational work of film theorists like Laura Mulvey, John Berger, and Christian Metz. For an important revision of this apparatus, see Mayne.

3. The quotation is from Metz 97; on the distinction between spectator and social audience, see Kuhn 442–47.

4. On the early histories of exploitation films, see Wood and Feaster.

5. A theater, usually in the inner city, that ran exploitation movies, so-called because they were often converted from defunct burlesque theaters.

6. The idea that Corman's films were B movies is inaccurate. B movies were more common in the 30s and 40s when studios would pair a first run A movie with a low budget studio film on a double bill. The B film rarely returned any profit. Exploitation movies like Corman's, shown as double features with other exploitation movies, could turn a profit for the producers, as Corman stresses in his memoir.

7. For a discussion of the presentism of teen culture and its relationship to cinematic medievalism, see Finke and Shichtman, *Cinematic Illuminations* 339–46.

8. On Corman's unhappiness with his special effects team, see 45.

9. This last from the trailer for *Viking Queen*.

10. Exploitation films evince a similar interest in the prehistoric. A year later, Corman made *Teenage Caveman* (Robert Vaughn's first movie), while Hammer scored a respectable hit in 1966 with *One Million Years B.C.* On popular culture fantasies of the Middle Ages, see Finke and Shichtman 15–22.

11. Corman claims that on this film he broke his own record for the most set ups in one day — seventy-seven (45). Corman was to return to Bronson Canyon a year later to film *Teenage Caveman*. See Corman's account of *Viking Women* 45–48.

12. We refer here both to the viewer implied by the film and its actual social audiences.

13. "I tried whenever possible, to frame shots with an interesting depth of field — placing objects or staging action from the foreground through the middle distances and out to the background" (29).

14. See Ahmed 2 and 14.

15. Christopher Lee and Peter Cushing made their reputations working for Hammer Films.

16. The film's theatrical trailer may be found at *http://www.youtube.com/watch?v=vMkQtpjj0b4* (accessed January 5, 2010).

17. If the name Priam seems out of place in a Celtic-Viking Britain, it is worth pointing out (as almost everyone who has seen the movie does) that the druids in their rituals call upon Zeus as their god. However, to enter into the spirit of this movie, one has to put aside the historical howlers, which are legion, beginning with the idea of a first-century British chieftain producing a child by a Viking woman. The film is a mashup of all sorts of classical and medieval mythologies: Roman, Greek, Celtic, Norse.

18. The screenplay for *Viking Queen* was written by Clarke Reynolds based on a story by John Temple-Smith, who also produced the film.

19. Including an arrogant upper class and a sullen, oppressed underclass.

20. To be sure, *Viking Queen* includes its share of trite iconographic flourishes. Maelgin's prediction that Selina will become queen is accompanied by a flash of lightning and clap of thunder to enhance the portentousness of the prophesy.

21. In the era of torture porn exploitations like the *Saw* franchise, it may be difficult to recapture the promise of the forbidden that these films were exploiting. Bear in mind that the censors refused to rate these films, while the original *Saw* was able to earn at least an NC-17 rating and *Saw 2* and *Saw 3* received relatively mild R ratings.

22. Michael Carreras, son of Hammer Films founder James Carreras, writes, "My father always started a film with a poster — and with a poster, drawing, piece of artwork, the way you did it was that if there was already a public image in some form then you weren't showing a potential backer something they've never seen." See also Corman.

23. Alberto Vargas and George Petty were among the best known "cheesecake" illustrators whose air-brushed girls in sexy poses were featured in men's magazines and calendars from the 1930s through the 1950s.

24. On the use of connotation to allude to homosexuality during the Production Code heyday, see Miller.

25. It would be instructive to compare this rape scene to the rape scene in Ingmar Bergman's 1960 *Virgin Spring*, in which Bergman forces his viewers to confront Karen's rape by filming it in a series of extremely long takes that prevent us from looking away; see our reading of this sequence in *Cinematic Illuminations* 293–96.

Works Cited

Ahmed, Sarah. *Queer Phenomenology: Orientations, Objects, Others*. Durham: Duke University Press, 2006.

Bakhtin, M. M., and Michael Holquist. *The Dialogic Imagination: Four Essays*, tr. Caryl Emerson and Michael Holquist. Austin: University of Texas Press, 1981.

Berger, John. *Ways of Seeing*. New York: Penguin, 1972.

Clark, Randall. *At a Drive-in Near You: The History, Culture, and Politics of the American Exploitation Film.* New York: Garland, 1995.

Corman, Roger, with Jim Jerome. *How I Made a Hundred Movies in Hollywood and Never Lost a Dime.* New York: Random House, 1990.

Finke, Laurie A., and Martin B. Shichtman. *Cinematic Illuminations: The Middle Ages on Film.* Baltimore: Johns Hopkins University Press, 2009.

Gray, Beverly. *Roger Corman: Bloodsucking Vampires, Flesh-Eating Cockroaches, and Thriller Killers.* New York: Thunder Mouth Press, 2004.

Harper, Sue. "The Scent of Distant Blood: Hammer Films and History." In Tony Barta, ed., *Screening the Past: Film and the Representation of History.* Westport, CT: Praeger, 1998.

Hillier, Jim. *The New Hollywood.* New York: Continuum, 1992.

Kuhn, Annette. "Women's Genres." In Ann E. Kaplan, ed., *Feminism and Film.* Oxford: Oxford University Press, 2000.

Mayne, Judith. "Paradoxes of Spectatorship." In Williams, *Viewing Positions.*

Metz, Christian. *The Imaginary Signifier.* Trans. Celia Britton, Annwyl Williams, Ben Brewster, and Alfred Guzzetti. Bloomington: Indiana University Press, 1982.

Miller, D. A. "Anal Rope." In Diane Fuss, ed., *Inside/Out: Lesbian Theories, Gay Theories.* London: Routledge, 1991.

Mulvey, Laura. "Visual Pleasure and Narrative Cinema." *Screen* 16 (1975): 6–18.

Nowell-Smith, Geoffrey. *Oxford History of World Cinema.* New York: Oxford University Press, 1995

Rafferty, Terrence. "The B King Takes His Place on the A List." *New York Times* 10 January 2010: MT7.

Schaefer, Eric. *"Bold! Daring! Shocking! True!": A History of Exploitation Films, 1919–1959.* Durham: Duke University Press, 1999.

Silver, Alain, and James Ursini. *Roger Corman: Metaphysics on a Shoestring.* Los Angeles: Silman-James Press, 2006.

Turner, Graeme. *Film as Social Practice.* 3d ed. London: Routledge, 1999.

Walsh, Frank. *Sin and Censorship: The Catholic Church and the Motion Picture Industry.* New Haven: Yale University Press, 1996.

Williams, Linda. *Viewing Positions: Ways of Seeing Film.* New Brunswick: Rutgers University Press, 1995.

Wood, Bret, and Felicia Feaster. *Forbidden Fruit: The Golden Age of the Exploitation Film.* Baltimore: Midnight Marquee Press, 1999.

Time Out of Joint:
Why a Gaul Fought the Normans
in *Astérix and the Vikings* (2005)

ANDREW B.R. ELLIOTT

"Far, far to the north lies an unforgiving land where the nights last several moons, and the winters are cruel: this is the land of the Vikings. Here, fierce chieftains lead their mighty warriors to battle." So begins the prologue to Stefan Fjeldmark and Jesper Møller's *Astérix and the Vikings* (*Astérix et les Vikings*, M6 Films, 2005), establishing the *mise-en-scène* for what appears to be yet another retelling of the familiar elements of the Viking story, drawing on cultural stereotypes of the Norsemen as brutal, fierce, fearless and savage invaders, marauding the coasts of Dark Age Europe in a ruthless and insatiable quest for plunder.

Indeed, throughout the opening scenes, the film relies on a pervasive intertextuality in the creation of the cinematic Norsemen. Viking raids are once again attributed to their inhospitable climate, the "unforgiving land" of the vague North, recalling Orson Welles' introduction to Fleischer's *The Vikings*, which equally cites the "cramped confines of their barren lands" as the motivation for their expansion. Pathetic fallacy — the staple of an alarming number of historical films — plays its part in the introduction too, using a dark color palette of grays and blacks which contrasts starkly with the icy seas to create a truly monochromatic Viking world. It thus stands apart as a world devoid of color and which somehow lacks the warmth, color and splendor remembered from the more familiar Disney animations depicting the Middle Ages of Western Europe.

The film's opening frames recreate a long, slow zoom from a bolt of lightning in the clouds down to the sea, and the clouds part to reveal the stern, impassive face of the Viking chieftain standing at the prow of his iconic longship, recalling the opening scenes of Patrick Bergin's Thorsson from *Berserker: Hell's Warrior*. As the voice-over mentions the word "battle," the ship runs aground onto the beach, and the invaders pour out onto the sand in a cinematographic nod to *Saving Private Ryan* (referred to in the comic as a Normandy Landing); running into the village, they begin to plunder and ransack at will (recalling the memorable introductory scene of *Erik the Viking*), burning and hacking at the flimsy huts and gardens. The punch line, however, is delivered by a slow track backwards from a close-up on one Viking's disappointed mien — as he kicks open a door, the frame remains empty; there is no one left to hack to pieces, no booty to plunder, no pillage and rape to be had anywhere in the village. It is clear that the villagers, unlike the Vikings of the twentieth-century imagination, know the meaning of fear and have turned tail and fled. The message of the film becomes clear from their "debriefing" session once back at the camp. Everyone is too scared to fight them, leaving their primitive urge to "do battle" distinctly unsatisfied.

The first few minutes of the film, then, already give us much food for thought. The degree of intertextuality indicates a relentless borrowing in the formation of a twenty-first-century representation of the Vikings and the unspoken acceptance of a Viking "iconography." The use of extradiegetic voice-over to narrate their history demonstrates our habitual trust of "impartial" historians and their retrospectively applied "motivations" which Stam describes as the "impersonal discourse of objective truth" (46). The unchallenged assumptions that Vikings were fierce barbarians reveal our unconscious acceptance of them as the dark other of our historical past, as a part of the "shaggy medievalism" memorably described by Eco (69). In addition, the re-use of many aspects of the typical Viking iconography in this short scene certainly indicates to us that — even if the film has little to contribute to a more rounded *historical* understanding of the Vikings — it has at least something to say about how we re-imagine them in the twenty-first century.

The degree of intertextual citation even within this opening sequence hints at a wider trend among the "reel Vikings," too, which suggests that Viking films are no longer looking *backwards* at their mythical, historical, or even their Victorian ancestry, but have been provided with a *parallel*, ready-made iconography from the great dream factories of Hollywood and beyond. They are perhaps just as often about other Viking *films* as they are about Vikings, drawing on their re-invention from film to film, which has been reworked to suit the narrative demands of previous directors. If such a proposition is true, then it does seem to suggest — along with other essays in this collection — that the re-interpretation of Vikings in film might, in some cases, be less about trying to get at the "truth" about the Vikings, nor even about maintaining fidelity to a source text or trying to achieve verisimilitude, but might instead be about drawing ideas from an cultural "imaginary" to which the cinema has itself contributed.[1]

The second issue that this essay will address is raised in the title of the film itself. If Astérix is a Gaulish warrior living and fighting on the periphery of the Roman Empire in 50 B.C., how does he come to be fighting Vikings in the first place? Aside from an intertextual historical basis (or perhaps as a result of it), the film also bears a similarity to the "peripatetic history" that can elsewhere be seen with Arthur and Robin Hood, by virtue of which a historical character (or group, in this case) becomes so engrained and re-used in the cultural imagination that the philological ties which root that character within a historical period become worn down. By continued re-use, they eventually fall away completely, extirpating the characters from any historical setting and leaving them free to wander throughout any given period of history. In *Astérix and the Vikings*, chronology has seemingly been set aside in favor of finding a worthy adversary for the plucky Gaul and his sidekick Obélix, and the stereotyping of the Vikings as fierce, courageous and cruel warriors made of them an excellent opponent ("at last, somebody worth killing," as the "Saxon" Cerdic might say).[2] Small matter, then, that what should keep them apart is not the icy North Sea but a little over eight centuries of history. Such an ahistorical approach (to borrow a term from Arthur Lindley[3]) thus characterizes a great deal of *Astérix and the Vikings*, and, indeed, Astérix creators Goscinny's and Uderzo's approach to history as a whole, viewing it as a great treasure trove of plots, characters and periods that can be freely combined and reconstituted so as to serve a narrative need rather than lecture on the niceties of a given historical period. As we shall see, such an approach also further reflects the insistence of modernity which so often impinges on our interaction with the past, throwing up intertextual references as well as condensing eons of history for the sake of narrative convenience.

In order, then, to understand the ubiquity of the Vikings, we must first place their reuse here in the context of Astérix's popularity, since it is not a film about Vikings *per se*, but rather about their appearance in the world of the Gauls. In the following analysis, then, I will first place Astérix into his cultural context — or rather contexts, given his continued popularity in Europe — and analyze the iconography of the Vikings whom he so inexplicably meets, before moving on to look at the intrusion of modernity that pervades not only in Uderzo and Goscinny's work, but that also affects a number of the directorial decisions in the comic's transition to the big screen. In the final section, I will use these arguments to show that the recreation and subversion of the Vikings is here not so much a slight on the Norsemen themselves, or the result of ignorance on the part of the creators, but is more than anything the result of historical pastiche, which places the Vikings at the confluence of a number of trends. The time that is out of joint, I will show, is less a conflict between warring tribes in the past, but rather a conflict between the past and the present, an example of what happens when our "conversation with the past" descends into heated debate.

Who Is *Astérix?*

The first question, however, for many non–Europeans might well be to ask "who is Astérix?" It is, if nothing else, a testament to the curious vagaries of comic book markets that — despite his status in France and Belgium as an instantly recognizable superstar — Astérix remains virtually unknown outside his native Europe. Celebrating his fiftieth birthday in 2009, Astérix originally rose from obscurity in the early 1960s and quickly became a rival among *bédéphiles* (comic aficionados) for the top spot among the bestsellers. His popularity has continued into the twenty-first century, too; even after the death of co-creator René Goscinny, *Astérix* comics show no sign of slowing down, but have instead seen their popularity grow more than ever.

Total sales of Astérix comics are estimated at over 300 million copies, and the publication of the latest installment, *Le ciel lui tombe sur la tête*, in 2005 sold 800,000 copies in the first three days.[4] With a series of video and board games, merchandising, clothing and eleven feature-length films, the Astérix industry has no shortage of devotees, either; the live-action film version, *Astérix et Obélix*, was seen in France by more viewers (9.9 million) than *Star Wars* (7 million), placing it firmly in the French number one box-office slot. Its sequel, *Astérix aux jeux Olympiques* (2008), saw even greater numbers, and with production costs in excess of €78 million, it remains the most expensive film to be made in the history of French cinema. Even with vigorous competition at the box office, over half of the production costs were nevertheless recouped in the opening weekend, and a third from home territory distribution alone (€23.4 million).[5]

The Gaulish warrior has no difficulties in his role as a rival to Disney off-screen, too, with his own shrewdly-marketed franchising including figurines and memorabilia, controversial Happy Meal toys, and even his own theme park, Parc Astérix, located just outside Paris and, tellingly, less than an hour's drive from the Eurodisney theme park. Having emerged during the same period as Tintin, and a product of the same Franco-Belgian imagination, the spirited Gaul has thus come to play a part in the French national identity, becoming "the ninth art's most widely recognized face, and an invaluable asset to Franco-

Belgian identity. Although he is a pre–Christian Gaulish warrior, Astérix is nonetheless a hero with whom almost everybody can identify, wherever they come from" (Screech 75).[6] It is clear from the outset that even within the big business of BDs (*bandes dessinées*) in France, Astérix is most certainly one of the comic book sector's biggest stars.[7]

As far as the character himself is concerned, the story of Astérix is relatively straight-forward. Living in a remote village in Armorica — modern day Brittany — Astérix and Obélix live ostensibly under the rule of Julius Caesar; at least, the Romans have conquered Gaul, save their tiny enclave that manages to resist domination thanks to a magic potion which gives them rejuvenating powers and formidable strength. Together they pass their days hunting wild boar, fashioning menhirs (a kind of tall, pointed rock), and raiding Roman camps for a good old-fashioned punch-up, in which the two Gauls unfailingly outmatch the legionnaires. Though, unsurprisingly, very little of Astérix's world has any basis in historical or archaeological evidence, the authorial choices made by Goscinny were not accidental; even though the choice of Armorica "was not historically correct, ... neither was it arbitrary. Their choice is in line with the popular French-speakers' perception of Brittany, which comes from Arthurian legend and Grail romances.... [Even today,] Brittany is widely regarded as a rebellious region which strongly opposes interference by outsiders, following its long-standing separatist tradition" (Screech 77).[8]

Such revealing choices in the inception of the character and stories of Astérix were, perhaps by nothing more than serendipity, to find deep resonance in the mentality of a proud nation in their struggle in the late 50s and 60s to balance the mixed blessing of American mass-culture with the emphasis placed on their own rich culture and heritage. So strong, in fact, was Astérix's role in this struggle that the phenomenon has later come to be named in his honor; "the Astérix syndrome" describes French artistic production as an *exception culturelle,* which plays a significant role in shaping identity in the face of mass-media and globalized popular culture. Thus in many ways, Astérix came to be seen as an iconic defender of French identity, so that "for many people in the 1960s, Astérix, like [General Charles] de Gaulle, was perceived to assert French national identity. At a time when French identity was increasingly challenged by Anglophone influences, the General and the Gaulish warrior were both putting up a robust resistance" (Screech 77).

The "syndrome," however, was not limited to resisting external influences. It also referred to the more potent internal debates taking place during the comic's emergence in the 1960s, against a backdrop of post–Occupation France and — more significantly — the Franco-Algerian War, twin historical forces that were to leave a lasting legacy on the nation and that presented fundamental challenges to core French identity.[9] As McKinney observes in respect to both Astérix and Tintin, "given the iconic status of these works, they have perhaps inevitably been read as incarnating various aspects of French and Belgian cultural identity. However, even during what is often considered a classical age of so-called Franco-Belgian comics (the 1950s–60s), such identities were problematic constructions, riddled with contradictions and shaped by tensions of various sorts, including ethno-linguistic, class, national and racial ones" (3). In recent years, too, the importance of the Gaulish warrior takes on even greater significance with the rise of extreme-right political factions such as Jean-Marie Le Pen's National Front, and the concomitant (though rather spurious) claims to "authentic" French identity "dating back to Clovis."[10] Viewed in this light, Goscinny and Uderzo's playful use of the mythical past can provide a useful parody — if not wholesale subversion — of such historical maneuvering, as well as a reassurance that identity was then, like now, a long way from being a fixed concept.

If Astérix can thus be understood as both a metonym for resistance to cultural saturation as well as a caricature of French identity, then *Astérix and the Vikings* can equally be seen as a demonstration of its playful *esprit gaulois* in the imagination of other nations and national caricatures. Just as assertions of French "purity" and pedigree are satirized in the comic, so too are national characteristics stereotyped, though "they are not stigmatised as being 'other.' Such good natured lampooning is easily understood in an age of rapprochement, European integration and mass tourism" (Screech 89). The names of the Gaulish warriors (all ending in "-ix") often play on a deft *jeu-de-mots* based on both character-types (such as the druid Getafix or the bard Cacofonix), and by their similarity to the real historical figure of Vercingetorix, familiar to every French schoolchild. So too, however, are the Roman and Viking names caricatured (as "-us" after Julius Caesar, and "-af," following Olaf), normalizations that are carried through into national archetypes, reflecting supposed national characteristics (so the chieftain becomes Timandahaf, followed by Polygraf, Telegraf, Cenotaf, and so on).[11] Although all racial groupings are thus subjected to the same generic naming patterns, the names of the Gauls are based on individual characteristics built up over the course of the series, whereas other racial groups tend to be established solely as a product of "foreign-ness." Such an emphasis on their ubiquity and homogeneity, however tongue-in-cheek, risks being construed as an attempt to paint the entire nation in the same tones, leaving little space for individuality and personal identity.

A similar approach to the imagination of the Vikings can be seen here throughout both comic and film, leaving little room for development of the individual characters (with the exception of the film's two inventions: Abba, the chieftain's "girl power" daughter, and Olaf, the slow-witted son of the Viking elder). Though the original title of the comic referred, correctly, to "the Normans" and not the Vikings, from the re-use of the standard iconography throughout the comic (and which is transferred whole cloth to the film), it is clear that the target of the pastiche was the modern image that we hold of the fierce Norsemen. If they remain the butt of the joke, after all, it seems to make little difference which term is used for them, since the horned helmets, the longboats and the bearded warriors clearly fill that same imaginary space in the popular memory. As Trafford and Pluskowski note, "Vikings ... are easily recognisable. Their appearance is distinctive and well-defined. Generally it is males who are portrayed; indeed the Viking is hyper-masculine. They are big and strong with blond or red hair, and equipped with swords or axes and winged or horned helmets.... Of course, little of this is supported by historical or archaeological evidence ... but that is rather beside the point. Even if the audience recognises ... the dubious historical accuracy of elements of this Viking kit, that does not mean it ceases to use, for instance, horned helmets as the central diagnostic symbols that 'mean' Vikings" (58).

Thus, their "dubious historical accuracy" notwithstanding, the inclusion of elements belonging to a popular understanding implies that Goscinny and Uderzo were not seeking to conduct a genuine revision — nor offer an apologetic reading — of the Vikings, but sought to re-use them as a straightforward national stereotype. Small matter, then, if the film refers to Vikings instead of Normans, since both were simply reprising their outward signs as what Samuels calls a visual "graphic" of history, functioning as "stock figures, our subliminal points of reference" within the narrative (27).

So if the stereotypical images that we hold about the Vikings are being reprised unchallenged here, the question of *why* they are being used in this way raises itself more insistently. To answer this question, we must first recognize that, like the adventure serials of the 1950s and 60s and a number of their comic book counterparts such as Conan *et al.*, the adventures of Astérix and Obélix rely on a series of shifting backgrounds and a character set of stereo-types that each provide a different danger, problem, or threat to be resolved. The comic version of *Astérix and the Normans* was released in 1966, and already, by the ninth title in the Astérix collection, the pair had fought Romans, Parisians, Britons, Goths, Gladiators and even Cleopatra's minions. In such a context, the inclusion of the Normans/Vikings presents an opportunity to provide a worthy adversary for the two warriors, putting up a much better fight than the Roman legions who disappear at the first sign of trouble, claiming, in their defense, that "never mind what Julius Caesar said, **not** going and **not** being seen is the best way **not** to get captured" (26).

Having been incarnated then simply to put up a good fight, the storyline that brings them to the Armorican coast (they take literally the adage that "fear gives you wings" and are searching for a "champion of fear" who will give them flying lessons) can be viewed as largely extraneous. Born of narrative necessity, their arrival does nothing to challenge the dominant stereotype, nor does it explore it to any great extent. Given that their "invasion" is motivated by such an unlikely quest, and not by dreams of domination or plundering, they thus represent no real threat to the status quo of the village (unlike the Romans, whom the villagers are busy thrashing when the Vikings first arrive). Perhaps, then, the question should not be why the stereotype passes unchallenged, but rather how and for what purposes the present is using this stereotype of the past. One of the most revealing answers to this latter question comes when we consider the part that the stereotype plays in the character arc of one of the central characters, Justforkix.

Justforkix: The Present in the Past

Though it is admittedly more prominent in the original comic, the plot of the film centers not on the "Viking invasion" but on the arrival of the chief's nephew, Justforkix, from the city of Lutetia (from Lutetia Parisiorum, the rough Gallo-Roman equivalent of Paris). Like many "fish out of water" comedies, a significant proportion of the jokes are initially predicated on the juxtaposition of the habits and customs of the "proto-metropolitan" world with those of the backward provincials. In the short scene covering his arrival in the village, the camera tracks the young Justforkix's open-topped, Italian sports chariot as it speeds through the forest and grinds to a halt outside the camp, a scene dealt with in the comic by a tightly-framed close-up of the chariot surrounded by skid marks. On his arrival, the hip Parisian continues to baffle the villagers by references to the modern, ultra-chic happenings of *la métropole*, from the latest music (by The Rolling Menhirs), American influences (*Oklahoma*'s signature tune becomes "I Want to Live in Armorica"), and the latest underground dancing crazes "from the catacombs." Given that the modernity of the comic relates to the 1960s, the film understandably updates these references to the realities of twenty-first-century life; Justforkix sends a message to his "babes" using a pocket messenger bird, SMS (Short Message Servix), teaches the young Armoricans breakdancing, and the Rolling Stones reference is transposed to Kool and the Gang's "Get Down on It" at the ball held in his honor. In-jokes further abound in the latent criticism of urban "slackers," such as the villagers' disapproval of the youngster's refusal to get up before noon, the emphasis that he places on appearance, and most especially of his vegetarian diet, a virtual blasphemy to the boar-devouring Obélix.

The character of the neophyte is thus played for laughs by the underlying — and initially unexpected — incompatibility between two lifestyles, which is predicated on its incongruity, "the common denominator of all comedic effects" (Müller 150). By parodying modern youth and lampooning late twentieth-century opprobrium of "the youth of today," it becomes clear that the film is only *pretending* to poke fun at the backwardness of the Gauls. As the plot unfolds, we quickly realize that, as is the case in many time-travel films, it is actually the modern day which is being subverted, and the criticism is actually of our loss of traditional values and core sense of self when faced with the relentless onslaught of the "cool" and the "chic." This criticism becomes particularly clear when Astérix and Obélix begin their task of making the youngster into a "real man," which they naturally interpret as a closer reflection of themselves. Where the comic perceives the training to be little more than giving him the "sound thrashing" so beloved of conservative patriarchal families in the postwar era, the film plays on more recent *Bildungsroman* motifs and uses a greater degree of intertextuality, eliding their progress into a fast-paced, *Rocky*-esque training montage set to an upbeat soundtrack.

The persistent intrusion of modernity in the film version can be seen less as an accidental, anachronistic oversight and more as a deliberate eschewal of the authenticity of history, which is dismissed in the comic as "gloomy classical allusion" (6), in order to rejoice in the unbridled subversion of the past. Goscinny, for example, acknowledges the importance of the past as a reference point, but nevertheless recognizes it as the contested site of an encounter between the past and the present: "I inform myself through a variety of sources, of which the keystone is naturally *The Gallic Wars*. But when I work, I close my books. My job is pastiche."[12] Pastiche, in fact, is precisely what gives the writers such freedom to play with the past, deliberately jumbling elements of a dim, mythological past together in order to suit narrative demands. Such an approach is no longer parody, which nevertheless requires strict adherence to the conventions and formulations of the original text, but a view of history informed by postmodern pastiche, "recuperating elements of a past, of different pasts. [It] is not about the claim to an authoritative view of history" (Hoesterey 52).

The reiteration of this reconstituted history without recourse to an original consequently absolves Astérix from the obligation to stick to "the historical facts," but chiefly its repetition works instead on what I would term "peripatetic history," in which vaguely or nominally historical figures are so frequently removed from a given historical milieu that they become extirpated from history altogether. Like *Conan the Barbarian*, rooted in mythical and not datable history, the character ceases to perform a historical function, but instead enters the achronic, atemporal "ahistoricism" which Lindley originally attributed to medieval film.

Deracinated from a real, datable and temporally-bound historical period, both Astérix and his Viking adversaries become free to wander at will through a vague mythological past, and they are no longer obliged to conform to the logic of a past world, but become roving signs of a generic "past-world," standing in parallel alongside us instead of temporally anchored behind us as a precedent. Such an anachronism also explains the insistent conflation of the past within the present, since it carries with it the implicit recognition that the past world is fictional and constructed in part *by the present*, which means that it will inescapably bear at least some of the signs of the modern era that created it. A criticism of Justforkix's shallow, chic existence thereby becomes a thinly-disguised condemnation of the urban "cool" of the 1960s (in the comic), and the detachment of postmodern youth in the film version. The inception of Justforkix as an anti-hero also contains a hint of wistful nostalgia which laments the loss of traditional values, and changing tastes which demand that "old-fashioned

From left to right, Justforkix, Astérix and Obélix in Stefan Fjeldmark and Jesper Moller's 2006 animated film *Astérix et les Vikings* (editor's collection).

heroic virtues like courage and duty give way to new ones like irony and detachment" (Segal 9).

Such a deliberate eschewal of historicity and verisimilitude in the chronology creates a striking contrast with the otherwise strong focus on accuracy in many other ways (such as the "gloomy classical allusions" and attention to detail in the evocation of Roman-occupied Gaul), presenting an interesting parallel with another Viking-influenced comic studied earlier in this collection of essays, *Prince Valiant*. In a section examining the modern uses of Vikings in the collective imagination, Matteo Sanfilippo describes Hal Foster's creation as the archetypal historical comic, praising its attention to the niceties of armor, settings and design, which help us to "overlook the absolute lack of verisimilitude in its chronology" (132).[13] It is perhaps revealing, then, to note that here too we find a mythological — and not historical — use of the Vikings as a one-size-fits-all barbarian for a potentially different era. By re-using popular iconography and not archaeological or historical documentation, the two comics serve to transpose the Norse warriors to a trans-historical sign, "recreating them without philological ties,"[14] reliant on the kind of peripatetic history mentioned above. The result is a jarring time difference between the civilized world of Western Europe (recreated through a prism of modernity so as to appear much closer to our own world) and the barbarism of the remote North (recreated as a remote and unrecognizable other). Our travels back and forth between the two worlds thus comes to resemble a form of cultural jetlag, in which the Vikings are simply set up as a barbarized opposition to demonstrate the innate superiority and precociousness of the heroes.

Why the Vikings?

All of which leads us to the second part of the question posed in the title of my essay: given the anachronism of their appearance in Gaul in the first place, why should we use the Vikings at all, and not some other "barbarian" tribe such as the Huns, the Alans — or, with a nod to Fuqua and Bruckheimer — the Sarmatians? The answer to this question lies, in part, in the narrative requirements of the film itself, and can also go some way to contributing to some of the overarching themes of this collection of essays, showing how the unthinking use of the Vikings "as a stick to beat the present" reveals their stereotypes and might in fact hold the key to their continuing fascination for twentieth- and twenty-first-century audiences.

In terms of plot, inherent within the structure of the narrative is the necessity to turn Justforkix "into a man," a coming-of-age plot-boiler that uses a standard range of narrative functions: a naïve youth, a tutor figure, a role model, and an "equal and opposite" mirror image. Given that throughout their previous incarnations, Astérix and Obélix have both proved their valor, it becomes clear that the concept of fear would be both alien to them and incongruous within the logic of their world, which depends on their ability to maintain courage in the face of an overwhelming Roman presence, not to mention the contradiction with the magic potion motif.[14] In order to measure the adept's progress, then, the plot requires some parallel character or group of characters — the mirror image mentioned above — who will mirror the protagonist's progression towards his goal by a regression themselves. An example of this parallel/mirror might be found in Chrétien de Troyes' *Perceval*, in which the young naïf's progress is demonstrated in part by Gauvain's fall from the ideal and neglect of his Quest for the Bleeding Lance. It is perhaps for this reason that Goscinny turns to the "Normans" (as proto–Vikings), since he was looking for a model of unchecked aggression and total fearlessness that would nonetheless embody the requisite "backwardness" that contrasts with Justforkix's *jeunisme* and urban savvy. The parallel structure of the plot consequently demands that for every example of progression in Justforkix's journey, the Vikings demonstrate a comparable regression to cowardice: this pattern is most visible in the comic, which finishes by Justforkix's metempsychosis, being reborn as a brave warrior at exactly the same time as the Vikings flee from battle in fear.

What is interesting here is that, despite the detailed research that the creators usually employed in their recreation of past figures, in this case they turned to the iconography of the Vikings as it has been assimilated into the modern mentality. This modern perception of the Vikings had already been re-interpreted in the nineteenth century, after which period they "have contributed colourfully to the modern Heritage industry. The iconography (long ships, horned helmets) that the Victorians developed for them remains instantly recognisable and wickedly deployed" (Wawn 372). Yet even so, it is clear from the events which follow that they have not been lifted wholesale from such a colorful iconography, for while the surface details may have remained intact (horned helmets, long beards, and so on), their underlying barbarity has been somewhat tempered. Where "history knows them as bloodthirsty and abominable barbarians, enemies of society capable of infamous, indefensible outrages" (Kendrick 12), both book and film have tried — though perhaps not wholly in earnest — to add a more human dimension to them. While they know no fear, and are introduced as those "bloodthirsty and abominable barbarians," by a process of humanization akin to that in *Erik the Viking,* they begin to emerge as more rounded characters, by putting on display those aspects of their lives which most closely resemble our own. In the comic, skulls are collected not for personal glory but as matching dinner sets (resulting in the care of Viking hostages since "the Chief doesn't like chipped glasses"), the Gauls and Vikings swap recipes for boar in cream sauce, and, most forcefully, the brutality of the Norsemen is motivated not by cruelty but because they do not understand the concept of fear, explained by their parting "gift" of gratitude — to slaughter all their hostages, so as to allow them to taste the finest dining at Odin's table in Valhalla.

The film, coming nearly forty years later, takes this concept further; their chief Timandahaf is presented as a hen-pecked husband trying to assert his patriarchal authority over his wife and daughter, and by the introduction of the character, Olaf, the slow-witted son of the chief's adviser, to whom much of the aggression is transferred with the excuse that he knows no better. Such inventions thus serve to expiate the brutality of the Vikings by transferring culpability to a marginal character, and consequently go a long way in rescuing the image of the Norse warrior ethos from wholesale condemnation. Given the cultural backdrop against which the comic emerged in 1967, it is perhaps no coincidence that such a revisionist stance towards the Viking warriors should come about — even in the service of comedy. Aberth notes that, after the late 1950s, traditional assumptions by historians about the brutality of the Vikings began to be reconsidered in the light of recent scholarship; with the publication of key studies by, among others, Brønsted, Gwyn Jones, Foote and Wilson, and P. H. Sawyer, there emerged a "sea change" of perception, "an overhaul of the Viking image [which] was long overdue" (31). Aberth further argues that "the cumulative effect of all their efforts is a more rounded and complex image of the Vikings that places as much emphasis on their peaceful, yet no less impressive, activities as traders, shipbuilders, settlers and explorers, as it does on their inescapable deeds as conquerors and pirates" (59).

As this collection of essays goes some way to show, such revisionism can be seen perhaps more than anywhere else in post–1960s popular films made about the Vikings in which their comedic invocations have tried to play down their violence in order to present a more human face behind their (perennially horned) helmets. "After *Erik the Viking,*" writes Aberth, "the old story of Viking pillagers and rapists is dead" (59), though perhaps we should now consider including *Astérix and the Vikings* in this category, since its brutal Vikings are shown to be only *too* human once they learn the meaning of fear. An interesting addendum to the comic that sadly was omitted in the film shows the Vikings' journey back from Gaul.[15] Having now learnt the concept of fear, they are shown to be bigger cowards than the newly-reformed Justforkix, being too scared to man the crow's nest alone, and asking the chief to stop shouting as he is "frightening the men" too much.

We must acknowledge here, however, that such a difference in endings between the comic and film versions, however, might be just as easily ascribed to a comic subversion rather than a historical revision. Such an iconoclastic stance towards "the facts," for example, can be traced throughout Fjeldmark's earlier subversion of tradition in *Quest for Camelot* and *Hjælp, jeg er en fisk/Help! I'm a Fish*. An important question thus arises concerning the potential for comedy to act as a corrective to other films' insistence on an unchallenged inheritance of outmoded beliefs; can subversions of such well-worn Viking platitudes really begin to "challenge audiences' expectations of typical Viking activity ... by making more movies that allow Vikings to do something besides rape, pillage and plunder"? (Aberth 60) Or is the comic representation of these Vikings in some ways merely a reflection of changing attitudes towards the Norsemen in the popular domain, brought about by other means such as *Erik the Viking*'s humanism or advertisements which hint that they might care about "What's in your wallet"?

Either way, the attempts of both comic and film to provide a more rounded view of the Vikings — however accidental — certainly speak volumes about the creators' attitudes towards them, as well as about directors Fjeldmark and Møller's aptitude for subversive humor, and can perhaps be seen as a surface indication of a gradual sympathy towards the Norsemen. The reassessment of traditional Viking imagery through a sympathetic lens seems on the surface to reflect a romanticized desire to see them as "not *that* bad after all," which could be argued to be just as distortive as former stereotypes. Instead of a forceful corrective to an ideologically-driven rewriting of history, we are perhaps being influenced by nostalgia for the bravery of the heroes of the eddas, a general courage and sense of duty which is often felt to be lacking in a post-heroic age. Seen this way, it becomes obvious why Goscinny might turn to the Vikings, who would service a nostalgic agenda in which the past was re-imagined as an idyllic, halcyon era of childhood innocence and values, and which becomes a handy shorthand for the fondly-remembered "good old days." If such were the case, then we must acknowledge it for what it is; when an idealized past is being used as a role model for the present, the real battle is no longer between past factions such as the Gauls and the Norsemen, but it is *really* between the present and the past. If Justforkix's urban chic is compared unfavorably with the heroic bravery of the Vikings, then the underlying moral is that modern era has much to learn before coming to maturation.

Again, either way, the use of the Vikings in the service of nostalgia can perhaps be seen here not as the unthinking re-use of a tired old stereotype, but as a testament to the power of their legacy, having entered our imagination as a fixed point of reference against which we should measure our progress. In a world of pastiche and intertextuality — in which free combinations of jumbled motifs and cultural borrowings from a range of media have been legitimized by "anything goes postmodernism" (Hoesterey 52) — perhaps the codification of the Vikings as an ahistorical, liminal imaginary is precisely what guarantees their success, in the same way as King Arthur, Grail stories and Robin Hood are indebted for their survival to their malleability. Such a manipulation of the generic Viking image in twenty-first century culture may well be an affront to the carefully researched "truth of the matter," but it is nevertheless the flexibility of the paradigms that allows them to find a home in a culture for whom bravery can be elided into raw aggression, curiosity into colonial expansion, and determination into callous brutality. Such is certainly the case with *Astérix and the Vikings*, since it is precisely their unreconstructed legacy as brutal, fierce Barbarians which causes the Vikings to be reprised in a wholly anachronistic setting.

Further, we must equally remember that Astérix's world view comes not from careful historical inquiry but from a comic and subversive perspective, which demands that historical "facts" be diluted by anomaly, anachronism, and incongruity in order to achieve their subversive effect, a dilution that allows them to survive. History, it seems, plays a much reduced role in such re-inventions, since "it is precisely because of this capacity to undergo cultural translation and modernisation that the old north has retained its power to attract and intrigue" (Wawn 371). In such a climate of anarchic subversion and contradiction, then, we ought not to be surprised to see "peripatetic" Vikings ransacking their way through Roman history, being transported forward to our own era, or even to see them become a vaguely historical presence on the fringes of our historical consciousness. Such a powerful legacy is thus a double-edged sword, on the one hand bestowing the freedom to participate in our cultural imagination over one millennium later, while on the other hand condemning them to the distortive transformation which comes along with it. Perhaps, then, these "reel Vikings" might even now begin to mutter their own prayers: "Protect us, O Lord, from the fury of the filmmakers."

Notes

1. My use of the term *imaginary* here is intended broadly to correlate with the explanation offered by Nickolas Haydock in *Movie Medievalism* (Jefferson, NC: McFarland, 2008), especially pp. 5–35, as well as that elaborated by François Amy de la Bretèque in *L'Imaginaire médiéval dans le cinéma occidental* (Paris: Champion, 2004).

2. Stellan Skarsgård in *King Arthur*, dir. Antoine Fuqua (Touchstone Pictures, 2004).

3. See Arthur Lindley, "The Ahistoricism of Medieval Film," *Screening the Past* 3 (May 1988).

4. Source: *http://www.actuabd.com/+Asterix-800-000-albums-vendus-en-trois-jours+*; accessed 4 January 2010.

5. Source: *www.the-numbers.com*; accessed 13 December 2009.

6. See especially Screech's third chapter, "A Hero for Everyone: René Goscinny's and Albert Uderzo's *Astérix the Gaul*," pp. 75–94.

7. For an excellent overview of the importance of comics in France and Belgium, see Mark McKinney, ed., *History and Politics in French-Language Comics and Graphic Novels*, especially Chapter One, "Representations of History and Politics in French-Language Comics and Graphic Novels," pp. 3–24.

8. See also Maryon McDonald, "*We Are Not French!" Language, Culture and Identity in Brittany* (London: Routledge, 1989).

9. See, for example, Todd Shepard, *The Invention of Decolonization: The Algerian War and the Remaking of France* (Ithaca: Cornell University Press, 2006); Lizabeth Zack, "Who fought the Algerian War? Political Identity and Conflict in French-Rules Algeria," *International Journal of Politics, Culture and Society* 16. 1 (Fall 2002): 55–97.

10. The original claim appears in *Le Monde*, 24 September 1991; for an interesting discussion (and debunking) of this claim, see Patrick Geary, *The Myth of Nations* (Princeton: Princeton University Press, 2003).

11. While many of the puns, such as the dog Idéfix (= *idée fixe*), are much funnier in the original French, for the sake of English-speaking readers, I have used the English versions of the names, as translated by Anthea Bell and Derek Hockridge. Nevertheless, the translators frequently merit particular praise with regard to these translations, and most particularly in the case of Idéfix, which becomes Dogmatix, playing both on the original French and the word *dog* itself. For a more in-depth listing of these, see *http://www.-asterix-obelix.nl/*, or Sudhakar Chandrasekhran and Ron Dippold's excellent annotations, downloadable in a number of formats at *http://asterix.openscroll.org/other_formats.html#notes-other-formats-table*.

12. "Je me documente à toutes sortes de sources…. Mais quand je travaille, je ferme mes bouquins. Mon boulot, c'est le pastiche" (translation mine; original quoted in Screech, p. 77).

13. "Senza badare all'assoluta inverosimiglianza della sua cronologia" (translation mine).

14. The ability of the Gaulish village to resist occupation is explained in an earlier comic by the discovery of a magic potion brewed by the druid Getafix (which explains his name), that gives superhuman strength to all who drink it. Obélix's supreme power works on a subversion of the Achilles mythos; having fallen into the cauldron as a child, he alone has permanent magical strength.

15. While I have tried to avoid simply listing differences between the comic and the film, it is perhaps worth explaining here that the trip by the Gauls to Scandinavia to rescue the kidnapped Justforkix was a complete invention on the part of the film. In *Astérix and the Normans*, the action takes place entirely on the beach of Armorica (described variously as a Normandy Landing, and a Norman Invasion), which leaves the Vikings sailing back to their homeland at the conclusion of the adventure.

Works Cited

Aberth, John. *A Knight at the Movies: Medieval History in Film*. New York: Routledge, 2003.

Astérix and the Normans. 1978; rpt. London: Knight Books, 1982.

Eco, Umberto. *Travels in Hyperreality: Essays*. London: Picador, 1987.

Hoesterey, Ingeborg. *Pastiche: Cultural Memory in Art, Film, Literature*. Bloomington: Indiana University Press, 2001.

Kendrick, T. A. *A History of the Vikings*. 1930; rpt. New York: Dover, 2004.

McKinney, Mark, ed. *History and Politics in French-Language Comics and Graphic Novels*. Jackson: Mississippi University Press, 2008.

Müller, Beate. *Parody: Dimensions and Perspectives*. Oxford: Blackwell, 1997.

Samuels, Raphael. *Theatres of Memory: Past and Present in Contemporary Culture*. London: Verso, 1994.

Sanfilippo, Matteo. *Il Medioevo secondo Walt Disney*. Roma: Castelvecchi, 1993.

Segal, Robert A. *Hero Myths: A Reader*. Oxford: Blackwell, 2000.

Screech, Matthew. *Masters of the Ninth Art: Bandes Dessinées and Franco-Belgian Identity*. Liverpool: Liverpool University Press, 2005.

Stam, Robert. *Subversive Pleasures: Bakhtin, Cultural Criticism, and Film*. Baltimore: Johns Hopkins Press, 1989.

Trafford, Simon, and Aleks Pluskowski. "Antichrist Superstars: The Vikings in Hard Rock and Heavy Metal." In *Mass-Market Medieval: Essays on the Middle Ages in Popular Culture*, ed. David W. Marshall. Jefferson, NC: McFarland, 2007.

Wawn, Andrew. *The Vikings and the Victorians: Inventing the Old North in Nineteenth-Century Britain*. Cambridge: D.S. Brewer, 2002.

Northern Lite: A Brief History of Animated Vikings

MICHAEL N. SALDA

Cartoon Vikings take a bewildering variety of forms. From agents of mindless destruction to heroic remnants of an ancient and noble race, the peoples of medieval Scandinavia have been portrayed by animators in conflicting ways since at least the late 1950s. Today both the berserking, horned-helmeted caricature and the lonely survivor of a bygone civilization can easily be found on Cartoon Network, Boomerang, YouTube, and elsewhere. Curiously, the inconsistent, if not indeed often bipolar characterization of the cartoon Viking seems to cause viewers no lasting confusion. We know a Viking when we see one, despite our inability to say exactly what defines him.

Searching online resources such as the Internet Movie Database (http://www.imdb.com) and the Big Cartoon Database (http://www.bcdb.com) for animated works featuring Vikings, Erik, Olaf, Leif, Thor, Odin, Loki, Beowulf, Valhalla, Asgard, and related terms exposes the leading edge of a large Nordic floe. Dozens of individual cartoons, animated series, and feature-length animated films emerge. In cartoons short and long, for theatrical release and television, the Viking proves to be a resilient, recurring character. Although his origins cannot be precisely identified, it comes as small surprise that cartoon Norsemen make their debut in the midst of a spate of blockbuster Viking feature films that begin with 1954's *Prince Valiant*.

The Beginnings

Arguably the most celebrated Viking cartoon is the theatrically released "What's Opera, Doc?" (Warner Bros., 1957), an energetic romp that also enjoys the distinction of being among the earliest of Viking cartoons. Chuck Jones's masterpiece presents Norse myth as reinterpreted by Wagner and reinterpreted once more by Michael Maltese, who provided the story and lyrics for Jones's direction. Elmer Fudd takes the role of the legendary Siegfried in three pursuits of eternal quarry Bug Bunny. First Elmer hunts Bugs in an attempt to "kill the wabbit," then he courts Bugs in drag disguise as the Valkyrie Brünnhilde, and finally he calls upon the heavens to strike down the deceptive lagomorph.

Norse elements filtered through Romantic opera abound. Elmer wears what comes to be an almost ubiquitous prop inherited ultimately from the nineteenth-century playhouse and more immediately from Hollywood's live-action Vikings: the nonhistorical horned helmet, always a sure sign that a cartoon Viking has arrived. For his part, Bugs (as Brünnhilde) sports a Valkyrie's winged headgear, another carryover from the stage and screen. At the cartoon's end, with Bugs killed by lightning that Elmer summoned, the victorious yet miserable Elmer carries his deceased "wuv" toward a light suggesting Valhalla. Throughout the cartoon, strains from Wagner's *Ring* cycle and other compositions rise to reinforce the idea that "What's Opera, Doc?" is an animated journey into Norse mythology.

Bugs returned to the Nordic sphere the following year in Friz Freleng's Oscar-winning "Knighty Knight Bugs" (Warner Bros., 1958). The short opens with an unnamed king — presumably Arthur — speaking: "Noble knights of the Round Table [burbling pause], ever since the accursed Black Knight captured our Singing Sword, evil times hath befallen us [more burbling]. One of ye knights must recover the Singing Sword." The task falls to court jester Bugs, to whom the king promises torture and death unless Bugs can recover the stolen item.

Cut to the Black Knight's castle. The Black Knight (Yosemite Sam, whose helmet has no horns though his exceptionally bushy red moustache fortuitously enhances his Viking aspect) and his "idyot" dragon slumber. Bugs sneaks into the castle, locates the Singing

Lobby card from "What's Opera, Doc?" (1957) (editor's collection).

Sword and — unimpressed by the weapon — wonders aloud why it is called what it is. The audience already knows. Theatergoers would recall the sword that Hal Foster had introduced into the Viking/Thule story line of his *Prince Valiant* comic strip in the late 1930s and that Twentieth Century–Fox had recently popularized again in *Prince Valiant*. As Robert Wagner's Valiant explains: "The Singing Sword will only give its power to its rightful owners. It will never sing in the hands of a traitor." And, as if in answer to Bugs's question, the sword in his hands begins to warble, making the sound of a musical saw. Its song wakes the knight and dragon. A conventional chase cartoon in a medieval setting follows: a drawbridge drops on the Black Knight's head, an ineptly aimed catapult launches him into a wall, a moat drenches the bungling knight repeatedly, and finally the dragon sneezes inside an anachronistic TNT storeroom to launch the castle's tower and its occupants into space. As a gloating Bugs leaves the castle and sets out for the horizon, the sword begins to sing once more. The premise — that Bugs must return the sword to the rather mean-spirited king who presides over the Round Table — seems to have been forgotten as the iris closes. Or perhaps there is no reason to return to the court, because the sword, now in Bugs's hands, has found its true owner.

Live-action features also contributed directly to a growing visual lexicon of the animated Viking. For 1958's *The Vikings*, animators at UPA created a two-minute title sequence and a minute of end credits that depict Norsemen who differ but little from the Normans (descendants of Norsemen) of the Bayeux Tapestry, the primary visual touchstone that guided the UPA animators. These UPA Vikings receive sober treatment: bearded and wearing unadorned helmets in keeping with the tapestry's style; reasonably accurate illustrations of the tapestry's stripe-hulled, stripe-sailed, shield-emblazoned, dragon-prowed longships that allowed Vikings to pillage other lands; and (from the animators' imaginations, not the tapestry) a pictorial narrative showing a horned-helmeted god Odin — sitting astride Sleipnir, his legendary eight-legged horse — whom courageous Vikings hope to meet in Valhalla after a hero's death.

But neither highbrow references to opera and museum artifacts nor middlebrow cinematic allusions to a recent Hollywood hit appeared in a 13-part (three and one-half minutes per segment) slapstick serial adventure that took Ruff, Reddy, and Prof. Gizmo to the frozen north on NBC television's *The Ruff and Reddy Show* (Hanna-Barbera, 1959). When Reddy's clumsiness botches the professor's mission to the moon and forces the spacecraft back to earth, they crash in an arctic wilderness. There they join forces with Olaf, a small yet relentlessly belligerent Viking lad. With Olaf at their side, they fight first a polar bear and then Capt. Greedy. Greedy has followed a radio signal to the craft, planning to steal its technology in a plot that mirrors similar Cold War fare from ABC's contemporaneous *Rocky and His Friends*. Viking know-how allows Olaf and his companions to overcome the villain by means of sword and shield, a trained falcon, an oliphant, charging like a bull with his horned helmet, a dragon-prowed longship, and finally the help of Olaf's bearded and plaited-haired adult Norse kinsmen. In the end, thanks to the little Viking, Gizmo's secrets are kept from falling into evil hands.

From such cartoons of the late 1950s, we first learned how to identify a cartoon Viking. In this composite portrait, the animated Viking often sports a beard, could wear a horned helmet, dresses in primitive clothing, expertly sails a longship, and fights fiercely. A pattern was taking shape.

The 1960s

However, in the United Kingdom, writer/illustrator Peter Firmin and scriptwriter Oliver Postgate brought to BBC television another view of early Norse civilization in the collage-animated series of *The Saga of Noggin the Nog* (Smallfilms, 1960). The half dozen 20-minute episodes — as well as the best-selling books that soon followed — tell of the good-hearted, gentle people of the medieval Northlands, the Nogs, under the benevolent rule of King Noggin. Although the Nogs face many internal and external threats to their peaceful existence, Noggin rarely draws his sword. Instead, the king relies primarily on his eponymous albeit sometimes addled noggin, with help from loyal guard Thor Nogson, bungling court inventor Olaf the Lofty, the wise and compassionate Queen Nooka, and Noggin's clever son Prince Knut.

Firmin and Postgate offered Vikings who ran counter to many of Hollywood's developing stereotypes. In addition to Noggin's desire to understand and negotiate his way out of troubles rather than fight, *Noggin the Nog* also suggested that helmets and beards might vary by a character's disposition: evil uncle Nogbad, for instance, sports a helmet with razor-sharp horns and wears a villain's twirled moustache; Thor (with heavy, groomed beard) and the Nog castle guards (with simple moustaches or clean-shaven) wear helmets with miniature wings or horns safety-capped by small balls. Harmless, clean-shaven Noggin himself wears only an inoffensive dome surmounted by a simple crown.

Noggin failed to stem the growing tide of Viking violence that flowed from America's shores. Bugs and his Warner pals continued to channel uniformly ferocious Viking spirit in Friz Freleng and Hawley Pratt's "Prince Violent" (Warner Bros., 1961) — a title that verbally plays on Hollywood's best-known Viking film. But the theatrical title of this Warner short proved unacceptable for network television, for which the cartoon was retitled "Prince Varmint" later in the decade. Horns bristle everywhere: on the helmet of Sam the Terrible (Yosemite Sam), on the dragon-prowed ship that he sails, and even on the helmet worn by the elephant that Sam rides. Sam's Viking look is balanced by his opponent Bugs, whose bunny ears thrust through a helmet to mirror his enemy's appearance.

Sam invades the land by longship, then moves like a whirlwind and gibbering à la another antagonistic Warner character, the Tasmanian Devil. As Sam and his sword pass over the hero's rabbit hole, Bugs is reminded of every household's must-have gadget of the era, an electric can opener. Bugs can see that Sam will be "troublesome," so he nonchalantly arms to deal with "the little monster." Sam's repeated assaults on the castle in which the local peasants have taken refuge meet with repeated failures. His bull-like charge at the castle gate ends with him stuck in the timbers. Next Bugs thwarts Sam's second charge, now with Sam astride the elephant, by mean of a *trompe l'oeil* gate painted on the castle wall. Then Sam puts his elephant to work launching stones over the battlements, forces him to charge across a drawbridge that cannot support the weight, and tries to employ the beast as a raft to cross the moat, all to no useful effect except to cause the abused, "stupid pachee-derm" to abandon his Viking master. Alone, Sam tries tunnels and explosives, finally gaining entrance to the castle, where he learns that the elephant — with a new, Marvin the Martian-style bristle-topped helmet to show his changed allegiance — has joined Bugs "on the good guys' side." Bugs and the elephant chase the invader back to his ship and out to sea, leaving Bugs to boast how much help he has been able to secure for "peanuts."

Comic book Vikings also came to life as animated Vikings on 1960s television. Secret-identity superhero Mighty Thor, one of Stan Lee's many contributions to the Marvel Comics universe, greeted 1966 by being given his own comic, *The Mighty Thor*, and a subseries slot on the syndicated *Marvel Superheroes Show* (Grantray-Lawrence Animation, 1966–68). Each week children tuned in to the cheaply animated six-minute adventures of Dr. Don Blake, who could transform to winged-helmeted Mighty Thor through the power of a cane that converts to the god's boomeranging hammer. In the series, the hero fights to keep the universe safe from various evils, often spawned by his adopted brother, the trickster Loki, in his many fruitless attempts to steal Thor's hammer. The series was produced on a shoestring budget, apparently by using preexisting Marvel comics as templates to produce extremely limited-animation, unattractive cartoons. The Viking lore imparted to viewers is shallow at best: a peppering of names (Asgard, Odin, Thor, Loki), but little else of interest to those who might want to learn about Viking culture or Norse myth from a comic book or its animated equivalent.

DC Comics countered Marvel in 1968 by introducing one of its own superheroes to villains disguised as Vikings in the seven-minute "Freeze's Frozen Vikings" on the CBS's *Batman/Superman Hour* (Ducovny Productions, 1968–69). One morning, an iceberg containing a Viking longship and its crew mysteriously floats into Gotham Harbor. The curator of the Gotham Museum seeks to defend the unprecedented find—as if it were a species needing protection—but Batman and Robin (as Bruce and Dick) doubt its authenticity. Their suspicions quickly prove justified. The "Vikings" are sinister Freeze's men staging an elaborate ruse. Soon, with sword and mace, they loot the Bank of Gotham and Gotham Department Store. The curator naively insists on shielding the "historical wonders" even as the crime spree unfolds, though at last he understands what Batman and Robin surmised from the start. In a final battle, Robin uses the villain's freeze-ray on the lead "Viking," whom the heroes then laughingly agree should be kept at the museum. The curator gets his specimen after all.

A short stretch from American comics is manga's *Astro Boy*, who, like Mighty Thor and Batman, was animated for television distribution in the 1960s. On NBC's half-hour episode of "The Viking King" (Mushi Productions, 1963), Astro Boy tangles with a band of pirates hijacking spaceships. However, these "Viking" pirates have no characteristics that actually identify them as *Vikings*. Although they do sail a ship (a spaceship), attack with swords (cutlasses), and come from a time earlier than Astro Boy's, nothing in the visuals concretely links these pirates to Norse forebears. (It seems to me only an ironic coincidence that the pirates follow a patch-eyed leader who could suggest to some viewers the one-eyed Odin.) I suspect these pirates became "Vikings" only in the dubbing studio. For example, when we learn that the pirate captain styles himself "the Viking King," a lackey enters to explain: "he says two kings are better than one king." Such English-specific word play—if not the entire idea of Vikings—seems to have been verbally grafted to this patently non–Viking *Astro Boy* episode to capitalize on American interest in Viking topics in the 1960s. One need not seek far in the era's similar shoddily dubbed Asian imports to understand influences that might spur Woody Allen to create 1966's *What's Up, Tiger Lily?*

Yet even Japanese filmmakers could be accused of inserting Vikings into places they perhaps did not logically belong. Case in point: Isao Takahata's feature-length anime *Taiyo no oji: Horusu no daiboken* (*The Prince of the Sun: The Adventure of Horus*) (Toei, 1968), released in America as *Little Norse Prince* in theaters and then *Little Norse Prince Valiant* on television to make the most of Viking themes that Western audiences would appreciate. Its considerable artistic merits aside—a young Hayao Miyazaki played a large role in the production—*Taiyo no oji* tells an odd tale, mixing aboriginal Japanese cultural traditions, costume, characters, and setting with the story of Horus (no relation to the Egyptian god), the last member of a Viking clan. The film does not explain how Horus's supposedly Norse ancestors, while fleeing a Chernabog-like demon, traveled from their village "on a quiet fjord way up north" to what the audience likely regards as wintry, northern Japan. However, *Taiyo no oji*'s Norse elements appear prominently throughout the film: a dilapidated, beached longship, long home to Horus's dying father; a Viking burial of sorts for the father, as Horus sets fire to the ship with father's corpse within; another, more modest, beached-ship burial in the fishing village where Horus finds a clan that takes him in; the hero's struggle with a monster (a giant fish) at the base of a waterfall, perhaps alluding to the Icelandic *Grettis Saga*; and a weapon inherited from his father, a small axe with a broken, stubby handle, that suggests Thor's hammer to an audience primed for allusions to Norse myth. The Vikings — if that is indeed who they are — receive a refreshingly realistic portrayal: rustic clothing made of skins, historically and culturally appropriate weapons (harpoons, axes), and nary a horned helmet, even in battle scenes.

Returning to North America, the talents of the Hardy Boys also brought them into contact with Viking culture in the late 1960s. The popular adventure-book heroes were rejuvenated as the animated bubblegum rockers "Hardy Boys Plus Three" (Joe and Frank, supplemented by pretty blonde Wanda, African American Pete, and the overweight Chubby) on ABC's *The Hardy Boys* (Filmation, 1969–71). The five travel the world, performing their songs and solving local mysteries between sets. In "The Viking Mystery Symbol" (1969), a concert tour — and gently educational adventure, in accord with the tone of the original 1963 book — through Canada's Northwest Territories leads to a mystery focused on a stolen Viking runestone that could lead to buried treasure. Although there are no living Vikings in the episode, "The Viking Mystery Symbol" taps into a popular notion of runestones as coded messages left behind by early Norsemen in their travels.

And there was animated evidence in the 1960s that the Norse traveled widely indeed — beyond the Middle Ages, Europe, North America, and even the planet according to "The Space Wolf" (circa 1967) on Canada's widely syndicated *Rocket Robin Hood* (Krantz Films, 1966–69). In the year 3000, descendants of Robin Hood and his merry men, now living on the New Sherwood Forest Asteroid, battle fresh incarnations of old foes: a new Prince John, a new Sheriff of N.O.T.T. (National Outerspace Terrestrial Territories), and the like. In this episode, first the Sheriff and then Robin and company encounter the Viking pirate Erik Arthur and his crew, who are pillaging interstellar shipping lanes in a rocket-powered longship equipped with a mix of modern weapons (tractor beam, "alpha attractor ray," and so on) likely borrowed from contemporaneous *Star Trek* episodes as well as venerable Norse standbys such as lightning from Thor's hammer. Realizing they have a common agenda, Robin partners with Erik to steal from Prince John, but when the double-crossing Viking breaks their deal, Robin takes all the gold and disables the alpha attractor ray to end Erik's piracy in the quadrant forever.

Back on earth, Warner-inspired zaniness continued with Peabody and Sherman's "Leif Ericson," Chilly Willy's "Vicious Viking," and *Arthur! and the Square Knights of the Round Table*'s "No Laugh Olaf." In the ABC short, Peabody and Sherman's time-travels take them on a pun-filled gambol to the year 995 to meet a heavily bearded, horned-helmeted, pseudo–Swedish-speaking ("Yumpin' yiminy!") explorer in "Leif Ericson" (1961), an episode of *Peabody's Improbable History* from *Rocky and His Friends* (Jay Ward, 1959–61). Leif and his crew are having difficulty keeping their ship afloat — and thus will be unable to discover Greenland — until Peabody and Sherman trace the trouble to Leif's 200-pound beard, which has led to the Norsemen's inability to achieve a precise (and nonsensical) ship-to-cargo balance. Much of the story revolves around attempts to shear Leif's facial hair, but ultimately another solution is found: grow the beard till it weighs 300 pounds and then discard the ship's 300-pound anchor to reach an ideal seafaring weight. The episode highlights Viking sailing and exploratory skills, though it must be admitted that the crew would not have traveled far without help from the future.

In the theatrically released "Vicious Viking" (Walter Lantz, 1967), while cutting ice blocks for a new igloo, Chilly and Smedley unearth a frozen Viking. They thaw him, releasing a throwback who could be *Ruff and Reddy*'s Olaf, all grown up. The Viking immediately begins brandishing his sword, spouting pseudo–Swedish, and trying to eat everything in sight to quell a hunger that has been building through 800 years in the ice. Wild, red-haired, bearded, horned-helmeted, and able to charge like a bull until Chilly makes him collide with an anvil, this berserking Norseman draws on nearly every caricature that had been developing for a decade. The Viking ends as he began, falling into frigid waters that again freeze him to await the day that some other animator would bring him back for more adventures. Chilly triumphantly dons the helmet and pseudo–Swedish diction as the cartoon comes to a close.

King Arthur's jester performed scenes from *Hamlet* for a horned-helmeted, oliphant-blowing, red-haired and -moustached, pseudo–Swedish-speaking Danish prince in the short "No Laugh Olaf" (c. 1967) on Australian television's *Arthur! and the Square Knight of the Round Table* (Air Programs International, 1966–68). Nonsense humor abounds as cowardly Arthur struggles to prevent Olaf's assault on Camelot. Because Arthur understands that the Viking's antagonism derives from a deep-seated inability to laugh, the jester is summoned to cure him. The "yester's" unfortunate choice of the melancholy Dane's "To be or not to be" soliloquy, however, fails to amuse the Danish prince before him. Then just as doom appears inevitable, the "Alas, poor Yorick" soliloquy — as the jester speaks directly to a skull — unintentionally tickles savage Olaf's funny bone. With Viking aggression tamed at last, Camelot is saved.

The Norsemen of "The Vikings" on the syndicated *Abbott & Costello* (Hanna-Barbera, 1967) have left scant trace of their existence beyond a website's report (http://www.pjfarmer.com/secret/Immortal/befuddled1d.htm) that the duo travels through time for an adventure in which Costello becomes a Viking chief and might have to marry an unsightly local. No further information about these undoubtedly comedic Vikings can be found. They likely share some stereotypical traits with the Norsemen of another Hanna-Barbera entry of the following year, 1968's "The Tiny Viking" on ABC's *The Adventures of Gulliver* (1968–70). In this half-hour episode, Gary Gulliver and his dog Tagg defend the good citizens of Lilliput against an old seafaring enemy "from an island in the north": tiny, pigtailed, winged-helmeted captain Thor and his crew of horned-helmeted marauders. From the safety of their dragon-prowed, stripe-sailed, shield-embellished longships, the Vikings launch stones into Lilliput and later stage a ground assault. Although there are setbacks, Gulliver and the spunky, ingenious Lilliputians successfully repel the invaders. Thor admits defeat to the "brave warrior" Gulliver, agrees to repair the damage the raid has done, swears never to attack again, and sails away.

A survey of the 1960s would be incomplete without an examination at the consciousness-raising episode of "The Lost Tribe of Golden Giants" (1967) from CBS's *The Lone Ranger* (Jack Wrather/Format Films, 1966–69). In this unusual short focused exclusively on Tonto's exploits, the Lone Ranger's "faithful Indian companion" rescues a Viking who has been forced to become the "stone-age, giant, freak" attraction in a traveling sideshow. As the angry sideshow operator pursues his escaped meal ticket and the "meddlin' redskin" across the desert, Tonto learns from Erik, his blond, bare-chested, horned-helmeted companion, of a tribe of Vikings descended from explorers long ago trapped in a hidden valley by a landslide. A recent earthquake allowed Erik to leave the valley, where he was promptly captured by the moustached villain who put him on display. Tonto pledges to help him return to his people. As they arrive at the valley and Erik rejoins his friends, the sideshow operator and his posse arrive with plans to enslave all the Vikings for future shows. Tonto explains that, to protect themselves, they now "must fight guns with wisdom and instinct." Tonto leads the Vikings to victory, then seals the valley again so that "ancient tribe safe from evils of civilization." In an episode where the only prominent white is a villain, "The Lost Tribe of Golden Giants" offers an intriguing narrative in which an honorable representative of one oppressed culture protects his equally honorable spiritual cousins from another culture from the evils of the white man. It was the Age of Aquarius.

The 1970s

Interest in seeing Vikings on American theater and television screens was waning significantly. The tide that had carried *The Vikings* (1958), *The Long Ships* (1963), and a formidable cinematic flotilla discussed elsewhere in this collection ebbed to a trickle by 1970. As producers of live-action films and television shows moved to other subjects, most animators followed suit. However, a smattering of Viking-themed cartoon episodes did premiere during the decade. The incongruous meeting suggested by "Tarzan and the Vikings" (1976) may initially seem as farfetched as the events that brought Tonto into contact with Vikings in the Old West, so the half-hour episode of CBS's *Tarzan, Lord of the Jungle* (Filmation, 1976–77) must explain how Norsemen came to establish an Amazonian outpost. Katrina gives the details: "The legends say that over a thousand years ago a Viking armada left our homeland to conquer the people to the south. But Odin grew angry at the small sacrifices taken, and sent the north wind to overtake them. The storm destroyed all but one longboat, and that was driven so far off course, the survivors were never able to find their way home again." Descendants of the original party have continued their Viking ways: building a new fleet of dragon-headed longships; dwelling in Norse-style cobblestone and timber dwellings; hunting with falcons; swearing by aspects of Asgard, Odin, and Thor; addressing their chieftain as *Jarl* Erik; and peppering their speech with other Scandinavian terms (delivered with Minnesotan accents). Belligerent men wear horned helmets, and social standing is reflected by the amount of hair on one's face. Oblivious to tropical heat, these Vikings dress in elegant, multilayered tunics that seem to have come from the pages of Foster's newspaper comic strip.

"Tarzan and the Vikings" traces Tarzan's enslavement by Torvald, the most aggressive of the tribe, to his eventual release by Erik. Along the way, Tarzan takes the side of young lovers Katrina and beardless Bjorn. The two cannot marry because Erik, Katrina's father, has already promised her to the fiercest of the Viking stock, Torvald, in a eugenics scheme aimed at keeping the Amazonian Vikings hardy for the next thousand years. Yet Erik needs to learn that Bjorn also possesses admirable qualities and to realize that Torvald seeks Katrina primarily as a stepping-stone to the throne (yes, there is a throne). Tarzan's presence in their community reveals Torvald's duplicity, allows Bjorn to shine and Katrina to change her marriage plans, and brings the Viking leader wisdom that he could gain only from spending time with the astute Lord of the Jungle.

The three "ghost Vikings" in "The Curse of the Viking Lake" (1978) on ABC's *Scooby's All-Star Laff-a-Lympics* (Hanna-Barbera, 1977–80) are, as always in the comedy-mystery series, no more than criminals in disguise — here, a Viking museum curator and two geologists posing as spirits. Their convoluted hoax relies on the curator's forged runic curse that warns people not to disturb a purported Viking burial ground; a fabricated shrine to Odin said to mark a Viking grave (to hide a secret passage into a mine); fake beards, animal-skin garb, and horned helmets presumably borrowed from the museum's exhibit; and a dragon-prowed longship, which the crooks are using to transport uranium from the alleged burial site. The Scooby bunch unravels the plot and then entrusts the two geologists and curator Hanson to Sheriff Svensen in a tale that appears to be set near Kensington, Minnesota, or a similar upper–Midwestern town known to celebrate its Scandinavian roots.

It took more than human sleuthing skills to stop "The Ghost Vikings" (1979) who appeared in a sunken Viking vessel off Norway's coast on ABC's *Spider-Woman* (DePatie-Freleng Enterprises, 1979–80). Here, Viking leader Valhammer sends three warriors from the year 952 through a "magic mirror" to a "magic time chest" in the sunken ship's hold in the present. The passage endows the three with extraordinary powers. Their flying longship allows the Vikings to harry the present, raiding London and Paris for treasure. Spider-Woman brings their wave of crime to an end, quashing Valhammer's plan to send an entire Viking army through time to conquer the world beyond the mirror.

Spider-Woman's Vikings are not far removed from *Star Trek*'s Klingons. Gruff, brutal, and entirely male (as far as can be observed in the scenes set in 952), raw Viking strength explicitly contrasts with Spider-Woman's superior feminine mental prowess and intuition. In this conflict, both sides also benefit from weapon upgrades courtesy of 1977's *Star Wars*: Viking swords sizzle electrically, a "light harpoon" is employed to snare a helicopter, and even Spider-Woman's webs fire with laser blaster sound effects. As is typical for the series, the suggestion of female superiority must be suppressed at the end: with the Viking threat eliminated, Spider-Woman returns to being newswoman Jessica, filing her nails and shopping.

Peabody's "Leif Ericson" and the Hardy Boys notwithstanding, animated works that overtly sought to *educate* school-age children about medieval Norse culture first appeared in the 1970s. "The Vikings" (1972) on *The Wonderful Stories of Professor Kitzel* (M. G. Animation, 1972–76) was one of dozens of short episodes from the series in which Prof. Kitzel introduced kids to history by way of his time-traversing electronic viewscreen. Kitzel, as his name suggests, often interrupts the viewscreen's reasonably reverent, "straight" history lesson (still images from a textbook) with wry remarks about the topic of the day — remarks that perhaps are meant to echo what was already in the mind of many a fifth-grader subjected to watching an unfunny series that was syndicated to television and sold to libraries for classroom use.

Across the Atlantic and similarly aimed at the education market, Albert Barillé launched the children's series *Il était une fois...* (Procidis) on France's FR3 in 1978. Its first subseries (*Il était une fois ... l'Homme*) provided an overview of human existence from the big bang to present. Episode 10 explores "L'Age des Vikings" with more or less "realistic" (albeit sanitized) cartoon depictions of PG-rated Norsemen and women, their customs, faith, culture, dwellings, and clothing, framed by the episode's narrative of a teacher explaining the day's lesson to his students. As edutainment, one can certainly do worse.

Continuing to court the youth audience, Japanese animators brought Runer Jonsson's Swedish children's book *Vicke Viking* (1963) to widespread Asian and European syndication in the mid–1970s with 78 half-hour episodes of *Chīsana baikingu Bikke* (Zuiyo, 1974–75; *Vicky the Viking* in Anglophone markets), the story of mild-mannered Bikke (Vicky), a boy who routinely uses his imagination rather than brute strength to help his one-eyed father and the rest of their horned-helmeted clan overcome various obstacles. Although not explicitly educational, in each episode Bikke serves up a lesson in proper, peaceful, thoughtful behavior to his own people and to others whom they meet. His pacifism recalls Noggin's.

Fewer outright silly Vikings came to the screen in the 1970s, but they occasionally made an appearance. The British Film Institute's online catalog describes John and Janice Watson's "Pillage Idiot" (1976)—a revealing title if ever one was—"about a dim-witted Viking and the various 'secret weapons' with which he plans to obliterate his British adversaries. Unfortunately, these ingenious devices never quite work as intended." One can only imagine....

The 1980s

Internationally syndicated anime Vikings continued to emigrate from Japan to markets around the globe in the 1970s and 1980s. Marine Boy's underwater excursion to the "Land of the Strange Vikings" (circa 1970) on *Marine Boy* (Japan Tele-Cartoons and Seven Arts, circa 1966–70) and LunLun's encounter with "The Viking Treasure" (1979) on *The Flower Child LunLun* (Toei, 1979–80) attest to the existence on Viking-themed anime in the 1970s, though reliable details about these episodes are unavailable. However, we are on surer ground with "The World of Odin" from the revitalized *Astro Boy* series (Tezuka Productions, 1980; dubbed for English distribution a few years later). This striking half-hour episode tells of the search for treasure reportedly left by King Erik in a lost Viking burial ground. The hunt leads to a surprising discovery: "Odin" is a stranded "explorer" robot from planet Xenon. The robot was worshiped as a god by medieval Vikings ("fools," Odin calls them) who did not comprehend the robot's technology when it crashed on earth over a millennium ago. Odin's desire to cannibalize Astro Boy's robotics to repair itself leads to a fight that Astro Boy wins by melting Odin in a sulfur spring—but not before we learn much about Vikings.

"The World of Odin" contains a hoard of authentic and fabricated Viking lore. Prof. Elefun's history lesson for Astro Boy sets the stage. He describes the warriors who sailed from Scandinavia to conquer regions in Europe. Some followed Erik to Greenland, where the king offered gold to Odin and inscribed stones that are now said to be located in a burial ground that even the Nazis could not find during World War II. We meet two warring Viking clans—one sails, is well-groomed, dresses in woven fabrics, and wears horned helmets; the other hirsute, helmetless, and dressed in rustic skins leads a primitive existence on the tundra—and both sides claim to be the true descendants of Odin and Erik. The first clan's chief is the one-eyed, one-armed Captain Claude, who suffered his injuries long ago in a duel with Zamara, chief of the primitives. A rematch, following an ancient rite that determines who will be *Gunnarr*, results in Zamara's death. But Claude will not be leader for long, as he dies soon afterward in a fight with robot Odin. Claude departs the scene aboard a ghostly longship that sails off the sea and into the sky, presumably bound for Valhalla. It then remains for Astro Boy to finish off the renegade robot.

Marvel superheroes and Viking gods once again clashed in "The Vengeance of Loki"

(1981), a half-hour episode of NBC's *Spider-Man and His Amazing Friends* (Marvel Productions, 1981–82). Loki's latest plot to defeat Mighty Thor and destroy mankind involves an iceberg, the powerful "twin diamonds" of the gods, a resurrected Erik, a flying longship, and lasers. Although the animation far surpasses that of *The Mighty Thor* series of the 1960s, the Viking world again springs primarily from the imaginations of Marvel staffwriters having a hard time taking the material seriously:

ERIK: Have I died and awakened in Valhalla?
FIRESTAR (aside, to Spider-Man): Valhalla is the Viking's heaven.
SPIDER-MAN (dismissively): Thanks. Now can you tell me the capital of Montana?

Beyond the decade's animated manga and comic book Norse excursions, the 1980s offered other Viking cartoons as well. In the half-hour "Olé the Red Nose Viking" from the syndicated *Yogi's Treasure Hunt* (Hanna-Barbera, 1985), a dozen Hanna-Barbera regulars seek the Chalice of Valhalla, an inverted horned helmet that will grant a wish to the first to drink from it. While Dick Dastardly and Mutley aim to find the prize for their own nefarious reasons, both the good and bad guys must contend with Olé—a close cousin to Chilly Willy's "Vicious Viking"—a voracious, pseudo–Swedish-speaking, horned-helmeted, longship-sailing Viking thawed from centuries in the ice and intent on using the chalice's one wish for world domination. But Snagglepuss's inadvertent sip from the cup and a trivial wish bring all grander plans to naught.

Stranded interplanetary traveler Alias of Zogma, covertly serving as King Arthur's court jester, faced off with Norseman Erik the Brainless in "The Viking Airship" and "Monster of the Lake" on British ITV's *Alias the Jester* (Cosgrove Hall Productions, 1985). These shorts present the stock comedic Viking caricature: horned helmets, thick beards, stupidity, and a pronounced inclination toward acquisition by means of violence, kidnapping, torture, and theft. From aboard their flying longship and a mechanized sea beast, Newcastle-twanged Erik and his first mate—whose nationality is determined more by exigencies of vituperative alliteration ("Swedish simpleton," "Norwegian numbskull," and "Danish dimwit") than geographic fidelity—seek Arthur's daughter, the Princess Amaranth. Alias stops them every time.

"The Littlest Viking" (1986), a half-hour episode on NBC's *Smurfs* (Hanna-Barbera, 1981–90), offered yet another encounter between a jester and Vikings. A raid on a seaside market and the unintended kidnapping of court jester Peewit and several Smurfs transport the cast to a Viking village. A range of Norsemen, good and bad, come into view. Leading the good is red-moustached, horned-helmeted King Derrick, whose singular integrity shows itself when he *pays* for merchandise that other Vikings have seized. Derrick rules a community of kind-hearted, rustic folk. Helmets aside, the men (usually bearded) wear clothes not substantially different from the vaguely medieval garb typical of humans in the *Smurfs*' cosmos. The women of the village dress in utilitarian peasant smocks and bonnets. Both women and men braid their hair. Animators portray the villainous Vikings of Erik's kingdom differently. The uncouth Olaf the Doubter, who led the furious sack of the market and secretly has eyes on Derrick's throne, goes about shirtless and helmetless, while his dim-witted yes-man Lars has a helmet with horns that curve inward to threaten only each other. Olaf is heavily bearded and, because he is bald (and thus must remain helmetless so that his pate remains exposed), plaits his whiskers. Lars is beardless, a further sign of his developmental retardation.

Into the middle of the power struggle between Derrick and Olaf falls Peewit, whose face the Vikings recognize from one carved on a runestone that prophesies Peewit as a great warrior who will save the people from the Storm King's frequent avalanches. Derrick's daughter Sigrid gives Peewit a Valkyrie's winged helmet to signal his hero's role. She also introduces him to "a delicacy my father discovered in a strange land across the seas": popcorn! By the end of the episode, Peewit and the Smurfs have negotiated an agreement: Olaf, Lars, and the Storm King swear allegiance to Derrick. As in many other episodes, Peewit and the Smurfs show that everyone can live peacefully, even Vikings.

Two feature-length Viking cartoons also opened in theaters in the 1980s. John Gardner's revisionist *Grendel* (1971) came to the screen in Australia's highly stylized musical adaptation *Grendel Grendel Grendel* (Victorian Film Corporation, 1981), a film that often calls to mind *Yellow Submarine* in its visual design and Monty Python in its intelligent, ironic outlook. The beleaguered Vikings of Hrothgar's meadhall are primarily background characters to Grendel's existential foreground. Yet within that sixth-century Scandinavian backdrop the animators offer many violent, greedy, bumbling, horned-helmeted and plaited-haired Vikings who fight to defend themselves against the Great Bogey from the mere. These Vikings inscribe their exploits on stone pillars, are entertained by a court "shaper" who sings of their deeds and, when the Bogey wins a fight, burn their dead on pyres.

Strategic reorganization of tales from the *Prose Edda* allowed Denmark's Swan Film Productions to focus on Thor's juvenile bondservants Tjalfe and Røskva and a toddler-like troll-giant named Quark in the ambitious, feature-length *Valhalla* (1986), which derives most immediately from Peter Madsen's 1970s Danish comic of the same name. The film offers many familiar episodes from Norse mythology: Thor and Loki's contests against the giants, the battle with the Midgard Serpent, and the goat-bone-breaking incident that forces the children into servitude, to name a few. However, *Valhalla*'s animators break from myth to offer many domestic scenes designed to hold the interest of children: Tjalfe and Røskva's time with their parents in a rustic peasant cottage, the antics of Thor and Sif's infant babies, Tjalfe and Røskva frolicking with Quark, and so on. And while the cataclysmic Ragnarok itself was no doubt too bleak a matter for *Valhalla*'s intended demographic, perceptive viewers realize that the first scene's Yggdrasil, the World Tree, is echoed in the final scene with Tjalfe, Røskva, and Quark living in a treehouse — suggesting that they are the ones who, like the *Edda*'s Lif and Leifthrasir, will survive the Norse apocalypse to carry on after the end-time of the gods.

As the decade came to an end, Hägar the Horrible stepped from the daily funnies to television for a half-hour CBS special in *Hägar Knows Best* (Hanna-Barbera/King Features, 1989). Returned from two years of pillaging ("a business trip," "taking souvenirs they didn't pay for"), Hägar readjusts to life at home with his wife and kids. During his absence, son Hamlet has turned from the pursuit of Viking ways to reading books; daughter Honi has become engaged at 16 (Hägar: "at long last"), though not to dad's favorite, the unkempt and dense Olaf, but to wimpy troubadour Lute. Although Hägar foresees the end of unciv-ilization as he knows it, he learns to accept his children for what they have become. The cartoon may hold a record for helmet variety: horned, spiked, antlered, funneled, and winged, worn by men, women, and pets, even to bed.

The 1990s to the Present

More cartoons have followed along paths blazed by earlier animated Vikings. The Fam-ily Channel aired 65 half-hour episodes of a complex soap opera of young adult angst and today's problems set in medieval Thule in *The Legend of Prince Valiant* (Sei Young Animation/Hearst Entertainment, 1991–94). Vikings, bad and good, some with horns but most without, populate a narrative designed to offer a family-friendly alternative to seamier contemporaneous primetime network fare such as *Beverly Hills, 90210* and *Melrose Place.*

Although the 1990s produced no feature films with cartoon Vikings, the first decade of the new millennium has spawned many. The direct-to-DVD *Leif Ericson: The Boy Who Discovered America* (Phil Nibbelink Productions, 2006) blended authentic incidents from the lives of Erik the Red and his son Leif with elements of Norse myth. The fusion allows Fenrir, the wolf bound by the gods, to occupy an island in the North Atlantic and offer life advice to Leif as he sails toward the New World and then returns home again.

Two beloved French icons also crossed paths with Vikings: resourceful albeit clumsy maid Bécassine is drawn into a crime caper that centers on a torque recovered from an ancient Viking hoard in *Bécassine: Le trésor Viking* (Ellipsanime, 2001); a Viking chieftain pursues Astérix across Gaul because he mistakenly believes that the diminutive hero can teach his warriors to fly in *Astérix et les Vikings* (M6 Studio, 2006). Robert Zemeckis's big-budget, computer-animated *Beowulf* (ImageMovers, 2007) offered a 3-D IMAX experience designed to appeal to viewers whose notions of Viking life spring primarily from graphic novels and video games.

As the decade closed, *The Secret of Kells* (Cartoon Saloon, 2009) traced a young monk's journey beyond cloister walls into an enchanted forest for adventures and knowledge that will allow civilization to survive the onslaught of the Northmen, depicted as brutish, angular, horned monoliths relentlessly burning their way across the landscape in search of gold. The Vikings of the 3-D *How to Train Your Dragon* (DreamWorks, 2010) received a more even-handed treatment in the tale of Hiccup, a reflective, inventive lad who befriends a wounded dragon and thereby manages to end a centuries-old conflict between his people and the beasts. Although the DreamWorks feature offers Vikings who dress and often comport themselves much as their animated precursors did, Hiccup demonstrates that Vikings are at heart no different from all of us once we get beyond surface details of horned helmets, rustic clothing, and studded battle gear.

Vikings have also often made appearances in dozens of shorter cartoons. The 1990s brought more escapades involving Viking treasures, marauders, horned helmets, time travel that transports medieval characters to the present or the reverse, isolated descendants of lost expeditions, pseudo–Swedish, and allusive use of Norse myth in episodes of *The Adventures of Don Coyote and Sancho Panda* ("Veni Vidi Viking"), *Where's Waldo?* ("Viking Fling"), *Young Robin Hood* ("The Viking Treasure"), *The Busy World of Richard Scarry* ("Young Vikings," "Viking Pigs"), *The New Adventures of Jonny Quest* ("Alligators and Okeechobee Vikings"), *Gargoyles* ("Eye of the Storm"), *Il était une fois … les Explorateurs* ("Erik the Red"), *Loggerheads* (the entire 1997 series), *Angry Beavers* ("Food of the Clods"), *Tommy & Oscar* ("The Secret of Olaf the Viking"), *Blazing Dragons* ("Erik the Well-Read"), *Histeria!* ("The Attack of the Vikings"), *Disney's Hercules* ("Hercules and the Twilight of the Gods"), *Animated Epics* ("Beowulf"), and *I am Weasel* ("I am Viking").

The new century has further enlarged this animated Viking smorgasbord with episodes of *Johnny Bravo* ("Thunder God Johnny"), *VeggieTales* ("Lyle, the Kindly Viking"), *Iron Nose* ("The Viking Giant," "Vikings on the Move"), *Samurai Jack* ("Jack and the Lava Monster"), *Horrible Histories* ("Vicious Vikings"), *Olliver's Adventures* ("Vikings from Outer Space"), *Robbie the Reindeer* ("Legend of the Lost Tribe"), *The Mythical Detective Loki Ragnarok* (the entire 2003 series), *Lilly the Witch* ("Lilly and the Vikings"), *The Backyardigans*

("The Viking Voyage"), *The Grim Adventures of Billy and Mandy* ("A Kick in the Asgard"), *Time Warp Trio* ("Viking It and Liking It"), *King Arthur's Disasters* ("The Viking Venture"), *Loonatics Unleashed* ("Loonatics on Ice"), *The Life and Times of Juniper Lee* ("It Takes a Pillage," "Trickster's in Town," "Citizen June," "Who's Your Daddy?"), *Random! Cartoons* ("Ivan the Unbearable"), and *SpongeBob SquarePants* ("Dear Vikings").

Although these animated Vikings of the past two decades often differ little in look and demeanor from their ancestors of the 1950s and 1960s, clever writers have found ever new puns to telegraph the berserking silliness to come in "Veni Vidi Viking," "A Kick in the Asgard," "It Takes a Pillage," and so on. While occasionally a few medieval Norseman with admirable attributes have also appeared in episodes such as "Erik the Well-Read" and "Lyle, the Kindly Viking," the "good" Viking remains a rare exception to time-honored rules for cartoon Viking deportment. These deviations from the expected entertain precisely because they openly flout the underlying stereotype of irrepressible violence and acquisition that viewers have come to anticipate over the past half century.

At press time, a healthy outlook for the animated Viking lies ahead. Flash-animated cartoon Norsemen have invaded the internet. Although one could easily cite many commendable entries, two deserve special note: Joel Trussell's music video for Jason Forrest's "War Photographer" (2005), which imagines a seaborne battle of Viking death metal bands, and "Scent of Valhalla" from Animatus Studio's *Derf the Viking* series (2008), an homage both to early Warner Bros. cartoons and the off-color humor of *Ren and Stimpy* and *South Park*. Still more animated Vikings seem certain to follow, thanks to YouTube tutorials such as Peter the Webcartoonist's "How to Draw a Cartoon Viking" (2008). Here future animators may learn the rudiments of bringing to life the next horned-helmeted, heavily bearded, jerkined warrior, stepped fresh from a longship that has sailed down the fjords with an armed Viking crew to pillage a town near you.

The Vikings on Film: A Filmography

Kevin J. Harty

The only previously published list of films about Vikings is Dag Sødtholt's very brief "Brede Seil over Nordsjø Går" in *Film og kino* 5 (September 2009): 49–51. The filmography below lists all full-length fiction films (animated and otherwise) that treat the Vikings or their legacy as an essential part of their plot. I have provided basic information about the film's production, a selection of reviews, and, where appropriate, bibliographic data on significant longer discussions of a film. The information that follows can be easily supplemented by a search of databases such as imdb.com, Lexis-Nexis, and ProQuest, as well as of the on-line versions of most major newspapers throughout the world, and of the numerous personal blogs and websites (albeit widely varying in their objectivity and value) that review, comment on, or discuss films.

Alfred the Great (1969)
Dir. Clive Donner; screenplay by Ken Taylor and James R. Webb, from a short story by James R. Webb. Great Britain: MGM/Bernard Smith-James R. Webb Productions.
The at-first reluctant Alfred becomes king and, during the early years of his reign, unites the Saxons against their common enemy the Viking Danes.
Reviews: *Film Daily* 22 October 1969: 4; *Films and Filming* 15 (September 1969): 59–60; *Films in Review* 20 (October 1969): 513–14; *Kinematograph Weekly* 19 July 1969: 23; *Monthly Film Bulletin* 36 (September 1969): 187; *Motion Picture Herald* 10 September 1969: Product Digest Section 269–70; *New York Times* 4 December 1969: 70; *Sight and Sound* 36 (Autumn 1969): 220; *Times* [of London] 17 July 1969: 9; *To-day's Cinema* 18 July 1969: 19; *Variety* 23 July 1969: 6.
Additional discussion: Young, Rob. "The Pattern under the Plough." *Sight and Sound* 20 (August 2010): 16–22.

And Trees Grow Out of Rocks (1965)
See *The Captive of the Dragon* (1965).

And Trees Will Even Grow Out of Rocks (1965)
See *The Captive of the Dragon* (1965).

Arthur the King (1982)
Dir. Clive Donner; screenplay by J. David Wyles. Great Britain and the United States: Martin Poll Productions, Comworld Films, and CBS-TV.
Alternate title: *Merlin and the Sword*.
King Arthur's court is overrun by guests and visitors, some expected and some not — including hundreds of Vikings.

Reviews: *Hollywood Reporter* 26 April 1985: 12; *New York Times* 26 April 1987: 3.30; *TV Guide* 33 (20–26 April 1985): A-144; *Variety* 8 May 1985: 162.
Additional discussions: Marill, Alvin H. *Movies Made for Television 1964–2004*. Lanham, MD: Scarecrow, 2005; Olton, Bert. *Arthurian Legends on Film and Television*. Jefferson, NC: McFarland, 2000.

As in Heaven (1992)
See *Svo á Jördu sem á Himni* (1992).

Astérix and the Vikings (2005)
See *Astérix et les Vikings* (2005).

Astérix et les Vikings (2005)
Dir. Stefan Fjeldmark and Jesper Møller; screenplay by Jean-Luc Goossens, based on the cartoon characters by Albert Uderzo and René Goscinny and adapted from their *Astérix et les Normands*, a volume in their series of Astérix *bandes dessinées*; feature-length animated film. France: SND, M6 Studio, Mandarin SAS, 2d3D Animations.
Alternate title: *Astérix and the Vikings*.
Astérix and Obélix seek to make a man out of the village chief's nephew as Viking marauders threaten their village.
Reviews: *Film français* 1 April 2006: 4; *Première* 351 (May 2006): 43; *Sight and Sound* 17 (March 2007): 46–47; *Télérama* 15 April 2006: 38; *Variety* 17 April 2006: 29.

The Attack of the Normans (1962)
See *I Normanni* (1962).

Beauty and the Beast (2002)
Dir. David Lister; screenplay by Paul Anthony. Great Britain: Peakingview/Crimson Knights Productions.
Alternate title: *Blood of Beasts* (2002).
Beowulf meets *Beauty and the Beast* when a Viking warrior is cursed for attempting to kill a beast scared to Odin. The curse is lifted when a Viking princess gives her life for the warrior whom she loves.
Reviews: *Screen Africa* September 2002: 5 and November 2002: 14.

Bécassine: Le Tresor Viking (2001)
Dir. Philippe Vial; screenplay by Beatrice Marthouret and Yves Coulon, from the comic strip by Jacqueline Rivière and Joseph Pinchon, which originally appeared in the first issue of *La Semaine de Suzette* on February 2, 1905; feature-length animated film. France: Christal Film.
The intrepid Breton nanny with her now-grown-up charge in tow travels through the sewers of Paris, among several Mediterranean ports, and across the frozen tundra of the Arctic regions in pursuit of a Viking treasure stolen from her employer.
Reviews: *Les Echos* [France] 13 December 2001: 45; *Le Figaro* 15 December 2001: n.p.; *Film-echo/Filmwoche* 17 May 2003: 31 and 31 May 2003: 28–29; *The Gazette* [Montréal] 11 October 2002: D6.
Additional discussion: Lehembre, Bernard. *Bécassine, une légende du siècle*. Paris: Hachette, 2005.

Beowulf (1998)
Dir. Graham Baker; screenplay by Mark Leahy from the Anglo-Saxon poem. United States, Great Britain, and France: Kushner-Locke Company, Capitol Films, Threshold Entertainment, and European Motion Picture Productions.
Baker offers his own spin on the details of the Anglo-Saxon film suggesting that larger threats to the comitatus come from within rather than from monstrous outside creatures like Grendel and his mother. Sexual transgression within the world of Hrothgar's court is the real cause of its downfall, and such transgression leads Hrothgar to father and then to reject Grendel.

Reviews: *Film Review* 600 (December 2000): 76; *Film tutti i film della stagione* 6 (July 1999): 54–55; *Première* 266 (May 1999): 77; *StarBurst* 269 (January 2001): 81; *Télérama* 5 May 1988): 38; *Variety* 7 June 1999: 30.

Additional discussions: Forni, Kathleen. "Graham Baker's *Beowulf*: Intersections between High and Low Culture." *Literature/Film Quarterly* 35 (July 2007): 244–49; Hughes, David. "An American Beowulf in Romania." *Fangoria* 198 (November 2000): 49–52.

Beowulf (2007)

Dir. Robert Zemeckis; screenplay by Neil Gaiman and Roger Avar—(very) loosely based on the Anglo-Saxon poem of the same title; feature-length animated, 3D digital film. United States: Paramount Pictures.

To save the aging King Hrothgar and his retainers, the eponymous hero, here not totally above-board in his motives, confronts a monster and his temptress mother, whose charms he cannot resist.

Reviews: *Empire* 223 (January 2008): 72 and 226 (April 2008): 136–37; *Entertainment Weekly* 965 (23 November 2007): 58; *Los Angeles Times* 15 November 2007: E1; *New York Times* 16 November 2007: E1, E18; *Newsweek* 150 (26 November 2007): 68; *Realms of Fantasy* 14 (December 2007): 8; *Screen International* 23 November 2007: 33; *Sight and Sound* 18 (January 2008): 61–62; *StarBurst* 357 (December 2007): 82–83 and 361 (April 2008): 114; *Time Out New York* 634 (22 November 2007): 130; *USA Today* 16 November 2007: E1; *Variety* 12 November 2007: 43, 49.

Additional discussions: Asma, Stephen T. "Never Mind Grendel. Can Beowulf Conquer the 21st-Century Guilt Trip?" *Chronicle of Higher Education* 7 December 2007: B14–15; Brown, William. "*Beowulf*: The Digital Monster Movie." *Animation: An Interdisciplinary Journal* 4 (July 2009): 153–68; Duncan, Jody. "All the Way." *Cinefex* 112 (January 2008): 44–50, 55–59; Kehr, Dave. "Duplicate Motion, Then Capture Emotion." *New York Times* 18 November 2007: Arts & Leisure 14–18; Lee, Chris. "Unusual Suspect." *Los Angeles Times* 15 November 2007: E1; Vaz, Mark Cotta, and Steve Starkey. *The Art of Beowulf*. San Francisco: Chronicle Books, 2007.

Beowulf and Grendel (2004)

Dir. Sturla Gunnarsson; screenplay by Andrew Rai Berzins based on the Anglo-Saxon poem *Beowulf*. Great Britain, Canada, and Iceland: Grendel and Beowulf Productions and Arclight Productions.

The familiar story is here offered with a twist: Grendel is a troll intent upon avenging the death of his father at the hands of Hrothgar.

Reviews: *Empire* 223 (January 2008): 194; *New York Times* 7 July 2006: B14; *Playback* 29 August 2005: 26; *Variety* 17 October 2005: 48.

Additional discussions: McFarlane, Brian. "Size Doesn't Matter." *Metro* [Australia] 144 (2004): 58–64; Ord, Wendy. "Lost in Iceland." *Take One* 14 (September–December 2005): 29–33.

Berserker (1987)

Dir. Jef Richard; screenplay by Jef Richard. United States: American Video Group/Paradise Filmworks.

A group of students camping in the woods are torn limb from limb by a Viking berserker who is cursed by the gods always to rise from the dead because in his first life he ate human flesh.

Review: *Variety* 27 May 1987: 38.

Berserker: Hell's Warrior (2001)

Dir. Paul Matthews; screenplay by Paul Matthews. Great Britain: Peakviewing Productions.

Two brothers, one cursed by Odin and turned into a blood-thirsty monster doomed to relive his life over and over, endlessly battle each other in the hopes that the curse can be lifted.

Review: *In Camera* April 2001: 10–11.

The Black Knight (1954)

Dir. Tay Garnett; screenplay by Alec Coppel. Great Britain: Warwick-Columbia.

Using Saracens disguised as Vikings, Sir Palamides, in league with King Mark, seeks to overthrow

Alan Ladd in the title role in Tay Garnett's 1954 film *The Black Knight* (editor's collection).

King Arthur's Camelot supplanting in the process Christianity with paganism. Their plans are foiled by a blacksmith named John who disguises himself as the mysterious Black Knight.

Reviews: *Film Daily* 21 October 1954: 6; *Harrison's Reports* 23 October 1954: 120; *Hollywood Reporter* 9 November 1954: 3; *Kinematograph Weekly* 26 August 1954: 21–22; *Monthly Film Bulletin* 21 (October 1954): 147; *Motion Picture Herald* 23 October 1954: Product Digest Section 185; *New York Times* 29 October 1954: 44; *To-day's Cinema* 25 August 1954: 10; *Variety* 8 September 1954: 6.

Additional discussion: Lupack, Alan. "An Enemy in Our Midst: *The Black Knight* and the American Dream." In Kevin J. Harty, ed. *Cinema Arthuriana, Twenty Essays.* 2002; rpt. Jefferson, NC: McFarland, 2010.

Blood of Beasts (2002)
See *Beauty and the Beast* (2002).

Brendan and the Secret of Kells (2009)
See *The Secret of Kells* (2009).

The Captive of the Dragon (1985)
Dir. Stanislav Rostotsky and Knut Andersen; screenplay by Stanislav Rostotsky and Knut Andersen. Norway and the USSR: Norsk Film and Gorky Film Studio.

Alternate titles: *And Trees Grow Out of Rocks, And Trees Will Even Grow Out of Rocks, The Captive of the Vikings, Dragens fange, Even on Rocks Trees Grow, I Na kamnjakh rastut derévja, Orangens fange.*

A Russian boy is kidnapped when Vikings raid his village and take him back to Norway where, once he grows up, he falls in love with a Viking princess.

Reviews: *Film og kino* 7 (October 1985): 258–59 and 8 (August 1985): 347, 368–69; *Scandinavian Film News* 5 (April 1985): 6; *Screen International* 19 October 1985: 306; *Soviet Film* 7 (July 1985): 12–15; *Variety* 28 August 1985: 12.

The Captive of the Vikings (1965)
See *The Captive of the Dragon* (1965).

I Coltelli del vendicatore (1965)
See *Knives of the Avengers* (1965).

Curse of the Viking Grave (1992)
Dir. Michael Scott; screenplay by Michael Scott. Canada and the United States: Muddy River Films and CanWest Broadcasting.

Alternate title: *Lost in the Barrens II: The Curse of the Viking Grave*

A teenager is tricked by a grifter into helping him find a white-gold cross supposedly buried in a Viking grave in rural Manitoba.

Review: *Toronto Star* 5 January 1992: C7 and 26 September 1993: E8; *Variety* 10 February 1991: 84.

Dragens fange (1965)
See *The Captive of the Dragon* (1965).

Erik the Conqueror (1961)
Dir. Mario Bava, screenplay by Piero Pierotti. Italy: Galatea Films.

Alternate titles: *Fury of the Vikings* and *Gli Invasori.*

A Viking orphan reared in England as a nobleman grows up to rescue his adopted mother when she is taken prisoner by Vikings and eventually saves his adopted homeland from further Viking raids and tyranny.

Reviews: *Daily Cinema* 26 April 1963: 6; *Film-echo/Filmwoche* 101 (19 December 1962): 7; *Kinematograph Weekly* 25 April 1963: 29; *Monthly Film Bulletin* 20 (June 1963): 86; *Motion Picture Herald* 18 September 1963: Product Digest Section 892; *Nuovo spettatore cinematografico* 30–31 (1962): 253–54; *Télérama* 26 March 1997: 123.

Additional discussions: Krafsur, Richard P., ed. *The American Film Institute Catalog of Motion Pictures, Feature Films 1961–1970.* New York: Bowker, 1976; Lucas, Tim. "Requiem for a Viking." *Video Watchdog* 25 (September-October 1994): 40–55; Poppi, Roberto, and Martin Pecorari. *Dizionario del cinema italiano. Vol. 3: I Film dal 1960 al 1969.* Rome: Gremese Editore, 1992.

Erik il vichingo (1964)
See *Vengeance of the Vikings* (1964).

Erik the Viking (1964)

See *Vengeance of the Vikings* (1964).

Erik the Viking (1989)

Dir. Terry Jones; screenplay by Terry Jones from a collection of short stories he originally wrote for children. Great Britain: Erik the Viking Productions and Prominent Features.

Erik finds himself a fish (or Viking) out of water when he rejects a life of rape and pillage as he sets out to awaken the gods to end a great winter that has buried his village in snow and ice.

Reviews: *Cinefantastique* 20 (November 1989); 26 and 20 (March 1990): 55; *Films and Filming* 419 (September 1989): 45; *Los Angeles Times* 1 November 1989: Calendar 3; *Monthly Film Bulletin* 56 (October 1989): 299; *New York Times* 28 October 1989: 13; *Positif* 345 (November 1989): 29–30; *Revue du cinéma* 454 (November 1989): 29–30; *StarBurst* 134 (October 1989): 22–23; *Sunday Times* [of London] 1 October C8; *Times* [of London] 28 September 1989: 22; *Variety* 6 September 1989: 22.

Additional discussion: Jones, Terry. *Erik the Viking*. New York: Applause Books, 1990. [Screenplay.]

Even on Rocks Trees Grow (1965)

See *The Captive of the Dragon* (1965).

Faintheart (2008)

Dir. Vito Rocco; screenplay by David Lemon and Vito Rocco. Great Britain: Odins Beard Ltd. and Channel Four Television Corporation.

Richard spends his weekends re-enacting Viking battles as he tries to win back his ex-wife and stare down those at work who bully him and his son because of his weekend activities.

Reviews: *Empire* 232 (October 2008): 63; *Sight and Sound* 18 (October 2008): 61–62: *Variety* 21 July 2008): 25.

Flight of the Raven (1984)

See *When the Raven Flies* (1984).

Full Moon (1990)

See *Runestone* (1990).

Fury of the Vikings (1961)

See *Erik the Conqueror* (1961).

Gisla Saga Surssonar (1981)

See *Útlaginn* (1981).

Grendel Grendel Grendel (1981)

Dir. Alexander Stitt; screenplay Alexander Stitt from the 1971 novel, *Grendel* by John Gardner, itself a reworking of the Anglo-Saxon poem *Beowulf*; feature-length animated film. Australia: Victorian Film Corporation and Animation Australia.

When Hrothgar summons Beowulf and his retainers to rid his land of the monster Grendel, it seems that man, not monster, is the truly destructive and frightening creature.

Reviews: *Cinefantastique* 12 (July-August 1982): 91; *Cinema Papers* 33 (July-August 1981): 286–87; *Hollywood Reporter* 14 April 1982: 9; *Metro* [Australia] 56 (Winter 1981): 64–65; *New York Times* 11 April 1982: 46 and 2A; *Variety* 4 November 1981: 26.

Hagbard and Signe (1967)

See *The Red Mantle* (1967).

Hammer of the Gods (2009)

See *Thor, Hammer of the Gods* (2009).

Här Kommer Bärsärkarna (1965)

Dir. Arne Mattsson; screenplay by Folke Nystrand. Denmark, Sweden, and Yugoslavia: Bison Film, Merry-Film, and Triglav Film.

Alternate title: *Here Come the Berserkers*.

Slapstick and what borders on soft-core pornography combine to give an atypical view of the supposed high jinx that punctuated lives of the Vikings as a group of berserkers led by Glum the Fly-infested and Garm the Stupid attack Rome, are sold into slavery as gladiators, end up bathing naked with Rome's most beautiful women, and leave half the city in ruins, before returning to Sweden to cause further mayhem. (In order to cut productions costs, the filmmakers used sets and props left over from Jack Cardiff's 1963 film, *The Long Ships*.)

Reviews: *Biografägaren* 40 (March 1965): 18–19; *Filmrutan* 8 (January 1965): 31.

Additional discussion: *Svensk filmografi 1960–1969*. Uppsala: Almqvist & Wiskell, 1977.

Here Come the Berserkers (1965)

See *Här Kommer Bärsärkarna* (1965).

Horus, Prince of the Sun (1968)

See *Taiyo no oji: Horusu no daiboken* (1968).

How to Train Your Dragon (2010)

Dirs. Dean DeBlois and Chris Sanders; screenplay by Will Davis, Dean DeBlois, and Chris Sanders from the children's books by Cressida Cowell; feature-length animated film. United States: Paramount/DreamWorks Animation.

The Vikings of the Isle of Berk join forces with their traditional fire-breathing, havoc-wracking dragon enemies, thanks to the efforts of their chief's seemingly unpromising scrawny son, Hiccup, and a wounded dragon pup, Toothless, to defeat a common enemy, a monster of behemoth proportions, thereby bringing lasting peace and harmony to the human and dragon inhabitants of Berk.

Reviews: *Entertainment Weekly* 1094 (19 March 2010): 80; *Hollywood Reporter* 12 March 2010: 35, 38; *Los Angeles Times* 26 March 2010: Calendar 1; *New York Times* 21 March 2010: Arts and Leisure 9 and 26 March 2010: C7; *San Francisco Chronicle* 26 March 2010: E1, E6, E8; *Sight and Sound* 20 (May 2010): 70 and 20 (June 2010): 90; *Time Out New York* 756 (25 March 2010): 67; *Variety* 15 March 2010: 20, 24.

Hrafninn Flygur (1984)

See *When the Raven Flies* (1984).

Den Hvite Viking (1991)

See *The White Viking* (1991).

I Na kamnjakh rastut derévja (1965)

See *The Captive of the Dragon* (1965).

I Skugga Hrafnsina (1988)

See *In the Shadow of the Raven* (1988).

In the Shadow of the Raven (1988)

Dir. Hrafn Gunnlaugsson; screenplay by Hrafn Gunnlaugsson. Iceland and Sweden: Cinema Art/F.I.L.M., with support from the Icelandic Film Fund and the Swedish Film Institute.

Alternate titles: *I Skugga Hrafnsina, Korpens Skugga*, and *The Shadow of the Raven*.

The story of Tristan and Iseult is retold against the back drop of feuding families in medieval Iceland.

Reviews: *Boston Globe* 24 May 1990: 84; *Chaplin* 219 (December 1988): 308–09; *Daily News* [New York] 12 July 1991: 55; *Filmrutan* 31.4 (1988): 35–36; *Hollywood Reporter* 9 October 1990: 11, 151; *New York Post* 12 July 1991: 29; *New York Times* 13 July 1991: 12; *Newsday* 12 July 1991: 71; *San Francisco Examiner* 31 August 1990: C7; *Variety* 19 October 1988: 249, 255; *Village Voice* 23 July 1991: 63.

Additional discussions: Chance, Jane, and Jessica Weinstein. "National Identity and Conversion through Medieval Romance." *Scandinavian Studies* 75 (Fall 2003): 417–38; Fridgeirsson, Asgeir. "The Bishop and the Actor." *Icelandic Review* 29.3 (1991): 37–40; Jónsdóttir, Solveig K. "Once Upon a Time in the North." *Icelandic Review* 25.4 (1987): 4–11.

The Incredible Hulk Returns (1988)

Dir. Nicholas Corea; screenplay by Nicholas Corea, based on the American televisions series that ran on CBS from 1978 to 1982, itself based on a Marvel Comics series. United States: New World Televisions and Bixby-Brandon Productions.

David Banner, transformed into the Hulk, teams up with the Viking god Thor to find a cure for the curse that causes Banner to shape shift into a monster.

Reviews: *Cinefantastique* 191 (January 1989): 116–17; *New York Times* 20 May 1988: C30; *Variety* 8 June 1988: 53, 56; *Washington Post* 22 May 1988: Y9.

Additional discussion: Marill, Alvin H. *Movies Made for Television 1964–2004.* Lanham, MD: Scarecrow, 2005.

Invasion of the Normans (1962)

See *I Normanni* (1962).

Gli Invasori (1961)

See *Erik the Conqueror* (1961).

The Island at the Top of the World (1974)

Dir. Robert Stevenson; screenplay by John Whedon, based on 1961 novel, *The Lost Ones* by Ian Cameron, one of the pseudonyms used by the English novelist Donald Gordon Payne. United States: Buena Vista/Walt Disney Productions.

In Edwardian times, a peer of the realm sets out for the Arctic regions by balloon to find his lost son only to discover the son living in a mysterious lush and temperate valley among Vikings who have inhabited the valley in isolation from the outside world since the tenth century.

Reviews: *CinemaTV Today* 21 December 1974: 15; *Hollywood Reporter* 26 November 1974: 3; *International Photographer* 476 (December 1974): 8–10; *Monthly Film Bulletin* 42 (January 1975): 10; *New York* 23 December 1974: 71; *New York Times* 21 December 1974: 18; *Time* 13 January 1975: 55; *Variety* 27 November 1974: 16.

Kilian's Chronicle (1994)

Dir. Pamela Berger; screenplay by Pamela Berger. United States: Lara Classics Productions.

Alternate title: *The Magic Stone.*

A young Irishman, kidnapped by Vikings and kept as a slave, escapes when they land in Vinland. Adopted into a tribe of Passamaquoddies, he helps them defeat a Viking berserker and eventually decides not to return to Ireland.

Reviews: *Boston Globe* 5 October 1994: 36; *Boston Phoenix* 14 October 1994: 3.10; *Daily News* [New York] 6 October 1995: 62; *New York Times* 6 October 1995: C12; *Variety* 10 October 1994: 85.

Additional discussions: Levich, Jacob. Ed. *The Motion Picture Guide: 1996 Annual (The Films of 1995).* New York: Cinebooks, 1996; Matchan, Linda. "Filming Viking Tale Rough Sailing." *Boston Globe* 27 October 1993: 32, 26; Sherman, Betsy. "The Berger Chronicles." *Boston Globe* 2 October 1994:

B1, B12; Wanat, Thomas. "Film Maker Focuses on American Before Columbus." *Chronicle of Higher Education* 19 October 1994: A8.

Knives of the Avengers (1965)

Dir. Mario Bava (as John Hold); screenplay by Mario Bava. Italy: Sider Film and P. T. Cinematografica.
Alternative titles: *I Coltelli del vendicatore* and *Raffica di cotelli.*
A stranded Viking defends a woman and child against their enemies. The woman's husband has been absent for years, but he returns in time to join forces with the Viking to right all the wrongs done to his family in his absence.
Reviews: *Fangoria* 206 (September 2001): 68; *Film-echo/Fimwoche* 49 (21 June 1967): 10; *Variety* 20 December 1967: 44.
Additional discussions: Lucas, Tim. "Requiem for a Viking." *Video Watchdog* 25 (September-October 1994): 40–55; Poppi, Roberto, and Martin Pecorari. *Dizionario del cinema italiano. Vol. 3: I Film dal 1960 al 1969.* Rome: Gremese Editore, 1992.

Korpen Flyger (1984)

See *When the Raven Flies* (1984).

Korpens Skugga (1988)

See *In the Shadow of the Raven* (1988).

Kristin Lavransdatter (1995)

Dir. Liv Ullmann; screenplay by Liv Ullmann from the 1921–1923 trilogy of the same title by Nobel laureate Sigrid Undset. Sweden and Norway: Lavransdatter AB and Norsk Film.
Kristan is bethrothed to the son of a wealthy landowner, flees to a convent to avoid marauding rapists, runs off with a knight with a reputation for being a lothario whom she does marry, and eventually dies of the plague in old age.
Reviews: *Catholic New Times* [Toronto] 24 September 1995: 8; *European Film Review* 6 (October 1996): 11; *Film og kino* 5 (May 1995): 24–25, 40–41; *Moving Pictures International* 11 (September 1995): 37; *Scandinavian Film News* 1 (August 1995): 7; *Variety* 11 September 1995: 111.

The Last of the Saxons (1910)

Dir. J. Stuart Blackton; screenplay uncredited. United States: Vitagraph Production Company.
Upon the death of King Edward, the Saxon Harold seizes the throne of England only to die on the field of battle at Senlac defending England from the invading troops of William of Normandy.
Reviews: *Bioscope* 12 January 1911: 36; *Motion Picture News* 15 October 1910: 8–9 and 5 November 1910: 16; *Moving Picture World* 8 October 1910: 824.

The Last of the Vikings (1960)

Dir. Giacomo Gentilomo; screenplay by Guido Zurli. France and Italy: Tiberius Films, Galatea Film, Les Films du cyclope, and Critérion Film.
Alternate title: *L'Ultimo dei vikinghi.*
A Viking prince returns home after years at sea to find his father murdered and his throne usurped. In the battles that follow, the murderer is slain, and the prince assumes his rightful place as king.
Reviews: *Daily Cinema* 19 March 1962: 5; *Film Daily* 120 (8 May 1962): 6; *Filmfacts* 5 (21 September 1962): 205; *Film français* 903 (22 September 1961): 31; *Intermezzo* 16 (April 1961): 6; *Kine Weekly* 23 March 1962: 10; *Monthly Film Bulletin* 29 (May 1962): 70; *New York Times* 27 September 1962: 33; *Video Watchdog* 23 (May-June 1994): 22–23.
Additional discussions: Lucas, Tim. "Requiem for a Viking." *Video Watchdog* 25 (September-October 1994): 40–55; Poppi, Roberto, and Martin Pecorari. *Dizionario del cinema italiano. Vol. 3: I Film dal 1960 al 1969.* Rome: Gremese Editore, 1992.

The Last Viking (1997)

See *Den Sidste Viking* 1997.

The Little Norse Prince (1968)

See *Taiyo no oji: Horusu no daiboken* (1968).

The Little Norse Prince Valiant (1968)

See *Taiyo no oji: Horusu no daiboken* (1968).

The Littlest Viking (1990)

See *Sigurd drakekreper* (1990).

The Long Ships (1963)

Dir. Jack Cardiff; screenplay by Berkeley Mather, based on the 1941 novel *Red Orm* by Frans Bengtsson. Great Britain: Avala Films-Warwick Film Production.

A Viking warlord and shipbuilder, who is also more than a little of a scoundrel, is captured by a Moorish prince with whom he does battle to obtain a fabled bell made of gold.

Reviews: *Daily Cinema* 26 June 1963: 14–15; *Film Daily* 11 June 1964: 4; *Hollywood Reporter* 29 May 1964: 3; *Kinematograph Weekly* 27 February 1964: 10–11; *Monthly Film Bulletin* 31 (April 1964): 57–58; *Motion Picture Herald* 24 June 1964: 73; *New York Times* 25 June 1964: 25; *Variety* 11 March 1964: 6.

Lost Colony: The Wraiths of Roanoke (2007)

Dir. Matt Codd; screenplay by Rafael Jordan. United States/Bulgaria: American World Pictures.
Alternate title: *The Wraiths of Roanoke*.

The lost colonists of Roanoke go missing when they encounter Viking wraiths cursed to wander the island and alienate the indigenous Crow tribes who might have helped them survive.

Review: *Newsday* 13 October 2007: B29.

The Magic Stone (1994).

See *Kilian's Chronicle* (1994).

Merlin and the Sword (1992)

See *Arthur the King* (1982).

I Normanni (1962)

Dir. Giuseppe Vari; screenplay by Nino Stresa. Italy and France: Galatea Film and Société Cinématographique Lyre.
Alternate titles: *The Attack of the Normans* and *Invasion of the Normans*.

In the ninth century, Viking tribes settle in England where they are blamed for killing the king by a ruthless Saxon baron, who is himself the real murderer. The Vikings join forces with those loyal to the murdered king and restore his daughter to the throne.

Reviews: *Cinématographie française* 10 November 6 April 1963: 10; *Daily Cinema* 8 November 1963: 7; *Film-echo/Filmwoche* 10 November 1962: 11; *Kine Weekly* 31 October 1963: 18; *Monthly Film Bulletin* 30 (December 1963): 173; *Télérama* 8 May 1996: 181.

Additional discussions: *Italian Film Production 1962.* Rome: Unitalia Film, 1963; Poppi, Roberto, and Martin Pecorari. *Dizionario del cinema italiano. Vol. 3: I Film dal 1960 al 1969.* Rome: Gremese Editore, 1992.

The Norsemen (1978)

Dir. Charles B. Pierce; screenplay by Charles B. Pierce. United States: American International Pictures.

Vikings set sail for North America to rescue their king and his retainers who, on an earlier voyage, were captured, blinded, and forced into servitude by native Americans.

Reviews: *Film Bulletin* October-November 1978: Reviews G; *Hollywood Reporter* 3 July 1978: 2; *Monthly Film Bulletin* 46 (March 1979): 48–49; *Variety* 5 July 1978: 16.

The Oath of a Viking (1914)

Dir. J. Searle Dawley; screenplay uncredited. United States: Picture Playhouse Films.

Olaf, a Viking exiled by his own tribe, is befriended by a rival tribe, whose chieftain's daughter he falls in love with, even though she is betrothed to another. Olaf tries to win her affection by deceit and treachery and is, as a result, returned to his own tribe for punishment.

Reviews: *Motion Picture World* 15 August 1914: 942; *Variety* 18 August 1915: 18.

Ofelaš (1987)

See *Pathfinder* (1987).

On Earth as in Heaven (1992)

See *Svo á Jördu sem á Himni* (1992).

Orangens fange (1965)

See *The Captive of the Dragon* (1965).

Outlander (2008)

Dir. Howard McCain; screenplay by Howard McCain and Dirk Blackman, (very) loosely based on the Anglo-Saxon poem *Beowulf.*

A space traveler from the future, Kainan, crashes to Earth in Viking times, unwittingly bringing with him a monstrous creature bent on killing him and destroying two warring tribes of Vikings. Both tribes unite under the leadership of Kainan to defeat the creature.

Reviews: *Deathray* 21 (October-November 2009): 106; *Dirigido por ...* 384 (December 2008): 24; *Empire* 243 (September 2009): 134 and 239 (May 2009): 54; *Fangoria* 285 (August 2009): 57; *New York Times* 24 January 2009: C13; *San Francisco Chronicle* 23 January 2009: E5; *Sight and Sound* 19 (June 2009): 74; *Variety* 25 August 2008: 84.

Outlaw (1981)

See *Útlaginn* (1981).

Pathfinder (1987)

Dir. Nils Gaup; screenplay by Nils Gaup from an early medieval Sami legend. Norway: Filmkameratene A/S, Norway Film Development Company A/S, and Norsk Film.

Alternate tiles: *Ofelaš* and *Veiviseren.*

A young Sami boy, having watched his family and neighbors all be killed by nomadic Tchude warriors, exacts his revenge upon them saving the inhabitants of several nearby villages in the process.

Reviews: *Cahiers du cinéma* 415 (January 1989): 57; *Film Journal* 93 (June 1990): 45; *Film og kino* (1988): 30–31, 52; *Filmrutan* 31.3 (1988): 38–39; *Films and Filming* 408 (September 1988): 36–37; *Kosmorama* 186 (Winter 1988): 49; *Los Angeles Times* 22 June 1990: Calendar 8; *Monthly Film Bulletin* 55 (September 1988): 278; *New York Times* 11 May 1990: C10; *Positif* 337 (March 1989): 78–79; *Scandinavian Film News* 6 (November 1986): 8; *Sunday Times* [of London] 25 September 1988: C8; *Times* [of London] 22 September 1988: 18; *Variety* 14 October 1987: 9.

Additional discussions: Cardullo, Bert. "Rites of Passage." *Hudson Review* 44 (Spring 1991): 96–104; *Pathfinder.* London: Guild Film Distribution, 1988. [Press book.]

Pathfinder (2007)

Dir. Marcus Nispel; screenplay by Laeta Kalogridis from the graphic novel of the same title by Laeta Kalogridis and Christopher Shy, loosely based on the plot of the 1987 film of the same title directed by Nils Gaup. United States: Twentieth Century–Fox/Phoenix Pictures.

A Viking boy is left behind in North America for showing cowardice during a Viking raid. Years later, after he has been adopted by a Wampanaog tribe, he helps them defeat the blood-thirsty, testosterone charged Viking berserkers who have returned to destroy everyone whom they encounter in the new world.

Reviews: *Empire* 215 (May 2007): 46 and 221 (November 2007): 186; *Entertainment Weekly* 931/932 (27 April–4 May 2007): 119; *Fangoria* 263 (May 2007): 6; *Los Angeles Times* 13 April 2007: E12; *New York Times* 13 April 2007: E17; *Sight and Sound* 17 (May 2007): 77–78; *StarBurst* 84 (November 2007): 97; *Time Out New York* 603 (19 April 2007): 105; *Variety* 13 April 2007: 8.

Additional discussion: Richards, Olly. "It's *Apocalypse Now* ... with Vikings." *Empire* 215 (May 2007): 92–96; Schurers, Fred. "Vikings on the Warpath." *American Cinematographer* 87 (September 2006): 60–69.

Prima Veras Saga am Olav den Hellige (1983)

Dir. Herodes Falsk; screenplay by the Prima Vera Troupe. Norway: Iste Klasses Film & Video and Norsk Film.

Alternative titles: *Prima Vera's Saga of Saint Olav* and *The Saga of the Viking Saint Olav.*

King, later Saint, Olav completes the conversion of Viking Norway to Christianity, albeit in a comedic scenario typical of Norway's answer to the Monty Python troupe.

Reviews: *Film og kino* 8 (1983): 287–88, 296; *Scandinavian Film News* 3 (May 1993): 3 and 3 December 1983: 5.

Prima Vera's Saga of Saint Olav (1983)

See *Prima Veras Saga am Olav den Hellige* (1983).

Prince of Jutland (1993)

Dir. Gabriel Axel; screenplay by Gabriel Axel and Erik Kjersgaard from the twelfth-century *Gesta Danorum* by the author known as Saxo Grammaticus. France, Great Britain, Denmark, and Germany: Les Films Ariane, Woodline Films, Kenneth Madsen Films, and Films Roses.

Alternate title: *Royal Deceit.*

In sixth-century Jutland, Prince Fenge murders his brother the king and beds his former sister-in-law, Gerruth, as his nephew, Amled, plots to revenge his father's murder. The film's source is, of course, the original version of the story of Hamlet.

Reviews: *Film-echo/Filmwoche* 24 (18 June 1993): 10; *Film français* 4 February 1994: 30; *Le Monde* 24 February 1994: 7; *Positif* 398 (April 1994): 58–59; *Screen International* 21 May 1993: 18; *Sight and Sound* NS 6 (February 1996): 60; *Télérama* 23 February 1994: 41; *Variety* 28 February 1994: 71.

Prince Valiant (1954)

Dir. Henry Hathaway; screenplay by Dudley Nichols, based on the long-running comic strip of the same title by Hal Foster. United States: Twentieth Century–Fox.

Exiled for a crime he did not commit, the eponymous Viking hero travels to King Arthur's court to clear his name. En route, he discovers a plot by an unidentified Black Knight to murder Arthur. In the course of the film, Valiant becomes a knight of the Round Table, returns home to free his countrymen from the tyranny of their new leaders, and sails back to Camelot to foil the plot to overthrow Arthur.

Reviews: *Film Daily* 2 April 1954: 6; *Films in Review* 5 (May 1954): 241–42; *Harrison's Reports* 3 April 1954: 55; *Hollywood Reporter* 2 March 1954: 3; *Kinematograph Weekly* 6 May 1954: 6; *Monthly Film Bulletin* 21 (July 1954): 85–86; *Motion Picture Herald* 3 April 1954: 30 and 10 April 1954: Product Digest Section 2254–55; *New York Times* 7 April 1954: 40; *New Yorker* 30 (April 1954): 93–94; *Times* [of London] 3 May 1954: 9; *To-day's Cinema* 29 April 1954: 6; *Variety* 7 April 1954: 6.

Prince Valiant (1997)

See *Prinz Eisenherz* (1997).

Prinz Eisenherz (1997)

Dir. Anthony Hickox; screenplay by Michael Beckner, Anthony Hickox and Carsten Lorenz, based on the long-running comic strip, *Prince Valiant* by Hal Foster. Germany: Constantin Films.

The eponymous hero sets out to save his country and learn the secrets of his past, while also retrieving Excalibur and Merlin's book of magic from Vikings in league with Morgan Le Fey. In the process he meets, falls in love with, and manages, with the help of the power of Excalibur, to raise the Princess Ilene of Wales, whom he will eventually marry, from the dead.

Reviews: *Cahiers du cinéma* 516 (September 1997): 82; *Empire* 103 (January 1998): 42; *Film Review* [Special Issue 22] February 1998: 76; *Film-echo/Filmwoche* 27 (5 July 1997): 51 and 29 (19 July 1997): 38; *Kino* [Germany] 3 (November 1996): 11; *Positif* 439 (September 1997): 48; *Sight and Sound* NS 8 (January 1998): 52.

Additional discussion: Alan Jones, "Prince Valiant." *Cinefantastique* 29 (March 1998): 52–53.

Raffica di cotelli (1965)

See *Knives of the Avengers* (1965).

The Red Mantle (1967)

Dir. Gabriel Axel; screenplay by Gabriel Axel from the twelfth-century *Gesta Danorum* by the author known as Saxo Grammaticus. Denmark, Sweden, and Iceland: ASA Filmudlejning, Movie Art of Europe, and Edda Films.

Dir. Alternate titles: *Den Røde kappe* and *Hagbard and Signe*.

In medieval Iceland, Hagbard and his brothers seeks to avenge the death of their father, King Hamund, by engaging in a blood feud with the family of his killer, King Sigvor. To settle the feud, Sigvor offers an alliance, which in turn leads to Hagbard falling in love with Sigvor's daughter Signe, whose hand in marriage is already promised to another. The blood feud then resumes; Hagbard disguises himself in a red mantle to visit Signe, is captured and hanged, as Signe sets fire to her room killing herself.

Reviews: *Filmfacts* 11 (August 1968): 203–04; *Film og kino* 9 (November 1967): 330; *Films and Filming* 15 (April 1969): 50–51; *Films in Review* 19 (June-July 1968): 377; *Hollywood Reporter* 15 August 1968: 3; *Kinematograph Weekly* 15 February 1969: 18; *Monthly Film Bulletin* 36 (March 1969): 60; *New York Times* 17 May 1968: 56; *To-day's Cinema* 7 February 1969: 9; *Variety* 25 January 1967: 21.

Additional discussions: Krafsur, Richard P., ed. *The American Film Institute Catalog of Motion Pictures, Feature Films 1961–1970.* New York: Bowker, 1976; *Svensk Filmografi 6: 1960–1969.* Uppsala: Svenska Filminstitutet, 1977.

The Raven Flies (1984)

See *When the Raven Flies* (1984).

Revenge of the Barbarians (1984)

See *When the Raven Flies* (1984).

The Robber's Daughter (1984)

See *Ronja rövardotter* (1984).

Den Røde kappe (1967)

See *The Red Mantle* (1967).

Ronja rövardotter (1984)

Dir. Tage Danielsson; screenplay by Astrid Lindgren from her 1981 novel of the same title. Sweden and Norway: Svensk Filmindustri and Norsk Film.

Alternate titles: *The Robber's Daughter* and *Ronya*.

The children of rival tribes of bandits grow up and fall in love. Fleeing to the forest, they eventually find that true love conquers family enmity.

Reviews: *Chaplin* 196 (February 1985): 50–51; *Film og kino* 1 (1985): 12–13 and 2 (1985): 75; *Film-echo/Filmwoche* 13/14 (7 March 1996): 17; *Filmrutan* 28.1 (1985): 5; *Levende billeder* 11 (January 1985): 57–58; *New York Times* 23 May 1986: C4; *Scandinavian Film News* 2 (Autumn 1983): 8 and 4 (December 1984): 4; *Variety* 19 December 1984: 88.

Ronya (1984)
See *Ronja rövardotter* (1984).

Royal Deceit (1994)
See *Prince of Jutland* (1994).

Runestone (1990)
Dir. Willard Carroll; screenplay by Willard Carroll, based on a novella of the same title by Mark E. Rogers. United States: Hyperion Pictures/Signature Productions.
Alternate title: *Full Moon*.
When a Viking runestone bearing a carving of a monstrous creature is discovered in Western Pennsylvania and brought back to New York City, the carving comes to life and wrecks havoc in Gotham.
Reviews: *Sight and Sound* NS 2 (August 1992): 67; *Hollywood Reporter* 14 February 1992: 13, 52; *Screen International* 10 March 1990: 15; *Variety* 17 February 1992: 69.

The Saga of Gisli (1981)
See *Útlaginn* (1981).

The Saga of the Viking Saint Olav (1983)
See *Prima Veras Saga am Olav den Helige* (1983).

The Saga of the Viking Women and Their Voyage to the Waters of the Great Sea Serpent (1957)
See *The Viking Women and the Sea Serpent* (1957).

Sea Dragon (1990)
Dir. Ágúst Gudmundsson; screenplay by Ágúst Gudmundsson, based on the 1977 novel, *Blood Feud* by Rosemary Sutcliff; originally released as a four-part television series and then as a film. Great Britain: Thames Television.
In the tenth century, Thormod and his slave, Jestyn the Briton, sail for England to avenge the murder of Thormod's father.
Reviews: *Screen International* 11 August 1990: 24; *Television Today* 29 November 1990: 25.

The Secret of Kells (2009)
Dirs. Tomm Moore and Nora Twomey; screenplay by Fabrice Ziolkowski; feature-length, Academy-Award nominated animated film. France-Belgium-Ireland: Les Armateurs, France 2 (Cinema)-Vivi Films-Cartoon Saloon, France 2 Cinéma.
Alternate title: *Brendan and the Secret of Kells*.
In the ninth century, Brendan, nephew of the abbot of Kells, assists his confreres in the scriptorium to copy and illustrate the famous book of gospels as Vikings menacingly surround and eventually sack the abbey.
Reviews: *Entertainment Weekly* 1094 (19 March 2010): 79; *L'Express* 12 February 2009: 22; *Film Comment* 46 (March-April 2010): 73; *Film Ireland* 127 (March 2009): 40; *The Irish Times* 6 March 2009: 13; *Los Angeles Times* 2 April 2010: Calendar 1; *Le Monde* 11 February 2009: 23; *New York Times* 5 March 2010: C6; *Positif* 576 (February 2009): 50; *San Francisco Chronicle* 1 April 2010: 96 Hours 20 and 2 April 2010: E8; *Screen International* 13 March 2009: 18; *Time* 175 (15 March 2010:53; *Time Out New York* 753 (4 March 2010): 54.

The Secret of the Forest (1955)

Dir. D'Arcy Conyers; screenplay by George Ewart Evans. Great Britain: Rayant Pictures.
Alternate title: *The Ship in the Forest*.
Two children uncover a hidden Viking treasure trove and must hide themselves and the trove from
   thieves who have buried their own loot at the same sight.
Reviews: *Monthly Film Bulletin* 23 (April 1956): 49; *Today's Cinema* 5 March 1956: 10.

Severed Ways: The Norse Discovery of North America (2007)

Dir. Tony Stone; screenplay by Tony Stone. United States: Heathen Films.
In a film without much dialog — and what dialog there is is in Old Norse and Abenaki — two Viking
   berserkers find themselves stranded in Newfoundland sometime in the eleventh century, where
   they maim or kill everyone whom they encounter, native peoples and even Irish missionaries, whose
   presence in Newfoundland is never quite explained.
Reviews: *Los Angeles Times* 17 July 2009: D6; *New York Times* 13 March 2009: C11; *Time Out New
   York* (12 March 2009): 70; *Variety* 25 June 2007: 47.

The Shadow of the Raven (1988)

See *In the Shadow of the Raven* (1988).

The Ship in the Forest (1955)

See *The Secret of the Forest* (1955).

Den Sidste Viking (1997)

Dir. Jesper Westerlin Nielsen; screenplay by Mikael Olsen. Denmark: Zentropa Entertainment.
Alternate title: *The Last Viking*.
At the end of the Viking Age, a tyrannical king and his army overrun a peaceful village, killing or
   enslaving the inhabitants. The son of the murdered chief of the village, although still a boy, avenges
   the evils done to his fellow villagers.
Review: *Scandinavian Film News* 8 (August 1995): 6.
Additional discussion: Jesper Andersen. "The Last Viking — A Timeless Story." *Scandinavian Film
   News* 5 (May 1994): 4–5.

Sigurd drakekreper (1990)

Dir. Lars Rasmussen and Knut Jorfald; screenplay by Lars Rasmussen, based on the 1982 young-
   adult novel of the same title by Torill Thorstad Hauger. Norway: Madiagjøglerne and Norsk Film.
Alternate titles: *Sigurd the Dragon Slayer* and *The Littlest Viking*.
Sigurd, the eleven-year old son of a Viking chieftain, must prove himself worthy to be his father's
   heir. A pacifist at first, the boy finally lives up to the reputation his name promises and becomes
   a wise and just ruler.
Review: *Variety* 18 April 1990: 24.

Sigurd the Dragon Slayer (1990)

See *Sigurd drakekreper* (1990).

A Sleeping Memory (1917)

Dir. George D. Baker; screenplay by Albert Shelby Le Vino, based on a 1902 novel of the same title
   by Edward Phillips Oppenheim. United States: Metro Pictures/De Luxe Productions.
Faced with the financial disgrace and suicide of her wealthy father, a young woman undergoes brain
   surgery as a cure for her depression only to discover that she has led any number of former lives
   including that of a cruel Viking queen.
Reviews: *Motography* 20 October 1917: 842; *Moving Picture World* 30 June 1917: 2134 and 10 November
   1917: 875, 920; *Variety* 19 October 1917: 31: *Wid's* 25 October 1917: 680.

Stara baśń: Kiedy słońce było bogiem (2003)

Directed by Jerzy Hoffman; screenplay by Jerzy Hoffman, from the nineteenth-century historical novel of the same title by Józef Ignacy Kraszewski. Poland: Zodiak-Jerzy Hoffman Film Production

Alternate title: *When the Sun Was God: An Ancient Tale.*

In what will become modern Poland, the tyrant Popiel hires Viking mercenaries further to oppress his people. Popiel meets his match at the hands of Ziemowit Piast, who has lived among the Vikings and who will go on to found Poland's first royal dynasty — Popiel is eventually eaten by mice. (Note: In the novel, the mercenaries are Germanic tribes, not Vikings, but this film, which was originally made-for-Polish television as a mini-series, was released as Poland was making a bid to enter the European Union, and the Polish authorities were wary of offending Germany, which could veto Poland's membership application.)

Reviews: *Dekada Literacka* 7–8 (July-August 2003), *Kino* 10 (October 2003): 50–51; *Kultura* 38 (August 2003): n.p.; *Przekrój* 38 (2003): 78.

Additional discussions: Cegiełkówna, Iwona. "Scenarzysty nic nie broni." *Kino* 9 (September 2003): 23–26; Cichowicz, Alicja. "A słonce było bogiem...." *Kino* 7–8 (July-August 2003): 38; Pietrasik, Zdzisław. "Makbeta zjadły myszy." *Polityka* 38 (20 December 2003): 62–64; Zarębski, Konrad J. "Trzeci raz się nie zastawię." *Kino* 7–8 (July-August 2003): 32–36.

Svo á Jördu sem á Himni (1992)

Dir. Kristin Jóhannesdóttir; screenplay by Kristin Jóhannesdóttir. Iceland: Tiu-Tiu Films.

Alternate title: *As in Heaven* and *On Earth as in Heaven.*

In parallel stories, a young girl comes of age in Iceland in the 1930s and in her past life there in the fourteenth century.

Review: *Variety* 24 August 1992: 63.

Additional discussion: Ómarsson, Thorfinnur. "Cinematic Resurgence." *Icelandic Review* 30.1 (1992): 20–25.

Taiyo no oji: Horusu no daiboken (1968)

Directed by Isao Takahata; screenplay by Kazuo Fukazawa; feature-length animated film. Japan: Toei Doga Films.

Alternate titles: *Horus, Prince of the Sun*; *The Little Norse Prince; The Little Norse Prince Valiant.*

A young prince sets out to avenge the death of his family and villagers at the hands of Viking raiders.

Reviews: *Première* 324 (February 2004): 44; *Sight and Sound* 16 (January 2006): 90; *UniJapan Film Quarterly* 11 (October 1968): 26.

Tarkan and the Blood of the Vikings (1971)

See *Tarkan Viking Kani* (1971).

Tarkan and the Vikings (1971)

See *Tarkan Viking Kani* (1971).

Tarkan versus the Vikings (1971)

See *Tarkan Viking Kani* (1971).

Tarkan Viking Kani (1971)

Dir. Mehmet Asian; screenplay by Sezgin Burak and Sadik Sendil. Turkey: IMWA.

Alternate titles: *Tarkan and the Blood of the Vikings, Tarkan and the Vikings,* and *Tarkan versus the Vikings.*

The peripatetic hero helps a Turkish princess overcome Viking invaders and assorted other enemies.

Review: *Video Watchdog* 20 (November-December 1993): 30–31.

Additional discussion: Balbo, Lucas. "Turkish délices." *CinémAction* 89 (1998): 91–94; Willeman, Paul. "The Zoom in Popular Cinema." *New Cinemas Journal of Contemporary Film* 1 (January 2002): 6–13.

I Tartari (1960)

See *The Tartars* (1960).

The Tartars (1960)

Dir. Richard Thorpe; screenplay by Sabatino Ciuffini, Ambrogio Molteni, Gaio Fratini, Oreste Palella, and Emimmo Salvi. Italy: Lux Film/MGM.

In medieval Russia, Vikings, who protect the native Slavic inhabitants, and marauding Tartars clash in a series of battles and orgies, and on some truly spectacular (for the time) burning sets.

Alternate title: *I Tartari*.

Reviews: *Daily Cinema* 29 November 1961: 17; *Harrison's Reports* 20 June 1992: 103; *Hollywood Reporter* 20 June 1962: 3; *Intermezzo* 16 (June 1961): 4; *Kinematograph Weekly* 23 November 1961: 27; *Monthly Film Bulletin* 29 (Jaunuary1962): 14–15; *Motion Picture Herald* 11 July 1962: Product Digest Section 611; *New York Times* 21 June 1962: 26; *Variety* 27 June 1962: 6.

Additional discussions: James, Howard. *The Films of Orson Welles*. New York: Citadel, 1991; Poppi, Roberto, and Martin Pecorari. *Dizionario del cinema italiano. Vol. 3: I Film dal 1960 al 1969*. Rome: Gremese Editore, 1992.

Il Tesoro della Foresta Pietrificata (1965)

Dir. Emimmo Salvi; screenplay by Luigi Tosi. Italy: Asteria Films.

Outraged gods in Valhalla clash with peaceful Viking villagers over possession of a vast horde of treasure.

Reviews: *Bianco e nero* 29 (May-June 1968): supplement 6; *Cahiers du cinéma* 179 (June 1966): 81; *Film-echo/Filmwoche* 7 (26 January 1968): 12; *Guia de filmes* [Portugal] 27 (May 1970): 114.

Additional discussion: Poppi, Roberto, and Martin Pecorari. *Dizionario del cinema italiano. Vol. 3: I Film dal 1960 al 1969*. Rome: Gremese Editore, 1992.

The 13th Warrior (1999)

Dir. John McTiernan; screenplay by William Wisher, Jr., from Michael Crichton's 1976 novel *Eaters of the Dead*, itself a loose adaptation of the Anglo-Saxon poem *Beowulf*. United States: Touchstone Pictures.

The Baghdad poet and ambassador Ahmed Ibn Fahdlan joins a band of twelve Viking warriors led by Buliwyf who are on a mission to rescue the court of Hrothgar from a horde of monstrous invaders.

Reviews: *Entertainment Weekly* 501 (3 September 1999): 43; *New York Times* 27 August 1999: E27; *Positif* 463 (September 1999): 38–39; *Screen International* 3 September 1999: 24; *Sight and Sound* 9 (September 1999): 57; *StarBurst* 254 (October 1999): 14–15; *Variety* 30 August 1999: 49–50; *Wall Street Journal* 27 August 1999: W1–2.

Thor, Hammer of the Gods (2009)

Directed by Todor Chapkanov; screenplay by Steve Bevilacqua and Rafel Jordan. United States; SyFy/NBC Universal Television.

Alternate title: *Hammer of the Gods*.

Vikings land on a mysterious island and are attacked by werewolves but are eventually saved when one of the Vikings proves to be a reincarnation of the god Thor.

Review: *Sun* [London] 21 November 2009: 17.

Thor il conquistatore (1982)

Dir. Teodoro Ricci; screenplay by Tito Carpi. Italy: Abruzzo Cinematografica.

At the beginning of time, Thor destroys his enemies in an epic battle among the Viking gods.

Reviews: *Écran fantastique* 27 (October 1982): 36; *Foreign Sales—Italian Movie Trade* 8 (October 1982): 58 and 9 (March 1983): 6.

Additional discussion: Poppi Robert. *Dizionario del cinema italiano: I film dal 1980 al 1989*. Rome: Germese Editore, 2000.

Timetrip: The Curse of the Viking Witch (2009)

Directed by Mogens Hagedorn; screenplay by Ina Bruhn. Denmark: Cosmo Film-TV2 and SF Film.
In the tenth-century, a spell grants a Viking sorceress and her lover, a Christian warrior, eternal life.
   In the twenty-first century, the lover, now a physicist, enlists the aid of two teenagers to travel
   back in time with him to recover a crucifix that can break the spell.
Reviews: *Børsen* [Denmark] 27 March 2009: 1; *Politiken* [Denmark] 27 March 2009: 2; *taz, die
   tageszeitung* 3 June 2010: 24–25; *Toronto Sun* 21 August 2009: 50.

L'Ultimo dei vichingi (1960)

See *The Last of the Vikings* (1960).

Útlaginn (1981)

Dir. Ágúst Gudmaundsson; screenplay by Ágúst Gudmaundsson, adapted from the medieval Icelandic
   Saga of Gísli Súrsson. Iceland: Isfilm Productions.
Alternative titles: *Gisla Saga Surssonar, Outlaw*, and *The Saga of Gisli*.
In defense of his honor, a man is forced to kill his brother-in-law for which he is subsequently
   branded an outlaw and forced to flee with a price on his head.
Reviews: *Filmrutan* 27.2 (1984): 32; *Icelandic Review* 24.2 (1986): 71–72; *Scandinavian Film News* 1
   (November 1981): 4 and 2 (February 1982): 2–3; *Variety* 31 March 1982: 26.

Valhalla (1986)

Dir. Peter Madsen and Jeffrey James Varab; screenplay by Peter Madsen and Henninge Kure; feature-
   length animated film based on a popular syndicated cartoon strip. Denmark: Swan Film Productions.
Two human children follow the gods Thor and Loki from Valhalla to Udgaard to defeat a race of evil
   giants.
Reviews: *Film-echo/Filmwoche* 63(7 November 1987): 18; *Kosmorama* 178 (December 1986) 10; *Variety*
   21 March 1986: 33.

Valhalla Rising (2008)

Directed by Nicholas Winding Refn; screenplay by Roy Jacobsen, Matthew Read, and Nicholas
   Winding Refn. Denmark: Scanbox-Vertigo-Nimbus Films.
With the aid of a young boy, a mute, one-eyed Viking warrior escapes from a long period of captivity
   in which he was kept as little more than a caged animal periodically let loose by his Scottish captors
   to fight their enemies and joins a troupe of Christian Vikings on Crusade to the Holy Land, but,
   thanks to a strange set of events, they all end up in North America instead.
Reviews: *Cineforum* 448 (October 2009): 53; *Empire* 251 (May 2010): 56; *Entertainment Weekly* 1112
   (23 July 2010): 68; *New York Times* 16 July 2010: C7; *Politiken* [Denmark] 16 August 2008: 2;
   Positif 589 (March 2010): 17–19; *Screen International* 2 October 2009: 32; *Sight and Sound* 20
   (April 2010): 79; *Time Out New York* 772 (15 July 2010): 57; *Total Film* 167 (June 2010): 56; *USA
   Today* 6 April 2010: 3D; *Variety* 25 August 2008: 22.
Additional discussion: Eisenreich, Pierre. "Nicolas Winding Refn." *Positif* 589 (March 2010): 20;
   Gombeaud, Adrien and Hubert Niogret. "Entretien avec Nicolas Winding Refn." *Positif* 589
   (March 2010): 21–26.

Veiviseren (1987)

See *Pathfinder* (1987).

Vengeance of the Vikings (1964)

Dir. Mario Caiano; screenplay by Arpad De Riso and Nino Scolaro. Italy and Spain: Nike Cinematografica and AS Films Producción.
Fleeing Danish tyranny, a Viking prince sets sail for the west and discovers a new land (North America), despite his cousin's attempt to make sure he never returns alive. After violent encounters with

The tethered One-Eye (Mads Mikkelsen) in Nicolas Winding Refn's 2009 film *Valhalla Rising* (editor's collection).

one tribe of native peoples and an unsuccessful attempt to form an alliance with another though marriage, the prince returns home and assumes the throne after his cousin's duplicity is exposed.
Alternate titles: *Erik il vinchingo* and *Erik the Viking*.
Reviews: *Daily Cinema* 3 July 1968: 3; *Kinematograph Weekly* 6 July 1968: 11; *Monthly Film Bulletin* 25 (August 1968): 118.
Additional discussions: *Cinéma espagnol*. Madrid: Uniespaña, 1966; *Italian Film Production 1965*. Rome: Unitalia Film, 1966; Poppi, Roberto, and Martin Pecorari. *Dizionario del cinema italiano*. *Vol. 3: I Film dal 1960 al 1969*. Rome: Gremese Editore, 1992.

Vicky the Viking (2009)

See *Wickie und die starken Männer* (2009).

The Viking (1928)

Dir. R. William Neill; screenplay by Randolph Bartlett and Jack Cunningham, based on a 1902 historical novel, *The Thrall of Leif the Lucky*, by Ottilie A. Liljencrantz. United States: MGM.
Vikings ravage the coasts of England taking back with them to Norway a number of captives, one of whom accompanies the secretly–Christian Leif Ericsson back to his pagan father's court in Iceland, where religious war breaks out. Leif sets sail west, lands in Newport, Rhode Island, and leaves a contingent of Vikings and slaves there as colonists, before he returns home to be reconciled with his father.
Reviews: *Bioscope* 3 July 1929: 43; *Film Spectator* 17 November 1928: 7; *Harrison's Reports* 15 December 1928: 199; *Kinematograph Weekly* 4 July 1929: 65; *New York Times* 29 November 1928: 32; *Variety* 5 December 1928: 12.
Additional discussions: Kalmus, T. J. "Technicolor Adventures in Cinemaland." *Journal of the Society*

of *Motion Picture Engineers* 30 (December 1938): 564–85; Klepper, Robert K. *Silent Film on Video.* Jefferson, NC: McFarland, 1996; Minden, Kenneth, ed. *The American Film Institute Catalog of Motion Pictures Produced in the United States, Feature Films 1921–1930.* New York: Bowker, 1971.

The Viking Queen (1914)

Dir. Walter Edwin; screenplay uncredited. United States: Edison.

Helga the Glorious, the Viking queen of one of the smaller Norse kingdoms, off marauding in neighboring kingdoms, faces an insurrection in her absence at home. She is eventually victorious against her enemies on both fronts.

Reviews: *Bioscope* 21 January 1915: 279; *Edison Kinetogram* 4 September 1914: Film 7722; *Kinematograph Monthly Record* 35 (March 1915): 83.

The Viking Queen (1967)

Dir. Don Chaffey; screenplay by Clarke Reynolds, from a short story by John Temple-Smith. Great Britain: Hammer Films.

Druids, the daughter of a Viking queen and her tribe, and Romans clash as treachery on all sides leads to the outbreak of a rebellion. The Viking princess falls in love with the Roman governor, but to no avail, as even their love cannot diffuse the tensions that lead to all-out war.

Review: *Daily Cinema* 8 March 1967: 6; *Film Daily* 12 September 1967: 6; *Filmfacts* 5 (April 1967): 400; *Hollywood Reporter* 30 August 1967 30 August 1967: 3; *House That Hammer Built* 6 (December 1997): 297–99; *Kine Weekly* 11 March 1967: 10; *Monthly Film Bulletin* 34 (April 1967): 64; *Motion Picture Herald* 13 September 1967: Product Digest Section 722; *Psychotronic Video* 39 (September 2003): 14; *Scarlet Street* 41 (2001): 25–26; *Variety* 30 August 1967: 6; *Video Watchdog* 63 (September 2000): 72–73.

Additional discussion: Krafsur, Richard P., ed. *The American Film Institute Catalog of Motion Pictures, Feature Films 1961–1970.* New York: Bowker, 1976

A Viking Saga (2008)

Dir. Michael Mouyal; screenplay by Michael Mouyal and Dennis Goldberg, based on events recorded as happening in the early to mid-ninth century in *The Russian Primary Chronicle*, originally compiled in Kiev in the early twelfth century. United States/Denmark: Supersonic Entertainment Films.

Alternate title: *A Viking Saga: Son of Thor.*

The sole survivor of a Viking raid on his village, the boy Helgi is adopted by his uncle, a traveling merchant. Years later, a trading mission takes Helgi (now known as Oleg) to a kingdom in the East ruled by the same raiders, where he meets the men who killed his family. After exacting his revenge, Helgi/Oleg establishes an elaborate system of trade routes from Scandinavia to the East that lead in turn to the founding of Viking Russia.

Reviews: on-line only.

A Viking Saga: Son of Thor (2008)

See *A Viking Saga* (2008).

The Viking Sagas (1996)

Dir. Michael Chapman; screenplay by Dale Herd and Paul R. Gurian. United States: New Line Cinema and Gurian Productions.

Kjartan, Prince of Iceland, seeks to avenge the murder of his father by the evil chieftan Ketil. After a series of trials and with the aid of a magic sword, Kjartan defeats Ketil, frees Iceland from his tyrannical rule, and wins a bride in the bargain.

Review: *StarBurst* 209 (1 January 1996): 47; *Sight and Sound* NS 6 (March 1996): 58.

The Viking Women (1957)

See *The Viking Women and the Sea Serpent* (1957).

The Viking Women and the Sea Serpent (1957)

Dir. Roger Corman; Screenplay: Lawrence Louis Goldman from a story by Irving Block. United States: Malibu/American-International Films.

Alternate titles: *The Saga of the Viking Women and Their Voyage to the Waters of the Great Sea Serpent* and *The Viking Women.*

Reviews: *Daily Cinema* 17 September 1985: 4; *Harrison's Reports* 26 April 1958: 68; *Kinematograph Weekly* 18 September 158: 28; *Monthly Film Bulletin* 25 (November 1958): 146; *Motion Picture Herald* 5 April 1958: Product Digest Section 785; *Video Watchdog* 114 (December 2004): 69–70.

Additional discussion: Mark Thomas McGee. *Roger Corman: The Best of the Cheap Acts.* Jefferson, NC: McFarland, 1988.

The Vikings (1958)

Dir. Richard Fleischer; screenplay by Calder Willingham from an adaptation by Dale Wasserman of the novel, *The Viking* by Edison Marshall. United States: United Artists.

Two half-brothers, neither of whom know of their relationship — one a slave and one a Viking prince — grow up to become mortal enemies as they fight for the hand of a Welsh princess.

Reviews: *Daily Cinema* 9 July 1958: 7; *Film Daily* 20 May 1958: 6; *Filmfacts* 1 (23 July 1958): 101–02; *Film in Review* 9 (August-September 1958): 402–03; *Harrison's Reports* 24 May 1958: 84; *Hollywood Reporter* 20 May 1958: 3; *Kinematograph Weekly* 10 July 1958: 21; *Monthly Film Bulletin* 25 (August 1958): 100–01; *Motion Picture Herald* 24 May 1958: Product Digest Section 840; *New York Times* 12 June 1958: 35; *Times* [of London] 9 July 1958: 6, 10; *Variety* 21 May 1958. 6.

Additional discussion: *The Vikings.* New York: Progress Lithographers, 1958. [Souvenir booklet.]

The Viking's Bride (1907)

Dir. Lewis Fitzhamon; screenplay uncredited. Great Britain: Williams, Brown & Earle Film Distributors and Hepworth Manufacturing Company.

When his new bride is kidnapped by the leader of a neighboring tribe, a Viking chieftain and his retainers rescue her.

Review: *Moving Picture World* 18 January 1908: 45.

Additional discussion: Savada, Elias. *The American Film Institute Catalog of Motion Pictures Produced in the United States: Film Beginnings, 1893–1910.* Metuchen, N.J.: Scarecrow, 1995.

The Viking's Daughter, the Story of the Ancient Norsemen (1908)

Dir. J. Stuart Blackton; screenplay uncredited. United States: Vitagraph Company of America.

Viking raiders take a Saxon prince prisoner. To her father's dismay, the daughter of the Viking chieftain falls in love with the prince. When the Saxon prisoner rescues the chieftain's daughter from a fire, her father relents, and the two are allowed to marry.

Review: *Moving Picture World* 1 August 1908: 92.

Additional discussion: Savada, Elias. *The American Film Institute Catalog of Motion Pictures Produced in the United States: Film Beginnings, 1893–1910.* Metuchen, N.J.: Scarecrow, 1995.

When the Raven Flies (1984)

Dir. Hrafn Gunnlaugsson; screenplay by Hrafn Gunnlaugsson. Iceland: F.I.L.M.

Alternate titles: *Flight of the Raven, Hrafninn Flygur, Korpen Flyger, The Raven Flies,* and *Revenge of the Barbarians.*

A ten-year-old boy witnesses Vikings murder his father and kidnap his sister. When he grows to manhood, he hunts down the Vikings who have murdered his father and rescues his sister who has been forced to marry one of those murderers.

Reviews: *El amante cine* 1 (July 1992): 60; *Film og kino* 6 (1985): 217–18; *Hollywood Reporter* 27 March 1985: 11; *Icelandic Review* 22.2 (1984): 2–3 and 24.2 (1986): 71–72; *Los Angeles Times* 21 March 1985: Calendar 2 and 27 March 1985: Calendar 7; *New York Times* 25 April: C2; *Scandinavian Film News* 3 (May 1983): 3 and 4 (April 1989): 6; *Variety* 21 March 1984; 17–18.

Additional discussions: Fridgeirsson, Asgier. "The Bishop and the Actor." *Icelandic Review* 29.3 (1991): 37–90; Gunnlaugsson, Hrfan. "A Film Director's Conversion." *Cinema Canada* 113 (December 1984): 13–14; Jónsdóttir, Solveig K. "Once Upon a Time in the North." *Icelandic Review* 25.4 (1987): 4–11.

When the Sun Was God: An Ancient Tale (2003)

See *Stara baśń: Kiedy słońce było bogiem* (2003).

The White Viking (1991)

Dir. Hrafn Gunnlaugsson; screenplay Hrafn Gunnlaugsson and Jonathan Rumbold. Norway and Iceland: Filmeffekt.

Alternate title: *Den Hvite Viking.*

The clash between traditional Viking paganism and the new Christian religion separates two young lovers in medieval Norway and Iceland.

Reviews: *Icelandic Review* 28. (1990): 52; *Variety* 16 March 1992: 61.

Additional discussions: Fridgeirsson, Asgier." "The Bishop and the Actor." *Icelandic Review* 29.3 (1991): 37–90; Vikingsson, Vidar. "New Venture into Virgin Territory." *Icelandic Review* 29.4 (1991): 22–28; *The White Viking* Oslo: Filmeffekt, 1991. [Souvenir booklet.]

Wickie und die starken Männer (2009)

Dir. Michael Herbig; screenplay by Michael Herbig from the series of children's books by Runer Jonsson. Germany: Rat Pack Filmproduktion.

A less-than-brave (or strong) Viking boy sets off with his elders on an adventure-laden odyssey which proves that they have underestimated his abilities as he frequently has to rescue his elders from danger.

Alternate title: *Vicky the Viking.*

Reviews: *EPD Film* 27 (September 2009): 52; *Film-dienst* 19 (September 2009): 20; *Frankfurter Rundschau* 22 May 2009: 26; *taz, die tageszeitiung* 3 September 2009: 24–25.

The Wraiths of Roanoke (2007)

See *The Lost Colony: The Wraiths of Roanoke* (2007).

Zvengoria (1928)

Dir. Alexander Dovzhenko; screenplay by Mikhail Johansen. USSR: VUFKU.

This combination fiction film and documentary recounts the search from the times of the Viking invasions to the present for a lost horde of treasure that is essential to the national identity of the Ukraine.

Reviews: *Close-Up* 3 (1928): 48–49; *Silent Film Monthly* 3 (December 1995): 12; *Sight and Sound* Supplement 12 (November 1947): 4.

Additional discussion: Kepley, Vance, Jr. "Folklore as Political Rhetoric: Dovzhenko's *Zvenigora*." *Film Criticism* 7 (October 1982): 37–46.

About the Contributors

Susan Aronstein is the author of *Hollywood Knights: Arthurian Cinema and the Politics of Nostalgia* (2005), as well as articles on medieval Arthurian romances, medievalism and popular culture, Monty Python, Disney, and Steven Spielberg. She is professor and directs the MA program in the Department of English at the University of Wyoming in Laramie.

Claudia Bornholdt is associate professor of German at the Catholic University of America in Washington, D.C. She has published several articles on German and Scandinavian medieval literature and is the author of *Engaging Moments: The Origins of Medieval Bridal-Quest Narrative* (2005). A second book, *Saintly Spouses: Chaste Marriage in Secular and Sacred Narratives from Medieval Germany*, is forthcoming from the University of Arizona Press.

Roberta Davidson is professor of English literature at Whitman College in Walla Walla, Washington. She has published on both medieval literature and popular culture representations of the Middle Ages in several journals, including *Studies in Medievalism*, *Arthuriana*, and *Translation and Literature*, among others. She is the coauthor, with John Kerwin, of a nonfictional account of teaching Shakespeare to maximum security inmates entitled *Macbeth for Murderers*, and is currently at work on a study of twentieth and twenty-first century representations of King Arthur.

Andrew B. R. Elliott is senior lecturer in media and cultural studies at the University of Lincoln in the United Kingdom, where he specializes in the representation of history in film and television. He has written elsewhere on the use of medieval philosophy in the television series *Monk* and re-writing history in James Cameron's films. His book *Remaking the Middle Ages: The Methods of Cinema and History in Portraying the Medieval World* (McFarland, 2011) further examines the representation of the Middle Ages in film.

Laurie A. Finke is professor of women's and gender studies at Kenyon College in Gambier, Ohio. With Martin B. Shichtman, she has coauthored *Cinematic Illuminations: The Middle Ages on Film* (2009), *King Arthur and the Myth of History* (2004), and numerous articles on medieval literature and culture. Their book, *Medieval Texts and Contemporary Readers* (1987), was the first collection of essays to provide a systematic representation of the diversity of contemporary critical debate about the nature of discourse and that debate's relevance to the study of medieval literature.

Joan Tasker Grimbert is professor of French in and former chair of the Department of Modern Languages and Literatures at the Catholic University of America in Washington, D.C. She has published extensively on Arthurian literature and film and is the author or editor of five books. She is currently translating the Burgundian prose work *Cligés*.

Kevin J. Harty is professor in and chair of the Department of English at La Salle University, Philadelphia. His previous publications include *The Reel Middle Ages* (1999), *King Arthur on Film* (1999), and *Cinema Arthuriana: Twenty Essays* (2002), all from McFarland. He is also president of the North American Branch of the International Arthurian Society and an associate editor of *Arthuriana*, the branch's quarterly scholarly journal.

Donald L. Hoffman is professor emeritus at Northeastern Illinois University in Chicago. In addition to having served as president of the IAS-NAB and reviewer for *Arthuriana*, he has published widely on Arthurian matters, especially on Malory and on the use of Arthurian materials in Caribbean and African American literature. His essay on "math anxiety" in *Good Will Hunting* appears in an anthology, *Math and Popular Culture*, edited by Jessica K. Sklar and Elizabeth Sklar, forthcoming from McFarland.

Kathleen Coyne Kelly is professor of English at Northeastern University in Boston. She has published in *Allegorica, Arthuriana, Assays, Exemplaria, Parergon, PRE/TEXT, Studies in Philology*, and *Year's Work in Studies in Medievalism*. She is the coeditor (with Marina Leslie) of *Menacing Virgins: Representing Virginity in the Middle Ages and Renaissance,* the coeditor (with Tison Pugh) of *Queer Movie Medievalisms*, and the author of *A.S. Byatt* and *Performing Virginity and Testing Chastity in the Middle Ages*.

Alan Lupack, director of the Rossell Hope Robbins Library and adjunct professor of English at the University of Rochester, is the author of *The Oxford Guide to Arthurian Literature and Legend*. A former president of the North American Branch of the International Arthurian Society, he is the coauthor, with Barbara Tepa Lupack, of *King Arthur in America*. He serves as the associate editor of the TEAMS Middle English Texts series, for which he has edited two volumes. His articles on Arthurian literature have appeared in *Arthurian Interpretations, Arthurian Yearbook, Studies in Medievalism, Cinema Arthuriana*, the Blackwell's *Companion to Arthurian Literature*, and elsewhere.

David W. Marshall is assistant professor of English at California State University, San Bernardino, where he specializes in medieval literature, medievalism, and literary adaptation. His edited collection *Mass Market Medieval* (McFarland, 2007) explores the breadth of medievalism in popular culture. Additionally, he has published articles on the use of medieval dragon legends in Young Earth Creationism, as well as on recent film adaptations of *Beowulf* and on the fourteenth-century John Ball letters.

Michael N. Salda is associate professor of medieval literature in the Department of English at the University of Southern Mississippi in Hattiesburg. He is the author of *La Bibliothèque de François Ier au Château de Blois*, the coeditor of *The Malory Debate: Essays on the Texts of Le Morte d'Arthur*, and a contributor to *Chaucer Review, Modern Philology, Arthuriana*, and other journals.

Martin B. Shichtman is professor of English at Eastern Michigan University in Ypsilanti. He has coauthored with Laurie A. Finke *Cinematic Illuminations: The Middle Ages on Film* (2009), *King Arthur and the Myth of History* (2004), and numerous articles on medieval literature and culture. He and Finke are also coeditors of the pioneering collection of essays *Medieval Texts and Contemporary Readers* (1987), the first such collection to examine the varieties of contemporary discourse about the Middle Ages.

Elizabeth S. Sklar is professor of English at Wayne State University, Detroit, where she teaches medieval literature. Her area of scholarly specialization is Arthurian studies. She has published extensively on the matter of Arthur, both medieval and modern, including essays on Arthurian film. Her coedited (with Donald L. Hoffman) book *King Arthur in Popular Culture* was published by McFarland in 2002. She is currently completing her second year as a member of the *Arthuriana* editorial board.

Christopher A. Snyder is professor of European history and director of the Honors Program at Marymount University in Arlington, Virginia. He is the author of several books, including *The World of King Arthur* (2000) and *The Britons* (2003), and the general editor of *The Early Peoples of Britain and Ireland: An Encyclopedia* (2008). A frequent lecturer at the Smithsonian Institution, Dr. Snyder has appeared on the History Channel, the Learning Channel, the National Geographic Channel, and BBC radio and television.

Joseph M. Sullivan is associate professor of German at the University of Oklahoma in Norman. While he has published on medieval and early modern religious literature, medieval Yiddish literature, and medieval-themed film, the main focus of his work is Middle High German Arthurian romance. Much of his most recent work has been on the Germanic rewritings of Chrétien de Troyes' *Yvain*.

Index